W9-BNY-983

BUTLER'S LIVES OF THE SAINTS

THE LIVES OF THE SAINTS

Originally Compiled by the

REV. ALBAN BUTLER

Now Edited, Revised, and Copiously Supplemented by

HERBERT THURSTON, S.J.

AND

DONALD ATTWATER

VOL. X

OCTOBER

Kenrick seminary library

Charles L. Souvay Memorial

WITHDRAWN

Ref
922.2
B986l
V. 10

2269

LONDON
BURNS OATES &
WASHBOURNE LTD

NEW YORK
P. J. KENEDY
& SONS

NIHIL OBSTAT:

Innocentius Apap, S.Th.M., O.P.,
Censor deputatus.

IMPRIMATUR:

✠ Joseph Butt,
Vic. Gen.

Westmonasterii,
die 4a Maii, 1936.

MADE AND PRINTED IN GREAT BRITAIN
FOR
BURNS OATES & WASHBOURNE LTD
PUBLISHERS TO THE HOLY SEE

PREFACE

IN the Bollandist *Acta Sanctorum* the month of October occupies no less than thirteen folio volumes. Seeing that at the beginning of the seventeenth century the saints of January were dealt with in two volumes, this seems to argue either a considerable increase in the entries of the calendar, or an enlargement of the plan of the editors as regards the reproduction of sources. Probably both causes have contributed to the result. Even before 1765, when the first volume for October appeared, a number of canonizations, beatifications and confirmations of *cultus* had taken place which more than a century earlier could not have been foreseen, and another century was to elapse before the end of the month of October was reached. During all this time new names were being added to the Church's roll of honour, and of late the causes introduced have multiplied still further, many of them reaching a decision with a minimum of delay. On the other hand the apparatus of scholarship has immensely developed, oriental sources have almost for the first time been explored, and the unremitting search for hagiographical documents in western libraries has brought numberless documents to light which were practically inaccessible to the early Bollandists. The ratio of two to thirteen is probably no exaggerated measure of the increase in the materials which the hagiographer has now to deal with.

When Alban Butler completed his *Lives of the Saints*, none of the October volumes of the *Acta Sanctorum* had yet appeared. He had therefore no help from this quarter in making his selection of the names to be included. He might perhaps in some cases have made a better choice than the martyrologium saints whose story is often legendary, not to say mythical, but he had to be content with the materials at hand. What was eventually printed was an unusually stout volume, including in the footnotes biographies of such eminent Christians as Father Louis of Granada, King Alfred the Great, and Baron de Renty, together with a number of dissertations on miscellaneous ecclesiastical subjects, for which unfortunately, as elsewhere in this new edition, no room can be found.

Mr. Attwater, in order to keep the bulk of the present volume within reasonable bounds, has often had to compress Butler's text,

v

and sometimes to omit his less important notices. The standing in popular estimation of the revered names of many of the saints belonging to this month is as great or even greater at the present day than it was two centuries ago. St Francis of Assisi, St Teresa of Avila, St Bridget of Sweden, St Bruno, St Francis Borgia, St Peter of Alcantara had necessarily to be treated in some detail, and there are in particular certain English saints, for example, St Edward the Confessor, St Wilfrid, and St Paulinus who could not be summarily dismissed. But there were also a number of additional names for which room had to be found—St Teresa of the Infant Jesus, St Margaret Mary Alacoque, St Gerard Majella, St Alexander Sauli, St Alphonsus Rodriguez, St Mary Frances of the Five Wounds, and a crowd of *Beati*, among whom the Blessed Antony M. Claret, beatified in 1934, is treated in an appendix. With one or two unimportant exceptions all the notices have been adapted from Butler's text or written afresh by Mr. Attwater. I am on the other hand responsible, as before, for the bibliographical notices.

HERBERT THURSTON, S.J.

CONTENTS OF VOLUME X

(The entries marked with an asterisk are additions to Butler's text. A few of his notices have been discarded and written anew; many have been supplemented, and all have been revised.)

CONTENTS OF VOLUME X

CONTENTS OF VOLUME X

CONTENTS OF VOLUME X

CONTENTS OF VOLUME X

CONTENTS OF VOLUME X

THE LIVES OF THE SAINTS

OCTOBER 1

ST REMIGIUS, or REMI, Bp. of Reims, Conf.
APOSTLE OF THE FRANKS

A.D. 533

ST REMIGIUS, the great apostle of the French, was illustrious for his learning, eloquence, sanctity, and miracles, which in his episcopacy of seventy years rendered his name famous in the annals of the Church. His father Emilius and his mother St Cilinia were both descended from noble Gaulish families, and lived at Laon, where Remigius seems to have been born in the year 439. He had a brother older than himself, St Principius, Bishop of Soissons, who was father of St Lupus of Soissons. An hermit named Montanus foretold the birth of Remigius to his mother, and the parents had a special care of his education, looked upon him as a child blessed by Heaven, and were careful to put him into the best hands. His nurse Balsamia is reckoned among the saints and is honoured at Reims, so that this child was surrounded not only by good but by the best possible influences in the persons of all these holy people. The boy made great progress in learning, and in the opinion of St Sidonius Apollinaris, who was acquainted with him in the earlier part of his life, he became the most eloquent person in that age. When only twenty-two, too young to be a priest much less a bishop, he was chosen by acclamation to fill the vacant see of Reims. But he was ordained and consecrated in spite of this impediment, and amply made up for his lack of experience by his fervour in prayer, meditation on the holy Scriptures, instruction of the people, and conversion of infidels, heretics, and sinners. St Sidonius, who had considerable practice in the use of words of commendation, was at no loss to find terms to express his admiration of the charity and purity with which this bishop offered at the altar an incense of sweet odour to God, and of the zeal with which by his words he subdued the wildest hearts and brought them under the yoke of

I

virtue. Sidonius had got a manuscript of his sermons from a man at Clermont (" I do not know how he got hold of it. Like a good citizen he gave it to me, instead of selling it "), and wrote to tell Remigius that in them he admired the loftiness of the thoughts, the judicious choice of the epithets, the gracefulness and propriety of the figures, and the justness, strength, and closeness of the reasoning ; the words flowed like a gentle river, but every part in each discourse was so naturally connected, and the style so even, that the whole carried with it an irresistible force. The delicacy and beauty of the thought and expression were so smooth that it might be compared to ice or crystal upon which a nail runs without meeting with the least unevenness. With this equipment of eloquence (of which unfortunately there is no specimen extant for us to judge its quality for ourselves) allied to the yet more valuable quality of personal holiness, St Remigius set out to spread Christianity among the Franks.

Clovis, king of all northern Gaul, was himself yet a pagan, though not unfriendly to the Church. A bishop, said to have been St Remigius, complained to him that one of his soldiers had looted a valuable vase from a church at Soissons, and Clovis tried to get it allotted to himself in order that he might return it. But the soldier broke it with his axe, saying, " You shall have the share that has fallen to you." Some time after Clovis detected the soldier in fault, and split open his head, exclaiming, " This is how you treated the vase at Soissons ! " Alban Butler and others have misunderstood this story. Its point lies not in the King's willingness to return the vase, but in the fact that the soldier had a customary legal right to his share of loot and that Clovis was not above taking a mean revenge. About 492 Clovis married St Clotildis, daughter of the Christian King of the Burgundians, and she made repeated attempts to convert her husband. He agreed to the baptism of their first-born, but when the child shortly after died he harshly reproached Clotildis, and said, " If he had been consecrated in the name of my gods, he had not died ; but having been baptised in the name of yours, he could not live." The Queen answered, " I thank God who has thought me worthy of bearing a child whom He has called to His kingdom." She afterwards had another son, whom she had baptised, and he also fell sick. The King said in great anger, " It could not be otherwise. He will die as his brother did through having been baptised in the name of your Christ." This child recovered, but it required a more striking manifestation of the might of the Christian God to convert the rough Clovis. It came in 496, when the Allemanni crossed the Rhine and the Franks marched out to drive them back. One account says that St Clotildis had said to him in taking leave, " My lord, to be victorious invoke the God of the Christians ; He is the sole Lord of the world and is called the God of battles. If you call on Him with confidence, nothing can resist you " ; and that the wary Clovis had promised that he would be a Christian if he were victorious. The battle was going badly against him when the King, either reminded of these words or moved by desperation, shouted to the Heavens, " O Christ, whom Clotildis invokes as Son of the living God, I implore Thy help ! I have called upon my gods, and they have no power. I therefore call on Thee. I believe in Thee ! Deliver me from my enemies and I will be baptised in Thy name ! " The Franks rallied and turned the tide of battle ; the Allemanni were overcome and slain in great numbers, and sued for a truce. It is said that Clovis, during his return from this expedition, passed by Toul, and there took with him St Vedastus, a priest who had led a retired life in that city, that he might be instructed by him in the faith during his journey. But Queen St Clotildis was not trusting to any enthusiasm of victory, and secretly sent for St Remigius, telling him to touch the heart of the King while he was well disposed. When Clovis saw her he cried out, " Clovis has vanquished the Allemanni and you have triumphed over Clovis. What you have so much at heart is done." The Queen answered, " To the God of hosts is the glory of both these triumphs due," and presented to him St Remigius as the most holy bishop in his dominions. This prelate continued his instruction in the faith and prepared him for baptism by the usual practices of fasting, penance, and prayer. Clovis suggested that perhaps the people would not be willing to forsake their gods, but said he would speak to them according to the Bishop's instructions. He assembled the chiefs and warriors, but they prevented his speaking, and cried out, " We abjure mortal gods, and are ready to follow the immortal God whom Remigius preaches." St Remigius and St Vedastus therefore instructed and prepared them for baptism. At this solemnity, in order to strike the senses of barbarous people and impress their minds, Queen Clotildis took care that the streets from the palace to the church should be adorned with hangings, and that the church and baptistery should be lighted with a great number of candles and scented with incense. The catechumens marched in procession, carrying crosses, and singing the litany ; St Remigius conducted the King by the hand, followed by the Queen and the people. At the font the Bishop is said to have addressed Clovis in words that are memorable, if not actually pronounced : " Bow down your head, O Sicambrian ! Adore what you have burned, and burn what you have adored." Words which may be emphatically addressed to every penitent, to express the change of his heart and conduct that is required of him. St Remigius afterwards baptised the King's two sisters and three thousand persons of his army, as well as women and children, with the help of the other bishops and priests present. Hincmar of Reims, who wrote a Life of St Remigius in the ninth century, is the first to mention a legend that at the baptism of Clovis the holy chrism for the anointing was found to be missing, whereupon St Remigius prayed and a dove appeared from the heavens, bearing in its beak an *ampulla* of chrism. A phial of oil, fabled to be the same, was preserved at the abbey of Saint-Remi and used in the consecration of the kings of France from Philip Augustus in 1180 to Charles X in 1824. It was broken up at the Revolution, but a piece of *la Sainte Ampoule* and its contents were saved and are kept in the treasury of Reims Cathedral. St. Remigius is also supposed to have conferred on Clovis the power of touching for the "king's evil" (scrofula), which was exercised by the kings of France at their coronation, again up to Charles X. This power was confirmed by St Marculphus, who died about 550.

The King after his baptism bestowed many lands on St Remigius, who distributed them to several churches, as he did the donations of others among the Franks, lest they should imagine he had attempted their conversion out of self-interest. He gave a considerable part to St Mary's church at Laon, where he had been brought up, and made his nephew Genebald the first bishop of that see. He also constituted Theodore first bishop of Tournai, St Vedastus first bishop of Arras and then of Cambrai, and he sent St Antimundus to restore the faith to the Morini and to found the church of Térouanne. When Clovis was preparing to march against Alaric II in 506, St Remigius sent him a letter of advice how he ought to govern his people so as to draw down upon himself and them the divine blessings. Clovis, after his victories over the Visigoths and the conquest of Aquitaine, sent a circular letter to all the bishops in his dominions in which he allowed them to give liberty to any of the captives he had taken, provided they made use of this privilege in favour only of persons of whom they had some knowledge. Under the protection of this monarch St Remigius spread the gospel of Christ by the conversion of a great part of the French nation, in which work God endowed him with an extraordinary gift of miracles, if we may trust his biographers on this point. The bishops who were assembled in a conference that was held at Lyons against the Arians in his time declared they were stirred to exert their zeal in defence of the Catholic faith by the example of Remigius, " Who," say they, " has everywhere destroyed the altars of the idols by a multitude of miracles and signs." He did his best to promote the cause of Catholic orthodoxy in Arian Burgundy, and at a synod in 517 converted an Arian bishop who came to it to argue with him. But the actions of St Remigius did not always meet with the approval of his brother bishops. Sometime after the death of Clovis the Bishops of Paris, Sens, and Auxerre wrote to him concerning a priest called Claudius, whom he had ordained at the request of the King. They blamed Remigius for ordaining a man whom they thought to be fit only for degradation, hinted that he had been bribed to do it, and accused him of condoning the financial malpractices of Claudius. St Remigius thought these bishops were full of spite and told them so, but his reply was a model of patience and charity. To their sneer at his great age he answered, " Rather should you rejoice lovingly with me, who is neither accused before you nor suing for mercy at your hands." Very different was his tone towards a bishop who had exercised jurisdiction outside his diocese. " If your Holiness was ignorant of the canons it was ill done of you to transgress the diocesan limits without learning them. . . . Be careful lest in meddling with the rights of others you lose your own."

St Remigius, whom St Gregory of Tours refers to as " a man of great learning, fond of rhetorical studies, and equal in his holiness to St Silvester," died on January 13 about the year 533. His feast is kept on the anniversary of the translation of his relics by Pope St Leo IX in 1049 to the abbey church of Saint Remi at Reims.

Cares and labours were sweet to this good bishop for the sake of the souls redeemed by the blood of Jesus Christ. Knowing how much He suffered for sinners throughout His mortal life, and how tenderly His divine heart is ever open to them, St Remigius was never weary in preaching, working, and praying for those committed to his charge. In imitation of the Good Shepherd and Prince of pastors he was always ready to lay down his life for their safety ; he bore them all in his heart and watched over them, trembling lest any should perish, especially through his neglect. As human endeavours are too weak to discover the wiles and repulse the assaults of the enemy without divine light and strength, he ever sought to obtain this aid by humble supplication : when he was not taken up in external service for his flock, he secretly poured forth his soul in devout prayer before God for himself and them and all men.

Although the enthusiastic letter in which Sidonius Apollinaris (who has, not unfairly, been described as an " inveterate panegyrist ") commends the discourses of St Remigius is authentic, most of the sources from which we derive our knowledge of the Saint are, to say the least, unsatisfactory. The short biography attributed to Venantius Fortunatus in not his, but of later date, and the *Vita Remigii*, written by Hincmar of Reims three centuries after his death, is full of marvels and open to grave suspicion. We have therefore to depend for our facts upon the scanty references in St Gregory of Tours (who declares that he had before him a life of St Remigius) and to supplement these by a phrase or two in letters of St Avitus of Vienne, St Nicetius of Treves, etc., together with three or four letters written by Remigius himself. The question in particular of the date, place and occasion of the baptism of Clovis has given rise to protracted discussion in which such scholars as Bruno Krusch, W. Levison, L. Levillain, A. Hauck, Godefroid Kurth, and Père Poncelet have all taken part. A detailed summary of the controversy, with bibliographical references will be found, under "Clovis," in the *Dictionnaire d'Archéologie*, vol. iii, cc. 2038–2052. It can safely be affirmed that no conclusive evidence has yet upset the traditional account given above, so far, at least, as regards the substantial fact that Clovis in 496, after a victory over the Alemanni, was baptised at Reims by St Remigius. As for more general matters, the principal texts, including the *Liber Historiæ*, have been edited by Bruno Krusch ; see the *Bibliotheca hagiographica Latina* (nn. 7150–7173). Consult also G. Kurth, *Clovis* (2nd edition, 1901), especially vol. ii, pp. 262–265 ; and cf. A. Hauck, *Kirchengeschichte Deutschlands*, vol. i (4th edition, 1904), pp. 119, 148, 217, 595–599. There are popular but uncritical lives of the Saints by Haudecœur, Avenay, Carlier, and others.

ST ROMANUS THE MELODIST, Conf.

Sixth Century

The composition of liturgical poetry has naturally had an attraction for many holy men, and Romanus the Melodist, the greatest of the Greek hymn-writers, is recognised and venerated as a saint throughout the Eastern Church. He was a Syrian Jew of Emesa, who was converted at an early age and became a deacon in the church of Beirut. During the reign of the Emperor Anastasius I he came to Constantinople. Beyond the writing of about a thousand hymns (some in dialogue form), nothing else is known of his life, except a story in the Greek *Menaion* which professes to give an account of his receiving the gift of sacred poetry at Constantinople. One eve of Christmas our Lady appeared to Romanus in his sleep and gave him a roll of paper, saying, " Take this paper and eat it." It appeared to him that he did so, and then he awoke and in great exaltation of spirit went down to the church of the All-holy Mother of God to assist at the Christmas Liturgy. When the gospel-book was about to be carried solemnly into the sanctuary, he went up into the deacon's ambo and extemporised the hymn beginning ἡ παρθένος σήμερον τὸν ὑπερούσιον τίκτει. " On this day the Virgin gives birth to

Him who is of a higher nature, and the earth offers a shelter to the Unattainable. Angels join with shepherds to glorify Him and the Magi begin to follow the star. For a new child is born to us, who was God before all ages." This hymn summarising the day's feast, said to be the first of its kind, is still sung in the Christmas offices of the Byzantine rite, and until the twelfth century it was solemnly sung on this festival at the banquet in the imperial palace by the combined choirs of the two greatest churches in Constantinople, the Holy Wisdom and the Apostles. Eighty other hymns of St Romanus survive, whole or in part, among them one composed for the feast of our Lady's Birthday, which is the earliest liturgical record of that feast. Some critics are inclined to see in St Romanus the greatest ecclesiastical poet of all ages, and it is not surprising that the Orientals, who are so passionately attached to liturgical worship, should observe his commemoration with considerable solemnity.

It would seem that the doubt whether St Romanus lived under the Emperor Anastasius I (491–518) or under Anastasius II (713–715) has not yet been finally decided. Krumbacher, who at first favoured the earlier date, later on inclined to the alternative view (see the *Sitzungsberichte* of the Munich Academy, 1899, vol. ii, pp. 3–156), but the more prevalent opinion connects Romanus with the sixth century. If he lived two hundred years later it would be strange that we find in his *Kontakia* no reference to iconoclasm. Much interest has of late years been taken in St Romanus by Byzantinists. See especially G. Cammelli, *Romano il Melode, Inni* (1930). In the *Byzantinische Zeitschrift*, vol. xi (1912), pp. 358–369, Father Petridès has printed a complete liturgical office of the Greek Church composed in honour of St Romanus. The thousand hymns he is said to have composed seems a large number, and it has been suggested by Père Bousquet, in *Échos d'Orient*, vol. iii (1900), pp. 339–342, that his output was not really a thousand hymns but a thousand strophes. The long-promised edition of the surviving *Kontakia*, begun by Krumbacher and taken over by M. P. Maas, does not yet seem to have seen the light.

ST BAVO, CONF.

c. A.D. 653

This famous hermit, also called Allowin, was a nobleman, and native of that part of Brabant called Hesbain, in the territory of Liége. After having led a very irregular life he was left a widower, and was moved to a sincere conversion to God by a sermon which he heard St Amandus preach. Amandus encouraged him by the consideration of the boundless mercy of God and set before his eyes the necessity of penance proportioned to his offences. Moved still more deeply by these instructions Bavo made his confession, and entered upon a course of canonical penance. Going home he distributed all his money among the poor, and settled upon St Amandus an estate at Ghent whereon he founded a monastery in honour of St Peter, which was afterwards called St Bavo's. Here Bavo received the tonsure at the hands of St Amandus and was animated to advance daily in the fervour of his penance and the practice of virtue. " It is a kind of apostasy," said his director to him, " for a soul which has had the happiness to see the nothingness of this world and the depth of her spiritual miseries not to raise herself daily more and more above them and to make continual approaches nearer to God." St Bavo accompanied St Amandus on his missionary journeys in France and Flanders, setting an example by the humiliation of his heart, the mortification of his will, and the rigour of his austerities. To satisfy his devotion, St Amandus after some time gave him leave to lead an eremetical life, and he is said first to have chosen for his abode a hollow trunk of a large tree, but afterwards built himself a cell in the forest of Malmédun near Ghent, where vegetables and water were his chief subsistence. He returned to the monastery of St Peter at Ghent, where St Amandus had appointed St Floribert the first abbot, and with his approval Bavo built himself a new cell in a neighbouring wood, where he lived a recluse until the end of his life. St Amandus and St Floribert attended him on his deathbed and his peaceful passage made a deep impression on all who were present. The monks of St Bavo's were secularised by Pope Paul III in 1536, at the request of the Emperor Charles V, who built a citadel in that part four years after and transferred the canons to St John's, which from that time possesses the relics and bears the name of St Bavo. When the bishopric of Ghent was erected by Paul IV in 1559, at the petition of King Philip II, this church was made the cathedral. As in the diocese of Ghent so in that of Haarlem in Holland, St Bavo is titular of the cathedral and the patron of the diocese.

The earliest life of St Bavo—there are two or three printed in the *Acta Sanctorum*, October, vol. i—has been re-edited by Bruno Krusch in the *Monumenta Germaniæ, Scriptores rerum meroving.*, vol. iv, pp. 527–546. He assigns it to the latter part of the ninth century and deems it to be of little value as a historical source. See also Van der Essen, *Étude critique sur les SS. méroving.*, pp. 349–357 ; and E. de Moreau, *St Amand*, pp. 220 *seq.* In art St Bavo is sometimes represented as a hermit, sometimes in ducal attire with a falcon on his wrist ; see Künstle, *Ikonographie*, ii, p. 121.

ST MELORUS, OR MELAR, MART.
EIGHTH CENTURY (?)

The church of the great nunnery at Amesbury in Wiltshire was dedicated in honour of our Lady and St Melorus, whose relics it claimed ; numerous places in the north and west of Brittany have St Mélar as their patron ; and a St Mylor was the patron of three churches in Cornwall, namely, Mylor, Linkinhorne, and Merther Mylor in the parish of St Martin-in-Meneage. The medieval Life of Melorus the Martyr, abridged from a French *vita* and probably written at Amesbury, states that he was of noble British blood, son of Melianus, Duke of Cornouaille (in Brittany). When he was seven years old his uncle Rivoldus murdered Melianus, usurped his power, and maiming Melorus by cutting off his right hand and left foot, confined him in a monastery. By the time the boy was fourteen his miracles earned him such honour that Rivoldus began to fear him, and bargained with his guardian Cerialtanus to get rid of him. Accordingly Cerialtanus smote off his head. The dead body of Melorus wrought several miracles, including the death of his murderers, and it was buried with honour. After many years missionaries brought the relics to Amesbury, whence they were supernaturally prevented from removing them. The legend current in Cornwall in the Middle Ages was substantially the same, but as written down by Grandisson, Bishop of Exeter, the events are staged in Devon and Cornwall. The Breton legend, as it appears in the pages of Albert le Grand in the seventeenth century, is longer and more detailed, some of the details being supplied out of the editor's head ; it gives the names of everybody concerned and localises all the events at definite places in Brittany. By it the head of St Mélar is said to be in the treasury of the Bishop of Cornouaille (Quimper) and his body in the church of Lanmeur, which is the great centre of the cult of the saint. Abbé Duine regarded this story of the " martyred " prince Malor as a " fable worked up out of bits of folk-lore and Celtic pseudo-genealogies, after the taste of the hagiographical romances of the eleventh and twelfth centuries " ; at the best it may have a quite forgotten foundation in fact in the murder of some innocent and noble youth.

During the reign of King Athelstan a large number of relics of Breton saints were brought to churches in the south and west of England, and Canon G. H. Doble suggests that among them some of St Melorus came to Amesbury and so established the connection between the saint and that place. The same authority is of the opinion that the Mylor of Cornwall originally had reference not to Melorus the martyr but to St Melorius (Méloir), a Breton bishop of an earlier date. He gives his name to Tréméloir and was a companion of St Samson of Dol, and the situation of the three Cornish Mylor dedications are favourable both to voyaging to and from Brittany and to association with St Samson. The patronal feast of Mylor by Falmouth was on August 21 (and not October 1 or 3, St Mélar's days), while that of Tréméloir is on the last Sunday in August. Both Mélar and Méloir must be distinguished from St Magloire (Maglorius, October 24); philologically the names are the same. The death of St Melorus is unanimously localised by very old traditions at Lanmeur, in the diocese of Dol, and they agree in saying that his severed members were replaced by a hand of silver and foot of brass, which were as useful as flesh and bone to him, even growing with the rest of his body. The idea is met with elsewhere in Celtic folk-lore. St Melorus was represented in the pictures on the walls of the English College chapel at Rome.

Canon Doble's booklet on *St Melor* in his series of *Cornish Saints* provides undoubtedly the most careful study that has been made of this rather obscure legend. He incorporates with his text a translation of an essay written by the late René Largillière. Notices of less value may be found in Baring-Gould and Fisher, *Lives of the British Saints*, vol. ii, p. 467 ; and in Stanton's *Menology*, p. 468. See also the *Analecta Bollandiana*, vol. xlvi (1928), pp. 411–412.

BD. NICHOLAS OF FORCA-PALENA, Conf.

A.D. 1449

After being a secular priest in his native town he went to Rome and became a Servite friar. Finding that he was called to a more eremetical life, he founded a society of hermits under the patronage of St Jerome and by the generous legacy of a friend was enabled to establish them at Santa Maria delle Grazie in Naples. Pope Eugenius IV gave him an empty monastery at Florence for a similar foundation there, and Blessed Nicholas then returned to Rome and formed another community on the Janiculum, at the church of Sant' Onofrio, which is now a cardinalatial title. At this time there was another congregation of hermits of St Jerome, with branches in Rome and elsewhere, recently founded by Blessed Peter Gambacorti, and with these Blessed Nicholas amalgamated his religious. He died in 1449 at the age of a hundred, and his *cultus* among the Hieronymites was confirmed in 1774.

The Bollandists could meet with no mediæval life of this hermit, but under September 29 they compiled a fairly copious account from later sources, notably from the *Historica Monumenta* of the Hieronymite monk, Sajanello. The evidence of *cultus* in the seventeenth century is good.

BD. JOHN OF DUKLA, Conf.

A.D. 1484

Among the many Poles in the Franciscan Order who adopted the stricter constitutions of the Observant friars in consequence of the preaching of St John Capistran was this John, who was born at Dukla in the year 1414. For long he lived the life almost of a recluse, but after being appointed guardian of the friary at Lwów (Lemberg) he gave himself to apostolic activity, and by his preaching and example brought back many schismatics to the Church from among the Russians and from the Hussite and other sects ; neither old age nor blindness could curb his zeal. He died on September 29, 1484, and the devotion of his people was answered with miracles ; in 1739 Pope Clement XII approved his *cultus* as a principal patron of Poland and Lithuania.

A tolerably full account of Blessed John is given by Dr. Kamil Kantak in the *Archivum Franciscanum Historicum*, vol. xxii (1929), pp. 434–437. Writing with a thorough knowledge of Polish sources, he complains of the scantiness of historical material. The facts he cites are drawn from the chronicle of John Komorowski, O.F.M., which was edited by Liske and Lorkiewicz in vol. v of their *Monumenta Poloniæ Historica* (1888), see especially pp. 246–249. John Komorowski, then Provincial, presided at the translation of the remains of the *beato* in 1522. A Life in Polish by Cyprian Damirski was published in 1672, but adds practically nothing. See also Léon, *Auréole Séraphique* (Eng. trans.), vol. ii, pp. 507–509.

THE CANTERBURY MARTYRS AND OTHERS

A.D. 1588

Reference has been made under date August 28 to the first group of martyrs who suffered in the renewal of persecution which took place following the Armada scare in July 1588. At the beginning of October there was a further batch of executions, seven *beati* being put to death to-day, four at Canterbury and three elsewhere. BLESSED ROBERT WILCOX was born at Chester in 1558. He was trained at the English College at Reims, where he received holy orders, and was sent on the mission in 1586. He began to labour in Kent, but in the same year was taken up and imprisoned in the Marshalsea. He was condemned to death and was hung, drawn, and quartered at Canterbury, on Oaten Hill, outside the city walls on the south side. With him died BLESSED EDWARD CAMPION, CHRISTOPHER BUXTON, and ROBERT WIDMERPOOL. Campion (*vere* Edwards) was born at Ludlow in 1552 and was for two years at Jesus College, Oxford. He was reconciled to the Church while in the service of Gregory, Lord Dacre, and went to Reims in 1586, when he assumed the name of Campion. He was ordained priest, " of the diocese of Canterbury," early in the following year and was at once sent to England. He was arrested at Sittingbourne and shut up first in Newgate and then the Marshalsea. Mr. Buxton was a Derbyshire man, born at Tideswell. He was at school there under the venerable martyr Nicholas Garlick and was sent to study for the priesthood at Reims and Rome. He was arrested and condemned soon after his return to England. These three secular priests all suffered for coming into the realm as seminary priests. Blessed Christopher was the youngest and it was thought that the sight of the barbarous execution of the others might frighten him into apostasy; when offered his life on that condition, he replied that he would rather die a hundred times. During his imprisonment in the Marshalsea he wrote out a *Rituale*, a relic which is still in existence. The fourth Canterbury martyr, Mr. Widmerpool, was a layman, born at Widmerpool in Nottinghamshire, educated at Gloucester Hall, Oxford, and a schoolmaster by profession. He was for a time tutor to the sons of the Earl of Northumberland, and his offence was that he had helped a priest by getting him shelter in the house of the Countess of Northumberland. Blessed Robert was hung, thanking God that he was privileged to die for the faith in the same city as St Thomas Becket.

On the same day were martyred, at Chichester, BLESSED RALPH CROCKETT and BLESSED EDWARD JAMES, and at Ipswich BLESSED JOHN ROBINSON. They were secular priests, condemned for their priesthood. Crockett and James were captured on board ship at Littlehampton upon coming into England, in April 1586. The one was born at Barton-on-the-Hill in Cheshire, educated at Christ's College, Cambridge and Gloucester Hall, Oxford, and was a schoolmaster in East Anglia before going to the college at Reims ; the other was born at Breaston in Derbyshire, brought up a Protestant, and educated at Derby Grammar School and St John's College, Oxford ; after his conversion he went to Reims and then to Rome, where he was ordained by Goldwell of Saint Asaph. After their capture they were committed to prison in London and remained there two and a half years, till after the Armada, when they were sent for trial to Chichester to be made an example. The story of Blessed John Robinson was similar. He was born at Ferrensby, in Yorkshire, and after the death of his wife went to Reims (he had a son, Francis, who also became a priest). He was ordained in 1585, was seized immediately on his arrival in England, and confined in the Clink in London. He was tried and condemned, and when the warrant for his execution at Ipswich arrived in September 1588, " the news did much to revive him, and to him that brought the warrant he gave his purse and all his money, and fell down on his knees and gave God thanks."

In addition to Challoner's *Memoirs of Missionary Priests* (ed. Pollen), pp. 146–150, consult Burton and Pollen, *Lives of the English Martyrs*, 2nd Series, vol. i, pp. 447–507.

OCTOBER 2

THE HOLY GUARDIAN ANGELS

ANGELS (ἄγγελος, messenger) are pure spirits, persons but bodiless, created by God with more acute intelligence and greater power than have human beings. Their office is threefold, namely, to praise God, to be His messengers, and to watch over man. That particular angels are appointed and commanded by God to guard each particular person that is born into the world is the general teaching of theologians, but the belief has not been defined by the Church and so is not of faith. These guardian angels lead the individual towards Heaven by defending him from evil, helping him in prayer, suggesting virtuous deeds, but acting upon the senses and imagination, not directly on the will, so that our co-operation is required. The psalmist assures us, " He hath given His angels charge over thee, to keep thee in all thy ways." And in another place, " The angel of the Lord shall encamp round about them that fear Him, and shall deliver them." The patriarch Jacob prayed his good angel to bless his two grandsons, Ephraim and Manasses, " The angel that delivereth me from all evils, bless these boys." Judith said, " His angel hath been my keeper, both going hence, and abiding there, and returning from thence hither." Christ deters us from scandalising any of His little ones, because their angels always behold the face of God, and they will demand punishment of God against any by whose malice precious souls, which were their wards, have perished. So certain and general was the belief of a guardian angel being assigned to every one by God, that when St Peter was miraculously delivered out of prison the disciples could not at first believe it, and said, " It is his angel."

St Bernard observes that we owe to our guardian angel " great reverence, devotion, and confidence ; reverence for his presence, devotion for his charity, and confidence in his watchfulness. Walk always with circumspection and awe, remembering the presence of angels to whom you are given in charge in all your ways. In every place, in every room, in every corner, pay respect to your angel. Dare you do before him what you durst not if I saw you ? . . . In God let us affectionately love the angels, those glorious spirits which are to be one day our companions in glory, at present appointed our tutors and guardians by our Father. Let us be devout, let us be grateful to such protectors ; let us love them, let us honour them as much as we are able."

We likewise ought to have confidence in the protection of our good angels, whom St Paul refers to as " ministering spirits, sent to minister for them who shall receive the inheritance of salvation." St Bernard writes in the same place, " Though we are so weak and our state so low, and though so long and dangerous a way lies before us, what can we fear under so great guardians ? As often as any tribulation or violent temptation assails you, implore your guardian, your guide, your assistant in distress and in all times of need." To deserve his help we must fly sin. " As smoke chases away bees and a vile smell doves, so the filth of sin drives away the angel, the keeper of life," says St Basil. God says (Exodus xxiii, 20) : " Behold I will send my angel, who shall go before thee, and keep thee in thy journey, and bring thee into the place that I have prepared. Take notice of him, and hear his voice, and do not think him one to be contemned : for he will not forgive when thou hast sinned, and My name is in him. But if thou wilt hear his voice, and do all that I speak, I will be an enemy to thy enemies and will afflict them that afflict thee. And My angel shall go before thee and shall bring thee " to the place prepared for those who faithfully serve God.

From early times liturgical honour was paid to all angels in the office of the Dedication of St Michael the Archangel *in Via Salaria* on September 29, and in the oldest extant Roman sacramentary, called Leonine, the prayers for the feast make indirect reference to them as individual guardians. But a separate feast of the Guardian Angels is not known before the sixteenth century, when it was local to Spain and observed on March 1. Pope Paul V authorised a special Mass and Office and at the request of Ferdinand II of Austria granted the feast to the whole Empire. Pope Clement X extended it to the Western Church at large as of obligation (it had been everywhere permissive since 1608) and fixed it for the present date, being the first free day after the feast of St Michael. Leo XIII raised its rank to that of a greater double.

An excellent article by Father J. Duhr, S.J., in the *Dictionnaire de Spiritualité*, vol. i (1933), cc. 580–625, treats exhaustively of devotion to the Guardian Angels. He points out *inter alia* that a votive Mass, *Missa ad suffragia angelorum postulanda*, had been in use at least from the time of Alcuin—he died in 804—who refers to the subject twice in his letters. Whether the practice of saying such a Mass originated in England is not clear, but we find Alcuin's text in the Leofric Missal (Section A) of the early tenth century. This votive Mass of the Angels was commonly allotted to the second day of the week (Monday), as for example in the Westminster Missal, written about the year 1375 ; but in Leofric it seems to be assigned to Thursday, by Alcuin to Tuesday, and in a ninth-century Tours missal to

Wednesday. In Spain it became customary to honour the Guardian Angels not only of persons, but of cities and provinces. An office of this sort was composed for Valencia in 1411. Even outside of Spain Bd. Francis of Estaing, Bishop of Rodez, obtained from Pope Leo X, a bull (dated 18 April 1518) which approved a special office for an annual commemoration of the Guardian Angels on March 1. In England also there seems to have been much devotion to the Angels. Herbert Losinga, Bishop of Norwich, who died in 1119, speaks eloquently on the subject ; and the well-known invocation beginning *Angele Dei qui custos es mei* is apparently traceable to the verse-writer Reginald of Canterbury, at about the same period. On the general question of the veneration of angels see also the *Dictionnaire de Théologie catholique*, vol. i, cc. 1222–1248 ; and on the liturgical aspect Kellner, *Heortology* (Eng. trans.), pp. 328–332. On the representation of angels in antiquity and art consult *Dictionnaire d'Archéologie*, etc., vol. i, cc. 2080–2161, and Künstle, *Ikonographie*, vol. i, pp. 239–264.

ST ELEUTHERIUS, Mart.

A.D. 303

" When the palace of Diocletian was burnt down at Nicomedia the holy soldier and martyr Eleutherius, with many others, was falsely accused of this crime. All of them were summarily put to death by order of the said cruel emperor. Some were cut down by the sword, others were burned, others thrown into the sea. In turn Eleutherius, the chief among them, whose valour long torture only increased, achieved his victorious martyrdom as gold tried in the fire." In these terms the Roman Martyrology refers to this martyr, but there are difficulties in the way of accepting the account given. He may be identical with the Eleutherius, a man of senatorial rank at Constantinople, mentioned in the martyrology on August 4. He was a chamberlain to the Emperor Maximian and was converted to Christianity. At the end of his catechumenate he went to his country house in Bithynia to be baptised, and provided a place of assembly there for the neighbouring Christians. He was betrayed by a servant, refused to sacrifice to the gods, and was beheaded and buried near his house. This was about the year 308. A church was built over his grave soon after the freeing of the Church by Constantine.

Although we know next to nothing of this martyr, we cannot with any certainty identify him with the martyrs honoured at Constantinople on August 4. The important fact is that on October 2 in the Syriac *breviarium* of the early fifth century we have the entry " at Nicomedia Eleutherius." From this the notice passed into the *Hieronymianum* ; see Delehaye's commentary, p. 537. The association of the martyr with the incident of the burning of Diocletian's palace is, as Dom Quentin has shown (*Les Martyrologes historiques*, pp. 615–616), simply an invention of the martyrologist Ado.

ST LEODEGARIUS, OR LEGER, Bp. OF AUTUN, MART.

A.D. 679

St Leodegarius was born about the year 616. His parents, who were of the Merovingian nobility, sent him to the court of King Clotaire II, who kept the young nobleman but a short time before he sent him to Dido, his uncle and bishop of Poitiers, who appointed a priest of learning to instruct him, and some years after undertook to finish his education himself. Leodegarius made great progress in learning and still more in the science of the saints. To walk in the presence of God and to be perfect are things inseparable, and it was by this constant union of his heart with God joined with self-denial and humility that Leodegarius attained in his youth to a considerable degree of Christian perfection. In consideration of his abilities and merit, his uncle dispensed with the canons and ordained him deacon when he was only twenty years old, and soon after made him archdeacon. When he had become a priest he retired to the monastery of St Maxentius, and soon after was obliged to take upon himself the government of that great abbey, which he held six years. Leodegarius was about thirty-five when he became abbot, and his contemporary biographer represents him as already a rather awe-inspiring person : " Being not uninformed in civil law he was a terrible judge of lay people and, learned in the canons, an excellent teacher of the clergy. Never having been softened by the joys of the flesh, he was strict in his treatment of sinners." He is said to have introduced the Rule of St Benedict into his monastery, which was in need of his reforming hand.

Clovis II dying in 658, left three sons, Clotaire, Childeric, and Theoderic, all under age. Clotaire III was proclaimed King, and his mother St Bathildis was regent, being assisted in the government by Erchinoald, mayor of the place, and the holy bishops St Eligius, St Ouen, and St Leodegarius, whose fame had reached the court whilst he governed his abbey in Poitou. He was called to the palace by St Bathildis, and in 663 nominated bishop of Autun. That see had been vacant two years whilst the diocese was miserably torn asunder by factions, of which one leader killed the other and so forfeited his claim to the see. The arrival of Leodegarius quieted all disturbances and reconciled the parties. He took care to relieve the poor, instructed his clergy, frequently preached to his people, adorned the churches, and fortified the town. He repaired the baptistery of his cathedral with great magnificence, caused the relics of St Symphorianus to be brought back, repaired the church of

St Nazaire, and built two other baptisteries. In a diocesan synod which he held at Autun, he enacted many canons for the reformation of manners and regarding the monastic order. He says that if the monks were what they ought to be their prayers would preserve the world from public calamities. By these ordinances they are enjoined to observe the canons and the Rule of St Benedict; to labour in common and to exercise hospitality; are forbidden to have property in anything and to go into cities, unless upon the business of the monastery : and in this case are commanded to have a letter from their abbot directed to the archdeacon. All clerics were directed to know by heart the Apostles' and Athanasian Creeds. This is the first mention of the latter under that name in France, and it is suggested that St Leodegarius was directing it against a possible spreading of the Monothelite heresy.

The saint had been bishop ten years when King Clotaire III died in 673. Upon this news he went at once to court, where one part of the lords declared for Childeric, who then reigned in Austrasia ; but Ebroin procured Theoderic, the other brother, to be proclaimed king, and was himself mayor of his palace. Leodegarius led the opposition against him, and this Austrasian and Burgundian party prevailing, Childeric was acknowledged king and would have put Ebroin to death if St Leodegarius and other bishops had not interceded that his life might be spared. He was exiled to the monastery at Luxeuil and Theoderic to St Denis. Childeric II governed well so long as he listened to the advice of St Leodegarius, who had so great a share in public affairs in the beginning of this reign that in some writings he is styled mayor of the palace. The King, being young and violent, at length abandoned himself to his pleasures and married his uncle's daughter without dispensation. St Leodegarius admonished him, without effect, and certain nobles took the opportunity to render the saint's fidelity suspect. At Easter 675, Childeric was at Autun and threatened the life of Leodegarius, who fled. He was pursued, captured, and banished to Luxeuil, where his opponent Ebroin still was. Childeric, having caused a nobleman called Bodilo to be publicly scourged, was slain by him. Theoderic was brought from Saint-Denis by the opponents of Ebroin and put on the throne, Leudesius being made mayor ; and St Leodegarius was restored to his see, and received at Autun with the greatest honour and rejoicing. Ebroin also left Luxeuil and, under pretence of a conference, murdered Leudesius. Then, to deal with St Leodegarius, his principal opponent and supporter of Theoderic III, he sent an army into Burgundy which marched to Autun. St Leodegarius would not fly, but distributed his plate among the poor to encourage them in defence of the city. He then ordered a fast of three days and a general procession, in which the relics of the saints were carried round the walls ; at every gate the bishop prostrated himself, and besought God that, if He called him to martyrdom, his flock might not suffer. He then called the people together into church and asked pardon of all those whom he might have offended by too great severity. When the enemy came up, the people shut their gates and made a stout defence. But St Leodegarius said to them, " Fight no longer. If it is on my account they are come, I am ready to give them satisfaction. Let us send one of our brethren to know what they demand." The army was commanded by Waimer, Duke of Champagne, who answered the citizens' herald that they would storm the town unless Leodegarius was delivered up to them. Leodegarius declared that he would rather suffer death than fail in his fidelity to his prince, and, the enemy continuing to press upon the city, he took leave of all his brethren, marched boldly out of the town, and offered himself to his enemies, who having seized on his person put out his eyes. This he endured without suffering his hands to be tied or emitting the least groan, singing psalms the while. Waimer carried St Leodegarius to his own house in Champagne, where he returned him the money he had taken from the church of Autun, which St Leodegarius sent thither to be distributed among the poor.

Ebroin, having deserted his own candidate for the throne, became mayor of the palace to Theoderic and absolute master in Neustria and Burgundy. He pretended a desire to revenge the death of King Childeric, and falsely accused St Leodegarius and his brother Gerinus of having concurred in it. When they were brought before Ebroin, St Leodegarius told him he would lose by his wickedness that dignity which he had usurped. The two brothers were separated, and Gerinus was tied to a post and stoned to death. During his execution he repeated the words, " Lord Jesus Christ, who camest not only to call the just but sinners, receive the soul of thy servant, to whom thou hast granted a death like that of the martyrs." Thus he continued in prayer till he died. This St Gerinus is mentioned as a martyr in the Roman Martyrology on this same day. St Leodegarius could not be condemned till he had been deposed in a synod, but he was dragged over rough ground where the soles of his feet were cut with sharp stones, and his tongue was maimed and his lips cut off ; after which he was delivered into the hands of Count Waringus, to be kept by him in safe custody. This Count honoured him as a martyr, took him into his own country, and placed him in the monastery of Fécamp in Normandy. The saint remained there two years, and when his wounds healed he was able to speak, as it was thought, miraculously. He instructed the nuns, every day offered the Holy Sacrifice, and prayed almost without ceasing. When St Gerinus was murdered he wrote a consolatory letter to his mother Sigradis, who was then a nun in the monastery of our Lady at Soissons. In it he congratulates with her upon her happy shelter from the world and comforts her for the death of Gerinus, saying that that ought not to be a grief to them which was an occasion of joy and triumph to the angels ; he speaks of himself with constancy and courage and, fearing lest she might be tempted to harbour resentment against their unjust persecutors, speaks of the forgiveness of enemies with tenderness and charity. He tells her that, since Christ set the example by praying on the cross for His murderers, it should be easy for us to love our enemies and persecutors. This letter is the effusion of a heart burning with charity and overflowing with Christian virtues, and there is not a word in it of the barbarous treatment to which he had himself been subjected.

Two years later Ebroin caused St Leodegarius to be brought to Marly, where he had assembled a small number of bishops that he might be deposed by their sentence. The saint was pressed to own himself privy to the death of Childeric, but he constantly denied it, calling God to witness that he was innocent. Those that were present rent his tunic from top to bottom, which was intended for a mark of his deposition. Then he was delivered to Chrodobert, count of the palace, to be put to death. Ebroin, fearing lest he should be honoured as a martyr, ordered him to be led into a wood and there executed and buried in secret. Chrodobert was so moved by the appearance and bearing of the martyr that he could not bear to see him put to death, and his wife wept bitterly. But the saint comforted her and assured her that God would bless her for her charity if she took care of his burial. Four executioners then carried him into a forest, where three of them fell at his feet, begging him to forgive them. He prayed for them and, when he said he was ready, the fourth cut off his head. The wife of Chrodobert had the saint interred in a small oratory at a place called Sarcing in Artois, but three years after his body was removed to the monastery of St Maxentius. The struggle between St Leodegarius and Ebroin is a famous incident in Merovingian history, and not all the right was on one side ; many good men, *e.g.* St Ouen, were supporters of the notorious Ebroin. It was inevitable in those days that bishops should take an active part in high politics, but, though the Roman Martyrology says St Leodegarius suffered *pro veritate*, it is not obvious why he should be venerated as a martyr.

In the *Acta Sanctorum* (October, vol. i, published in 1765) Father C. De Bye devotes more than a hundred folio pages to the history of this saint. Two early lives are printed which, though they are by no means always in agreement, he believed to be the work of contemporaries. It was reserved for B. Krusch in the *Neues Archiv.*, vol. xvi (1890), pp. 565–596, to explain more or less satisfactorily the problem presented by their textual identity in some passages and their divergences in many others. He holds that neither was of contemporary origin, but that there was a third Life of which a considerable portion is preserved in a Paris MS. (Latin 17002), and that this was written some ten years after the death of Leodegarius by a monk of Saint-Symphorien who aimed at excusing the conduct of St Leodegarius's successor in the see. The Lives published by the Bollandists were compiled from fifty to seventy years later, with this as a basis, but are still of historical importance. Krusch (in *Monumenta Germaniæ, Scriptores rerum Meroving.*, vol. v, pp. 249–362) has reconstituted the text of what he believes to have been the original Life. Let us add that the letter of Leodegarius to his mother Sigradis is unquestionably an authentic document, whereas the will attributed to him is open to grave doubt. See further the *Analecta Bollandiana*, vol. xi (1890), pp. 104–110, and Leclercq in the *Dictionnaire d'Archéologie*, etc., vol. viii, cc. 2460–2492. Pitra's *Histoire de S. Léger* (1846) is now out of date, though it called attention to some new texts. Père Camerlinck, O.P., who has contributed a Life to the series "Les Saints" (1910), is inclined to panegyric and sometimes uncritical, but he gives an acceptable account of this tragic history. As the calendars show, Leodegarius was honoured in England from quite early times, mostly on October 2, but also on October 3.

OCTOBER 3

ST TERESA-OF-THE-CHILD-JESUS, Virg.

A.D. 1897

THE spread and enthusiasm of the *cultus* of St Teresa-of-the-Child-Jesus, a young Carmelite nun not exteriorly distinguished from hundreds of others, is one of the most impressive and significant religious phenomena of contemporary times. Within a few years of her death in 1897, under the name of " the Little Flower," she became known throughout the world ; her " little way " of simplicity and perfection in the doing of small things and discharge of daily duties has become a pattern to numberless " ordinary " folk ; her autobiography, written at the command of her superiors, is a famous book ; miracles and graces without number are attributed to her intercession. A contrast with a yet more famous Teresa forces itself : both were Carmelites and both were saints—and both have left long autobiographies in which may be traced the great external and temperamental and spiritual divergences and the inner common ground of their respective lives.

The parents of the saint-to-be were Louis Martin, a watchmaker of Alençon, son of an officer in the armies of Napoleon I, and Azélie-Marie Guérin, a maker of *point d'Alençon* in the same town, whose father had been a *gendarme* at Saint-Denis near Séez. Five of the children born to them survived to maturity, of whom Teresa was the youngest. She was born on January 2, 1873, and baptised Marie-Françoise-Thérèse. Her childhood was happy, ordinary, and surrounded by good influences ; " my earliest memories are of smiles and tender caresses." She had a quick intelligence and an open and impressionable mind, but there was no precocity or priggishness about the little Teresa ; when the older sister Léonie offered a doll and other playthings to Céline and Teresa, Céline chose some silk braid, but Teresa said, " I'll have the lot." " My whole life could be summed up in this little incident. Later . . . I cried out, ' My God, I choose all ! I don't want to be a saint by halves.' " In 1877 Madame Martin died, and M. Martin sold his business at Avignon and went to live at Lisieux (Calvados), where his children might be under the eye of their aunt, Madame Guérin, an excellent

woman. M. Martin had a particular affection for Teresa, but it
was an elder sister, Marie, who ran the household and the eldest,
Pauline, who made herself responsible for the religious upbringing
of her sisters. During the winter evenings she would read aloud to
the family, and the staple was not some popular manual or effer-
vescent " pious book " but the *Liturgical Year* of Dom Guéranger.
When Teresa was nine this Pauline entered the Carmel at Lisieux
and Teresa began to be drawn in the same direction. She had
become rather quiet and sensitive, and her religion had really got
hold of her. About this time she one day offered a penny to a lame
beggar, and he refused it with a smile. Then she wanted to run
after him with a cake her father had given her ; shyness held her
back, but she said to herself, " I will pray for that poor old man
on my first Communion day "—and she remembered to do it, five
years later : a day " of unclouded happiness." For some years she
had been going to the school kept by the Benedictine nuns of Notre-
Dame-du-Pré, and among her remarks about it she says : " Observing that some of the girls were very devoted to one or other of the
mistresses, I tried to imitate them, but I never succeeded in winning
special favour. O happy failure, from how many evils have you
saved me ! " When Teresa was nearly fourteen her sister Marie
joined Pauline in the Carmel, and on Christmas Eve of the same
year Teresa underwent an experience which she ever after referred
to as her " conversion." " On that blessed night the sweet infant
Jesus, scarcely an hour old, filled the darkness of my soul with
floods of light. By becoming weak and little, for love of me, He
made me strong and brave ; He put His own weapons into my
hands so that I went on from strength to strength, beginning, if I
may say so, ' to run as a giant.' " Characteristically, the occasion
of this sudden accession of strength was a remark of her father
about her child-like addiction to Christmas observances, not intended
for her ears at all.

During the next year Teresa communicated to her father her
wish to become a Carmelite, and M. Martin agreed ; but both the
Carmelite authorities and the Bishop of Bayeux refused to hear of
it on account of her lack of age. A few months later she was in
Rome with her father and a French pilgrimage on the occasion of
the sacerdotal jubilee of Pope Leo XIII. At the public audience,
when her turn came to kneel for the Pope's blessing, Teresa boldly
broke the rule of silence on such occasions and asked him, " In
honour of your jubilee, allow me to enter Carmel at fifteen." Leo
was clearly impressed by her appearance and manner, but he upheld
the decision of the immediate superiors. " You shall enter if it be

God's will," he said, and dismissed her with great kindness. The Pope's blessing and the earnest prayers made at many shrines during this pilgrimage bore their fruit in due season. At the end of the year the bishop, Mgr. Hugonin, gave his permission, and on April 9, 1888, Teresa Martin entered the Carmel at Lisieux whither her two sisters had preceded her. " From her entrance," deposed her novice mistress, " she surprised the community by her bearing, which was marked by a certain majesty that one would not expect in a child of fifteen."

During her noviciate Père Pichon, S.J., gave a retreat to the nuns and he testified in the cause of Teresa's beatification : " It was easy to direct that child. The Holy Spirit was leading her and I do not think that I ever had, either then or later on, to warn her against illusions. . . . What struck me during that retreat were the spiritual trials through which God wished her to pass." St Teresa was a most assiduous reader of the Bible and a ready interpreter of what she read (her *Histoire d'une Âme* is full of scriptural texts), and, in view of the fact that her *cultus* has obtained the dimensions of a " popular devotion," it is interesting to notice her love for liturgical prayer and her appreciation of its unsurpassed significance for the Christian. When she was officiant for the week and had to recite the collects of the Office in choir she reflected " that the priest said the same prayers at Mass and that, like him, I had the right to pray aloud before the Blessed Sacrament and to read the gospel when I was first chantress." In 1889 the three sisters in blood and in Carmel sustained a sad blow when their beloved father's mind gave way following two paralytic attacks and he had to be removed to a private asylum, where he remained for three years. But " the three years of my father's martyrdom," wrote St Teresa, " seem to me the dearest and most fruitful of our life. I would not exchange them for the most sublime ecstasies." She was professed on September 8, 1890. A few days before she wrote to Mother Agnes-of-Jesus (Pauline) : " Before setting out my Betrothed asked me which way and through what country I would travel. I replied that I had one only wish : to reach the height of the mountain of Love. . . . Then our Saviour took me by the hand and led me into a subterranean way, where it is neither hot nor cold, where the sun never shines, where neither rain nor wind find entrance : a tunnel where I see nothing but a half-veiled light, the brightness shining from the eyes of Jesus looking down. . . . I wish at all costs to win the palm of St Agnes. If it cannot be by blood it must be by love. . . ." One of the principal duties of a Carmelite nun is to pray for priests, a duty which St Teresa discharged with great fervour at all times ;

something she had seen or heard when visiting Italy had for the first time opened her eyes to the fact that the clergy need prayers as much as anybody else, and she never ceased in particular to pray for the good estate of the celebrated ex-Carmelite Hyacinthe Loyson, who had apostatised from the faith. Although she was delicate she carried out all the practices of the austere Carmelite rule from the first, except that she was not allowed to fast. " A soul of such mettle," said the prioress, " must not be treated like a child. Dispensations are not meant for her."—" But it cost me a lot," admitted Teresa, " during my postulancy to perform some of the customary exterior penances. I did not yield to this repugnance because it seemed to me that the image of my crucified Lord looked at me with beseeching eyes, begging these sacrifices." However, the physical mortification which she felt more than any other was the cold of the Carmel in winter, which nobody suspected until she admitted it on her death-bed. " May Jesus grant me martyrdom either of the heart or of the body, or preferably of both," she had asked, and lived to say, " I have reached the point of not being able to suffer any more—because all suffering is sweet to me."

The autobiography which St Teresa wrote at the command of her prioress, *l'Histoire d'une Âme*, is an unique and engaging document, written with a delightful clarity and freshness, full of surprising turns of phrase, bits of unexpected knowledge and unconscious self-revelation, and, above all, of deep spiritual wisdom and beauty. She defines her prayer and thereby tells us more about herself than pages of formal explanation : " With me prayer is a lifting-up of the heart ; a look towards Heaven ; a cry of gratitude and love uttered equally in sorrow and in joy. In a word, something noble, supernatural, which enlarges my soul and unites it to God. . . . Except the Divine Office, which in spite of my unworthiness is a daily joy, I have not the courage to look through books for beautiful prayers. . . . I do as a child who has not learnt to read— I just tell our Lord all that I want and He understands." Her psychological insight is keen : " Each time that my enemy would provoke me to fight I behave like a brave soldier. I know that a duel is an act of cowardice, and so, without once looking him in the face, I turn my back on the foe, hasten to my Saviour, and vow that I am ready to shed my blood in witness of my belief in Heaven." She passes over her own patience with a joke. During meditation in choir one of the sisters continually fidgeted with a rosary, till Teresa was sweating with the irritation. At last, " instead of trying not to hear it, which was impossible, I set myself to listen as though it had been some delightful music, and my meditation—which was *not* the 'prayer of quiet'—was passed in offering this music to our Lord." The last chapter is a veritable pæan of divine love, and concludes, "I entreat thee to let thy divine eyes rest upon a vast number of little souls ; I entreat thee to choose in this world a legion of little victims of thy love." St Teresa numbered herself with these little souls : "I am a very little soul, who can only offer very little things to our Lord."

In 1893 Sister Teresa was appointed to assist the novice mistress and was in fact mistress in all but name. On her experience in this capacity she comments, "From afar it seems easy to do good to souls, to make them love God more, to mould them according to our own ideas and views. But coming closer we find, on the contrary, that to do good without God's help is as impossible as to make the sun shine at night. . . . What costs me most is being obliged to observe every fault and smallest imperfection and wage deadly war against them." She was only twenty years old. In 1894 M. Martin died and soon after Céline, who had been looking after him, made the fourth Martin sister in the Lisieux Carmel. Eighteen months later, during the night between Maundy Thursday and Good Friday, St Teresa heard, "as it were, a far-off murmur announcing the coming of the Bridegroom" : it was a hæmorrhage at the mouth. At the time she was inclined to respond to the appeal of the Carmelites at Hanoi in China, who wished to have her, but her disease took a turn for the worse and the last eighteen months of her life was a time of bodily suffering and spiritual trials. The spirit of prophecy seemed to come upon her, and it was now that she made those three utterances that have gone round the world. "I have never given the good God aught but love, and it is with love that He will repay. After my death I will let fall a shower of roses." "I will spend my Heaven in doing good upon earth." "My 'little way' is the way of spiritual childhood, the way of trust and absolute self-surrender." In June 1897 she was removed to the infirmary of the convent and never left it again ; from August 16 on she could no longer receive holy Communion because of so frequent sickness. On September 30, with words of divine love on her lips Sister Teresa of Lisieux died.

So unanimous, swift, and impressive was the rise of the *cultus* of Teresa, miracles at whose intercession drew the eyes of the whole Catholic world upon her, that the Holy See, ever attentive to common convictions expressed by the acclamation of the whole visible Church, dispensed the period of fifty years which must ordinarily elapse before a cause of canonisation is begun. She was solemnly beatified by Pope Pius XI in 1923, and in the year of Jubilee 1925

the same pope declared Teresa-of-the-Child-Jesus to have been a
saint. Her feast was made obligatory for the whole Western Church,
and in 1927 she was named the heavenly patroness of all foreign
missions with St Francis Xavier. These recognitions were grate-
fully received and acclaimed not only by Catholics but by many
non-Catholics, whose attention had been called to her hidden life
and who had read her autobiography. In appearance St Teresa was
slight, with golden hair and grey-blue eyes, eyebrows very slightly
arched, a small mouth, delicate and regular features. Something of her quality can be seen in prints taken from original photographic negatives, beside which the current composite pictures of
her are insipid and lacking in human character.

St Teresa quite definitely and consciously set out to be a saint.
Undismayed by the apparent impossibility of attaining so great a
height of disinterestedness, she said to herself : " ' The good God
would not inspire unattainable desires. I may then, in spite of my
littleness, aspire to sanctity. I cannot make myself greater ; I must
bear with myself just as I am with all my imperfections. But I
want to seek a way to Heaven, a new way, very short, very straight,
a little path. We live in an age of inventions. The trouble of
walking upstairs no longer exists ; in the houses of the rich there
is a lift instead. I would like to find a lift to raise me to Jesus,
for I am too little to go up the steep steps of perfection.' Then I
sought in the holy Scriptures for some indication of this lift, the
object of my desire, and I read these words from the mouth of the
Eternal Wisdom : 'Whosoever is a *little one*, let him come to Me ' "
(Isaias lxvi 13).

The books and articles devoted to Ste Thérèse of Lisieux are wellnigh
countless, but they are all based upon her autobiography and her letters,
supplemented in some cases by the evidence given in the process of her
beatification and canonisation. These last documents printed for the use of
the Congregation of Sacred Rites are very important, for they let us see that,
even among religious pledged to the austerities of the Carmelite rule, the
frailties of human nature may still betray themselves, and that part of the
work of this innocent child was to be, by force of example, the silent re-
former and restorer of strict observance in her own convent. Among the
best biographies of the saint, though not by any means the longest, may be
mentioned that of Père H. Petitot, O.P., *Sainte Thérèse de Lisieux, une
renaissance spirituelle* (1925), that of Baron Angot des Rotours in the series
" Les Saints," that of Fernand Laudet, de l'Institut, *L'Enfant chérie du
Monde* (1927), and among the most recent the volume of Henri Ghéon
(1933), which has been translated into English by Mr. Attwater, *The Secret
of the Little Flower*. The more official publications, if one may so speak, are
represented by *Sainte Thérèse de l'Enfant Jésus, Histoire d'une Âme*, which
in its latest edition runs to over six hundred pages ; and Mgr Laveille,
Sainte Thérèse de l'Enfant Jésus ; d'après les documents officiels du Carmel de

Lisieux, 1925. The former of these is available in a translation, made from an earlier edition by Father T. N. Taylor. As a curious demurrer to the enthusiasm evoked by the canonisation mention may be made of the article in the Catalan journal, *Estudis Franciscans*, vol. xxx, by the Capuchin Père Ubald d'Alençon, but this should not be read without reference to the reply published in the same periodical by the Vicar-General of Bayeux.

ST HESYCHIUS, Conf.

End of the Fourth Century

Mention of this holy monk is made in the Life of St Hilarion (October 21), whose faithful disciple he was. He accompanied his master when he left Palestine for Egypt, and when Hilarion, being unwilling to return to Gaza, where he was so well known, fled secretly across the sea to Sicily, Hesychius sought him for three years. He could hear no word of him either in the desert or the ports of Egypt, so he made his way into Greece, where at last a rumour reached him that a wonder-working prophet had arrived in Sicily. He went thither, and tracked Hilarion to his retreat, where "he fell on his knees and watered his master's feet with tears." Continuing the vain search for complete solitude they went together to Epidaurus in Dalmatia and then to Cyprus. After two years St Hilarion sent Hesychius to Palestine to salute the brethren there, report on their progress, and visit the old monastery near Gaza. On his return in the spring he found that Hilarion, worried by the press of people, wanted to escape to yet another country, but he was now considerably advanced in age and Hesychius persuaded him to be content with a place of retreat deeper in the island which he had found for him. Here Hilarion died. St Hesychius was again in Palestine at the time and directly he heard the news he hurried back to Cyprus to watch over the body lest it be taken away by the people of Paphos. He found that his beloved master had left a letter bequeathing to him all his worldly goods, namely, a book of the gospels and some clothes. To allay the suspicions of those who jealously guarded the hermitage he pretended that he was going to live there, but after ten months he was able, with great difficulty and risk, to carry off the body of St Hilarion and convey it back to Palestine. It was met by crowds of monks and lay people who accompanied it for burial to the monastery which he had established at Majuma, and there some years later Hesychius himself died.

From the virtues of humility and charity, which Christ declares to be the foundation of His spirit in a soul, arose the meekness, peace, fortitude, and constancy, with the whole train of virtues exhibited by the Fathers of the Desert. By their conversion from the world they were interiorily changed and became new men, endued with a temper truly heavenly and animated with the spirit of Christ. The light of faith spreads its beams upon our souls, but has not produced the same reformation and change in our wills and affections. This it cannot do whilst we refuse to open our hearts to this grace and to set ourselves to remove all self-love and passion. Till this change be wrought in our affections we are earthly, strangers to the spirit of Christ, and want the mark of meekness and charity by which those are to be known that belong to Him. A Christian is not a mere name or empty profession : it is a great and noble work, a work of difficulty which requires application and continual pains, and in which the greater our endeavours and advances have been with the greater ardour do we continually strive to go up higher towards perfection.

A sufficient account of St Hesychius is provided in the *Acta Sanctorum*, October, vol. ii. It is mainly derived from St Jerome ; but see later under Hilarion, October 21.

THE TWO EWALDS, Marts.

c. A.D. 695

Soon after St Willibrord with eleven companions in the year 690 had opened the spiritual harvest in Friesland, two brothers, both priests from Northumbria, followed their example and went over into the country of the Old Saxons in Westphalia to preach the gospel. They had previously been for some time in Ireland to improve themselves in sacred learning. Both had the same name Ewald, or Edwald ; for distinction the one was called the Black, the other the White Ewald, from the colour of their hair. The first was more learned in the holy Scriptures, but both were equal in fervour of devotion and zeal. The two brothers arrived in Germany about the year 694 and met a certain steward, whom they desired to conduct them to his lord, because they had tidings for his advantage. The man invited them into his house and kept them there for several days, promising to take them to his master. The two missionaries passed the time in prayer and in singing psalms and hymns, and every day offered the sacrifice of the Mass, for which purpose they carried with them sacred vessels and a consecrated altar-stone. The barbarians observing this, and fearing lest the preachers might prevail upon their chief to forsake their gods for a new religion, resolved to murder them both. The White Ewald they killed by the sword upon the spot, but inflicted on the Black cruel torments before they tore him limb from limb. The lord of the territory when he heard of what had happened was furious that the two strangers had not been brought to him : he put the murderers to the sword and burned their village. The bodies of the martyrs, which had been thrown into the river, were discovered by a heavenly light which shone over them ; an English monk, Tilman, was warned in a vision what this column of light portended and gave the bodies honourable burial. St Bede says this river was the Rhine, but the traditional place of the Ewalds' martyrdom is at Aplerbeke on the Embscher, a tributary, near Dortmund. The Ewalds were at once honoured as martyrs, and Pepin had their bodies taken up and enshrined in the church of St Cunibert at Cologne. They are named in the Roman Martyrology and venerated as the patrons of Westphalia ; their feast is also kept by the Premonstratensian canons regular, for whom St Norbert obtained some of their relics in 1121.

In the calendar known as St Willibrord's, which must have been written in the early years of the eighth century (probably before 710), we have under October 4 the entry, *natale sanctorum martyrum Heuualdi et Heualdi*. The assignment to October 4, instead of October 3, may be due to an oversight of the scribe, for the Fulda Martyrology and that preserved in Anglo-Saxon both agree with Bede's History in naming October 3 as the proper day. See also the notes of C. Plummer's edition of Bede's History, especially pp. 289–290 ; and H. A. Wilson in *The Calendar of S. Willibrord* (H. Bradshaw Society, 1918), p. 41.

ST GERARD OF BROGNE, ABBOT AND CONF.

A.D. 959

The county of Namur gave birth to this saint, who was nearly related to Haganon, Duke of lower Austrasia, educated in military service, and given a post in the household of Berengarius, the sovereign count of Namur. An engaging sweetness of temper gained him the esteem and affection of everyone, and his courtesy and beneficence gave charm to his virtue and made it shine. He gave alms to the utmost extent of his means and knew no imaginary necessities which serve so often for pretences to withhold charities. He knew that a man gains nothing by cheating his own soul, for it is the truth that will judge us, which can neither be altered nor weakened by the excuses of the passions or the prejudices of men. One day as Gerard returned from hunting, whilst the rest went to take refreshment, he stole into a retired chapel at Brogne, which was part of his own estate, and remained there a long time in prayer. He found so much interior sweetness therein that he rose from it with sadness and said to himself, " How happy are they who have no other obligation but to praise the Lord night and day, and who live always in His presence." To procure this happiness for others and their incessant tribute and honour to the supreme majesty of God, he founded several benefices and built a church there. He is alleged also to have been told by St Peter in a vision to bring thither the relics of St Eugenius, a companion of St Dionysius of Paris. Later the monks of Saint-Denis gave him what purported to be the relics of this martyr and St Gerard enshrined them with great pomp at Brogne. Thereupon he was accused to the Bishop of Liége of promoting the veneration of relics of doubtful authenticity. But the bishop was satisfied by the miraculous intervention of St Eugenius.

In 918 Gerard's sovereign, who from the experience which he had of his prudence and virtue placed entire confidence in him, sent him to the court of France upon an important commission. At Paris, leaving his attendants in the city, he retired to an abbey, where he was edified with the fervour and solitude of the monks and desired to dedicate himself to God there. For this the consent of his sovereign was necessary, which upon his return to Namur he got from him, though with great difficulty. His uncle Stephen being bishop of Tongres, he went thither to receive his blessing and advice, and, having settled his temporal affairs, went back with great joy to the monastery to make the sacrifice of himself at the foot of God's altar.

Gerard after his profession laboured every day with greater fervour to carry Christian virtues to their noblest heights, and in due course he received priestly orders, though his humility was not overcome in his promotion without difficulty. When he had lived eleven years in this monastery he was sent by his abbot to found an abbey of monks upon his estate at Brogne. This done, and finding the dissipation of receiving visitors and the charge of a numerous community break in too much upon his retirement, he built himself a cell near the church and lived in it a recluse. God some time after called him to an active life for the greater advancement of His glory, and Gerard was obliged to undertake the reformation of the regular canons at St Ghislain, six miles from Mons, in which house he established the Rule of St Benedict and the most admirable discipline ; the canons had been in the habit of carrying the relics of their holy founder about the countryside, and exposing them for money which they put to bad uses. St Gerard carried out this difficult work with such prudence that the Count of Flanders, Arnulphus, whom the saint had miraculously cured of the stone and whom he had engaged to take up a penitential life, committed to him the general inspection and reformation of all the abbeys in Flanders. In the course of the next twenty years or so he introduced new and exact discipline in eighteen monasteries, all which houses honoured him as their abbot and second founder. Monasteries of Champagne, Lorraine, and Picardy also received his attention, and he was honoured on all hands as the restorer of the discipline of the monks of St Benedict. No fatigues made the saint abate anything of his own austerities or interrupt the continual communication of his soul with God. When he had spent almost twenty years in these trying labours and was broken with old age, he made a general visitation of all the monasteries that were under his direction, and when he had finished shut himself up in his cell at Brogne to prepare his soul to go to receive the reward of his labours, to which he was called on October 3 in 959.

The Life (compiled a century after the death of St Gerard and printed by Mabillon and in the *Acta Sanctorum*, Oct., vol. ii) which Alban Butler has here summarised, has been the subject of much discussion in recent years. It depends, no doubt, upon some earlier account which has perished, but it is in many respects untrustworthy. The document known as the *Virtutes S. Eugenii* (*Analecta Bollandiana*, vol. iii, pp. 29–57, and v, pp. 385–395) seems clearly to prove that there were no secular canons who preceded the monks at Brogne. So again it was not at St Denis that Gerard became a monk, and the journey to Rome is apocryphal ; moreover, there is much confusion in the chronology. See on all this Dom U. Berlière in the *Revue Bénédictine*, vol. ix (1892), pp. 157–172. Sackur (*Die Cluniazenser*, vol. i, pp. 366–368) takes a rather more favourable view of the *Vita S. Gerardi*.

ST FROILAN, BP. OF LEON, AND ST ATTILANUS, BP. OF ZAMORA, CONFS.

A.D. 1006 AND 1009

These two bishops were among the greatest figures of the early days of the reconquest of Spain from the Moors, and both find a place in the Roman Martyrology, Froilan to-day and Attilanus on the 5th. Froilan came from Lugo in Galicia and at the age of eighteen went to live as a hermit in the wilderness ; among his disciples was Attilanus, who came to him from Tarazona when he was only fifteen. Together they organised their followers into a regular monastic community at Moreruela on the river Esla in Old Castile, Froilan being the first abbot and Attilanus his prior. They were promoted to the episcopate together, and both consecrated on the same day, June 8, 990, to the adjoining sees of Leon and Zamora. St Froilan was one of the principal restorers of monasticism in Spain, and the martyrology speaks of his great charity to the poor. When the end of the tenth century was at hand and there was the usual excitement and fear among the ignorant and superstitious (and others as well) in view of the expected end of the world also, St Attilanus went about his diocese reassuring the people and taking the opportunity to exhort them to penance in view of the uncertainty of life, being himself the first to set an example of penitential works. He died in 1009, three years after his friend Froilan, and was canonised by Pope Urban II about ninety years later.

The account of these saints in the *Acta Sanctorum*, Oct., vol. iii (under Oct. 5), is mainly based upon Lobera, *Historia de las Grandezas . . . de Leon y de su Obispo S. Froylan* (1596) ; though some mild satire is aimed at that writer's belief that when a wolf killed the donkey which carried the bishop's luggage, St Froilan compelled the wolf to do penance by serving him for many years in the same capacity of beast of burden. A Latin life (tenth century ?) is printed in Florez, *España Sagrada*, vol. xxxiv, pp. 422–425. See also a Life by A. Lopez Pelàez (1910), and another booklet by the same author, *El culto de S. Froylan* (1911). It does not even seem certain that the main object of the *cultus* was not another Bishop Froilan who lived a century later.

ST THOMAS CANTELUPE, Bp. of Hereford, Conf.

A.D. 1282

The Cantelupes were Normans, who came over with the Conqueror and received from him great estates and honours which they exceedingly increased, becoming by marriages heirs of the Strongbows and Marshals, Earls of Pembroke, of the Fitzwalters, Earls of Hereford, and of the Braoses, lords of Abergavenny. The father of St Thomas was steward of Henry III's household, and his mother, Millicent de Gournay, dowager Countess of Evreux and Gloucester. His parents had four other sons and three daughters, towards whom Thomas was not very friendly when he grew up. He was born about the year 1218 at Hambledon, near Great Marlow, and his education was entrusted to his uncle Walter, Bishop of Worcester. He sent Thomas to Oxford when he was nineteen, where he studied under Robert Kilwardby the Dominican, afterwards archbishop of Canterbury and cardinal-bishop of Porto. This experienced tutor found no obstacle or opposition to his instructions in the heart of his pupil, but he did not stay at Oxford long, going on to Paris with

his brother Hugh for their philosophy and other studies.* Here
the young patricians lived in considerable state, and in 1245 accompanied their father, who was one of the English envoys, to the
thirteenth General Council at Lyons. Here Thomas was made a
chaplain to Pope Innocent IV, was probably ordained, and received
dispensations to study civil law and to hold a plurality of benefices,
a permission of which he afterwards freely availed himself. At
Lyons he became acquainted with the most eminent pastors and
theologians of the Church, by whose conversation he much improved
himself, and then, after reading his civil law at Orleans, returned to
Paris, where he received a visit from St Louis IX. After getting
his licence he came back to Oxford to lecture there in canon law,
and in 1262 was chosen chancellor of the University. St Thomas
was always noted for his charity to poor students ; he was also a
strict disciplinarian. There were fifteen thousand undergraduates
in residence ; they were allowed to carry arms and were divided
into opposing camps of northerners and southerners. St Thomas
had an armoury of weapons, confiscated for misuse. When Prince
Edward camped near the city and the whole University was " gated,"
the young gentlemen burned down the provost's house, wounded
many of the townspeople, and emptied the mayor's cellar (he was
a vintner). Unlike his grandfather, who had been a strong supporter of King John, Thomas the Chancellor was with the barons
against Henry III, and was one of those sent to plead their cause
before St Louis at Amiens in 1264. After the defeat of the King
at Lewes, St Thomas was appointed chancellor of the kingdom.
His prudence, courage, indefatigable application, scrupulous justice,
and disregard of human respect and of the least bribe which could
be offered him even in the most indirect manner, completed the
character of an accomplished magistrate ; the King himself experienced his inflexibility. He urged the banishment of the Jews, because
by their usuries, extortions, and base coin they were a public nuisance
to the state. But he did not hold office long, being dismissed after
the death of Simon de Montfort at Evesham, though it was provided
that he should remain in the privy council, which he did till his
death. The saint was then about forty-seven years old, and he
retired to Paris, making books and his devotions his only pleasure.

* The University was turned upside down about this time, which may
account for Thomas's short sojourn there. The brother of the papal legate,
Cardinal Otto, had thrown soup over an Irish undergraduate who annoyed
him, whereupon a Welsh undergraduate shot the legate's brother. The
University protected its student and the Cardinal left the city in great anger,
threatening an interdict.

He came back to Oxford after some years, was re-appointed chancellor there, and took his D.D. in the church of the Dominicans: on which occasion Robert Kilwardby, his old friend and director, then archbishop-elect of Canterbury, declared in his public oration that the candidate had lived without reproach and never forfeited his baptismal innocence. In 1274 he was called by Pope Gregory X to the second General Council of Lyons, assembled for the reunion of the Greeks. His papal chaplaincy was confirmed, and he continued to demonstrate that pluralism is not necessarily inconsistent with sanctity, for in addition to being archdeacon of Stafford and precentor of York, he held four canonries and seven or eight parochial livings. These he administered by competent and properly paid vicars, and he was in the habit of making unannounced visits to see how the souls and bodies of their flocks were being cared for. In the year after the council he was chosen bishop of Hereford by the chapter of that church, and consecrated in Christ Church at Canterbury. On that occasion St Thomas commented on the fact that his episcopal brethren from across the Welsh border were not present; he was not pleased.

Owing to the civil wars and the pusillanimity of his two predecessors the large and wealthy diocese of Hereford was in a bad state when St Thomas came to govern it. One after another he met, defied, and overcame the lords, spiritual and temporal, who encroached on its rights and possessions: Baron Corbet, Llewellyn of Wales (whom he excommunicated), Lord Clifford (who had to do public penance in Hereford Cathedral), the Bishop of Saint Asaph, the Bishop of Menevia (who tried by force to prevent him from consecrating the church of Abbey Dore in the Golden Valley), each in turn experienced the firmness of this feudal prelate, baron and bishop, who " was by nature careful and prudent in things pertaining to this world, and more so in those that pertained to God." One of them said to him, " Either the Devil is in you, or you are over familiar with God." There was a lively struggle with Gilbert de Clare, Earl of Gloucester, who insisted on hunting in the western side of Malvern chase, which the Bishop claimed. Gilbert replied to his warning by calling him a " clergiaster " and threatening to beat him. The unseemly epithet (it has a horrid sound) not unnaturally annoyed St Thomas, and he began a suit against the Earl of which one result can be seen to this day in the " Earl's Ditch," running along the top of the Malvern Hills. The original ditch is much older than Gilbert de Clare, but he repaired and palisaded it, to mark his boundary and to keep his deer from straying on to the episcopal lands. Among the numerous habits and traits of St Thomas recorded in the process of his canonisation is that when he travelled in his diocese he asked every child he met if he had been confirmed, and if not the Bishop at once supplied the omission. Public sinners he rebuked and excommunicated, equally publicly, particularly those who in high places set a bad example to those below them. Pluralism without the proper dispensation he would not permit, and among those whom he deprived of benefices in his diocese were the dean of Saint Paul's and the archdeacons of Northampton and Salop.

Unhappily, during the last years of his life there was dissension between St Thomas and John Peckham, the Franciscan Archbishop of Canterbury, first on some general questions of jurisdiction and then on particular cases arising in the diocese of Hereford. In a synod held at Reading in 1279 St Thomas was leader of the aggrieved suffragans, and in due course Rome gave them the reliefs they asked ; but in his personal dispute he was threatened with suspension by the primate and withdrew for eighteen months to Normandy, while his representative carried the case to Rome. He came back in 1282, but after a brief reconciliation the trouble broke out afresh, and the Bishop of Hereford was excommunicated. Some bishops refused to publish the sentence, and St Thomas publicly announced his appeal to Pope Martin IV, whom he set out to see in person. Some of Peckham's letters to his procurators at Rome are extant, but in spite of their fulminations St Thomas was very kindly received by the Pope at Orvieto. Pending the consideration of his cause he withdrew to Montefiascone, but the fatigues and heat of the journey had been too much for him and he was taken mortally sick. It is related that, seeing his condition, one of his chaplains said to him, " My lord, would you not like to go to confession ? " Thomas looked at him, and only replied, " Foolish man." Twice more he was invited, and each time he made the same reply. The chaplain was not aware that his master went to confession every day. Commending his soul to God, St Thomas died on August 25, 1282, and was buried at Orvieto ; soon his relics were conveyed to Hereford, where his shrine in the cathedral became the most frequented in the west of England (Peckham had refused to allow their interment until he had seen the certificate of absolution from the papal penitentiary). Miracles were soon reported (four hundred and twenty-nine are given in the acts of canonisation) and the process was begun under Pope Clement V at the request of King Edward I ; it was achieved in the year 1320. He is named in the Roman Martyrology on the day of his death, but his feast is kept by the Canons Regular of the Lateran and the dioceses of Birmingham,

Salford, and Shrewsbury on this October 3, by Cardiff on the 5th, and Westminster on the 22nd.

The Bollandists, who had access to the process of canonization, have given a very full account of St Thomas in the first volume of the *Acta Sanctorum* for October. Father Strange, S.J., who published in 1674 his *Life and Gests of St Thomas of Cantelupe*, had to be content with such materials as Capgrave and Surius were able to furnish. This English account by Father Strange was reprinted in the Quarterly Series in 1879, but it is now quite inadequate. An immense amount of fresh material has of late years been rendered accessible through the publication of Cantelupe's episcopal register by the Cambridge and York Society, of *Bishop Swinfield's Household Expenses* (Camden Society), of Archbishop Peckham's correspondence (Rolls Series), etc. etc., while nearly all the monastic chronicles of the period furnish more or less frequent references to the same holy Bishop of Hereford. Professor Tout's article in the *Dictionary of National Biography*, vol. viii, pp. 448–452, is not only thorough but admirable in tone. The same, however, can hardly be said of the well-informed notice in A. T. Bannister, *The Cathedral Church of Hereford* (1924).

BD. DOMINIC SPADAFORA, Conf.

A.D. 1521

Was born at Messina of a family which had come from somewhere in the East to Sicily in the thirteenth century. He received the habit of the Order of Preachers in St Zita's priory at Palermo and after his ordination was sent to the house of studies at Padua, where he took his degrees and spent some years teaching. He was then sent back to Palermo, where he preached with much fruit and at length obtained the degree of master in theology. Shortly after Blessed Dominic was sent for to Rome to be on the staff of the master general, Father Joachim Torriano, who was soon to be in trouble over the affair of Savonarola. But before this came to a head Blessed Dominic had left Rome to take charge of a new Dominican foundation at the shrine of our Lady of Grace near Monte Cerignone. He remained here for the rest of his life, twenty-eight years, undertaking long missionary journeys and winning many souls to Christ. Blessed Dominic died suddenly and without apparent illness. After Vespers on December 21, 1521, he summoned his friars and gave them his last instructions, asked for the last sacraments, and quietly died. He was beatified exactly four hundred years after by Pope Benedict XV.

The decree confirming the *cultus* of Blessed Dominic is printed in the *Acta Apostolicæ Sedes*, vol. xiii (1921), pp. 104–108. It contains a biographical summary. A short Life was published by R. Diaccini in 1921.

OCTOBER 4

ST FRANCIS OF ASSISI, Conf.
Founder of the Friars Minor
A.D. 1226

IT has been said of St Francis that he entered into glory in his lifetime, and that he is the one saint whom all succeeding generations have agreed in canonising. This over-statement has sufficient truth in it to provoke another, namely, that he is the one saint whom, in our day, all non-Catholics have agreed in canonising. Certainly no other has so appealed to Protestants and even to non-Christians. He captured the imagination of his time by presenting poverty, chastity, and obedience in the terms of the troubadours and courts of love, and that of a more complex age by his extraordinary simplicity. Religious and social cranks of all sorts have appealed to him for justification, and he has completely won the hearts of the sentimental. But the idylls that are associated with his name—the marriage with Lady Poverty, the listening birds, the hunted leveret, the falcon, and the nightingale in the ilex-grove, his " love of nature " (so uncommon in the thirteenth century, when " nature " was still regarded as natural), his romance of speech and action, these were only, so to speak, " trimmings " of a character which was wholly imbued with the supernatural, inspired by Christian dogma, and devoted not merely to Christ but to the crucified Christ. St Francis was born at Assisi in Umbria in 1181 or 1182. His father, Peter Bernardone, was a merchant, and his mother was called Pica ; some say she was gently born and of Provençal blood. His parents were persons of probity, and were in good circumstances. Much of Peter's trade was with France, and his son having been born while he was absent in that country, they called him *Francesco*, "the Frenchman," though the name of John had been given him at his baptism. In his youth he was much led away with amusements, and was devoted to the ideas of romantic chivalry propagated by the troubadours ; he had plenty of money and spent it lavishly, even ostentatiously. He was uninterested alike in his father's business and in formal learning. He was simply bent on enjoying himself. Nevertheless, he was not licentious, and would never refuse an alms to any poor man who asked it of him for the love of God. When he was about twenty strife broke out between the cities of Perugia and Assisi, and Francis, with several others, was carried away prisoner by the Perugians. This he suffered a whole year with great cheerfulness and good temper, and comforted his companions who chafed at their confinement. But as soon as he was released he was struck down by a long and dangerous sickness, which he suffered with so great patience that by the weakness of his body his spirit gathered greater strength and became more serious. On his recovery he determined to join the forces of Walter de Brienne, who was fighting for the Pope against the Germans in southern Italy. He bought himself expensive equipment and handsome outfit, but as he rode out one day in a new suit of clothes, meeting on the road a gentleman reduced to poverty and very ill clad, he was touched with compassion and changed clothes with him. That night he seemed to see in his sleep a magnificent palace, filled with rich arms, all marked with the sign of the cross ; and he thought he heard one tell him that these arms belonged to him and his soldiers. He set out exultingly for Apulia, but never reached the front. At Spoleto he was taken ill again, and as he lay there a heavenly voice seemed to tell him to turn back, " to serve the master rather than the man." Francis obeyed. At first he returned to his old life, but more quietly and with less enjoyment. His preoccupation was noticed, and he was told he was in love. " Yes," he replied, " I am going to take a wife more beautiful and worthy than any you know." He began to give himself much to prayer and to have in his soul a contempt of transitory things, and a desire to sell his goods and buy the precious jewel of the gospel. He knew not yet how he should do this, but by certain strong inspirations our Lord made him understand that the spiritual warfare of Christ is begun by mortification and victory over one's self. Riding one day in the plains of Assisi he met a leper, whose sores were so loathsome that at the sight of them he was struck with horror. But overcoming himself, he dismounted, and as the leper stretched out his hand to receive an alms, Francis, whilst he bestowed it, kissed the man and embraced him with great tenderness.

Henceforward he often visited the hospitals and served the sick, as if in them he served Christ himself, kissing the hands of the lepers with great affection and humility. He gave to the poor sometimes his clothes and sometimes money. He made a journey to Rome to visit the tombs of the apostles, and finding a multitude of poor before the door of St Peter's, he gave his clothes to one whom he thought to be most in need, and clothing himself with the rags of that poor man he remained all day in the company of those beggars. One day as he was praying in the church of St Damian, outside the walls of Assisi, he seemed to hear a voice coming from the crucifix, which said to him three times, " Francis, go and repair My house, which you see is falling down." The saint, seeing that church was old and ready to fall, thought our Lord commanded him to repair that. He therefore went home, and in the simplicity of his heart took a horseload of cloth out of his father's warehouse and sold it, with the horse, at Foligno. The price he brought to the poor priest of St Damian's, asking to be allowed to stay with him. The priest consented, but would not take the money, which Francis therefore left on a window-sill. His father, hearing what had been done, came in great indignation to St Damian's, but Francis had hid himself. After some days spent in prayer and fasting, he appeared again in the streets, though so disfigured and ill-clad that the people pelted him and called him mad. Bernardone, more annoyed than ever, carried him home, beat him unmercifully (Francis was about twenty-five !), put fetters on his feet, and locked him up, till his mother set him at liberty while his father was out. Francis returned to St Damian's. His father, following him thither, hit him about the head and insisted that he should either return home or renounce all his share in his inheritance and return the purchase-price of the goods he had taken. Francis had no objection to being disinherited, but said that the other money now belonged to God and the poor. He was therefore summoned before Guido, Bishop of Assisi, who told him to return it and have trust in God ; " He does not wish His Church to profit by goods which may have been gotten unjustly." Francis did as he was told and, with his usual literalness, added, " The clothes I wear are also his. I'll give them back." He suited the action to the word, stripped himself of his clothes, and gave them to his father, saying cheerfully, " Hitherto I have called you father on earth ; but now I say, ' Our Father, who art in Heaven.' " Pietro Bernardone left the court, " burning with rage and with an exceeding sorrow." The Bishop admired the young man's fervour, covered him with his cloak and, shedding tears, ordered some garment or other to be brought in for him. The frock of a labourer, a servant of the Bishop, was found, and Francis received this first alms with many thanks, made a cross on the garment with chalk, and put it on.

Francis went out of the Bishop's court in search of some convenient shelter, extemporising and singing the divine praises along the highways. He was met by a band of robbers in a wood, who asked him who he was. He answered with confidence, " I am the herald of the great King." They beat him and threw him into a ditch full of snow. He went on singing the praises of God. He passed by a monastery, and there received alms and a job of work as an unknown poor man. In the city of Gubbio, one who knew him took him into his house, and gave him a tunic, belt, and shoes, such as pilgrims wore, which were decent though poor and shabby. These he wore two years, and he walked with a staff in his hand like a hermit. He then returned to San Damiano at Assisi and was welcomed by the priest there. For the repairs of the church he gathered alms and begged in the city of Assisi, where all had known him rich, bearing with joy the railleries and contempt with which he was treated by some. For the building he himself carried stones and served the masons and helped put the church in good repair. Having a strong devotion to St Peter, he next did the same for an old church which was dedicated in honour of that apostle. After this he retired to a little church called Portiuncula, belonging to the abbey of Benedictine monks on Monte Subasio, who gave it that name probably because it was built on so small a parcel of land. It stands in a plain, two miles from Assisi, and was at that time forsaken and in a ruinous condition. The retiredness of this place appealed to St Francis, and he was delighted with the title which the church bore, it being dedicated in honour of our Lady of the Angels. He repaired it in the same manner he had done the two others, and fixed his abode by it. Here, on the feast of St Matthias in the year 1209, his way of life was shown to St Francis. In those days the gospel of the Mass on this feast was Matt. x 7–19 : " And going, preach, saying : The kingdom of heaven is at hand. . . . Freely have you received, freely give. . . . Do not possess gold . . . nor two coats nor shoes nor a staff. . . . Behold I send you as sheep in the midst of wolves. . . ." The words went straight to his heart and he asked an exposition of them. Then, applying them literally to himself, he gave away his shoes, staff, and leathern girdle, and left himself with one poor coat, which he girt about him with a cord. This was the habit which he gave to his friars the year following : the undyed woollen dress of the shepherds and peasants in those parts. Thus garbed, he began to exhort the people to penance with such energy that his words pierced the hearts of his hearers. As he passed them on the road he saluted the people with the words, " Our Lord give you peace." God had already favoured the saint with the gifts of prophecy and miracles. When he was begging alms to repair the church of St Damian, he used to say, " Help me to finish this building. Here will one day be a monastery of nuns by whose good fame our Lord will be glorified over the whole Church." This was verified in St Clare five years after. A man in Spoleto was afflicted with a cancer, which had disfigured his mouth and cheeks in a hideous manner. Having without receiving any benefit made a pilgrimage to Rome for the recovery of his health, he met St Francis and would have thrown himself at his feet ; but the saint prevented him and kissed his diseased face, which was instantly healed. " I know not," says St Bonaventure, " which I ought most to wonder at, such a kiss or such a cure."

Many began to admire the heroic virtue of this great servant of God, and some desired to be his companions and disciples. The first of these was Bernard da Quintavalle, a rich tradesman of Assisi and a person of prudence and of authority in the city. He watched the career of Francis with curiosity, he invited him to his house and had a bed made ready for him near his own. When Bernard seemed to be fallen asleep, the servant of God got up and, falling on his knees, passed a long time in prayer, frequently repeating aloud the words, *Deus meus et Omnia*, " My God and my All." The ardour with which he poured forth his soul expressed how strongly divine love filled his heart. Bernard secretly watched, saying to himself, " This man is truly a servant of God," and admiring the happiness of one whose heart was filled with God and to whom the whole world was as nothing, Bernard asked the saint to make him his companion. They heard Mass together, and searched the Scriptures that they might learn the will of God. The *sortes biblicae* being favourable, Bernard sold all his effects and divided the sum among the poor in one day. Peter of Cattaneo, a canon of the cathedral of Assisi, desired to be admitted with him, and Francis " gave his habit " to them both together on April 16, 1209. The third person who joined them was the famous Brother Giles, a person of great simplicity and spiritual wisdom, who came to St Francis in his cell at the Portiuncula. When his followers had increased to a dozen, Francis drew up a short informal rule consisting of the gospel counsels of perfection, to which he added things necessary for uniformity in their manner of life. He exhorts his brethren to manual labour, but will have them content to receive for it things necessary for life, not money. He bids them not to be ashamed to beg alms, remembering the poverty of Christ ; and he forbids them to preach in any place without the bishop's licence. Incidentally, it provided that " should any one of them stray from the Catholic faith or life in word or in deed, and will not amend, he shall be altogether cast out of the brotherhood." He carried his rule to Rome to obtain the Pope's approbation. Innocent III appeared at first averse, and many of the cardinals alleged that the orders already established ought to be reformed and their number not multiplied, and that the intended

poverty of this new institute was impracticable. Cardinal John
Colonna pleaded in its favour that it was no more than the evangelical counsels of perfection. The Pope consulted for some time,
and had the affair recommended to God. He afterwards told his
nephew, from whom St Bonaventure heard it, that in a dream he
saw a palm tree growing up at his feet, and in another he saw
St Francis propping up the Lateran church, which seemed ready to
fall (as he saw St Dominic in another vision five years after). He
therefore sent again for St Francis, and approved his rule, but only
by word of mouth, tonsuring him and his companions and giving
them a general commission to preach penance. St Francis now left
Rome with his twelve disciples, and returned with them first to the
valley of the Nera and thence to Assisi, where they lived together
in a little cottage at Rivo Torto, outside the gates of the town. They
sometimes went into the country to preach, Francis first preparing
them by speaking of the kingdom of God, contempt of the world,
the renouncing their own will, and the mortification of the senses.
After a time they had trouble with a peasant who wanted the cottage
for the use of his donkey. " God has not called us to prepare a
stable for an ass," observed Francis, and went off to see the abbot
of Monte Subasio. The abbot definitely handed over the Portiuncula chapel to St Francis, upon condition that it should always
continue the head church of his order. The saint refused to accept
the property " in fee simple " but would only have the use of the
place ; and in token that he held it of the monks, he sent them
every year as an acknowledgment a basket of fish caught in a neighbouring river. The monks always sent the friars in return a barrel
of oil. This custom is now revived between the friars of Santa
Maria degli Angeli and the Benedictines of San Pietro at Assisi.
Round about the chapel the brothers built themselves huts of wood
and clay. St Francis would not suffer any dominion or property
of temporal goods to be vested in his order, or in any community
or convent of it, and he called the spirit of holy poverty the foundation of his order, and in his dress, in everything that he used, and
in all his actions he showed the reality of his love for it. St Francis
would call his body Brother Ass, because it was to carry burdens,
to be beaten, and to eat little and coarsely. When he saw anyone
idle, profiting by other men's labour, he called him Brother Fly,
because he did no good, but spoiled the good which others did and
was troublesome to them. As a man owes charity to his own body,
the saint a few days before he died asked pardon of his for having
treated it perhaps with too great rigour. Indiscreet or excessive
austerities always displeased him. When a brother through

immoderate abstinence was not able to sleep, Francis brought him food and, that he might eat it with less confusion, began himself to eat with him. At the beginning of his conversion, finding himself assailed with violent temptations against purity he sometimes cast himself naked into ditches full of snow. Once, under a more grievous trial than ordinary, he began to discipline himself sharply, and when this failed of its effect threw himself into a briar-patch and rolled therein. The humility of Francis was no emotional self-depreciation, but grounded in the certainty that " what each one is in the eyes of God, that he is and no more." He never proceeded in holy orders beyond the diaconate, not daring to be ordained priest. When asked how one who is truly obedient ought to behave, he said he ought to be like a dead body. He had no use for singularity. In a certain convent he was told that one of the friars was a man of admirable virtue and so great a lover of silence that he would only confess his faults by signs. The saint did not like it, and said, " This is not the spirit of God but of the Devil. A temptation, not a virtue." Because he humbled himself, and his heart was disengaged from the love of all creatures, God exalted Francis above others. He illuminated the understanding of His servant with a light and wisdom that is not taught in books, but comes down from Heaven. When a certain brother asked leave to study, Francis told him that if he would often repeat the *Gloria Patri* with devotion he would become very learned before God. He was himself an example of knowledge so attained. His love for and power over the lower animals were noted and often referred to by those who knew him : his rebuke to the swallows while he was preaching at Alviano, " My sisters the swallows, it is now my turn to speak. You have been talking enough all this time " ; the birds that perched around him while he told them to praise their Creator ; the rabbit that would not leave him at Lake Thrasymene ; and the tamed wolf at Gubbio, which some maintain is an allegory and others a plain fact.

The early years at Santa Maria degli Angeli was a time of training in poverty, mutual help, and brotherly love. For their daily bread the brothers worked at their trades and in the fields for neighbouring farmers. When work was lacking, they begged from door to door, and even then were strictly forbidden to accept money. They were always at the service of their neighbours, and particularly of lepers and similar sufferers. These, St Francis insisted, should be referred to and addressed as " my brother-Christians," with that same instinctive delicacy of mind which makes many country people in England and Wales to-day refer to tramps not as " tramps " but as " travellers." Recruits continued to come, and among them the

" Three Companions," Angelo Tancredi, Leo, and Ruffino, who were afterwards to write the Life of their seraphic father ; and the " renowned jester of the Lord," Brother Juniper, of whom St Francis said, when he had been even more " simple " than usual, " I would that I had a forest of such junipers ! " He was the man who, when a crowd of people was waiting to receive him at Rome, was found playing seesaw with some children outside the walls. St Clare called him " God's plaything." This young girl left her home in Assisi to be a follower of St Francis after hearing him preach in the church of St George, in the spring of 1212. He established her with other maidens at San Damiano, which soon became to the Franciscans what the nuns of Prouille were to the Dominicans : a tower of womanly strength and sense, an enclosed garden of supporting prayer. In the autumn of the same year, Francis, not content with all that he did and suffered for souls in Italy, resolved to go and preach to the Mohammedans. He embarked with one companion at Ancona for Syria, but they were driven straight on to the coast of Dalmatia and wrecked. The two friars could get no further and, having no money for their passage, travelled back to Ancona as stowaways. After preaching for a year in central Italy, during which the lord of Chiusi put at the disposal of the Franciscans as a place of retreat Monte Alvernia in the Tuscan Apennines, St Francis made another attempt to reach the Mohammedans, this time in Morocco by way of Spain. Urged on by the spirit of the apostolate and martyrdom, his companions could scarce keep up with him on the road as they walked on day after day. But again he was disappointed in his object, for somewhere in Spain he was taken ill, and when he recovered he returned into Italy, where again he laboured strenuously to advance the glory of God among all Christian people.

Out of humility he gave to his order the name of Friars Minor, desiring that his brethren should really be below their fellows and seek the last and lowest places. Many cities were now anxious to have the once-despised brothers in their midst, and small communities of them sprang up throughout Umbria, Tuscany, Lombardy, and Ancona. In 1215 St Francis went to Rome to be present at the General Council of the Lateran, where for the first time he probably met his fellow-friar St Dominic, who had been preaching faith and penance in southern France while Francis was still a " young man about town " in Assisi ; and in the following year he begged from Pope Honorius III that indulgence of the Portiuncula of which an account has already been given under August 2. At Pentecost in 1217 the first general chapter of the Friars Minor was held at Assisi.

They were now so numerous that some organisation and systematic control was imperatively necessary. The order was therefore divided into provinces, each in charge of a minister provincial, to whom was committed " the care of the souls of the brethren, and should anyone be lost through the minister's fault and bad example, that minister will have to give an account before our Lord Jesus Christ." The order was now to be extended beyond the Alps, and missions were sent to Spain, Germany, and Hungary. Francis himself proposed to go to France, but was dissuaded by Cardinal Ugolino (afterwards Pope Gregory IX) ; so he sent instead Brother Pacifico and Brother Agnello, who was afterwards to bring the Franciscans to England, St Francis now submitted his brotherhood to the direction and protection of the good and prudent Ugolino, and he presided in 1219 at the second general chapter, called " of Mats," because of the number of huts of wattles and matting hastily put up to shelter the brethren. There were five thousand of them present, and it was inevitable that among so many were some for whom the original spirit of Francis himself was already diluted. He was too haphazard, that is, in this case, too trusting in God, for them ; they agitated for more " practicalness." Francis was moved to indignation. " My brothers," he replied, " the Lord has called me by the way of simplicity and humbleness, and this is the way He has pointed out to me for myself and for those who will believe and follow me. . . . The Lord told me that He would have me poor and foolish in this world, and that He willed not to lead us by any way other than by that. May God confound you by your own wisdom and learning and, for all your fault-finding, send you back to your vocation whether you will or no." And to those who wished him to obtain for them of the Pope a licence to preach everywhere without the leave of the bishops of each diocese, he answered, " When the bishops see that you live holily, and attempt nothing against their authority, they will themselves entreat you to work for the salvation of the souls committed to their charge. Let it be your singular privilege to have no privilege. . . ." St Francis sent some of his friars from this chapter on their first missions to the infidels, to Tunis and Morocco, reserving to himself a mission to the Saracens of Egypt and Syria. Innocent III's appeal at the Lateran Council for a new crusade had resulted only in a desultory attempt to bolster up the Latin kingdom in the East : Francis would wield the sword of the word of God.

He appointed two vicars to have care of the order during his absence, and set sail with twelve friars from Ancona in June 1219. After calling at Cyprus and Acre they came to Damietta on the Nile delta, before which the crusaders were sitting in siege. Francis was profoundly shocked by the dissoluteness and self-seeking of the soldiers of the Cross. When in August a big attack was planned he foresaw its failure and tried to dissuade the leaders from giving battle. He was not heard, and the Christians were driven back with the loss of six thousand men. However, they continued the siege, and took the city on November 5 the same year. In the meantime St Francis, burning with zeal for the conversion of the Saracens, desired to pass to their camp, though he was warned that there was a price on the head of every Christian. Permission was given him by the papal legate and he went with Brother Illuminato among the infidels, crying out, " Sultan ! Sultan ! " Being brought before the Sultan, Melek el-Kamil, and asked his errand, he said boldly, " I am sent not by men but by the most high God, to show you and your people the way of salvation by announcing to you the truths of the gospel." Discussion followed, and other audiences. The Sultan was somewhat moved and invited him to stay with him. Francis replied, " If you and your people will accept the word of God, I will with joy stay with you. If you yet waver between Christ and Mohammed cause a fire to be kindled, and I will go into it with your priests that you may see which is the true faith." The Sultan answered that he did not believe any of their *imams* would be willing to go into the fire, and that he could not accept his condition for fear of upsetting the people. He offered him many presents, which the saint refused, and after some days Melek el-Kamil, fearing lest some should be converted and desert to the Christians, sent Francis, escorted by a strong guard, back to their camp before Damietta. Disappointed that he could do so little either with the crusaders or their opponents, St Francis returned to Acre, whence he visited the Holy Places and preached in Syria. Then, summoned by an urgent message of distress, he returned to Italy.

Francis found that in his absence his two vicars, Matthew of Narni and Gregory of Naples, had introduced certain innovations whose tendency was to bring the Franciscans into line with the other religious orders and to confine their proper spirit within the more rigid framework of monastic observance and prescribed asceticism. With the sisters at San Damiano this had taken the form of regular constitutions, drawn up on the Benedictine model by Cardinal Ugolino. When St Francis arrived at Bologna he was amazed and grieved to find his brethren there housed in a fine convent : he refused to enter it, and lodged with the Friars Preachers, from whence he sent for the guardian of his brethren, upbraided him for his perfidy and ordered the friars to leave that house. St Francis saw these events as a betrayal : it was a crisis that might transform or destroy his followers. He went straight to the Holy See, and obtained from Honorius III the appointment of Cardinal Ugolino as official papal protector and adviser to the Franciscans, for he was a man who believed in St Francis and his ideas while being at the same time an experienced man of affairs. Then he set himself to revise the rule, and summoned another general chapter, which met at the Portiuncula in May, 1221. To this assembly he presented the revised rule, which abated nothing of the poverty, humbleness, and evangelical freedom which characterised the life he had always set before them : it was Francis's challenge to the dissidents and legalists who now, beneath the surface, were definitely threatening the peaceful development of the Franciscans. Chief among them was Brother Elias of Cortona, who, as vicar of St Francis at the Portiuncula, was in effect minister general of the brethren ; but he did not dare too openly to oppose himself to the founder whom he sincerely respected. The order had in fact become too big. "Would that there were fewer Friars Minor," cried Francis himself, "and that the world should so rarely see one as to wonder at their fewness !" At the end of two years, throughout which he had to cope with the growing tendency to break away from his ideas and to expand in directions which seemed to him to compromise the Franciscan vocation, Francis retired to Monte Rainerio, near Rieti, once again to revise his rule for solemn approbation by the Holy See. This done, he handed it to Brother Elias for communication to the ministers. It was promptly lost, and St Francis had again to dictate it to Brother Leo, amid the protests of many of the brethren who maintained that the forbiddance of holding corporate property was impracticable. In the form in which it was eventually solemnly approved by Pope Honorius III in 1223, it represented substantially the spirit and manner of life for which St Francis had stood from the moment that he cast off his fine clothes in the bishop's court at Assisi. So much so that Brother Elias refused to consider himself bound by it, and maintained in after years that he had never professed it. About two years earlier St Francis and Cardinal Ugolino had drawn up a rule for the fraternity of lay people who associated themselves with the Friars Minor in the spirit of Francis's " Letter to all Christians," written in the early years of his mission—the Franciscan tertiaries of to-day. These congregations of lay penitents, bound to a life very different from that of their neighbours, grew to be a significant power in the religious life of the Middle Ages, and in canon law tertiaries, of whatever order, still have a status differing in kind from that of members of pious confraternities and sodalities.

St Francis spent the Christmas of that year at Grecchio in the valley of Rieti where, he told his friend Giovanni da Vellita, " I would make a memorial of that Child who was born in Bethlehem and in some sort behold with bodily eyes the hardships of His infant state, lying on hay in a manger with the ox and the ass standing by." Accordingly a " crib " was set up at the hermitage, and the peasants crowded to the midnight Mass, at which Francis served as deacon and preached on the Christmas mystery. The custom of making a crib was probably not unknown before this time, but this use of it by St Francis is said to have begun its subsequent popularity. He remained for some months at Grecchio in prayer and quietness, and the graces which he received from God in contemplation he was careful to conceal from men. Brother Leo, his secretary and confessor, testified that he had seen him in prayer sometimes raised above the ground so high that he could only touch his feet, and that sometimes he was raised much higher. Towards the festival of the Assumption of the Blessed Virgin in 1224, St Francis retired to Mount Alvernia, which had been made over to his use by the lord of Chiusi in 1213, and there made a little cell. He kept Leo with him, but forbade any other person to come to him before the feast of St Michael. Here it was, on or about Holy Cross day 1224, that happened the miracle of the *stigmata*, of which an account has been given on September 17, when it is commemorated throughout the Western Church. Having been thus marked with the signs of our Lord's passion, Francis tried to conceal this favour of Heaven from the eyes of men, and for this purpose he ever after covered his hands with his habit, and wore shoes and stockings on his feet. Yet having first asked the advice of Brother Illuminato and others, he with fear disclosed to them this wonderful happening, and added that several things had been manifested to him which he never would disclose to anyone. It would seem that the gift of the *stigmata* was in part a recompense of the great love which St Francis bore to the Cross of Christ. From the beginning of his conversion his heart so burned with this divine love that the sufferings of his Saviour continually filled his thoughts. It was to render himself more perfectly conformed to his crucified Jesus that he stripped himself of everything, made of his body a victim of penance, and thrice sought among the infidels an opportunity of giving his life for Christ by martyrdom. The Passion was all his learning, all his glory, all his joy, all his comfort in this world. To soothe him during illness he was one day asked to let someone read a book to him ; but he answered, " Nothing gives me so much consolation as to think of the life and passion of our Lord. Were I to live to the end of the world I should stand in need of no other books." It was in contemplation of Christ naked and crucified, and crucified again in the persons of his suffering poor, that Francis came so to love poverty as to look on her as his lady and mistress. And he extended his rule of poverty to what is interior and spiritual, fearing lest anyone among his friars should regard his personal abilities and attainments as his own property, for so they feed self-love and produce complacency and secret attachments contrary to that entire disengagement of the heart which opens it to the divine grace. Francis did not despise learning, but he feared it for his followers. Studies were good as a means to an end, if they spent still more time in prayer, and studied not so much how to speak to others as how to preach to themselves. Studies which feed vanity rather than piety he abhorred, because they utterly extinguish charity and devotion, and drain and puff up the heart; but above all he feared the Lady Learning as a rival of the Lady Poverty. "Wheedled by the evil spirits, these brethren of mine will leave the way of holy simplicity and most high poverty," he groaned, as he watched their anxiety for books and schools. Before he left Alvernia St Francis composed that poem which has been called the "Praise of the Most High God," then, after the feast of St Michael, he came down from the mountain, bearing in his flesh the marks of the sacred wounds, and healed the sick who were brought to him in the plain below.

The two years that remained of his life were years of suffering and of happiness in God. His health was getting worse and worse, the *stigmata* were a source of physical pain and weakness, and his sight was failing. He got so bad that in the summer of 1225 Cardinal Ugolino and the vicar-general, Elias, obliged him to put himself in the hands of the Pope's physicians at Rieti. He complied with great simplicity, and on his way thither paid his last visit to St Clare at San Damiano. Here, almost maddened with pain and discomfort he triumphed again over his body, and made the "Canticle of Brother Sun," which he set to a tune and taught the brethren to sing. He went to Monte Rainerio to undergo the agonising treatment prescribed, and got but temporary relief. "O Lord," he prayed, "I return Thee thanks for the pains which I suffer. I pray that Thou add to them a hundred times, if such be Thy holy will. I am joyful that Thou art pleased to afflict me without sparing my body here; what sweeter comfort can I have than that Thy will be done!" He was taken to Siena to see other physicians, but he was dying. He dictated a message to his brethren, to love one another, to love and observe the Lady Poverty, and to love and honour the clergy of the Church. Some time before his death he made a longer testament for his religious brethren in which he recommends to them that they always honour the priests and pastors of the Church as their masters, that they faithfully observe their rule and work with their hands, not out of a desire of gain but for the sake of good example and to avoid idleness. " If we receive nothing for our work, let us have recourse to the table of the Lord, begging alms from door to door." Then he went to Assisi and was lodged in the bishop's palace. The doctors there, pressed to speak the truth, told him he could not live beyond a few weeks. " Welcome, Sister Death ! " he exclaimed, and asked to be taken to the Portiuncula. As they came on the way to a hill in sight of Assisi he asked for the stretcher to be put down, and turning his blind eyes towards the town called down the blessing of God upon it and upon his brethren. Then they carried him on to the Portiuncula. When he knew the end was close at hand, Francis asked that they would send to Rome for the Lady Giacoma di Settesoli, who had often befriended him, and ask her to come, bringing with her candles and a grey gown for his burial, and some of the cake that he liked so well. But the lady arrived before the messenger started. " Blessed be God," said Francis, " who has sent our Brother Giacoma to us. Bring her in. The rule about women is not for Brother Giacoma." He sent a last message to St Clare and her nuns, and bade his brethren sing the verse of the song he had made to the Sun which praises Death, and while they were singing he began the 141st psalm, " I cried to the Lord with my voice ; with my voice I made supplication to the Lord." Then he called for bread and broke it and to each one present gave a piece in token of mutual love and peace. He insisted upon being laid on the ground and covered with an old habit, which the guardian lent him. In this posture he exhorted his brethren to the love of God, of poverty, and of the gospel " before all other ordinances," and gave his blessing to all his disciples, the absent as well as those that were present. The passion of our Lord in the gospel of St John was read aloud, and in the evening of Saturday, October 3, 1226, St Francis died.

He had asked to be buried in the criminals' cemetery on the Colle d'Inferno, but the next day his body was taken in solemn procession to the church of St George in Assisi. Here it remained until two years after his canonisation when, in 1230, it was secretly removed to the great basilica built by Brother Elias. For six hundred years it was not seen by the eyes of man, till in 1818 after fifty-two days' search it was found deep down beneath the high altar in the lower church. St Francis was only forty-four or forty-five years old at the time of his death. This is not the place to relate, even in outline, the chequered and glorious history of the order which he founded; but in its three branches of Friars Minor, Friars Minor Capuchin, and Friars Minor Conventual, together making the one Franciscan Order, it is the most numerous religious institute in the Church to-day.

So vast and ever-growing is the literature associated with the life of St Francis, and so intricate are the problems presented by some of the principal sources, that it would be impossible to enter into any detail in the space available here. Let it be noted in the first place that we have certain small ascetical writings of the saint himself. They have been critically edited by Père Edouard d'Alençon, and have been translated into English, e.g. by Father Paschal Robinson in America, and by the Countess de la Warr in England. Secondly there is a series of *legendæ* (a phrase which here implies no suggestion of a fabulous origin), in other words the primitive biographies. The most certainly attested are three documents attributed to Thomas of Celano, the *Vita prima*, written before 1229; the *Vita secunda*, a supplement composed between 1244 and 1247; and the *Miracula*, dating from about 1257. Then we have the official Life by St Bonaventure, *c.* 1263 (a critical text appeared first in vol. viii of his *Opera omnia*, edited at Quaracchi), from which the *legenda minor* was afterwards compiled for liturgical use. This Life by St Bonaventure was written with a view to pacification. A heated controversy had broken out in the Order between the "Zelanti," or "Spiritual" friars, and those who favoured a mitigated observance. The former appealed to acts and sayings of the founder which were on record in certain earlier writings. Many of these incidents were suppressed in the Bonaventure Life, and in order that such occasions of discord might not be revived, directions were issued that the older *legendæ* should be destroyed. The MSS. representing this earlier tradition are therefore rare, and in many cases they have only been brought to light by modern research. Brother Leo, the special confidant of St Francis, undoubtedly wrote certain *ceduli* or *rotuli* about his seraphic father, and the great mediævalist Paul Sabatier always maintained that the substance of these writings was preserved in a document known as the *Speculum Perfectionis*. His final revision of this work was edited by A. G. Little and brought out by the British Society of Franciscan Studies in 1931. Its origin and date have been much controverted, and, on the other hand, a text discovered of late years at Perugia by Père F. M. Delorme—he printed it in 1926 under the name *Legenda antiqua*—has, Delorme avers, a much better claim to be regarded as Brother Leo's long-lost work. Among other primitive and important texts is the *Sacrum Commercium*, "the Converse of Francis and his sons with holy Poverty," which may well have been written, so it has been suggested, by Blessed John Parenti as early as 1227, and of which an excellent translation was published by Montgomery Carmichael in 1901. Then we have the *Legenda Trium Sociorum*, the *Legenda Juliani de Spira* and other similar compositions, as well as the *Actus beati Francisci*, which last, under the name given it in its Italian adaptation, the *Fioretti*, is familiar everywhere, and has been translated into every language. Of the innumerable modern Lives of St Francis it will be sufficient to mention a few best worthy of notice. In the first place, there is the English Life by Father Cuthbert, the Capuchin, which has gone through several editions and has been supplemented by other books of the same author dealing with the early Franciscan history and spirit. Another Catholic Life is that of John Jörgensen which has appeared in many European languages ; unfortunately the English translation is not altogether satisfactory. On the other hand, Mr. G. K. Chesterton's sketch, though brief in compass, is admirably written and leaves a vivid impression. M. Paul Sabatier is not a Catholic, but he writes most sympathetically in his biography of St Francis. It was first printed in 1894, but the " édition définitive " appeared only after the author's death in 1931. To these may be added two excellent Italian Lives by V. Facchinetti (1921) and D. Sparacio (1928), and one in Spanish by L. de Sarasola (1929). The admirable *Short Introduction to Franciscan Literature* by Father Paschal Robinson (1907) is now somewhat out of date, but V. Facchinetti's *Guida bibliografica* (1928) is full and useful.

ST AMMON THE GREAT, Conf.

c. A.D. 350

It is often stated that St Ammon was the first of the Egyptian fathers to establish a monastery in Nitria ; this is by no means certain, but it is beyond doubt that he was one of the most famous hermit monks to live in that desert. After the death of his wealthy parents, his uncle and other relatives forced Ammon, when he was twenty-two years old, into matrimony. But he read to his wife what St Paul wrote in commendation of the state of virginity, by which she was persuaded to consent to their living together in perpetual continence. They thus lived eighteen years under the same roof. He was severe in his mortifications so as gradually to inure and prepare his body to bear the austerity of the desert. Having spent the day in hard labour tilling a large garden in which he planted and cultivated balsam, at evening he supped with his wife on vegetables or fruit, and afterwards retired to prayer in which he passed a great part of the night. When his uncle and others who opposed his retreat were dead, he retired to Nitria with his wife's consent, and she assembled in her house a number of religious women, who were visited and directed by St Ammon once every six months.

Nitria, now called the Wady Natrun, is about seventy miles south-east from Alexandria and has been described as " a poisonous marsh overgrown with weeds, full of reptiles and blood-sucking flies. There are good and evil oases. This was the marsh that gave its name to Nitria—the soda marsh. The hermits chose it because it was even worse than the desert." Palladius visited it fifty years after the time of St Ammon. " On the mountain," he writes, " live some five thousand men with different modes of life, each living in accordance with his own powers and wishes, so that it is allowed to live alone or with another or with a number of others. There are seven bakeries in the mountain, which serve the needs both of these men and also of the anchorites of the great desert, six hundred in all. . . . In this mountain of Nitria there is a great church, by which stand three palm trees, each with a whip suspended from it. One is intended for the solitaries who transgress, one for robbers, if any pass that way, and one for chance comers ; so that all who transgress and are judged worthy of blows are tied to the palm tree and receive on the back the appointed number of stripes and are then released. Next to the church is a guest-house, where they receive the stranger who has arrived until he goes away of his own accord, without limit of time, even if he remains two or three years. Having allowed him to spend one week in idleness, the rest of his stay they occupy with work either in the garden or bakery or kitchen. If he should be an important person they give him a book, not allowing him to talk to anyone before the hour. In this mountain there also live doctors and confectioners. And they use wine and wine is on sale. All these men work with their hands at linen manufacture, so that all are self-supporting. And indeed at the ninth hour it is possible to stand and hear how the strains of psalmody rise from each habitation, so that one believes that one is high above the world in Paradise. They occupy the church only on Saturday and Sunday. There are eight priests who serve the church, in which so long as the senior priest lives no one else celebrates or preaches or gives decisions, but they all just sit quietly by his side " (*Lausiac History*, Lowther Clarke's trans.). Thus lived the monks and anchorites who, in the words of St Athanasius, " came forth from their own people and enrolled themselves for citizenship in Heaven."

St Ammon's first disciples lived dispersed in separate cells, till St Antony the Great advised him to assemble the greater part of them under the eye of an attentive superior, though even then the monastery was no more than a fortuitous aggregation of private cells. Antony himself selected the site for their group and set up a cross there, and he and Ammon often exchanged visits. St Ammon lived in great austerity. When he first retired into the desert he took a meal of bread and water only once a day ; this he afterwards extended to two and sometimes to three or even four days. St Ammon wrought many miracles, one of which is recorded by St Athanasius in his Life of St Antony and elsewhere. He was going to cross a river when the banks were overflowed with Theodore his disciple, and they withdrew from one another to undress. But St Ammon even when alone was too shy to swim across naked, and while he stood trying to make up his mind he found himself on a sudden transported to the other side. Theodore coming up and seeing he had got over without being wet, asked him how it was done, and pressed him so earnestly that Ammon confessed the miracle, making him first promise not to mention it to anyone till after his death. St Ammon died at the age of sixty-two years ; and St Antony, at the distance of thirteen days' journey from him, knew the exact time of his death, having seen in a vision his soul ascend to Heaven.

The spirit of the monastic state being that of penance and retirement, the primitive founders were particularly watchful entirely to shut the world out of their monasteries and to guard all the avenues through which it could break in upon their solitude. Its breath is always poisonous to those who are called to a life of quiet. Charity may call a monk abroad to serve his neighbour in spiritual functions ; but that person only can safely venture upon external employment who is dead to the world, and who tries to preserve in it interior solitude and recollection, having his invisible food and secret manna, and making it his delight to converse secretly in his heart with God and to dwell in Heaven.

Our information comes mainly from the *Lausiac History* of Palladius, but one or two miracles may be added from the document now commonly known as the *Historia Monachorum*. The Greek text of this last was edited by Preuschen in his book *Palladius und Rufinus* (1897). See also the *Acta Sanctorum*, October, vol. ii, and Schiwietz, *Das morgenländische Mönchtum*, vol. i, p. 94.

ST PETRONIUS, Bp. of Bologna, Conf.

c. A.D. 445

There was a Petronius who was prefect of the *prætorium* in Gaul at the beginning of the fifth century, and this saint was probably his son. A reference in a letter of St Eucherius of Lyons suggests that the younger Petronius also at one time held an important civil office, for he is said, like St Hilary of Arles, to have passed from a position of secular rank to the service of the Church, and then became renowned in Italy for his virtues. While a young man he is said to have made a journey to Palestine, " where he passed many days collecting all the vestiges of Christian antiquity " and acquiring information which he was afterwards to put to practical use. He visited the colonies of hermit monks in the Holy Land and Egypt, and the *Lives of the Monastic Fathers of Egypt* has been attributed to him ; it was, however, written by Rufinus of Aquileia, probably from information furnished by

St Petronius. About the year 430 he was appointed bishop of Bologna, and when he had taken possession of his pontifical throne he devoted his attention first of all to the repair of churches, which were in a ruined condition owing to the recent ravages of the Goths. "He built a monastery outside the city towards the east, in honour of the protomartyr St Stephen: a spacious building with lofty walls, and built with many columns of porphyry and precious marbles, having capitals carved with the figures of men, animals, and birds. He devoted the greatest attention to this building, and with special care in the reproduction of the Lord's sepulchre, of which he set out the work himself with a measuring rod. . . . The buildings extended to the place which represented Golgotha, where the cross of Christ stood." In all there were seven churches and the system of buildings reproduced in general lines the Holy Places at Jerusalem. It is even said that the Bishop peopled it with Syrian monks, but it was eventually handed over to the Benedictines; the Englishman who became Pope Adrian IV was at one time a monk there. St Petronius made the church of San Stefano his cathedral, and it was so used by the bishops of Bologna until the tenth century, in the fourth year of which Emilia was ravaged by the Huns and the buildings of Petronius destroyed. They were rebuilt and restored at various times during the Middle Ages, and during the twelfth century San Stefano achieved great popularity as a place of pilgrimage for those who could not go to the East. In 1141 some new representations were set up which were probably fruitful in putting false relics into circulation. Rather conveniently, the relics of St Petronius himself were discovered at the same time, and a Life of the saint was written in which fables and nonsense make up for lack of precise information. In a much-modified form the *Nuova Gerusalemme* of Bologna remains to this day a monument to the enthusiasm of one of its earliest bishops and the principal patron of the city.

The document printed in the *Acta Sanctorum*, October, vol. ii, as a life of St Petronius, is of no historical value. It was fabricated only in the twelfth century. A compilation in Italian written one hundred and fifty years later is equally worthless. The whole question has been thoroughly investigated by Mgr. Lanzoni in his monograph *S. Petronio, vescovo di Bologna nella storia e nella leggenda* (1907). See also Delehaye's review in *Analecta Bollandiana*, vol. xxvii (1908), pp. 104–106. In the periodical *Romagna*, vol. vii (1910), pp. 269–277, Mgr. Lanzoni carries his investigation further. He seems very doubtful whether Petronius ever visited Palestine.

OCTOBER 5

ST PLACIDUS AND HIS COMPS., MARTS.

c. A.D. 546

IN consequence of the reputation of the great sanctity of St Benedict whilst he lived at Subiaco, the noble families in Rome brought their children to him to be educated in his monastery. Equitius committed to his care his son Maurus when twelve years of age, and the patrician Tertullus his son Placidus, who was no more than seven. In his *Dialogues* St Gregory relates that Placidus having fallen into the lake at Subiaco as he was fetching some water in a pitcher, St Benedict, who was in the monastery, immediately knew of the accident, and calling Maurus said to him, " Brother, run ! Make haste ! The child has fallen into the water." Maurus ran to the lake and walked on the water a bow-shot from the land to the place where Placidus was struggling, and, taking hold of him by the hair, returned with the same speed. When he got to the shore and looked behind him he saw he had walked upon the water, which he had not noticed till then. St Benedict ascribed this miracle to the disciple's obedience, but St Maurus attributed it to the command and blessing of the abbot, maintaining that he could not work a miracle without knowing it. This miraculous corporal preservation of Placidus may be regarded as a symbol of the preservation of his soul by divine grace from the spiritual shipwreck of sin. He advanced daily in wisdom and virtue so that his life seemed a true copy of that of his master and guide, St Benedict. He, seeing the progress which grace made in his heart, loved Placidus as one of the dearest among his children and probably took him with him to Monte Cassino when he went there in 528. This place is said to have been given to St Benedict by Tertullus, the father of Placidus. This is all that is known of St Placidus, who was venerated by the Benedictines as a confessor before the ninth century.

But the feast kept by the Western Church to-day is of St Placidus, " a monk and disciple of the blessed abbot Benedict, together with his brothers Eutychius and Victorinus, their sister the maiden Flavia, Donatus, Firmatus the deacon, Faustus, and thirty other monks," who, we are told, were martyred by pirates at Messina. Of these

57

it may be said that certain early martyrologies mention on this date the martyrdom in Sicily of SS. *Placidus*, Eutychius, and their companions, who probably suffered under Diocletian. The present confusion in the liturgical books of the Benedictine Placidus with a number of martyrs who died two hundred years before he was born and in a place which, so far as we know, he never went near, appears to have its origin in a deliberate forgery of the early twelfth century. At that time Peter the Deacon, a monk of Monte Cassino and librarian of that house, gave to the world an account of the life and passion of St Placidus, whose martyrdom nobody had hitherto heard of. He claimed to have got his information from one Simeon, a priest of Constantinople, who had inherited a contemporary document. This purported to have been written by a servant of Placidus called Gordian, who had escaped from the slaughter of Placidus and his companions in Sicily, fled to Constantinople, and there written the account, which he gave to Simeon's ancestors in whose house he lodged. This story was at first received with the suspicion it deserved, but like others of the same sort it gradually succeeded in imposing itself and was eventually accepted by the Benedictines and throughout the West. According to it St Placidus was sent into Sicily where he founded the monastery of St John the Baptist at Messina. Some years later a fleet of Saracen pirates from Spain descended on the island, and when the abbot, his brothers and sister, and his monks would not worship the gods of the king, Abdallah, they were put to the sword. There were, of course, no Moors in Spain in the sixth century, and no Saracenic descents on Sicily from Syria or Africa are recorded before the middle of the seventh. Additional evidence, of equally suspicious sort, was duly forthcoming, including a deed of gift from Tertullus to St Benedict of lands in Italy and Sicily, but it was not till 1588 that the veneration of St Placidus spread to the faithful at large. In that year the church of St John at Messina was rebuilt, and during the work a number of skeletons were found interred beneath the apse. These were hailed as the remains of St Placidus and his martyred companions, and Pope Sixtus V approved their veneration as those of martyrs. The feast was given the rank of a double and inserted in the Roman Martyrology, which causes the Bollandists to question if the Pope acted with sufficient prudence. Among the Benedictines the feast of St Placidus and his Companions, Martyrs, is a double of the second class. When their kalendar was recently undergoing revision the editors proposed to suppress this feast entirely, and to join the commemoration of St Placidus, as abbot and confessor, to that of St Maurus on January 15. The Congregation of Sacred Rites, however, directed that there was to be no innovation in respect of this feast until it could be brought into line with the decision of the historico-liturgical question involved which would be dealt with in the revision of the Roman Breviary (whose third lesson for the feast summarises Peter the Deacon's Life). The Benedictines accordingly retained the name and rank of the feast, but suppressed the proper office, replacing it by the common office of several martyrs, with a general collect that does not mention either St Placidus or martyrs.

The whole story of this fabrication has been very carefully investigated by Dom U. Berlière in the *Revue Bénédictine*, vol. xxxiii (1921), pp. 19–45 ; an article in which the liturgical as well as the historical aspects of the case have been taken into account. The spuriousness of the narrative attributed to " Gordian " had previously been convincingly demonstrated by E. Caspar, *Petrus Diaconus und die Monte Cassineser Fälschungen* (1909), see especially pp. 47–72. The text of the pseudo-Gordian *Passio* will be found in the *Acta Sanctorum*, October, vol. iii. Consult also Delehaye's commentary on the *Hieronymianum*. The names of the martyrs in Peter the Deacon's forgery are all taken from the entry for October 5, in this martyrologium, though Firmatus and Flaviana or Flavia are there expressly stated to have suffered at Auxerre in France.

ST APOLLINARIS, Bp. of Valence, Conf.

A.D. 520

St Hesychius, Bishop of Vienne, brother of St Sidonius Apollinaris, had two sons, of whom the younger was the great St Avitus of Vienne and the elder was this Apollinaris of Valence. He was born in the year 453, educated under St Mamertus, and consecrated bishop by his brother before he was forty years old. Owing to the disorderly life of a previous prelate the see of Valence had been vacant for a number of years, and the diocese was in a deplorable state of ill-living and heresy. St Apollinaris applied himself to the restoration of morals and ecclesiastical discipline and to the rooting out of Arianism, in which he displayed great learning and wisdom. In the year 517 a synod at Epaon condemned an official of Sigismund, King of Burgundy, for having contracted an incestuous marriage. The culprit refused to yield, Sigismund supported him, and the bishops concerned were banished. St Apollinaris spent a year in exile. The occasion of his recall is said to have been the illness of Sigismund. The Queen thought that her husband's malady was a divine punishment for his persecution of the bishops, and she sent to St Apollinaris to come to court. He refused. Then she asked for his prayers and the loan of his cloak, and this being laid upon the sick king he recovered. Thereupon Sigismund sent a safe-conduct to the bishop and expressed contrition for his contumacy.

Some letters are extant which passed between St Apollinaris and St Avitus, which show mutual affection between the brothers and amusing touches of playfulness. In one of them Apollinaris reproves himself for having forgotten to observe the anniversary of the death of their sister Fuscina (whom Avitus praises in a poem); and in another Avitus accepts an invitation to the dedication of a church, but suggests that on this occasion too much revelry should be avoided. Being forewarned of his death, St Apollinaris went to Arles to visit his friend St Cæsarius and the tomb of St Genesius. His progress down and up the Rhône was marked by marvels of dispersing storms and exorcising demons, to which the Roman Martyrology refers, and on his return to Valence he died, about the year 520. He is venerated as the principal patron of Valence, under the popular name of " Aiplonay."

The Life printed in the *Acta Sanctorum*, October, vol. iii, is there attributed to a contemporary, but this does not seem very probable. See Bruno Krusch in *Mélanges Julien Havet* (1895), pp. 39–56, and in *Monumenta Germaniae, Scriptores rerum Meroving.*, vol. iii, pp. 194–203, where the text is critically edited. *Cf.* also Duchesne, *Fastes épiscopaux*, vol. ii, p. 446.

ST GALLA, Widow

Middle of the Sixth Century

Among the victims of Theodoric the Goth in Italy was a noble patrician of Rome, Quintus Aurelius Symmachus, who had been consul in 485. He was put to death unjustly in 525 and left three daughters, Rusticiana (the wife of Bœthius), Proba, and Galla, who is mentioned in the Roman Martyrology to-day. A reference to her life and a brief account of her death are given in the *Dialogues* of St Gregory the Great. Galla within a year of her marriage was left a widow and, though young and wealthy, she determined to retire from the world, to become a bride of Christ rather than again enter into that natural matrimony which, as St Gregory says in a generalisation that he would have found hard to substantiate, "always begins with joy and ends with sorrow." She was not to be turned from her resolve even by the warning of her physicians that if she did not marry again she would grow a beard. She there-fore joined a community of consecrated women who lived close by the basilica of St Peter, where she lived for many years a life of devotion to God and care of the poor and needy.

Eventually she was afflicted with cancer of the breast, and being one night unable to sleep for pain she saw standing between two candlesticks (for she disliked physical as well as spiritual darkness) the figure of St Peter. " How is it, master ? " she cried to him. " Are my sins forgiven ? " St Peter inclined his head. " They are forgiven," he said. " Come, follow me." But Galla had a dear friend in the house named Benedicta, and she asked that she might come too. St Peter replied that Galla and another were called then, and that Benedicta should follow after thirty days. Then the vision vanished and St Galla summoned the superior and the sisters and told them what had passed. And accordingly three days later Galla and another were taken to God, and Benedicta after thirty days. St Gregory, writing fifty years after, says that " the nuns now in that monastery, receiving them by tradition from their predecessors, can tell every little detail as though they had been present at the time when the miracle happened." The letter of St Fulgentius, Bishop of Ruspe, " Concerning the state of Widowhood," is supposed to have been addressed to St Galla ; her relics are said to rest in the church of Santa Maria in Portico.

Little seems to be known beyond what is recorded in the *Acta Sanctorum*, October, vol. iii. It is probable that the church known as St Salvator de Gallia in Rome really perpetuated the name of this saint. The French had a hospice at St Salvator in Ossibus near the Vatican. They had to move and settled close to St Salvator de Galla, which consequently came to be known as de Gallia instead of Galla. See P. Spezi in *Bulletino della Com. archeolog. com. di Roma*, 1905, pp. 62–103 and 233–263.

ST MAGENULPHUS, or MEINULF, Conf.

c. A.D. 857

Magenulphus was born of a noble Westphalian family ; on the death of his father, his mother, Wigtrudis, fled to the court of Charlemagne to escape the unwelcome attentions of her brother-in-law. Local tradition has it that Magenulphus was a posthumous child, born while his mother was on the way to the King at Stadberg, beneath a lime tree that is still shown near Bödeken. Charlemagne made him his godchild and sent the boy to the cathedral school at Paderborn. A conference of the bishop, Badurad, on the text, " The foxes have holes and the birds of the air nests : but the Son of Man hath not where to lay His head," determined him to enter the ranks of the clergy, and on receiving minor orders he was presented to a canonry in the cathedral of Paderborn. He was ordained deacon and then made archdeacon.

It was the desire of St Magenulphus to apply his riches to the foundation of a monastery for women on his own estates, and he chose as the site a spot in the forest where the deer came to drink at a brook. His choice was confirmed, it is said, by seeing a stag which displayed a cross between its antlers, like those of St Eustace and St Hubert. The monastery was duly founded at Bödeken and peopled with canonesses from Aix-la-Chapelle, for whose life he drew up a rule and constitutions. He made the monastery a centre from which he preached the gospel over the surrounding country, and he is accounted one of the apostles of Westphalia. St Magenulphus died and was buried at Bödeken. A story, perhaps invented in view of some local dispute, says that while being carried to burial he sat up on the bier and exclaimed, " Tell the Bishop of Paderborn not to interfere in the election of a new superior ! " Other miracles were reported at his tomb, and these, with the memory of his humbleness and generosity, caused him soon to be venerated as a saint. His relics were translated to the Bussdorf church in Paderborn in 1803. Magenulphus is called St Méen in France, and must be distinguished from the better-known St Méen (Mevennus, June 21) who founded a monastery near Rennes.

St Magenulphus was a rich young man who devoted both his wealth and himself entirely to the service of Christ, refusing the secular advancement that was open to him that he might become a director of nuns and a preacher to the people. " O you souls who have the true faith," cries the great St Teresa, " what blessings can you seek that can be compared to the least of those which God gives to His servants even in this life ? Even here He gives Himself to those who forsake all for love of Him. He is no respecter of persons : He loves all and there can be no exception, even of the most wicked. It is beyond my power to declare what a soul finds in herself when our Lord is pleased to confide these hidden things to her : a delight far above all that can possibly be imagined. And yet what proportion of these heavenly consolations is God pleased to bestow in this life ? No more than as it were a single drop of water of the mighty river that is prepared for us. It is a shame that we should desire such transcendent blessings and endless glory, all at the cost of the good Jesus, and not at least weep over Him with the daughters of Jerusalem. If we will not help Him to carry the cross, how can we think of coming to enjoy that which He purchased for us at the price of blood ? "

A Life of this saint seems to have been written about the year 895 when his remains were first exhumed for veneration, but this has not been preserved to us. It was, however, utilized by a certain Siegward who compiled a wordy but inadequate biography, *c.* 1035. Yet a third life was written from these materials and from his own acquaintance with the history of the period by Gobelinus Persona. It must have been produced, as Löffler has shown in the *Historisches Jahrbuch* for 1904 (pp. 190–192) between 1409 and 1416. The text of both Siegward and Gobelinus is printed in the *Acta Sanctorum*, October, vol. iii.

BD. RAYMUND OF CAPUA, Conf.

A.D. 1399

The family of delle Vigne was one of the noblest of Capua ; Peter delle Vigne had been chancellor to the Emperor Frederick II (his conduct in that office is defended by Dante in the *Inferno*), and among his descendents was Raymund, born in 1330. While a student at the University of Bologna he became a Dominican, and in spite of the continual handicap of bad health made steady progress in his order. When he was thirty-seven he was prior of the Minerva at Rome, and afterwards was lector at Santa Maria Novella in Florence and then, in 1374, at Siena. Here he met St Catherine who, assisting at his Mass on St John the Baptist's day, heard as it were a voice saying to her, " This is my beloved servant. This is he to whom I will entrust you." Father Raymund had already been chaplain to the Preacheresses at Montepulciano and so had experience of religious women, but he had never before met one like this young tertiary : she was twenty-seven, sixteen years younger than himself. He was a cautious, deliberate man, and did not allow himself either to be carried away by her vehemence or put off by her unusualness ; he did not at once recognise her mission, but he did recognise her goodness, and one of the first things he did on becoming her confessor was to allow her holy Communion as often as she wished. For the six last and most important years of her life Raymund of Capua was the spiritual guide and right-hand man of Catherine of Siena, and would be remembered for that if he had done and been nothing else of note.

Their first work in common was to care for the sufferers from the plague by which Siena was then devastated. Father Raymund became a victim and had symptoms of death : Catherine prayed by his couch for an hour and a half without intermission, and on the morrow he was well. Thenceforward he began to believe in her miraculous powers and divine mission, and when the pestilence was stayed he co-operated in her efforts to launch a new crusade to the East, preaching it at Pisa and elsewhere and personally delivering Catherine's famous letter to that ferocious freebooter from Essex,

John Hawkwood. This work was interrupted by the revolt of Florence and the Tuscan League against the Pope in France, and they turned their efforts to securing peace at home. Father Raymund went to Avignon with a letter from Catherine to Gregory XI, and when she herself came thither presented her to him and seconded those efforts which resulted in the Pope's return to Rome in 1377. Still striving for peace with Florence, Catherine sent Father Raymund from Rocca d'Orcia with " certain proposals " to Gregory, and while he was in Rome the master general of his order appointed him once more prior at the Minerva. Then Gregory XI died, Urban VI succeeded him, the opposition party elected Clement VII, and the Schism of the West began. St Catherine and Blessed Raymund had no doubt as to which was the legitimate pope, and in December 1378 Urban sent him to France to preach against Clement and to win over King Charles V. Catherine was in Rome and had a long farewell talk with this faithful friar who had been active in all her missions for God's glory and had sometimes sat from dawn till dark hearing the confessions of those whom she had brought to repentance ; on the quayside, " We shall never again talk like that," she said, and fell on her knees in tears.

At the frontier Blessed Raymund was stopped by Clementine soldiers and his life threatened. He returned to Genoa, where he received a letter from St Catherine, disappointed at his failure. Pope Urban wrote telling him to try and reach France through Spain, but this also was useless ; Catherine sent him another letter of stinging reproach for what she considered his faint-heartedness. Raymund remained at Genoa as vicar of the Dominican province, preaching against Clement and studying for his mastership in theology. While in Pisa, on April 28, 1380, he " heard a voice, which was not in the air, speaking words which reached my mind and not my ears," and those words were, " Tell him never to lose courage. I will be with him in every danger : if he falls, I will help him up again." A few days later he heard that St Catherine was dead and that she had spoken those words of him to those who stood by. He succeeded to the charge of her *famiglia*, that is, the little group of clerics and lay-people who had helped and hindered her in all her undertakings, and he continued all his life her labours for the ending of the schism. But for the next nineteen years Blessed Raymund was conspicuous also in a new sphere of activity. At the time of St Catherine's death he was elected master general of the Urbanist part of the Dominican Order, and he set himself to restore its fervour, grievously impaired by the schism, the Black Death, and general debility. He particularly sought to revive the more specifically monastic side of the order, and established a number of houses of strict observance in several provinces, whose influence was intended to permeate the whole. The reform was not completely successful, and it has been made a reproach to Blessed Raymund that his provisions tended to modify and lessen the studies of the friars ; on the other hand they also formed many holy men, and it is not for nothing that the twenty-third master general has been popularly called the second founder of his order. To spread the third order in the world was also part of his scheme, in which he was particularly supported by Father Thomas Caffarini, to whose relentless urging-on we owe the fact that Blessed Raymund persevered with and completed his Life of St Catherine. He also wrote, in his earlier and less burdened years, a Life of St Agnes of Montepulciano.

Blessed Raymund of Capua died on October 5, 1399, at Nuremberg, while working for Dominican reform in Germany. His body was translated to the church of St Dominic at Naples, and he was beatified by Pope Leo XIII in 1899.

No formal biography of Blessed Raymund is preserved to us from early times, but the sources for the life of St Catherine of Siena necessarily tell us a great deal about him (see April volume, p. 344). There are also his writings, collected in the volume *Opuscula et Litteræ* (1899) and the, unfortunately incomplete, *Registrum Litterarum* of the Dominician masters general edited by Fr. Reichert, O.P. These official documents are of great importance for their bearing on the reform movement in the Order which Raymund initiated. There is a good modern biography by Père Cormier, *Le bienheureux Raymond de Capoue* (1899), and the Beato occupies a conspicuous place in the third volume of Père Mortier's *Histoire des Maîtres Généraux*, O.P. See further the article by Bliemetzrieder in the *Historisches Jahrbuch*, vol. xxx (1909), pp. 231–273.

BD. FELICIA MEDA, Virg. and Abbess

A.D. 1444

Felicia Meda was born at Milan in 1378, the eldest of three children of good family. The sudden death of both her parents when she was a child disposed her mind to serious things, and soon after she was twelve she bound herself to a life of chastity and direct service of God, which she followed in the world for ten years. Then she gave away her estate to her family and to the poor, and became a Poor Clare in the convent of St Ursula at Milan ; shortly afterwards her sister followed her example and her brother became a Friar Minor. For twenty-five years Blessed Felicia lead the hidden and austere life of her order, remarkable in the community for her faultless observance of the rule and her perseverance in prayer and penance in spite of the diabolical influences that were active against her. Evil spirits are said to have appeared to her in terrifying forms and to have made physical assaults upon her, but the gentle nun overcame these fierce trials, and her experience and tempered character caused her to be elected abbess. Under her loving and skilful direction the devotion and virtue of the nuns of St Ursula's became famous, and when, some fourteen years later, in 1439, the wife of Galeazzo Malatesta, the Duke of Pesaro, wished to found a Poor Clare convent in that city she asked St Bernardino of Siena, minister of the Observants, for an affiliation from Milan. St Bernardino sent Blessed Felicia herself to make the new foundation, with seven of her nuns. The sadness with which the Milanese nuns parted from their abbess was equalled by the rejoicing with which she was received at Pesaro, whither her reputation had preceded her. The wife of Galeazzo, accompanied by the townspeople, came out to meet her and her nuns, but could not persuade them to get into the ducal carriages and drive in in state, so they made their entry into the city all together on foot. Blessed Felicia presided over the new convent for only four years, in which time she filled it with devoted religious, and died on September 30, 1444. The people of Pesaro, who had attributed their deliverance from war and plague to her prayers, flocked to venerate her tomb and were rewarded by many miracles. This ancient *cultus* was approved by Pope Pius VII in 1812.

In the *Acta Sanctorum*, September, vol. viii, a tolerably full account, based mainly on Mark of Lisbon, is given of this *beata*. An article, however, in the *Archivum Franciscanum Historicum*, vol. xx (1927), pp. 241–259, supplies a more thorough discussion of the sources, and points out that the sending of Blessed Felicia to Pesaro depended ultimately upon the Franciscan minister-general, Fra Guglielmo da Casale, whose letter imposing this obedience is still preserved. A Life of the *beata* by Fra Agostino Gallucci was printed in 1637.

THE LONDON MARTYRS OF 1588
(SECOND GROUP)

The first group of "Armada martyrs" in London suffered on August 28 and 30, 1588, and three more *beati* achieved their crowns on the following October 5. BLESSED WILLIAM HARTLEY was of yeoman stock, born about 1557 at Wilne, Derbyshire, in the same parish as Blessed Edward James. He was educated a Protestant and went up to St John's College, Oxford, where he ultimately became a chaplain. He was ejected by the vice-chancellor in 1579, went to Reims, was ordained at Châlons in 1580, and came back to England in the same year. For a time he helped Blessed Robert Campion and Father Parsons in their printing and publishing activities, but in eighteen months he was apprehended in the house of the Lady Stonor. For three and a half years he was in prison in London, the last twelve months in irons, having been caught saying Mass before other prisoners in his cell. At the beginning of 1585 he was deported, without trial, but, when he had recovered his health at Reims and made a pilgrimage to Rome, he returned secretly to London. In September 1588, Blessed William was arrested in Holborn, and a rumour was spread that he had apostatised. This was effectually contradicted by the heroic way in which he met his death, by hanging, " near the Theatre " in Shoreditch, and in the presence of his own mother. " He was a man," says a contemporary, " of the meekest disposition and naturally virtuous, modest, and grave, with a sober and peaceful look."

BLESSED JOHN HEWETT, who was hanged on the same day at Mile End Green for his priesthood, was son of a York draper and had been a student at Caius College, Cambridge. While yet a deacon he was arrested, put in prison at York, and then banished. After ordination to the priesthood at Reims in 1586, he came back to London and was seized in Grays Inn Lane in the following year. At that time he went under the name of John Weldon (*alias* Savell) and in that name he was again sent into exile. But he was arrested on a false charge in the Netherlands by the Earl of Leicester, who sent him to London for trial. Here he was tried and sentenced (as John Weldon) for being a seminary priest in England.

BLESSED ROBERT SUTTON, a schoolmaster of Paternoster Row, was hanged at Clerkenwell for being reconciled to the Church, he having been brought up a Protestant at his birthplace, Kegwell in Leicestershire. An eye-witness of his martyrdom, William Naylor, wrote : " . . . the sheriff promised to procure his pardon if he would but pronounce absolutely the word *all :* for he would that he should acknowledge the Queen to be supreme head in all causes without any restriction ; but he would acknowledge her to be supreme head in all causes temporal ; and for that he would not pronounce the word *all* without any restriction, he was executed. This I heard and saw."

Besides the account which is given in Challoner's *Missionary Priests* and in Stanton's *Menology*, see *The Lives of the English Martyrs*, second series (ed. Burton and Pollen), vol. i, pp. 508–536. A few other details may be gleaned in vol. v of the publications of the Catholic Record Society, e.g. pp. 20, 158, 291, etc.

OCTOBER 6

ST BRUNO, Conf.
Founder of the Carthusians
A.D. 1101

THE religious and learned Cardinal Bona, a great man not only of the Cistercian Order but of the whole Church, speaking of the Carthusian monks, of whose institute St Bruno was the founder, calls them, "the great miracles of the world: men living in the flesh as out of the flesh; the angels of the earth, representing John the Baptist in the wilderness; the greatest ornament of the Church; eagles soaring up to Heaven whose state is justly preferred to the institutes of all other religious orders." The originator of this remarkable body of men came of a good family and was born at Cologne about the year 1030. While still young he left home to finish his education at the cathedral school of Reims, at that time under the direction of Herimanus and one of the best schools in Europe. He did well in both classical and sacred studies, and returned to Cologne where he was ordained and was given a canonry in the collegiate church of St Cunibert (he may have held this even before he went to Reims). In 1056 he was invited to go back to his school as a professor, and when Herimanus retired in the following year, Gervasius, Archbishop of Reims, made Bruno rector, to which dignity then belonged the direction of the studies and all the great schools of the diocese. The fact that he was appointed to the charge of so famous a school when only about twenty-seven years old shows that he was no ordinary man, but at the same time does not suggest the way in which he was to become really distinguished in the memory of Christians. He personally taught "the most advanced, the learned, not young clerics," and in all his lessons and precepts he had chiefly in view to conduct men to God, and to make them know and respect his holy law. Many eminent scholars in philosophy and divinity did him honour by their proficiency and abilities, and carried his reputation into distant parts; among these Odo de Châtillon became afterwards a beatified pope under the name of Urban II. Robert of Burgundy, bishop of Langres, and cardinal Rangerius, and Archbishop of Reggio; while many other learned prelates of that age mention it as a particular honour and happiness that they had been Bruno's scholars. Such was his reputation that he was looked upon as " the light of churches, the doctor of doctors, the glory of the two nations of Germany and France, the ornament of the age, the model of good men, and the mirror of the world," to use the expressions of an ancient writer. He taught in and maintained the reputation of the school of Reims for eighteen years, when he was appointed chancellor of the diocese by Manasses, the successor of Gervasius, a man whose life made him utterly unfit to be in holy orders at all, much less an archbishop. Bruno soon learned the truth about him and Hugh of St Die, the pope's legate, summoned Manasses to appear at a council which he held at Autun in 1076, and upon his refusing to obey the summons declared him suspended from his functions. St Bruno, another Manasses, the provost, and Pontius, a canon of Reims, accused him in this council, and Bruno behaved with so much prudence and dignity that the legate, writing to the Pope, extolled his virtue and wisdom, styling him the most worthy doctor of the church of Reims, and recommending him as one excellently qualified to give good counsel and to assist in promoting the cause of God in the churches of France. Manasses, exasperated against the three canons who had appeared against him, caused their houses to be broken open and plundered, and sold their prebends. The persecuted priests took refuge in the castle of the Count of Rouçy, and remained there till the simoniacal archbishop, by deceiving Pope St Gregory VII (no easy matter), had been restored to his see, when Bruno went to Cologne. In 1080 Manasses was again excommunicated, and he fled to the court of the Emperor Henry IV. St Bruno then came back to Reims, not to be archbishop as many hoped, but as a step towards leaving it for ever.

Some years before he had come to a decision to abandon the active ecclesiastical life, of which he himself gives an account in his letter to Raoul or Ralph, provost of Reims. St Bruno, this Ralph, and another canon of Reims, named Fulcius, in a conversation which they had one day together in the garden of Bruno's landlord, discoursed on the vanity and false ambitions of the world and on the joys of eternal life, and being strongly affected by their serious reflections, promised one another to forsake the world. They deferred the execution of this resolve till Fulcius should return from Rome, whither he was going ; and he being detained there, Ralph slackened in his resolution and continued at Reims, became a monk there, and was afterwards made archbishop of that see. But Bruno persevered in his intention of embracing a state of religious retirement. He forsook the world in a time of flattering prosperity, when he enjoyed in it riches, honour, and the favour of men, and when the church of Reims was ready to choose him archbishop (if the King of France would have permitted). He resigned his benefice and renounced whatever held him in the world, and persuaded some of his friends to accompany him into solitude. They first put themselves under the direction of St Robert, abbot of Molesmes (who was afterwards to found Cîteaux), and then lived in a hermitage at Sèche-Fontaine near by.* In this solitude Bruno, with an earnest desire for true perfection in virtue, considered with himself and deliberated with his companions what it was best for them to do, seeking the will of God in the exercises of solitude, penance, and prayer. He at length decided that their present home was unsuitable and to apply to St Hugh, bishop of Grenoble, who was truly a servant of God and a person better qualified than any other to assist him; moreover, he was told that in the diocese of Grenoble there were woods and deserts most suitable to his desire of finding perfect solitude. Six only of those who had accompanied him in his retreat now attended him, namely Landuin, who afterwards succeeded him as prior of the Grande Chartreuse; Stephen of Bourg and Stephen of Die, both canons of St Rufus in Dauphiné; Hugh, whom they called "the Chaplain" (all most learned men), and two laymen, Andrew and Guerin. St Bruno and these six companions arrived at Grenoble about midsummer in 1084, and came before St Hugh, begging of him some place where they might serve God, remote from worldly affairs and without being burdensome to men. Hugh received them with open arms, for these seven strangers had been represented to him in a vision he had the night before in his sleep: wherein he thought he saw God Himself building a church in the desert called the Chartreuse, and seven stars rising from the ground and forming a circle which went before him to that place as it were to show him the way to the church. He embraced them very lovingly and assigned them that desert of Chartreuse for their retreat, promising his utmost assistance to establish them there. But that they might be armed against the difficulties they would meet with, lest they should enter upon so great an undertaking without having well considered it, he at the same time warned them of its situation, most difficult of access among the mountains, beset with high craggy rocks, almost all the year covered with snow. St Bruno accepted the offer with joy, and St Hugh made over to

* The often repeated story of the conversion of St Bruno by being a witness of the declaration of the dead Raymond Diocres that he was a lost soul is not mentioned by himself or any of his contemporaries. It was deleted from the Roman Breviary as apocryphal by Pope Urban VIII.

them all the rights he had in that forest, as did the abbot of Chaise-Dieu in Auvergne, who was joint lord. Bruno and his companions immediately built an oratory there, and small cells at a little distance one from the other, like the ancient *lauras* of Palestine. Such was the origin of the order of the Carthusians, which took its name from this desert of Chartreuse.* St Hugh, by a charter in the month following, forbade any woman to go into their lands or any person to fish, hunt, or drive cattle that way. The monks first built a church on a summit and cells near it, in which they lived two together in each cell (soon after, alone), meeting in church at Matins and Vespers ; other hours they recited in their cells. They never took two meals in a day except on the great festivals, on which they ate together in a refectory. On other days they ate in their cells as hermits. Everything amongst them was extremely poor : even in their church they would have no gold or silver, except a silver chalice. They scarcely ever spoke to one another, save by signs, and seemed to have no other use for their bodies than to afflict and humble them with austerities. Labour succeeded prayer. It was a chief work to copy books, by which they endeavoured to earn their subsistence, and, if all else was poor, the library was rich. The soil of their mountains was bad and its climate hard, so they had few cornfields, but they bred cattle as a source of income. Blessed Peter the Venerable, abbot of Cluny, some twenty-five years after St Bruno, writes of them : " Their dress is poorer than that of other monks ; so short and thin and so rough that the very sight frightens one. They wear hair shirts next their skin and fast almost perpetually ; eat only bran-bread ; never touch flesh, either sick or well ; never buy fish, but eat it if given them as an alms. . . . Their constant occupation is praying, reading, and manual labour, which consists chiefly in transcribing books. They say Mass only on Sundays and Festivals." This manner of life they followed without any written rule, though they conformed to that of St Benedict in some points which were compatible with an eremitical life. St Bruno made his disciples fervent observers of the customs and practices he had established, which Guigo, fifth prior of the Chartreuse, drew up in writing in 1227. The Carthusian is the only old religious order in the Church which never had any reform and has never stood in need of any, owing to the entire sequestration from the world and to the vigilance of superiors and visitors in never allowing a door to be opened for mitigations and dispensations to creep in. This institute has been regarded by the Church as the most perfect model of a penitential

* As does each separate monastery of Carthusians, *e.g.* in Italian, *certosa*, in Spanish, *cartuja*, in English, *charterhouse.*

and contemplative state, and yet St Bruno when he established his hermit-monks had no intention of founding a new religious order. That they spread beyond the mountains of Dauphiné is due, under God, to a call which came to him only six years after he went to the Chartreuse and which was as unwelcome as it was unexpected. He had " to come down again to these prisoners and to have part in their toils and honours."

St Bruno was styled by the writers of that age master of the Chartreuse, and sometimes prior, for being the person who led the rest into that life he was looked upon by them as their superior ; and as he was the most learned, so he also excelled them in fervour. St Hugh became so great an admirer of his virtue that he took him for his father and spiritual director, and without regard to the difficulty of the way often went from Grenoble to the Chartreuse, to enjoy the conversation of St Bruno and improve himself by his advice and example. But his fame went beyond Grenoble and reached the ears of Odo de Châtillon, his former pupil at Reims and now Pope Urban II. Hearing of the holy life which he led, and being from his own personal acquaintance fully convinced of his great prudence and learning, the Pope sent him an order to come to Rome that he might assist him by his counsels in the government of the Church. Bruno could have scarcely met with a more severe trial of his obedience or made a greater sacrifice. Nevertheless, without further deliberation he set out early in 1090, having nominated Landuin prior at the Chartreuse. The departure of the saint was an inexpressible grief to his disciples, and some of them went away. The rest, with Landuin, followed their master to Rome, but they were prevailed upon by Bruno to return to their former habitation, of which the monks of Chaise-Dieu had taken possession upon their leaving. They recovered their former cells, which were restored to them by the Abbot of Chaise-Dieu, to the joy of St Hugh and of Hugh, Archbishop of Lyons, legate of the Holy See, who both conducted them back and saw them again settled there. St Bruno, meanwhile, had permission to occupy a hermitage among the ruins of the Baths of Diocletian, where he would be close at hand when required by the Pope. Exactly what part he played in the papal activities of the time we do not know. Work formerly attributed to him is now recognised as having been done by his namesake, St Bruno of Segni, but he certainly helped in the preparation of various synods in which Blessed Urban aimed at the reformation of the clergy. That Bruno should efface himself and that his influence should be hidden is what is to be expected from so contemplative a spirit. Soon, however, the papal court had to remove to the south of Italy, and Bruno with it. Here Urban pressed him to accept the archbishopric of Reggio in Calabria, but the saint excused himself with so great earnestness, and redoubled his importunities for the liberty of living in solitude, that the Pope at length consented that he might retire into some wilderness in the mountains of Calabria where he would be at hand, but not to the Chartreuse—that was too far off. Count Roger, brother of Robert Guiscard, gave him the beautiful and fertile valley of La Torre, in the diocese of Squillace, where he settled with some new disciples whom he had gained in Rome. Here he betook himself to the exercises of a solitary life with more joy and fervour than ever. Remembering the resolve which his old friend Ralph of Reims had made to embrace a solitary life, he wrote him from this place a tender letter inviting him to his hermitage, putting him in mind of the obligation he had taken upon himself, and giving him an agreeable and cheerful description of his desert, and of the joy and delight which he and his companions found in it. This letter it was which caused Ralph to become a monk in the monastery of Saint-Rémi. Its tone shows how far the saint was from the least disposition of melancholy, moroseness, or harsh severity. Gaiety of soul, which always attends true virtue, is particularly necessary in all who are called to a life of solitude, in which nothing is more pernicious than sadness, and to which nothing is more contrary than a tendency to morbid introspection. In the year 1100 Landuin, prior of the Chartreuse, went into Calabria to consult St Bruno about the form of living which he had instituted, for the monks were desirous not to depart in the least from the spirit and rule of their master. St Bruno wrote them a letter full of tender charity and the spirit of God, which he sent by Landuin when he returned ; in it he instructed them in all the practices of a solitary life, solved the difficulties which they proposed to him, comforted them in their troubles, and encouraged them to perseverance and watch against all the attacks of their enemies. By the establishment of this second charterhouse, St Stephen's, at La Torre, the Carthusian life was extended beyond the fastness of the mountains of Dauphiné, which but for St Bruno's ready obedience to the call of the Holy See might never have happened. He established in it that spirit which guided the monks of the Grande Chartreuse, and on its temporal side he was mostly generously helped by Count Roger, with whom he formed a close friendship. Bruno would visit Roger and his family at Mileto, when there was a baptism or some such matter toward, and Roger would frequently go and stay at La Torre ; and they died within three months of one another. On one occasion, while besieging Capua, Roger was saved from the treachery of one of his officers by being warned by St Bruno in a dream. The treachery was verified and the man condemned to death, but he was pardoned at Bruno's request.

His last sickness came upon him towards the end of September 1101, and when he saw death near he gathered his monks about his bed, and in their presence made a public confession of his life and a profession of faith, which his disciples set down and preserved. It is very clear and explicit on the mysteries of the Trinity and Incarnation, and in condemning the heresy of Berengarius, which had lately raised trouble in the Church. He thus expressed his faith in the Sacrament of the Altar : " I believe in the Holy Sacrament which the Church believeth, namely, that the substance of bread and wine is changed on the altar, so as to be after consecration the true Body of our Lord Jesus Christ ; His true Flesh and His true Blood, which we receive for the remission of our sins and as a pledge of eternal life." He resigned his soul to God on Sunday, October 6, 1101. An account of his death was sent by his monks of La Torre in an encyclical letter to the chief churches and monasteries of Italy, France, Germany, England, and Ireland according to custom to recommend the souls of persons deceased to their prayers. This mortuary-roll of St Bruno, with the *elogia* written thereon by the one hundred and seventy-eight recipients, is one of the fullest and most valuable of such documents extant. St Bruno has never been formally canonised, the Carthusians being averse from all occasions of publicity ; but in 1514 they obtained leave from Pope Leo X to keep his feast, and in 1623 Gregory XV extended it to the whole Western Church. In Calabria he enjoys all the veneration of a " popular " saint ; the contrast of contemplative and active in his life is thus mirrored in the circumstances of his *cultus*.

St Bruno had often in his mind the words of the Psalmist : " My eyes prevented the watches. I was troubled and I spoke not. I thought upon the days of old and I had in my mind the eternal years. . . . Lo ! I have gone far off, flying away, and I abode in the wilderness." This constant meditation on eternity animated him with fervour and the spirit of penance, and made him pass whole nights in tears calling down God's mercy on himself and on the world. For all men to converse much in Heaven, by the constant union of our hearts to God, is the shortest road to Christian perfection. Those who are employed in the active life ought to learn the art of accompanying all their actions with a lively attention to the divine presence, just as our guardian angels are faithful in discharging every duty of that external ministry which God has committed to them, yet so as never to intermit the contemplation of the Godhead

and the incessant homage of praise and love which are the uninterrupted occupation of their happy state. Without this precaution,
by the hurry of worldly affairs, of studies, and even in the discharge
of the sacred ministry itself, the spirit of piety and devotion is extinguished in the heart and the most sacred functions are easily profaned.

Although there is nothing in the nature of a contemporary Life of
St Bruno, a good deal of information is available from other sources.
The *Vita Antiquior*, printed by the Bollandists, October, vol. iii, cannot
have been written before the thirteenth century, and it begins with the
story of the conversion of Bruno through the miracle of the dead man's
avowal that he was buried in Hell, a story now generally discredited, as
pointed out above. But in Guibert de Nogent's autobiography, in Guido's
account of St Hugh of Grenoble, and in contemporary chronicles and
letters (including two letters of Bruno himself), etc., a vivid picture of
the saint is presented. These materials have been collected and turned
to account both in the *Acta Sanctorum* under this day, in the *Annales
Ordinis Cartusiensis* of Dom Le Couteulx, vol. i, and in several modern
Lives. Mention in particular should be made of H. Löbbel, *Der Stifter
des Carthäuser-Ordens* (1899) ; and of the somewhat less critical *Vie de
S. Bruno*, by a monk of the Grande Chartreuse (1898). See also the
slighter sketches by M. Gorse and Boyer d'Agen, both published in 1902.
St Bruno's authentic works, mostly Scripture commentaries, were reprinted
by the Carthusians at Montreuil-sur-Mer in 1891–2. On his relations with
Archbishop Manasses in the earlier part of his life reference may be made
to Wiedemann, *Gregor VII und Erzbischof Manasses I von Reims* (1885),
together with Hefele-Leclercq, *Conciles*, vol. v, pp. 220–226. A tolerably
full bibliography of writings concerning St Bruno is contained in the
article " Chartreux " in the *Dictionnaire de Théologie*, vol. ii, cc. 2279–2282.

ST FAITH, VIRG. AND MART.

A.D. 287 ?

When this maiden was summoned to answer for her Christianity
before the procurator Dacian at Agen she signed herself with the
cross and called to Heaven for help in these words : " Lord Jesus,
who art always ready to assist Your servants, fortify me at this hour
and enable me to answer in a manner worthy of You." Thus
strengthened, she turned to Dacian, who asked her, " What is your
name ? " She answered, " My name is Faith (*Fides*) and I endeavour
to have that which I am named." Then he asked, " What is your
religion ? " and she said, " I have served Christ from my infancy.
and to Him I have consecrated my whole soul." Dacian was disposed to be merciful, and appealed to her. " Come, child, remember
your youth and beauty. Renounce the religion you profess and
sacrifice to Diana ; she is a divinity of your own sex and will bestow

on you all sorts of good things." But Faith replied, " The divinities of the Gentiles are evil. How then can you expect me to sacrifice to them ? "—" You presume to call our gods evil ! " exclaimed Dacian. " You must instantly offer sacrifice, or die in torments." The saint, remembering the courage of the martyrs and the glorious crown promised to those who persevere to the end, felt herself inflamed with a new desire to die for her Lord. " No ! " she cried, " I am prepared to suffer every torment for Christ. I long to die for Him." Dacian ordered a brazen bed to be produced and the saint to be bound on it with chains. A fire was kindled under, the heat of which was made still more intolerable by the addition of oil. Some of the spectators, struck with pity and horror, exclaimed, " How can he thus torment an innocent girl only for worshipping God ! " Thereupon Dacian arrested certain of them, and as these refused to sacrifice they were beheaded with St Faith. The legend of St Faith is late and untrustworthy and confused with that of St Caprasius (October 20) and the apocryphal duplicate SS. Primus and Felician, but her *cultus* was widespread in Europe during the Middle Ages. The chapel in the eastern part of the crypt of St Paul's Cathedral in London is still called St Faith's. Its predecessor before the Fire was the church of the parishioners of St Faith's parish in Faringdon Ward Within, their parish church having been pulled down when the choir of the cathedral was lengthened in the year 1240.

The legend of St Faith and of the miracles worked at her shrine was unusually popular in the Middle Ages. In the *Bibliotheca Hagiographica Latina* thirty-eight distinct Latin texts, nn. 2928–2965, are enumerated, and these gave rise to a considerable literature in the vernacular which is of great philological interest. See, for example, Hoepfener and Alfaric, *La Chanson de Sainte Foy*, 2 vols. (1926), and the review of the same work in the *Analecta Bollandiana*, vol. xlv (1927), pp. 421–425. An early and relatively sober text of the *passio* (which does not mention St Caprasius by name) is printed in the *Acta Sanctorum*, October, vol. iii. *Cf.* also Bouillet-Servières, *Sainte Foy* (1900) and Duchesne, *Fastes Épiscopaux*, vol. ii, pp. 144–146. The mention of St Faith in the *Hieronymianum* affords some presumption that she did actually suffer at Agen, but the date is problematical.

ST NICETAS, CONF.

c. A.D. 838

Among the courtiers of the Empress Irene, the great upholder of the Catholic doctrine and practice of the veneration of images of our Lord and the saints, was a young patrician named Nicetas. He came of a Paphlagonian family related to the Empress, and is said to have been sent by her to the second œcumenical Council of Nicæa, in the acts of which, however, he is not mentioned as one of her two official representatives.   In the palace revolution which put Nicephorus I on the throne Nicetas retained his office as prefect of Sicily (his feast is kept at Messina), perhaps at the cost of taking part against his patroness, but when Nicephorus was slain in the year 811 he entered the monastery of Chrysonike in Constantinople. Here he remained until the Emperor Leo the Armenian began his attack on the holy images, when Nicetas and other monks retired to a country house, taking with them a very precious *ikon* of our Lord.   When the Emperor heard of this he sent a company of soldiers, who took away the picture by force, and Nicetas was forbidden to leave his place of refuge.   Nothing more is known of him for over a dozen years, when the Emperor Theophilus called on him to recognise the communion of the Iconoclast patriarch Antony.   This St Nicetas peremptorily refused to do, and with three other monks he was driven from his monastery.   As there was a penalty attached to giving shelter to defenders of the images they had great difficulty in finding another refuge ;   they were pursued from place to place, till at last St Nicetas found peace and security on a farm at Katisia in his native Paphlagonia.   Here he built a church in honour of the Holy Angels and lived for the rest of his life.

A brief account of this Nicetas, based mainly upon the Greek *Menæa*, is given in the *Acta Sanctorum*, October, vol. iii.   *Cf.* also the *Constantinople Synaxary*, edited by Delehaye, cc. 115–6.

ST MARY-FRANCES, Virg.

A.D. 1791

Barbara Basinsin, mother of this saint, had much to suffer before the child's birth, from the roughness and bad temper of her husband, Francis Gallo, and from horrible dreams and delusions.   In her distress she opened her heart to the Franciscan St John-Joseph-of-the-Cross and the Jesuit St Francis-Jerome.   They reassured and comforted her and are moreover said to have prophesied the future holiness of the unborn babe, who was born at Naples in 1715 and baptised Anne Mary Rose Nicolette.   Her family was *bourgeois*, and when Anne was sixteen her father set his heart on her marrying a wealthy young man of rather better family, who was most anxious to have the virtuous and attractive girl as his wife.   But she had already made up her mind to give herself to Christ only.   From her earliest years she had been unusually religious : she had been admitted to holy Communion at seven years of age, and it was popularly said that she was instructed in the faith by her guardian angel himself. Anne therefore resolutely opposed her father in this matter, to his great indignation. His brutal temper carried him away, and he beat the girl with a cord and locked her in her room with only bread and water. She was glad enough to suffer thus for her faithfulness to God's call, while her mother tried to persuade Francis Gallo to let Anne have her wish of enrolling herself among the tertiaries of St Francis. To help her she called in Father Theophilus, a friar of the Observance, who at length made Gallo see that his conduct was unjust and unreasonable, and got him to drop his insistence on the advantageous match.

Accordingly, on September 8, 1731, Anne received the habit of the third order secular in the Franciscan church of the Alcantarine reform at Naples. As a testimony to her devotion to our Lord's passion she took the name of Mary-Frances-of-the-Five-Wounds. In accordance with a practice then not entirely obsolete she continued to live at home, wearing the habit of her order and devoting herself to a religious life of piety and material usefulness ; during the last thirty-eight years she directed the household of a secular priest, Don John Pessiri. Sister Mary-Frances displayed in herself a number of the physical phenomena of mysticism in a marked degree. While making the stations of the cross, especially on Fridays and particularly the Fridays of Lent, she would experience pains corresponding to those of the Passion : of the agony in the garden, the scourging, the crowning with thorns, and so on week by week in order, culminating in an appearance of death. She is said to have received the *stigmata*. But the most remarkable occurrences were with reference to the Blessed Sacrament to which she had a very deep devotion, being allowed to receive It every day. It is alleged that three times the sacred Host came to her mouth without visible agency : once from the celebrant's fingers as he said *Ecce Agnus Dei*, once from the ciborium, and once the piece which is broken off the larger Host to be put into the chalice. But the Barnabite Blessed Francis-Xavier Bianchi testifies to even more astonishing things when he says : " During my Masses God allowed her to partake of the Precious Blood that was in the chalice. In truth, the archangel Raphael, after the consecration and my communion, took the chalice from the altar and carried it to the residence of the servant of God, who was kept there by illness, and communicated her. Sometimes she drank very little, hardly three sips, but another time she drank about half. I was well aware of the disappearance of part of the

78

KENRICK SEMINARY LIBRARY
7800 KENRICK ROAD
ST. LOUIS, MISSOURI 63119

Precious Blood. When I questioned her about what had happened, she replied, ' Father, if the archangel St Raphael had not warned me that the Sacrifice was not completed I should have drunk the whole.' " At the Christmas of 1741 Sister Mary-Frances received the mystical espousals. While praying at the crib she seemed to see our Lord in glory stretching out His right hand to her and to hear the words, " This night you shall be my bride." The experience brought on a temporary loss of sight, which lasted till the next day. She was favoured with other visions and was very frequently wrapt away in ecstasy.

To the sufferings that have been referred to were added bodily ill-health and distress caused by the unkindness to her of her father and other members of her family. But St Mary-Frances did not think these enough, and added to them severe voluntary austerities, at the same time asking God that she might take upon herself the pains of those in Purgatory (including, eventually, her own father) and of her sick and sinful neighbours. Her confessor one day exclaimed that he wondered there were any souls left in Purgatory at all. Several times, it is said, dead persons appeared to her, asking for particular prayers to be said on their behalf. " With her eyes fixed on Heaven," says another confessor, " she offered all her sufferings to the Eternal Father in union with those of Jesus Christ, blessing and praising Him and ready for yet more." To the Theatine provincial, Father Gaetano Laviosa, she said that she had endured all that could be endured. Priests, religious, and lay people came to her for help and direction. To Friar Peter-Baptist, of the Alcantarines, she said, " Take care, father, not to let jealousies arise among your penitents. We poor women are very subject to it, as I know by experience ; I have suffered from it. I thank God for prompting my confessor to act in the way he did. He told me to come to confession after all his other penitents, and when I went in he often only said to me sharply, ' Go to Communion.' Then the Devil whispered in my ear how little sympathy my confessor had for me, how he ignored what I suffered at home from my father and sisters when they complained angrily at my coming back from church so late. But what troubled me most were the remarks of the neighbours because I went to confession so often. I tell you this both that you may be careful and gentle, and also not spare those who need a little severity."

St Mary-Frances lived till the early years of the French Revolution, and she clearly foresaw in a general way some of the events that were to come. " I can see nothing but disasters," she said more than once. " Troubles in the present, greater troubles in the future. I pray God that I may not live to witness them." She died on October 6, 1791, and was buried in the church of Santa Lucia del Monte at Naples. She had promised Blessed Francis-Xavier Bianchi that she would appear to him three days before his death, and is said actually to have done so on January 28, 1815. St Mary-Frances was beatified in 1843 and canonised in 1867.

A short biography by Father Laviosa, who had known the saint personally, was published not long after her death, and this was revised and issued again in 1866, in anticipation apparently of the canonization which took place next year (1867), for it bears the title : *Vita di Santa Maria Francesca delle Cinque Piaghe di Gesù Cristo*, and she is called " Santa " throughout. This Life was also translated into French ; and from the same source was abbreviated the account in Léon, *Auréole séraphique* (Eng. trans.), vol. iii, pp. 278–286. Another Life by Luigi Montella was published at Naples in 1866. For the physical phenomena see Imbert-Gourbeyre, *La Stigmatisation* (1892), vol. i, pp. 436–441.

OCTOBER 7

THE MOST HOLY ROSARY OF THE BLESSED VIRGIN MARY

POPE ST PIUS V in 1571 ordered an annual commemoration of our Lady of Victory to be made to implore God's mercy on the Church and all the faithful, and to thank Him for His protection and numberless benefits, particularly for His having delivered Christendom from the arms of the infidel Turks by the sea victory of Lepanto in that year, a victory which seemed a direct answer to the prayers and processions of the Rosary Confraternities at Rome made while the battle was actually being fought. Two years later Gregory XIII changed the name of the feast to that of the Rosary and granted it to all churches which had an altar dedicated in honour of the Rosary, fixing it for the first Sunday in October (the day of Lepanto). On August 5, the feast of the dedication of St Mary Major, in the year 1716, again while the Marian processions were taking place, the Turks were again signally defeated, by Prince Eugene at Peterwardein in Hungary. In thanksgiving therefor, Pope Clement XI decreed that the feast of the Holy Rosary should be observed throughout the Western Church. Pope Leo XIII raised its rank to that of a double of the second class and added the invocation " Queen of the most Holy Rosary " to the Litany of Loreto. The feast is now kept on the date of the battle of Lepanto, October 7 (except by the Dominicans, who observe the original first Sunday of the month), and a *toties quoties* plenary indulgence may be gained on that day on the usual conditions by those visiting a church in which the Rosary Confraternity is erected.

The rosary is a practice of devotion in which, during fifteen " Our Fathers " and " Glorias " and one hundred and fifty " Hail Marys," divided into ones and tens, the faithful are taught to honour our divine Redeemer by meditating on the fifteen principal mysteries of His sacred life and of His holy Mother. It is therefore an abridgement of the gospel, a history of the life, sufferings, and triumphant victory of Jesus Christ, and an exposition of what He did in the flesh which He assumed for our salvation. The principal object of the devotion of every Christian ought to be always to bear in mind these mysteries, to return to God a perpetual homage of love, praise, and thanksgiving for them, to implore His mercy through them, to make them the subject of meditation, and to mould his affections, regulate his life, and form his spirit by the impressions which they make on his soul. The rosary as a method of doing this is easy in itself and adapted to the slowest or feeblest capacity ; and at the same time sublime and faithful in the exercise of all the highest acts of prayer, contemplation and interior virtues. These are admirably comprised in the prayer which our Lord Himself vouchsafed to teach us, which those who penetrate the spirit of each word can never weary in repeating. To obtain mercy and grace no prayer can be offered to God more efficacious or pleasing than that which is put into our hearts and mouths by His Son, our blessed Redeemer Himself. All other good prayers are but paraphrases or expositions of it, and it is more especially pleasing to God and beneficial to us when it is offered in honour of the mysteries of our redemption, to pay the homage of our love and thanksgiving for them, and to ask God's mercy, love, and compassion by them. The " Hail Mary " is often repeated in the rosary because, as it contains praise for the Incarnation, it best suits a devotion instituted to honour that mystery. Though it be addressed to the Mother of God, with an invocation of her intercession, it is chiefly a praise and thanksgiving to the Son for the divine mercy therein. The Holy Ghost is the principal author of this prayer, which the archangel Gabriel, the messenger of the Blessed Trinity, began ; St Elizabeth, another mouthpiece of the Holy Ghost, continued, and the Church finished it ; for the first and second part consist of the praises bestowed on the Blessed Virgin by St Gabriel and by St Elizabeth inspired by the Holy Ghost ; the last part was added by the Church, with the petition for her intercession and styling her Mother of God.

According to the tradition of the Order of Preachers, recognised by many popes and accepted in the Roman Breviary, the rosary, just as we know it, was devised by St Dominic himself, and used by him in his missionary work among the Albigensians, in consequence of a vision in which our Lady revealed it to him. No tradition of the kind has been more passionately supported and few have been more devastatingly attacked. Its truth was first questioned some two hundred years ago, and the resulting controversy has been carried on at intervals ever since. It is well known that the use of beads or similar objects as a device for aiding the memory and keeping count is not only pre-Dominican but pre-Christian ; and the monks of the Eastern Church use a rosary of ancient origin, having 100 or 103 beads, on a quite different plan from and entirely independent of the Western devotion. Nor is it now disputed that the custom of saying a number of *Paters* or *Aves* (often 150, corresponding to the number of the psalms), and keeping count of them by means of a string of beads, etc., was widespread in the West before the thirteenth century. Such an article was found with the relics of St Rosalia (see September 4), and the famous Lady Godiva of Coventry, who died about 1075, left by will to a certain statue of our Lady " the circlet of precious stones which she had threaded on a cord in order that by fingering them one after another she might count her prayers exactly " (William of Malmesbury). Moreover there is no doubt that such strings of beads were used for long only for the counting of *Paters*. In the thirteenth century and throughout the Middle Ages such articles were called " paternosters " ; their makers were " paternosterers " ; and in London they worked in the street we still call Paternoster Row. A learned Dominican bishop, Mgr. Esser, maintained that meditation while reciting numerous *Aves* was first practised by certain Carthusians in the fourteenth century. None of the stories about the origin of the rosary current before the fifteenth century mention St Dominic, and for another hundred years there was no uniformity in the way it was said, even among the Friars Preachers themselves. Negatively, none of the early accounts of St Dominic make any mention of the rosary, either in referring to his methods of prayer or to anything else ; the early constitutions of his order are quite silent about it ; and there is little trace of a rosary in early Dominican iconography, from Fra Angelico's paintings down to St Dominic's sumptuous tomb at Bologna (finished in 1532).

Under stress of the facts just summarised recent opinion regarding the origin of the rosary has diverged considerably from the views which prevailed at the close of the sixteenth century. Writing in 1922, Dom Louis Gougaud, O.S.B., states that " the various elements which enter into the composition of that Catholic devotion commonly called the Rosary are the product of a long and gradual development which began before St. Dominic's time, which continued without his having any share in it and which only attained its final shape several centuries after his death." Father Getino, O.P., considers that St. Dominic was the originator of the devotion on the ground that he presumably popularized the practice of reciting multiplied *Aves*, without, however, any special direction as to the number of repetitions or the systematic insertion of *Paters*. Father Bede Jarrett, O.P., on the other hand, considers that St. Dominic's special contribution was the breaking up of the *Aves* into groups of ten by the insertion of *Paters* ; while Père Mortier, O.P., asserts with all the emphasis of italics that the rosary as conceived by St. Dominic was not properly speaking *a devotion, a formula of prayer ; it was a method of preaching.*

If it be necessary to abandon the idea of its invention and even propagation of its use by St Dominic himself, the Western rosary is none the less properly distinguished as the Dominican rosary ; the friars of his order gave it the form it now has and for four hundred and fifty years have zealously spread its use throughout the world, bringing thereby unnumbered blessings to countless souls and sending up a ceaseless pæan of worship before God. No Christian is too simple or unlettered to make use of the rosary ; it may be the vehicle of high contemplation as well as of the simplest petition or aspiration ; as a form of private prayer it comes only after the biblical psalms and those prayers with which the Church as Church praises almighty God and His Christ. It is only fitting that so great a means of good should be publicly celebrated in her liturgy.

As to the origin of this feast consult Benedict XIV, *De Festis*, Bk. II, ch. 12, n. 16 ; and Esser, *Unseres Lieben Frauen Rosenkranz*, p. 354. The case against the claim made for St Dominic in the matter of the institution of the rosary will be found most fully presented in the *Acta Sanctorum*, August, vol. i, pp. 422, *seq.* ; in *The Month*, October 1900 to April 1901 ; and in Father Holzapfel, O.S.F., *S. Dominikus und der Rosenkranz* (1903). There have, of course, been many attempted vindications of the Dominican tradition, but it is instructive to contrast the uncompromising tone of such books as that of Père Mézard, O.P., *Étude sur les Origines du Rosaire* (1912), of that of Father W. Lescher, *St Dominic and the Rosary* (1902), with the attitude of Père Mortier, O.P., *Histoire des Maîtres Généraux, O.P.*, vol. i (1903), pp. 15–16 and vol. vii, p. 189 n., or of Father Bede Jarrett, *Life of St. Dominic* (1924), p. 110. See also *The Month*, October 1924 ; Dom Gougaud in *La Vie et Les Arts liturgiques*, October 1922, and July 1924 ; and Jean Guiraud in his *Life of St Dominic*, p. 11, and in his *Cartulaire de Prouille*, Preface, pp. 328–330.

SS. SERGIUS AND BACCHUS, MARTS.

A.D. 303

These martyrs were officers of the Roman army on the Syrian frontier, Sergius being described as commandant of the recruits' school and Bacchus as his subaltern. They were personal favourites of the Emperor Maximian, until one day when he went into the temple of Jupiter to sacrifice he noticed that they stopped outside. They were ordered to come in and take part in the sacrifice. On their refusal, they were stripped of their arms and badges of rank, dressed up in women's clothes, and so paraded through the streets.

They were then despatched to Resapha in Mesopotamia, where the governor had them so severely scourged that St Bacchus died under the lash, on October 1, 303. His body was thrown out on to the highway, where the dogs protected it from the attacks of vultures, an incident recorded of several other martyrs. St Sergius was made to walk a long distance in shoes with nails thrust through into his feet, and on October 7 was beheaded. The martyrdom of these two officers is very well attested by the evidence of the martyrologies and early writers, but the particulars of their passion are far from trustworthy. In the year 431 Alexander, Metropolitan of Hierapolis restored and beautified the church over their grave, whose walls in the middle of the sixth century were plated with silver. Alexander was very annoyed when, three years after he had spent so much money on it, Resapha was taken from his jurisdiction and made a bishopric. The Emperor Anastasius I renamed the place Sergiopolis, and Justinian fortified it and greatly honoured the memory of the martyrs. The church of SS. Sergius and Bacchus was dedicated in Rome in the seventh century, but they are not mentioned in the oldest Roman sacramentaries ; their liturgical commemoration in the West dates only from the eleventh or twelfth century. They have now a commemoration on October 7.

If we may trust the *Voyage Archéologique* of Le Bas and Waddington, vol. iii, n. 2124, a church in Eastern Syria, dedicated to these two martyrs in 354, affords the earliest known example of this form of recognition of sanctity. Their " Acts " are preserved in Latin, Greek and Syriac. See the *Analecta Bollandiana*, vol. xiv (1895), pp. 373–395, and, for a list of the various recensions, the *Bibliotheca Hagiographica* in its three divisions, *Latina*, *Græca* and *Orientalis*. Père Delehaye in his *Origines du Culte des Saints*, pp. 242–244 calls attention to the extraordinary popularity of St Sergius in the East as evidenced not only by the number of churches and sanctuaries dedicated in his honour either alone or jointly with St Bacchus, but also by the prevalence of Sergius as a baptismal name. On Resapha, or, as it is also written, Rosapha, etc., consult Spanner and Guyer, *Rusafa* (1926), Herzfeld, *Archæologische Reise* (1911–1922) and Peeters in *Analecta Bollandiana*, xlv (1927), pp. 162–165.

ST JUSTINA, VIRG. AND MART.
A.D. 304 (?)

She probably suffered at Padua in the persecution of Diocletian. St Venantius Fortunatus, Bishop of Poitiers in the six–seventh century, ranks her among the most illustrious virgins whose sanctity and triumph have adorned the Church, saying that her name makes Padua famous, as Euphemia does Chalcedon and Eulalia the city of Merida. And in his poem on the life of St Martin he bids those who visit Padua to kiss the sacred sepulchre of the blessed Justina, on the walls of which they will see the actions of St Martin represented in figures or paintings. A church was built at Padua in her honour about the middle of the fifth century, and herein in 1177 her alleged relics were found. About the same time appeared a very clumsily forged account of her passion, which pretends that St Justina was baptised by St Prosdocimus, " a disciple of the blessed Peter," who gave his information to the writer. This Prosdocimus, we are told, was the first bishop of Padua and a martyr under Nero, and St Justina was slain by the sword for her faithfulness to Christ, with a number of particulars for the truth of which there is no evidence.

The fifteenth-century Benedictine " reform " of St Justina (now the Italian Cassinese congregation) took its name from the church of this saint at Padua, where it was inaugurated.

See the *Acta Sanctorum*, October, vol. iii, but there is an older text of the *Passio* printed in the *Analecta Bollandiana*, vol. x (1891), pp. 467–470 ; and *ibid.*, vol. xi (1892), pp. 354–358, an account of the alleged discovery of her relics in 1117. See also Allard, *Histoire des Persécutions*, vol. iv, pp. 430 *seq.*, and Trifone's three articles in the *Rivista Storica Benedettina*, 1910 and 1911.

ST MARK, POPE AND CONF.

A.D. 336

St Mark was by birth a Roman and served God with fervour among the clergy of that church. Advancing continually in humility and the sense of his own weakness and imperfections, he strove every day to surpass himself in the fervour of charity and zeal. Mark was the first pope to be elected after the freeing of Christianity by Constantine. He did not let the new conditions relax his watchfulness, but endeavoured rather to redouble his zeal during the peace of the Church ; knowing that, if men cease openly to persecute the faithful, the Devil never allows them any truce, and his snares are generally most to be feared in the time of a calm. The saint contributed very much to advance the service of God during the pontificate of St Sylvester ; after whose death he was himself placed in the apostolic chair on January 18, 336. He held the dignity only eight months and twenty days, dying on October 7 following. According to the *Liber Pontificalis* he built two churches, one over the cemetery of Balbina between the Via Appia and the Via Ardeatina, where he was afterwards buried ; another within the walls, near the Capitol, the cardinalatial titular of San Marco. He is also said to have conferred the *pallium* on the Bishop of Ostia together with the right to consecrate the Bishop of Rome ; later bishops of Ostia certainly exercised this right, but the conferring of the *pallium* at this date cannot be verified. A fragmentary poem on a St Mark by Pope St Damasus, which some authorities refer to this pope, extols his disinterestedness and contempt of earthly things, and the spirit of prayer by which he drew down on the people abundant blessings. It was by constant watchfulness over themselves, by self-denial, and by humble prayer that all the saints triumphed over their spiritual enemies. They never laid down their arms. A Christian ought to be afraid of no enemy more than himself, whom he always carries about with him and whom he is not able to flee from. He should therefore never cease to cry out to God, " By myself I can do nothing to prevent myself falling through my own weakness. Unless thou, O Lord, art my light and my strength I watch and fight in vain."

In the *Acta Sanctorum*, October, vol. iii, will be found what little is known of St Mark. See also the *Liber Pontificalis* (Ed. Duchesne), vol. i, pp. 202–204.

ST OSYTH, or SYTHE, Virg. and Mart.

c. A.D. 675

According to her legend St Osyth was the daughter of a Mercian chief, Frithwald, and his wife Wilburga, said to have been a daughter of Penda of Mercia. She was brought up in a nunnery, perhaps at Aylesbury, and wished herself to become a nun ; but her parents affianced her to Sighere, King of the East Saxons. If this is the Sighere mentioned by St Bede, he apostatised from the faith during a pestilence about 665, but was, presumably, reconciled by the bishop Jaruman. This man had a passion for hunting, and during his wedding-breakfast went off in pursuit of a stray stag ; on his return he found his bride had gone. She made her way to the East Anglian bishops, Acca of Dunwich and Bedwin of Elmham, and Sighere, realising that it was better to have no wife than an unwilling one, let them clothe her with the religious habit. He himself gave to St Osyth some land at a place called Chich, on a creek of the Colne between Brightlingsea and Clacton, and here she established her monastery. She governed it for some years with great prudence and holiness, but it was situated in a dangerous place and disaster soon overtook it. In a raid of the Danes the marauders tried to carry St Osyth off, and when she fiercely resisted they smote off her head.

The body of St Osyth was taken to Aylesbury, but afterwards brought back to Chich, where a priory of Austin canons under her invocation was established in the twelfth century. Near it grew up the present village of Saint-Osyth, and the memory of the martyred abbess is preserved in several other local place-names, St Osyth Creek, St Osyth Marsh, St Osyth Wick, and St Osyth's Well. Saint Osyth is locally pronounced "Toosey."

There is a notice in the *Acta Sanctorum*, October, vol. iii, but the difficulties of the case are more clearly presented in Stanton, *Menology*, pp. 477 and 673, and in *Dict. Nat. Biog.*, vol. xlii, p. 337. The calendars collated by Mr. Edmund Bishop, which are noted in the former of these, point to the conclusion that there was a very definite *cultus* in East Anglia. This, however, was of late growth, for there seems to be little or no trace of it before the Norman Conquest. In calendars and other references the name of this saint is frequently disguised under the form "Sythe" or some equivalent spelling.

BD. ARTALDUS, or ARTHAUD, Bp. of Belley, Conf.

A.D. 1206

Blessed Artaldus was born in the castle of Sothonod in Savoy. At the age of eighteen he went to the court of Duke Amadeus III, but a year or two after he gave up his estates and secular career to become a Carthusian at Portes, not far from his home. After many years, being a priest and an experienced and holy religious, he was sent by the Prior of the Grande Chartreuse to found a charterhouse in the diocese of Geneva. The site chosen was a valley in the Valromey, significantly called "the Cemetery," and here Artaldus established himself with six of his brethren from Portes. The community was no sooner well settled down than their buildings were destroyed by fire, and Blessed Artaldus had to begin all over again. He chose a fresh site, on the Arvières river, which was given to him by Duke Amadeus, several other lords and prelates came to his aid, and his second foundation was soon built and occupied. But a Carthusian cell could not contain the ever-increasing reputation of Artaldus : like his master St Bruno, he was consulted by the pope, and when he was over eighty he was called from his monastery to be bishop of Belley, in spite of his vehement and reasonable protests. However, after less than two years of episcopate his resignation was accepted, and he thankfully returned to Arvières, where he lived in peace for the rest of his days. During his last years he was visited by St Hugh of Lincoln, who had come into France, and who, while he was prior of the charterhouse of Witham, had induced Henry II to become a benefactor of Arvières. Blessed Artaldus died in 1206, on October 6, but his feast is kept on the 7th at Belley and by the Carthusians ; he is said to have been 105 years old. His relics were enshrined in 1824 and the *cultus* confirmed by Pope Gregory XVI ten years later.

There is a short medieval Life in the *Acta Sanctorum*, October, vol. iii, but a fuller account is obtainable from Dom Le Couteulx, *Annales Ordinis Carthusiensis*, vols. ii and iii. The *Magna Vita* of St Hugh of Lincoln records a gentle rebuke administered by Hugh when Blessed Artaldus asked him for political news in the presence of a community who had turned their backs upon the world to give themselves entirely to God.

BD. MATTHEW CARRERI, CONF.

A.D. 1470

John Francis Carreri was a native of Mantua and received the name Matthew when he joined the Order of Preachers. He was a successful preacher, preparing himself for that ministry by long periods of recollection, and an upholder of strict observance in his order, but very few facts of external interest are recorded of his life, except the incident of his capture by pirates. This happened while on a voyage from Genoa to Pisa. The friar was set free, but when he saw that among the other prisoners were a woman and her young daughter, he went back to the pirate captain and offered himself in their place. The ruffian was so astonished at the request that he let all three of them go. Blessed Matthew met Blessed Stephana Quinzani, while she was still a child, and it is said that he promised her that she should be his heiress. Nobody knew what a mendicant friar could mean by this remark, but after Blessed Matthew's death she began regularly every Friday to have terrible pain in her bosom, in exactly the same way as he had formerly done as a testimony of his devotion to the Passion. Blessed Matthew died (after having asked his prior's permission so to do) at Vigevana on October 5, 1470, and twelve years later Pope Sixtus IV allowed his solemn translation and a liturgical commemoration.

An account of this *beato* is furnished in the *Acta Sanctorum*, October, vol. iii ; but see further the *Monumenta Ordinis Prædicatorum Historica*, vol. xiv, pp. 115 *seq.* A brief sketch in English will be found in Procter, *Dominican Saints*, pp. 281–283.

OCTOBER 8

ST BRIDGET OF SWEDEN, Widow

A.D. 1373

ST BIRGITTA, more commonly called Bridget, was daughter of Birger, governor of Upland, the principal province of Sweden, and his wife Ingeborg, daughter to Sigrid the Fair whom his brother had married. Both her parents were devout and God-fearing people. Ingeborg, who had several other children, died about the year 1315, some twelve years after the birth of Bridget, who thenceforward was brought up by an aunt. She did not begin to speak till she was three years old, and then she spoke quite clearly and unhesitatingly, rather than confusedly like a child ; her goodness and devotion matched her speech. But she tells us that in her youth she was inclined to be proud and overbearing towards her inferiors in rank. At ten years of age she was deeply affected by a sermon which she heard on the passion of Christ, and the night following seemed to see Him hanging upon His cross and she thought she heard Him say to her, " Look upon Me, my daughter."—" Alas," said she, " who has treated You thus ? " She seemed to herself to hear Him answer, " They who despise Me, and are insensible to My love for them." The impression made upon her mind was never effaced, and from that time the sufferings of her Redeemer became the centre of her spiritual life. Before she was fifteen, Bridget married Ulf Gudmarrson, Prince of Nierck, who was himself only eighteen, and the marriage subsisted happily for twenty-eight years. They had eight children, four boys and four girls, of whom one is venerated as St Catherine of Sweden. For some years Bridget led the life of a feudal lady on her husband's estate at Ulfsa, with the difference that she cultivated the friendship of a number of learned and virtuous men, notably Blessed Nicholas Hermansson, the Bishop of Linköping, who had been tutor to her children.

About the year 1335 St Bridget was summoned to the court of the young king of Sweden, Magnus Eriksson, to be principal lady-in-waiting to his newly wedded queen, Blanche of Namur. Before she had been long at Stockholm Bridget found that her responsibilities could not stop at the duties of her office. Magnus was weak and tended to be wicked ; Blanche was good-willed but irresponsible and luxury-loving. The saint bent all her energies to developing the better side of the Queen's character and to establishing an influence for good over both of them. As so often happens in such cases, she earned the love and respect of the young sovereigns, but did not succeed in making much difference in their lives ; they could not or would not take her altogether seriously. The personal revelations which later were to make St Bridget so famous were already supporting her, and concerned matters so far apart as the necessity of washing and terms for peace between England and France, " which if the English king does not accept, he will prosper in none of his affairs, but will end his life in grief and leave his realm and children in tribulation and anguish." But the court did not seem susceptible to these influences : " What was the Lady Bridget dreaming about last night ? " became a sort of byword. And St Bridget had troubles of her own. Her eldest daughter had married a riotous noble whom his mother-in-law refers to as " the Brigand " ; and about 1340 the youngest son, Gudmar, died. St Bridget thereupon made a pilgrimage to the shrine of St Olav of Norway at Trondhjem, and on her return, fortified thereby, she made a further attempt to curb the excesses of Magnus and Blanche. Meeting with no more success than before, she got leave of absence from the court, and with Ulf and their children went on pilgrimage to Compostela, visiting on their way the shrines of the Magi at Cologne and of St Mary Magdalen and others in Provence. On the way back Ulf was taken ill at Arras, where he lodged with his wife and children first in the street of the Lombards and afterwards at the house of a canon of the cathedral. He received Viaticum and Extreme Unction from the hands of the Bishop of Tournai, and all seemed over. But Bridget spared neither pains nor prayers for his recovery. Ulf promised that if he were spared to return to his own land he would go into a monastery, and she received an assurance of it by a revelation of St Denis. He was in fact restored again to health and arrived in Sweden, where he died in 1344 in the monastery of Alvastra, of the Cistercian Order, where his son Benedict was a student. Ulf was at Alvastra only a twelvemonth, Bridget living near by, and was clothed just before his death.

St Bridget continued to live at Alvastra for two years, having renounced the rank which she held in the world, and taken upon herself the state of a penitent. Her husband's estates she divided among her children according to the laws of justice and equity, and from that day seemed to forget what she had been in the world. She changed her manner of dress, using no more linen except for a veil to cover her head, wearing a rough hair-shift and cords full of knots for a girdle. The austerities which she practised were so excessive that she made herself ill, and her confessor interfered to modify them. Her visions and revelations now became so insistent that she was alarmed, fearing to be deluded by the Devil or by her own imagination. But a thrice-repeated vision told her to submit them to Master Matthias, a canon of Linköping and a priest of experience and learning, and he pronounced them to be of God. From now to her death she communicated them as they occurred to Peter, prior at Alvastra, who wrote them down in Latin. Those of this period culminated in a command of our Lord to go to the royal court and warn King Magnus of the judgement of God on his sins. She did so, and included the Queen, the nobles, and the bishops in her denunciation. For a time Magnus mended his ways, and liberally endowed the monastery which St Bridget now founded at Wadstena, on Lake Wetter.

In this house St Bridget placed sixty nuns, and in a separate enclosure canons, to the number of thirteen priests, in honour of the twelve Apostles and St Paul, four deacons, representing the Doctors of the Church, and eight choir-brothers not in orders, making the number of our Lord's apostles and disciples, eighty-five, in all. She prescribed them the Rule of St Augustine, with certain particular constitutions which are said to have been dictated to her by our Saviour in a vision. This circumstance is neither mentioned by Boniface IX in the bull of her canonisation, nor by Martin V in the confirmation of her order ; and the popes when they speak of this rule mention only the approbation of the Holy See, without making reference to any such private revelation. In this institute, as in the Order of Fontevrault, the men were subject to the abbess of the nuns in temporals, but in spirituals the women were under the jurisdiction of the canons, because the order was principally instituted for women and the men were admitted only to afford them spiritual ministrations. The convents of the men and women were separated by an inviolable enclosure, but had the same church, in which the nuns' choir was above in a gallery, so they could not even see one another. There are now no men in the Order of the Most Holy Saviour, or Bridgettines as they are commonly called, and where formerly there were seventy houses of nuns there are to-day but about a dozen. All surplus income had every year to be given to the poor, and ostentatious buildings were forbidden ; but each religious could have as many books for study as he or she pleased.* During the fifteenth century Wadstena was the literary centre of Sweden.

In consequence of a vision St Bridget wrote a very outspoken letter to Pope Clement VI, urging him to abandon Avignon for Rome, and to bring about peace between Edward III of England and Philip IV of France. The Pope declined to leave Avignon, but sent Hemming, Bishop of Abö, to Philip's court, where, however, he could do nothing. King Magnus, meanwhile, who valued Bridget's prayers if not her advice, asked for her interest in a projected crusade against the pagan Letts and Esthonians, which was really a disguised plundering expedition. The saint saw through it, and tried to dissuade him, offering her two surviving sons as securities to his creditors who were pressing him. She was now very out of favour at the Swedish court, but was beloved by the people, among whom she went travelling about the country and looking after their temporal and spiritual welfare. Many of them were not long converted, and she enforced the preaching of her chaplains by miracles of healing. In 1349, in spite of the Black Death that was ravaging Europe, she decided to go to popeless Rome for the holy year of Jubilee in 1350. With her confessor, Peter Olavsson of Skening, and others, she embarked at Stralsund, amid the tears of the people who were never to see her again : for at Rome she settled down, to work among the people and for the return of the popes to their City. She lived by a rule, hearing Mass at five o'clock every morning ; it is said she went to confession every day and to Communion several times a week. The brightness of her virtue shone doubly in contrast to the degradedness of Rome in those days, where open robbery and violence were rife, vice no less open and unashamed, the churches falling through neglect, and the people uncared for except to be exploited. The austerity of her way of living, the fervour of her devotion, her love of the holy shrines, her severity to herself and kindness to others, her tirelessness in serving the sick, the poor, and pilgrims, made her loved by all in whom the light of Christianity was not entirely extinguished. She made the care of her fellow-countrymen her particular charge, and every day she fed Swedish pilgrims in her house near St Laurence in Damaso. Nor did she confine her good works and exhortations to holy living to the poor and humble. For

---

* The Bridgettine community at South Brent in Devon has unbroken organic identity with a pre-Reformation community, and is the only English religious community of which this is true. It was founded by King Henry V at Syon House, Isleworth, in 1415. The nuns took refuge at Dendermonde in Flanders at the dissolution under Henry VIII, after various vicissitudes settled at Lisbon, and returned to England (Spettisbury in Dorset) in 1861.

example, when her daughter Catherine came on a visit to Rome, Bridget was away, and she eventually found her mother at the monastery of Farfa, whither she had gone to remonstrate with the abbot, " a very worldly man, who did not trouble about souls at all." Bridget persuaded her daughter not to return to Sweden, and St Catherine remained her helper and dear companion throughout the remainder of her life. Among the places particularly associated with St Bridget in Rome are the churches of St Paul's-outside-the-Walls and San Francesco a Ripa. In the first is the most beautiful crucifix of Cavallini, before which she prayed and which is said to have spoken to her, and in the second she had a vision of St Francis, who said to her, " Come and eat and drink with me in my cell." She took this to be an invitation to go to Assisi and gain the Portiuncula indulgence, which she accordingly did with her household, making it into a tour of shrines in Italy which lasted for two years. The Franciscans claim St Bridget as a tertiary of their order. The saint's prophecies and revelations had reference to most of the burning political and religious questions of her time, both of Sweden and Rome. She prophesied that Pope and Emperor would shortly meet amicably in Rome (which Blessed Urban V and Charles IV did in 1368), and the using of her by factions did somewhat to abate her popularity among the Romans. Her prophecies that their iniquities would be visited with condign punishments had the same effect, and several times her ardour drew down persecution and slander upon her. She was turned out of her house at a month's notice, and more than once she and Catherine found themselves seriously in debt ; they sometimes even had to beg for food at a convent of Poor Clares. St Bridget's joy at the coming of Pope Urban V was short-lived, for he soon retired to Viterbo and Montefiascone, and it was rumoured he was going back to Avignon. On her return from a pilgrimage to Amalfi she had a vision in which our Lord appeared to tell her to go to the Pope, warn him that his death was near, and show him the rule of the religious at Wadstena. This rule had already been submitted to Urban when he arrived in Rome, and he had done nothing about it. So now Bridget set off to Montefiascone, and as a result of her audience the Pope gave a general approval to her rule and monastery. Four months later Urban was dead, and St Bridget three times wrote to his successor at Avignon, Gregory XI, warning him to come back to the apostolic see, which he eventually did four years after her death.

In the following year, in consequence of another vision, St Bridget embarked on the last of her journeys, a pilgrimage to the Holy Places, taking with her St Catherine, her sons Charles and Birger, Peter of

Alvastra, and others. The expedition started inauspiciously, for at Naples Charles got himself entangled with Queen Joanna I, that Mary Stuart of the South. Although his third wife was still alive in Sweden, Joanna wanted to marry him, and he was far from unwilling. His mother was horror-stricken, and set herself to ceaseless prayer for the resolution of the difficulty. It came about in an unexpected and tragic way. Charles was struck down by a fever, and after a fortnight's illness died in the arms of his mother. He was, with St Catherine, her favourite child, and Bridget after his funeral went on in deepest grief to Palestine. Here, after being nearly drowned in a wreck off Jaffa, her progress through the Holy Places was one long succession of visions of the events that had happened there and other heavenly consolations. On her way back, in the autumn of 1372, she landed at Cyprus where she denounced the wickedness of the royal family and the citizens of Famagusta, and then passed on to Naples, where her warnings were read by the clergy from the pulpit but with little effect on their uninstructed and erring congregations. The party arrived back in Rome in March 1373. Bridget had been ailing for some months, and now she got weaker every day till, having received the last Sacraments from her faithful chaplain, Peter Olavsson, she died on July 23 in her seventy-first year. She was temporarily buried in the church of St Lawrence in Panisperna ; four months after, the body was taken up and, in the care of St Catherine and the prior of Alvastra, it was carried in triumphal progress by way of Dalmatia, Austria, Poland, and Danzig to Wadstena, where it was laid to rest in the abbey. St Bridget was canonised in 1391 and is the patron saint of the kingdom of Sweden.

Nothing is more famous in the life of St Bridget than the many revelations with which she was favoured by God, chiefly concerning the sufferings of our Saviour and events which were to happen in certain kingdoms. By order of the Council of Basle, the learned John Torquemada, afterwards cardinal, examined the book of St Bridget's revelations, and approved it as profitable for the instruction of the faithful, and this approbation was admitted by the council as competent and sufficient. It, however, amounts to no more than a declaration that the doctrine contained in that book is conformable to the orthodox faith, and that the revelations are credible upon a historical probability. Pope Benedict XIV referred specifically to the revelations of St Bridget, among others, when he wrote that, " Even though many of these revelations have been approved, we cannot and we ought not to give them the assent of divine faith, but only that of human faith, according to the dictates of prudence whenever these dictates enable us to decide that they are probable and worthy of pious credence." It is noticeable of St Bridget that, with true simplicity of heart, she always submitted her revelations to the judgement of the pastors of the Church ; and she was far from ever glorying in any extraordinary graces, which she never desired and on which she never relied except to be obedient thereto and to increase her love and humility. If her revelations have rendered her name famous, it is by her heroic virtue that it is venerable to the whole Church. To live according to the spirit of the mysteries of religion is something much greater and more sublime than to know hidden things or to be favoured with the most extraordinary visions. To have the knowledge of angels without charity is to be only a tinkling cymbal ; both to have charity and to speak the language of angels was the happy privilege of St Bridget. The book of her revelations was first printed at Lübeck in 1491, and has been translated into several languages. They were known in England in the year of the saint's death, and part were translated by the Bridgettine Richard Whytford in 1531. The lessons at Matins in the Bridgettine breviary are taken from the revelations on the glories of our Lady, according to the alleged words of our Lord to St Bridget, "I will send My angel who will reveal to you the lection that shall be read at Matins by the nuns of your monastery, and you shall write it as he tells you." Alban Butler pertinently remarks that had the revelations all been written down by St Bridget herself, instead of passing through the mind and translation of Peter of Alvastra and, in part, Alphonsus of Vadaterra, "it would have been compiled with more simplicity and with greater life and spirit, and would have received a higher degree of certainty."

The life and sufferings of our divine Redeemer are the book of life, in which both souls which now begin to serve God and those who have long exercised themselves in the practice of virtue find the most powerful incentive and means of spiritual improvement. The astonishing example which our Saviour set us of infinite meekness and humility in becoming a helpless babe will, if seriously considered and meditated upon, reach the very bottom of our hearts and totally reform our innermost affections. That inordinate self-love and pride, which seems almost interwoven in our very frame, will be beaten down ; the poison of our passions will be expelled ; and penitence, humility, and contempt of the world will possess our affections. The more a soul advances in the school of Christian virtues, the more she will find every circumstance in these sacred mysteries to be an unfathomed abyss of love and an inexhaustible source of spiritual riches. By this meditation she daily learns more perfectly the spirit of our divine Redeemer and puts on that blessed mind which was in Christ Jesus. In this interior conformity to Him consists our reformation and perfection : this resemblance, this image of our divine original formed in us, is what entitles us to participate in our Lord's promises.

Owing to the immense interest which of late years has been taken in St Bridget by Scandinavian scholars of all creeds, the materials formerly available in the various editions of the *Revelationes Ste Birgittæ* and in the *Acta Sanctorum*, October, vol. iv, have to a large extent been superseded. The oldest Life, which was compiled immediately after her death by her confessor Peter of Alvastra and Peter of Skänning who was the spiritual director at Wadstena, was only printed for the first time in 1871 in the collection *Scriptores rerum Sueciarum*, vol. iii, part 2, pp. 185–206. Other Lives, such as that by Birger, Archbishop of Upsala, will be found in the Bollandists and in the publications of Swedish learned societies. But the most valuable material of all is furnished by the depositions in the process of canonisation. A scholarly edition of the whole collection of these canonisation documents has recently been compiled by Isak Collijn, *Acta et Processus canonizacionis Beate Birgitte*, Upsala (1921–1931). There are furthermore a number of biographies and of studies of special aspects of the saint's career, mostly in Swedish ; notably an account of the historical personages connected with her life in Sweden and in Rome. This, published under the title *Birgittinska Gestalter* (1929), is also by Collijn. One historically excellent Swedish Life by E. Fagelklou (not a Catholic), has been translated into German (1929) by M. Loehr. Among French biographies that written by Comtesse de Flavigny, *Sainte Brigitte de Suède, Sa Vie, ses Révélations et son Œuvre* has reached a third edition (1910) and may be recommended as having made good use of Swedish sources. It seems rather doubtful whether the *Révélations* have not been to some extent coloured by the prepossessions of her confessors who took them down or translated them into Latin. The most reliable text is said to be that of G. E. Klemming in Swedish (1857–1884), of which a modernised selection has been edited by R. Steffen (1909). An English Life of St Bridget was contributed to the Quarterly Series in 1888 by F. Partridge, and more recently, *The Story of the English Bridgettines* (1933) has been briefly told by Canon J. R. Fletcher.

HOLY SIMEON, Prophet

First Century

It is recorded in the Gospel of St Luke that Simeon was a citizen of Jerusalem, a just and devout man who awaited the consolation of Israel. And the Holy Ghost was in him, and had told him that he should not die before he had seen the Anointed of the Lord. When therefore Joseph and Mary brought the infant Jesus to be presented to God in the temple, Simeon also was moved by the Spirit to come in. And he took the Child in his arms and praised God in those words which are known after him as the Canticle of Simeon, the

Nunc Dimittis sung by the Church at the office of Compline. And he prophesied of the Child and His mother, saying : " Behold ! this Child is set for the fall and for the resurrection of many in Israel, and for a sign which shall be contradicted. And thy own soul a sword shall pierce, that out of many hearts thoughts may be revealed." There are several apocryphal references and traditions about Holy Simeon, but nothing more is known of him than is stated above. He is named in the Roman Martyrology to-day and his feast is kept in several places in the West, but by the Byzantines on February 3.

There is a lengthy discussion in the *Acta Sanctorum*, October, vol. iv, but the modern commentators on St Luke's gospel have a fuller knowledge of the references to Simeon in early apocryphal literature. See *e.g.* Lagrange, *L'Evangile selon S. Luc* (1921), pp. 83–84.

ST REPARATA, VIRG. AND MART.

c. A.D. 250

The Reparata mentioned in the Roman Martyrology to-day was a virgin martyr at Cæsarea in Palestine during the persecution of the Emperor Decius. Her spurious Acts state that she was twelve years old and of a lively disposition. Being denounced as a Christian she was brought before the prefect, who was moved by her beauty and tried to win her over with fair words. Reparata argued with him and was therefore subjected to various tortures. As these failed to have any effect on her she was thrown into a furnace of fire where, like the three holy children of Juda, she stood unharmed and sang the praises of God. The prefect again tried to induce her to sacrifice to the gods, but Reparata only answered him back from within the furnace, till in desperation he commanded the guards, " Take the talkative and horrid creature and cut off her head, and don't let me lay eyes on her again." So she was led away, still singing, and as her head was smitten off " her soul was seen to go out from her body and ascend to Heaven in the form of a dove." The body of St Reparata was taken up and buried by the Christians ; later her alleged relics were translated to Italy, where the martyr is greatly venerated in several dioceses.

One text of the legendary *passio*, of which there are various recensions, is printed in the *Acta Sanctorum*, October, vol. iv. It would seem that St Reparata's story was sometimes confused with that of St Pelagia or Margaret. *Cf.* Delehaye, *Légendes hagiographiques* (1927), p. 188.

ST THAÏS, Penitent

Fourth Century

According to the legend there lived in Egypt during the fourth century a famous courtesan named Thaïs, who had been educated a Christian. Her infamy came to the ears of St Paphnutius at his hermitage in the Thebaïd, and he determined to try and redeem her. He put off his penitential garb, dressed himself in such a manner as to disguise himself, and, going to her house (probably at Alexandria), was introduced to her room. He told her he desired to talk with her, but wished it might be in some more private place. " What is it you fear ? " said Thaïs. " If men, no one can see us here ; but if you mean God, no place can hide us from His eye." " What ! " replied Paphnutius, " do you know there is a God ? " " Yes," said she, " and I moreover know that Heaven will be the portion of the good and everlasting Hell for the punishment of the wicked." " Is it possible," mused aloud the hermit, " that you should know these truths and yet dare to sin and to draw so many after you, before Him who knows and will judge all things ? " Thaïs was overcome by the reproach of so venerable an old man, and at the same time the Holy Ghost who moved Paphnutius to speak enlightened her understanding to see the baseness of her sins, and softened her heart by the touch of His grace. Filled with confusion at her crimes and with bitter sorrow, detesting her ingratitude against God, she burst into tears and, throwing herself at the feet of Paphnutius, cried, " Father, tell me what to do. Pray for me, that God may show me mercy. I want only three hours to settle my affairs, and then I am ready to do all you shall counsel me." Paphnutius appointed a place to meet and went away.

Thaïs got together all her jewels, furniture, clothes, and the rest of her ill-gotten wealth, and making a great pile in the street burnt it publicly, inviting all who had made her those presents and been the partners of her sin to join her in penance. Then she hastened to Paphnutius, and was by him conducted to a monastery of women. There he shut her up in a cell, putting on the door a seal of lead as if that place had been her grave, nevermore to be opened. He ordered the sisters to give her every day bread and water through the window, and she asked him, " Father, teach me how I am to pray." Paphnutius answered, " You are not worthy to call upon God by uttering His holy name, because your lips have been filled with iniquity ; nor to lift up your hands to Heaven, for they are defiled with impurities ; but turn yourself to the east, and

repeat these words : ' Thou who hast created me, have pity on me.' "
Thus she continued to pray with continual tears, and when she had
persevered with fervour in this life for three years, St Paphnutius
went to St Antony to ask his advice whether this penitential course
did not seem sufficient to prepare her for reconciliation and holy
Communion. St Antony and his monks passed the night together
in prayer, and in the morning St Paul the Simple, his oldest disciple,
said that God had prepared a place in Heaven for the penitent.
Paphnutius therefore went to her cell to release her from her penance.
Thaïs said that from the time of her coming thither she had never
ceased bewailing her sins, which she had always weighing as a burden
on her. " It is on that account," said Paphnutius, " that God has
blotted them out." She therefore left her prison to live with the
rest of the sisters, but God withdrew her out of this world fifteen
days after her release, it is said about the year 348. She is honoured
in the Greek menologies on October 8, but though her story has
been known in the West since the middle of the sixth century,
St Thaïs is not named in the Roman Martyrology.

The more important texts, Greek, Latin and Syriac, which refer to
Thaïs, were brought together by the Abbé F. Nau in the *Annales du Musée
Guimet*, vol. xxx, part 3 (1903), pp. 51–112. The historical character of
the narrative of her conversion is, however, extremely doubtful. To begin
with, the identity of name with that of the famous courtesan who was
associated with Alexander the Great, is at least suspicious. Mgr. Batiffol,
after a careful discussion of all the available evidence, in the *Bulletin de
Littérature ecclésiastique*, 1903, pp. 207–217, came to the conclusion that
the story was simply " une moralité," a pious fable, and in this verdict
Delehaye (*Analecta Bollandiana*, xxiv, p. 400) and Dom Leclercq (*Dictionnaire d'Archéol.*, I, c. 2339) entirely concur. The texts vary in assigning the
conversion of Thaïs to Paphnutius, Serapion or Bessarion ; but a sensation
was caused when it was announced at the beginning of this century that
the mummified remains of Serapion and Thaïs had been discovered at
Antinoë in Egypt and were actually on view in the Musée Guimet at Paris.
See the account by A. Gayet in the *Annales du Musée Guimet*, vol. xxx,
part 2, pp. 35 *seq.* ; or better in his brochure, *Antinoë et les sépultures de
Thaïs et de Sérapion* (1902). Undoubtedly the names Θαιας and Σαραπιων
are attached to their respective graves, but there are difficulties about the
interpretation of the fragmentary inscriptions. Serapion was an ascetic,
for iron instruments of penance were found on the body. The so-called
Thaïs had with her an apparatus like a cribbage-board, pierced with holes,
which has been explained as a " *compte-prière*," a sort of rosary. But there
is really nothing which would require us to connect these two interments,
or identify them with the personages named in the legend.

ST DEMETRIUS, Mart.
A.D. 306 (?)

This Demetrius was probably a deacon martyred in the persecution of Diocletian at Sirmium in Dalmatia. A prefect of Illyria, Leontius, introduced his cult to Salonika and translated some of his relics thither, building a basilica in his honour in either city. From the fifth century Salonika was the great centre of the cult of St Demetrius : he was the local patron and heavenly protector, and huge crowds of pilgrims flocked to his tomb, where a miraculous oil was said to exude from the relics, whence he was called *Myrobletes*. His great church was burnt down only in 1917. According to the Salonika legend St Demetrius was a citizen of the place, who was arrested for preaching the Gospel and speared, without trial, while temporarily shut up in a room of the public baths. The earliest account, not older than the sixth century, says that the order for his murder was given by the Emperor Maximian in a fit of temper, consequent on the slaying of his favourite gladiator by an amateur called Nestor. In subsequent fictitious accounts the deacon of Sirmium (if such he was) becomes a proconsul (so styled in the Roman Martyrology) and a warrior-saint, in which capacity his popularity was exceeded only by that of St George ; both were adopted by the Crusaders and were supposed to have been seen in their ranks at the battle of Antioch in 1098. The popular St Demetrius is an entirely imaginary character : like St Procopius, St Menas, St Mercurius, and others, a genuine martyr of whom little or nothing was known was by a series of fabrications transformed into a literal warrior of Christ, a military martyr, and the patron and reinforcement of soldiers and chivalry. His feast is kept with solemnity throughout the East on October 26 and he is named in the preparation of the Byzantine Liturgy.

An excellent account of this martyr, including Greek texts of the two principal families of the *Passio*, is printed in the *Acta Sanctorum*, October, vol. iv ; but Père Delehaye, in his *Légendes grecques des Saints militaires* (1909), pp. 103–109 and 259–263, has gone over the ground again and has furnished a critical revision of the earlier document. He calls attention to the fact that Demetrius is commemorated in the Syriac *breviarium* and is there connected with Sirmium at a date previous to the building of the great basilica at Salonika by Leontius. At Ravenna, no doubt through Byzantine influence, the cult of St Demetrius seems to have established itself before it was known elsewhere in Italy ; the earliest chapel in Ravenna was dedicated in his honour (see Delehaye in *Analecta Bollandiana*, vol. xlvii, 1929, pp. 11–12). For the representations of St Demetrius in art consult Künstle, *Ikonographie*, vol. ii, pp. 179 *seq.*

ST PELAGIA, Penitent
Fourth Century

Pelagia, more often called Margaret, on account of the magnificence of the pearls for which she had so often sold herself, was an actress of Antioch, equally celebrated for her beauty, her wealth and the disorder of her life. A synod having been called in that city by the patriarch, a group of bishops were sitting in the portico of the basilica of St Julian the Martyr, listening to the words of the greatly respected bishop from Edessa, St Nonnus. While he was speaking, Pelagia, surrounded by her admirers and attendants, rode by on a white donkey; she was wearing her famous jewels, her face, arms, and shoulders were bare as if she were a common courtesan, and she looked around her with bold and provoking glances. St Nonnus stopped speaking and his auditors turned away their eyes, but he watched her till she was out of sight, and then asked, " Did not that woman's beauty please you ? " The bishops were puzzled by the question and made no reply. And St Nonnus said, " I was well pleased to see her, for it seems to me God sent her as a lesson to us. She goes to an infinity of trouble to keep herself beautiful and to perfect her dancing, but we are considerably less zealous in the care of our dioceses and of our own souls." That night Nonnus had a dream, in which he was celebrating the Liturgy but was much disturbed therein by an unclean and offensive dove that fluttered around the altar. When the deacon dismissed the catechumens the dove went away also, but came back again after the Liturgy and the dreamer caught it and threw it into the fountain in the atrium of the church. It came out of the water gleaming like snow and, flying up into the heavens, disappeared. The next day being Sunday, all the bishops assisted at the Liturgy of the patriarch, and St Nonnus was asked to preach. His words went straight to the heart of Pelagia, who had been moved to come to the basilica though she was not even a catechumen, and she wrote a note asking him to speak with her. St Nonnus agreed, on condition that the other bishops should be present, and coming in she threw herself on her knees before him and asked for baptism, beseeching him to come between her and her sins, which would otherwise recoil on his head. The patriarch was asked to provide a sponsor, and when he had appointed the senior deaconess, Romana, St Nonnus baptised the actress in her true name of Pelagia, confirmed her, and gave her holy Communion.

When the news of this conversion got about Antioch the debauched men-about-town were very annoyed with the bishops, and threatened them in the streets, and tried to induce Pelagia to come back to her old haunts and life. But she repudiated them with the sign of the cross. On the eighth day after her baptism, when she had given up all her property to Nonnus for distribution to the poor, she laid aside her white garments, put on men's clothes, and disappeared from the city. She made her way to Jerusalem and there, in a cave on the Mount of Olives, lived as a solitary, being known and reverenced among the people as Pelagius, " the beardless monk." Three or four years later, James, the deacon of St Nonnus, visited her, and while he was there St Pelagia died. When those who came to bury her discovered her sex, they cried out, " Glory be to Thee, Lord Jesus, for Thou hast many hidden treasures on earth, as well female as male."

The original of this circumstantial narrative was written by one who claimed, falsely, to be the deacon James just mentioned, and the whole story as it stands must be set aside as a work of fiction, a religious romance. Père Delehaye the Bollandist detects in it two elements, the first and essential one of which comes from the sixty-seventh homily on St Matthew of St John Chrysostom. There he speaks of an Antiochene actress, whose infamy was known throughout Cilicia and Cappadocia, who underwent a sudden conversion ; after her baptism she lived for many years a life of extreme austerity as a recluse. Chrysostom does not mention her name and there is no reason to suppose that she was ever the object of a religious *cultus.* " James's " reliance on this story is obvious. Whether he deliberately adopted the second element also, or whether it is an accidental development, is not so certain. Pelagia the penitent has been confused with a real St Pelagia. She was a virgin martyr of Antioch who was celebrated in that city in the fourth century on October 8 (in the Roman Martyrology, June 9) ; she is mentioned both by St John Chrysostom and St Ambrose, with particulars of her passion.*

" If there is any item of religious interest to be deduced from all this," writes Père Delehaye after discussing the development of the tale at some length, " it is the fact that a traditional *cultus* may have the life crushed out of it by legend." He sees in this popular romance

* A third Pelagia, of Tarsus, named in Eastern kalendars also on October 8 (Roman Martyrology, May 4), seems to be a combination of the true and the false Pelagias of Antioch. The pseudo-Pelagia of Antioch is the only one of the three mentioned in the Roman Martyrology on October 8 ; her feast is celebrated liturgically not only by the Byzantines, but by the Latins of Jerusalem as well (on October 26).

of the " Repentance of Pelagia " the starting-point of the tales of a whole group of imaginary saints, of whom a characteristic example is St Marina (July 17). The legend of the saint of Antioch " lost by degrees every vestige of historical fact ; even the account of the conversion became eliminated and the purely legendary residuum passed under various names . . . thanks to which we have the saints Mary or Marina, Apollinaria, Euphrosyne, and Theodora, who are simply literary replicas of the Pelagia of the self-styled James ; or else, as in the case of St Eugenia, the theme of a woman hiding her sex was tacked on to other narratives having for their hero some historic personage " (*Legends of the Saints*, p. 203).

As Père Delehaye points out in the work just quoted (3d. French Edition, 1927, p. 190), the historical Pelagia, who is commemorated on this day in the Syriac *breviarium* of the early fifth century, was not a penitent but an innocent maiden fifteen years of age. When summoned before the tribunal of the persecutor, she made an excuse that she must first attire herself in her bravest apparel, and then, knowing the outrages to which in such cases Christian virgins were constantly subjected, she threw herself headlong from the roof of the house. This is the true story of St Pelagia as known both to St Ambrose (P.L., xvi, cc. 229 and 1093) and to St John Chrysostom (P.G., l, cc. 579–585), neither of whom condemns her act, but extols it as a noble example of the love of chastity. It is curious that the original text of Alban Butler completely ignores the true Pelagia and assumes the truth of the extravagant legend. The text of the fictitious Acts may be found in the *Acta Sanctorum*, October, vol. iv, but better in H. Usener, *Legenden der hl. Pelagia* (1897). The attempt of the last-named scholar to explain the *cultus* of St Pelagia as a survival of the worship of Aphrodite has been dealt with by Delehaye in the book cited above. See also in the present series the bibliographical notes appended to St Marina, July 17, p. 229 ; St Margaret, July 20, p. 290 ; and St Pelagia of Tarsus, May 4.

ST KEYNE, Virg.

Fifth Century ?

The memory of St Keyne (Keyna or Cain) has been preserved in England by the verses which Robert Southey wrote about her holy well in the parish of Saint-Keyne near Liskeard in Cornwall, the properties of which were known in the Middle Ages, though the story of the canny Cornish bride is probably a local joke of more recent date. St Keyne was very well known in parts of South Wales and the west of England, but it is difficult, if not impossible, to find out anything authentic about her. In the Welsh lists (but not in the list which William of Worcester copied in Cornwall) of the twenty-four children of Brychan of Brecknock, she appears as a daughter of that liberal father of saints, and we learn that she was venerated " between the forks of the Ogmore " river, in Morgannwg. The account of her given in her *vita*, edited probably by John of Tynemouth in the fourteenth century from an earlier and longer Life, is as follows.   The father of the blessed Keyne was King Brychan Brycheiniog, who had twelve sons and twelve daughters. Before her birth her mother Gwladys dreamed that her womb was full of myrrh and balm, her breasts emitting light, and that she gave birth to a white dove.   Keyne grew into a very beautiful young woman, but resolutely refused all suitors and took a vow of virginity ; therefore she was called in Welsh *Cain Wyry*, Keyne the Maiden. Then she resolved to become a solitary and, crossing the Severn, she took up her abode in the forests on the left bank.   The place was infested with snakes, which she turned into stone, " for the stones in the fields and villages there have the form of serpents, as if they had been carved by mason's art, to this very day."*   She lived there for years, making many journeys and founding oratories, till at St Michael's Mount she met her nephew St Cadoc, who persuaded her (with the help of an angel) to return to Wales.   " She made for herself a habitation in a certain hillock at the roots of a certain great mountain," and there caused a healing well to spring up.   Just before her death she told St Cadoc that that place would fall into the hands of a sinful race, whom she would root out and lead thither other men, who would find her forgotten tomb, " and in this place the name of the Lord shall be blessed for ever."

Camden records the tradition that the place of St Keyne's hermitage in England was at Keynsham in Somerset, near where the Avon falls into the Severn, but there was no known *cultus* of the saint in that county until, curiously enough, modern times : she is now commemorated throughout the diocese of Clifton on this day. The site of her final resting-place in South Wales has been the subject of much discussion.   For a time it was thought to be Llangenny, between Abergavenny and Crickhowell, where there is an old well, but this was through an erroneous identification of St Keyne with St Ceneu.   Canon G. H. Doble has made out a strong case for Llangeinor in Glamorgan.   The name is a corruption of Llan-gainwyry, the Church-place of the Virgin Cain ; topographically it meets all the requirements ; and in a lonely place on Mynydd Llangeinor is a holy well whose waters are still credited with salutary properties. It is impossible to tell how much (or little) of the *vita* of St Keyne

---

* And to this day.   There are plenty of the fossils called " ammonites " in the quarries around Keynsham, and their mythical origin is remembered locally.

is true. Canon Doble concludes that she was one of a band of missionaries who in the fifth century came from Breconshire into the parts of Herefordshire east of the Black Mountains ; from there she visited and founded churches in South Wales, Cornwall, and perhaps Somerset : he has found her name in one form or another in at least seven places. But he ends up by querying if St Keyne were not rather a man than a woman, seeing the amount of hard travel and work this founder (if there were only one) must have got through.

The Life attributed to John of Tynemouth is printed with a commentary in the *Acta Sanctorum*, October, vol. iv, but Canon Doble, as an expert in Celtic topography and philology, has been able to trace the slender clues to the saint's activities far more thoroughly than was possible for any foreign scholar in the eighteenth century. His account of St Keyne was first published in the *Downside Review* for January 1931, pp. 156–172, and since then the essay on " the Children of Brychan," of which this forms a part, has been issued separately.

OCTOBER 9

ST DIONYSIUS THE AREOPAGITE, Bp. of Athens, Mart.

First Century

WHILE St Paul, having had to leave Berea, was waiting at Athens for Silas and Timothy, "his spirit was stirred within him, seeing the city wholly given to idolatry." He therefore went into the market-place and the Jewish synagogue to talk with the people, and certain Epicurean and Stoic philosophers, hearing him, came to him and asked, " May we know what this new doctrine is, which thou speakest of ? " Paul therefore went with them to the Areopagus, or the Hill of Mars, the meeting-place of the Athenian council, where, says St Luke, " all the Athenians and strangers that were there employed themselves in nothing else but either in telling or in hearing some new thing." And the Apostle announced before these philosophers and sophists the Christian doctrines of repentance, purity of manners, the unity and omnipresence of God, His judgements, and the resurrection of the dead. The divine fire with which he delivered these great truths was an eloquence with which they were unacquainted, and, though the doctrine of the resurrection of the dead shocked many, others were exceedingly moved with the sublimity of this new doctrine and with the marks of a divine mission with which the preacher spoke ; and they said they would hear him again upon that subject on some other day. Some, whose hearts were touched by grace and who with simplicity sought after the truth, without delay addressed themselves to St Paul and received from him full evidence of the divine revelation which he preached to them. Among these there was a woman named Damaris and a man named Dionysius, who, being a member of the council, which was called after the hill whereon it assembled, was distinguished as " the Areopagite."

That is all that is known with complete certainty of St Dionysius the Areopagite. Eusebius gives the testimony of St Dionysius of Corinth that he became first bishop of Athens, appointed by St Paul himself according to the " Apostolic Constitutions " of the fourth century. St Sophronius of Jerusalem and others call him a martyr, the Menology of Basil adding that he was burned alive at Athens under Domitian. In all ancient kalendars the day of his feast is October 3, on which date it is still observed by the Byzantines and Syrians. Nowhere before the seventh century at the earliest is there any suggestion that St Dionysius the Areopagite ever left Greece, but afterwards his name is found connected with Cotrone in Calabria, Geneva, and, of course, Paris. His identification with St Dionysius (Denis) of France, referred to below, is still recorded in the Roman Martyrology and in the liturgy of the day* ; and the sixth lesson at Matins ends with the words : " He wrote admirable and truly heavenly books on the Divine Names, on the Celestial and Ecclesiastical Hierarchies, on Mystical Theology, and divers others." This is a reference to another error of the Middle Ages concerning St Dionysius the Areopagite, namely, that he was the author of four treatises and ten letters which, from the end of the seventh until the fifteenth century, were among the most valued and admired theological and mystical writings, both in the East and West, and exercised an immense influence on the Scholastics. The growing conviction that they were not the work of a disciple of St Paul, but written much later by one who falsely attributed them to the Areopagite, caused them to be long under a cloud ; but in modern times their own intrinsic worth and the strong evidence produced that they are genuine works, but of the fifth century, has to a certain extent restored them to the honour and use which their value demands.

In the *Acta Sanctorum* a long dissertation of more than one hundred and sixty folio pages is mainly devoted to proving that the Dionysius converted by St Paul was not the writer of the book on " the Divine names " and of other treatises attributed to the same authorship. There can be no question, however, that pseudo-Dionysius wished to be identified with the Dionysius of the Acts of the Apostles. In the very earliest known mention of these writings, we find them brought forward (at the conference held at Constantinople in A.D. 532) as the work of " Dionysius the Areopagite," and rejected by Hypatius as forgeries. An immense literature has grown up around them, but that hardly concerns us here. The true author has never been identified. The attempt made by Father Stiglmayr, S.J. (in *Scholastik*, vol. iii, 1928), to father them upon Severus of Antioch has been courteously but effectively refuted by J. Lebon, the editor of Severus (see the *Revue d'Histoire ecclésiastique*, vol. 26, 1930, pp. 880–915). The pseudo-Dionysius claims that when at Heliopolis he witnessed the eclipse of the

---

* Alban Butler could not bring himself to admit this openly. In a footnote he says, " Hilduin . . . upon the authority of spurious and fabulous records, pretends that St Dionysius, the first bishop of Paris, is the same person with the Areopagite ; of which mistake, *some traces are found in certain other writings* " (italics ours). Their identity was not questioned in the West from the ninth to the seventeenth century.

sun which occurred during the crucifixion of our Lord, and also that he was present at the death of the Blessed Virgin. All this is pure invention ; and *cf.* the article of P. Peeters in the *Analecta Bollandiana*, vol. xxix (1910), pp. 302–322, who there draws inferences very unfavourable to the literary honesty of Hilduin, Abbot of Saint-Denis, the first Latin translator of pseudo-Dionysius, and seemingly also the first to proclaim his identity with Dionysius, Bishop of Paris. As to Hilduin, we must await the final conclusions of the series of *Études dionysiennes* (vol. i appeared in 1932) which Père G. Théry, O.P., is engaged in publishing, after contributing two preliminary articles to the *Revue d'Histoire ecclésiastique* for 1925, as well as other earlier essays on the subject to other periodicals.

ST DEMETRIUS, Bp. of Alexandria, Conf.

A.D. 231

He is said to have been the eleventh successor of St Mark the Evangelist, and is certainly the first bishop of Alexandria of whom anything is known, chiefly in his relations with Origen. When Clement withdrew from the direction of the catechetical school of Alexandria about the year 203, Origen assumed his place and was confirmed in it by St Demetrius, with whom he was then on terms of close friendship ; the Bishop even defended him against those who had condemned the bodily mutilation to which he had voluntarily submitted himself. During the persecution of Caracalla Origen went to Cæsarea in Palestine and accepted an invitation to preach before the bishops there. St Demetrius protested, for Origen was yet a layman, and, in spite of the defence of him made by St Alexander, Bishop of Jerusalem, and Theoctistus, Bishop of Cæsarea, recalled him to Alexandria. Fifteen years later Origen set out for Athens, furnished with a letter of recommendation from St Demetrius, and on his way through Cæsarea was ordained priest, without the leave of his own bishop. Thereupon Demetrius convened a synod which sentenced him to banishment, and later on a formal condemnation was promulgated, from which it may be gathered that there was question of unorthodox teaching as well as of uncanonical ordination.

St Demetrius is said to have erected the first three suffragan sees of Alexandria and to have written to Pope St Victor I about the computation of the date of Easter. He vigorously opposed Gnosticism and is often credited, on the authority of St Jerome, with having sent St Pantænus on his mission to Yemen and Ethiopia. But this probably took place before St Demetrius was a bishop. He governed the see of Alexandria for forty-two years and died in the year 231, at the age of 105, revered by his people and also feared, on account of the gift which was his of reading men's secret sins and thoughts.

There is little to add to the data collected in the *Acta Sanctorum*, October, vol. iv. See also the articles on Demetrius and on Origenes in the *Dict. Christ. Biog.*, and on the letters of Demetrius in *Dict. d'Archéol.*, *etc.*, vol. viii, cc. 2752–2753.

SS. DIONYSIUS, or DENIS, Bp. of Paris, RUSTICUS, and ELEUTHERIUS, Marts.

c. A.D. 275

There is no mention of St Dionysius of Paris until the sixth century (St Gregory of Tours) and the first account of his life and martyrdom, dating from a little later, is a document confused with worthless legends, so that his true history is uncertain. St Gregory says he was born in Italy and sent into Gaul with six other missionary bishops about the year 250. Of these, the one who carried the Gospel furthest into the country was St Dionysius, who with the priest St Rusticus and the deacon St Eleutherius penetrated to Lutetia Parisiorum and established Christian worship on an island in the Seine. Other foundations of his, according to the traditions of the church of Paris, were Notre-Dame-des-Champs, whose crypt he is supposed to have dedicated in honour of our Lady, a chapel to St Stephen (afterwards St Etienne-des-Grès), and a chapel to the Blessed Trinity (afterwards St Benoît). St Dionysius preached with so great effect and made so many conversions that the pagan priesthood was alarmed. At their instigation the Roman governor Fescenninus Sisinnius arrested him with Rusticus and Eleutherius and, after a long imprisonment, all three were beheaded. Their *acta* say that the bodies of the martyrs were thrown into the Seine, from which they were rescued and given honourable burial by a Christian lady called Catulla. A small chapel was built over their tomb, around which arose the great abbey of Saint-Denis.

This monastery was founded or greatly benefited by King Dagobert I (*d.* 638), and it is possible that soon after this time the identification of St Dionysius with Dionysius the Areopagite began to gain currency, or at least the idea that he was sent by Pope Clement I in the first century. But it was not everywhere or even widely accepted until the time of Hilduin, abbot of Saint-Denis. In the year 827 the Emperor Michael II sent as a present to the Emperor of the West, Louis the Pious, copies of the writings ascribed to

St Dionysius the Areopagite (see above, p. 107). By an unfortunate coincidence they arrived in Paris and were taken to Saint-Denis on the eve of the feast of the patron of the abbey. Hilduin translated them into Latin, and when some years later Louis asked him for a Life of St Dionysius of Paris, the abbot produced a work which persuaded Christendom for the next nine hundred years that Dionysius of Paris, Dionysius of Athens, and the author of the " Dionysian " writings were one and the same person. In this " Areopagitica " Abbot Hilduin made use of spurious and worthless materials and it is difficult to believe in his complete good faith. He ascribed the *acta* to a son of Dionysius's first convert, but false attributions of that sort were common among hagiographers of the early Middle Ages and have not quite the same damning significance that they would have to-day. But Hilduin's Life is a tissue of fables. The Areopagite, having handed over the church of Athens to St Publius of Malta, visited Jerusalem and Ephesus in order to call on our Lady and St John ; then he comes to Rome where Pope St Clement I receives him and sends him to evangelise the Parisii. They try in vain to put him to death by wild beasts, fire, and crucifixion ; then, together with Rusticus and Eleutherius, he is successfully beheaded on Montmartre (actually *Mons Martis*, not *Mons Martyrum*). The dead body of St Dionysius rose on its feet and, led by an angel, walked the four miles from Montmartre to where the abbey church of Saint-Denis now stands, carrying its head in its hands and surrounded by singing angels, and so was there buried. Of which marvel the Roman Breviary makes mention.

The *cultus* of St Dionysius, better known, even in England, as Denis, was very strong during the Middle Ages ; he is one of the Fourteen Holy Helpers and invoked against headache. He is popularly regarded as the patron saint of France.

Another long dissertation is devoted to St Dionysius, Bishop of Paris, in the *Acta Sanctorum, ubi supra.* The earliest *passio*, attributed of old, but erroneously, to Venantius Fortunatus, has been re-edited by Bruno Krusch, *M. G. H. Auctores Antiq.*, vol. iv, part 2, pp. 101–105. This ascribes the sending of Dionysius into Gaul, as Bishop of Paris to Pope St Clement in the first century, but it does not identify him with the Areopagite, neither does it mention Catulla by name. See also what has been said about the Areopagite above (p. 107) and consult J. Havet, *Œuvres*, vol. i, pp. 191–246 ; G. Kurth in *Études Franques*, vol. ii, pp. 297–317 ; L. Levillain in the *Bibliothèque de l'Ecole des Chartes*, vol. 82 (1921), pp. 5–116 ; vol. 86 (1925), pp. 5–97, with others more recent ; and Dom Leclercq in *Dict. d'Archéol.*, etc., vol. iv, cc. 588–606. On St Dionysius in art see Künstle, *Ikonographie*, vol. ii.

ST PUBLIA, Widow

c. A.D. 370

St Publia, mentioned in the Roman Martyrology to-day as an
" abbess " who made a bold confession of the Faith under the
Emperor Julian the Apostate, is referred to by the historian Theodoret as a woman of good family in Antioch who in the prime of
life was left a widow. Her only son John became a distinguished
priest in the city, and she gathered together in her house a number
of consecrated virgins and widows who wished to live a common
life of devotion and charity. In the year 362 Julian came to Antioch
to prepare for his campaign against the Persians, and as he was
passing by the house of Publia one day he stopped to listen to the
inmates, who were singing the praises of God in their oratory. It
so happened that they were singing the 115th Psalm, and the Emperor
distinguished the words, " The idols of the Gentiles are silver and
gold, the works of the hands of men : they have mouths and speak
not," and so on to the verse, " Let them that make them become
like unto them, and all such as trust in them." He was furious at
what he took to be a personal insult, and bade the women be silent,
then and in the future. They replied by singing, at the word of
their mistress Publia, Psalm 67 : " Let God arise and let His enemies
be scattered." Thereupon Julian ordered her to be brought before
him, and in spite of her sex, age, and venerable appearance allowed
her to be struck by his guards. Not thus could the choral prayer
of the religious be silenced, and it is said that the Emperor intended
to have put them all to death when he came back from Persia. But
he was destined never to return alive and St Publia and her companions finished their course in peace.

See the *Acta Sanctorum*, October, vol. iv, where Theodoret's account
(*Hist. Eccles.*, iii, 19) is quoted.

SS. ANDRONICUS, Conf., AND ATHANASIA, Matron

Fifth Century

Andronicus was a native of Alexandria who settled in Antioch
to carry on the business of a silversmith and banker. He was very
happily married to a young woman named Athanasia, they had two
children, John and Mary, and their trade flourished. It is said that
Andronicus divided his income into three equal parts, of which he

reserved the first for the family requirements, one for the relief of the poor, and the other to lend without interest to those tradesmen and others who were in difficulties. When they had been married for twelve years both their children suddenly died on the same day, and Athanasia thereafter spent much of her time weeping at their grave and praying in a neighbouring church. She was here one day when suddenly a strange monk stood before her, who asked her why she wept, and when she told him assured her that John and Mary were happy in Heaven. Then he left the church, Athanasia following to speak more with him, but when she asked the porter which way the monk had gone she was told that there had been no monk there. Then Athanasia knew that she had seen a vision of St Julian Sabas, patron of children, in whose memory the church was dedicated ; and she went home rejoicing to her husband, who bore his grief with patience and resignation, and suggested to him that the time had come for them to renounce the world and prepare for their end. Andronicus agreed, and they pensioned off their servants and divided their goods, keeping for themselves only what was necessary. And as they left their home, leaving the door standing open, St Athanasia called down the blessing of the God of Abraham and Sara upon herself and her husband, beseeching Him that, " as we leave this house door open for love of Thee, so open to us the gates of Thy kingdom." Then, by way of Jerusalem, where they visited the Holy Places, they made their way into their native land of Egypt, where they sought out St Daniel, known as " of Many Miracles," among the solitaries of Skete. They told him of their resolve, and he sent St Andronicus to the great monastery of Tabenna, which St Pachomius had founded on an island in the Nile near Thebes, and St Athanasia to be an anchoress in the wilderness, dressed in the habit of a man. And so they lived the austere life of the Egyptian monks for twelve years.

At the end of that time St Andronicus received permission again to visit the Holy Places of Palestine, and on his way he fell in with a beardless old monk, who said that his name was Athanasius and that he also was going to Jerusalem. They therefore travelled together, made their religious exercises together, and returned once more to the place where they had met. Then they realised that they had a great regard and affection one for another and were unwilling to be parted, so they both went back to Tabenna, and a cell was found there for Father Athanasius near to that of Andronicus. When the time came for Athanasius to die it was seen that he was weeping, and a monk asked him why he wept when he was about to go to God. " I am grieved for my father Andronicus," was the reply,

" for he will miss me. But when I am gone, give him the writing that you will find under my pillow." After he was dead the writing was found, and when he read it St Andronicus knew—what the other had known since they met on the way to Jerusalem—that Athanasius was his wife Athanasia. Then the monks came, dressed in white and carrying branches of palm and tamarisk, and bore the body of St Athanasia to burial. A monk stopped with St Andronicus in his cell until they had celebrated the seventh day of Athanasia, and then tried to persuade the old man to come away with him; and he would not. So the monk departed alone, but he had not gone a day's journey when a messenger overtook him, saying that Father Andronicus was ill and at the point of death. He hurried back, summoning the other monks, and St Andronicus died peacefully amid the prayers of his brethren. They buried him beside his wife.

The Copts, Ethiops, and some of the Byzantine churches keep the feast of " Our holy father Andronicus and his wife Athanasia," and they were entered in the Roman Martyrology (with the place of death given as Jerusalem) by Cardinal Baronius.

Although a Greek version of this story is printed in the *Acta Sanctorum*, October, vol. iv, from the *Menæa*, the saints in question do not seem to have enjoyed any great popularity in Byzantine circles. There is only the barest mention of them in the *Synaxarium Constantinopolitanum* (see Delehaye's edition, c. 501, under March 2). On the other hand the whole story is told at length in the lectionaries of Abyssinia, and may be read in Budge's translation—*The Ethiopic Synaxarium*, p. 1167. The feast was there kept on the 28th Hamle, corresponding roughly to August 1.

ST GISLENUS, OR GHISLAIN, ABBOT AND CONF.

c. A.D. 680

Having led for some time an eremitical life in a forest in Hainault this Frankish saint founded there, for the benefit of many who desired to serve God under his direction, a monastery in honour of SS. Peter and Paul. He governed it with great sanctity and prudence for thirty years, from about the year 650; the abbey was long known as The Cell (now Saint-Ghislain, near Mons), and its church was consecrated by St Authbertus of Cambrai. The original name of the place was Ursidongus, that is, " the bear's den," whence arose the legend that a bear, hunted by King Dagobert I, took refuge with St Gislenus and showed him the site of his future monastery. St Gislenus is said to have had great influence on St Vincent Madelgarus and his wife St Waldetrudis and their family; with his encouragement

Waldetrudis founded the convent at Castri Locus (Mons), where Gislenus had had his first hermitage, and her sister St Aldegondis the convent of Maubeuge. With the last-named he was united in a very close friendship, and when they were both too old conveniently to make the journey to one another's monasteries, they built an oratory in honour of St Quintinus in between, and would there meet to converse of God and matters connected with their respective communities. When St Aldegondis had her vision of the death of St Amandus, it was St Gislenus who explained to her that this was a warning of her own approaching death also.

The Roman Martyrology says that St Gislenus resigned a bishopric before becoming a hermit. This refers to the quite apocryphal legend that he was born in Attica, became a monk there, and was elevated to the see of Athens. In consequence of a vision he resigned this office, went on a pilgrimage to Rome with other Greek monks, and while there received divine direction to go on into Hainault, which he did with two companions. There he met St Amandus, and was encouraged by him to settle down by the river Haine. In accordance with this tale we are told that the monks of the monastery of St Gislenus at first lived according to the Rule of St Basil; their rule actually seems to have been indeterminate, for in the tenth century St Gerard of Brogne imposed that of St Benedict on the abbey of Saint-Ghislain. The legend also explains why the eldest sons of a certain family at Roisin were all called Baldericus (Baudry). When the mysterious Greek stranger was on his way to give an account of himself to the bishop St Aubertus at Cambrai, he received hospitality at Roisin, and during the night his host's wife was overtaken by a difficult labour. The husband appealed for his prayers to Gislenus, who handed him his belt, saying, " Put this round your wife like a baldric (*baudrei*), and she will safely give birth to a son." The saint's promise was verified, and the grateful parents gave him two estates for the endowment of his monastery. Roisin is still a place of pilgrimage for pregnant women, and mothers whose children are troubled by convulsions bring them to be blessed with a relic of the saint.

There is no very satisfactory account of the career of St Gislenus. An anonymous Life is printed by Mabillon and the Bollandists; and another, by Rainerus, a monk of Saint-Ghislain in the eleventh century, has been edited by Poncelet in the *Analecta Bollandiana*, vol. vi (1887), pp. 209–302. See also Van der Essen, *Étude critique sur les Saints Mérovingiens*, pp. 249–260; Berlière, *Monasticon Belge*, vol. i, pp. 244–246; and Berlière in *Revue liturgique et monastique*, vol. xiv (1929), pp. 438 *seq*. The story, as told in the early biographies, is very improbable.

ST SAVIN, CONF.

EARLY NINTH CENTURY?

This saint is venerated as the apostle of the Lavedan, that district of the Pyrenees at one end of which is situated the town of Lourdes. He was born of a good family at Barcelona and brought up very carefully by his widowed mother, who when he became a young man sent him to the care of his uncle Hetilius at Poitiers ; he is called count of that place. Being appointed tutor to his young cousin, Savin so impressed him by his religious example and inspiring words that the youth secretly left home one night and went to the great Benedictine monastery at Ligugé. When the flight and its object were discovered, Hetilius and his wife besought Savin to use his influence with their son to induce him to return home. But he refused, quoting the words of our Lord that He must be loved even more than father and mother, and furthermore announced his intention of becoming a monk at Ligugé himself. The cousins were clothed together with the habit of St Benedict.

St Savin is sometimes said to have become abbot of Ligugé ; eventually he left there with the object of becoming a solitary. He walked to Tarbes and from thence made his way to the place in the Lavedan then called Palatium Æmilianum, where Charlemagne had recently founded a monastery for Benedictines. The abbot, Forminius, received him kindly and showed him a place a little way off in the mountains well suited to his design. Here St Savin built himself a cell, which he afterwards exchanged for a pit in the ground, saying that everyone should expiate his own sins in the way and the measure that seems to himself called for. This in reply to Forminius, who on one of his frequent visits to the hermit expressed the opinion that his austerities were becoming exaggerated. Savin preached to the peasants of the neighbourhood by his mouth and by the example of his kindly and penitential spirit, and many and remarkable were the miracles with which they credited him. For example, a farmer having roughly stopped him from crossing his land to reach a spring, he struck water from the rocks with his staff ; and one night, having no dry tinder, he lit his candle by the flames from his own heart ! He wore only one garment, summer and winter, and that lasted him for thirteen years.

St Savin was forewarned of his death and sent a message to the monastery, and he was surrounded by clergy, monks, and devoted people when his peaceful end came. His body was enshrined in the abbey church, which was afterwards called

St Savin's, and the name extended to the adjacent village, Saint-Savin-de-Tarbes.

No reliance can be placed upon the short text of uncertain date printed in the *Acta Sanctorum*, October, vol. iv (*cf.* Mabillon, *Annales Benedictini*, vol. i, p. 575); even the century in which the hermit lived is a matter of pure conjecture. Poncelet, instead of speaking of Charlemagne, prefixes to his notice the time-heading : " Saec. V ? " The proper names here printed " Hetilius " and " Forminius," are given as Eutilius and Fronimius by both Mabillon and the Bollandists. It is characteristic of the methods of a certain type of hagiographer that out of these scanty materials a writer in the so-called *Petits Bollandistes* has evolved a biography of seven closely printed pages (over 4,500 words) in which he speaks with the same detail and definiteness of statement as he might have used in providing a summary of the career of Napoleon I.

BD. GUNTHER, Conf.

A.D. 1045

The first part of the life of Gunther, who was a cousin of St Stephen of Hungary and related to the Emperor St Henry, was by no means inspired by the holiness of his relatives, for until his fiftieth year he was a worldly and ambitious nobleman, and none too scrupulous at that. He then came under the influence of St Gothard of Hildesheim, at that time abbot of Niederaltaich and engaged in reforming the monastery of Hersfeld. This prelate succeeded also in reforming Gunther, who made up his mind to expiate his sins by becoming a monk. He devoted all his property to the endowment of Hersfeld, with the exception of an endowment for the abbey of Göllingen in Thuringia, of which house he retained the ownership in spite of the protests of St Gothard. Gunther then went on pilgrimage to Rome in the year 1006, and on his return entered Niederaltaich as a monk. But his conversion had not been complete, his humble position did not satisfy his ambition, and he insisted on being allowed to be made abbot of Göllingen. The experiment was not successful : there was friction between him and his monks, and the monastery began seriously to suffer. Aided perhaps by an illness which overtook Gunther, St Gothard succeeded by persuasion and rebuke in inducing him to resign his abbacy, and he returned to Niederaltaich. His turning to God was at last wholehearted, and whereas formerly the status of a simple monk had been too modest for him he now wished for an even more humble and retired life. Accordingly in 1008 he went to live as a hermit in the forest of Lalling, where a reputation of sanctity soon brought him

disciples. Three years later he moved with them to the neighbourhood of Rinchnach on the Regen in Upper Bavaria, where cells were
built and a church, dedicated in honour of St John the Baptist ; this
foundation developed into a regular monastery and was endowed by
the Emperor Conrad II.

Blessed Gunther in the meanwhile continued his eremitical existence, going from place to place to beg alms for the poor, and,
encouraging his cousin Stephen in the christianisation of his realm.
It is said that Gunther received the gift of infused knowledge and
became a powerful preacher though deficient in ordinary ecclesiastical
learning : he could probably neither read nor write. He atoned for
the excesses of his earlier years by severe mortification, and he exercised a rigid discipline over his followers, to the extent of rationing
the amount of water which each of his monks might have at disposal.
Blessed Gunther died at about the age of ninety, on October 9, 1045,
at Hartmanitz in Bohemia, in the presence of Duke Brzetislav of
Poland. He was buried at Brzevnov, near Prague (where his relics
were destroyed by the Hussites in the fifteenth century), and the
reputation of the last thirty-five years of his life together with the
wonders that were reported at his tomb led to a popular *cultus :* it
is recognised liturgically at Passau and elsewhere.

The main facts in the Latin biography printed both by Mabillon and
the Bollandists are probably reliable. This compilation seems to be based,
at least in part, upon statements taken from the writings of Wolfher, a
canon of Hildesheim, who was a contemporary. See also Grauert, in the
Historisches Jahrbuch, vol. xix (1898), pp. 249–287 ; and Oswald, *Das
Kloster Rinchnach* (1902).

ST LOUIS BERTRAND, Conf.

A.D. 1581

Louis was the son of John Bertrand, a royal notary, and was born
at Valencia in Spain on January 1, 1526. He was related through
his father to St Vincent Ferrer and was baptised at the same font as
that saint had been a hundred and seventy-five years before ; and
was the eldest of nine children, who, being all remarkable for their
goodness, were a proof of how deep root virtue may take in the heart
of youth when it is imprinted in them by the good example and early
instruction of their parents. Louis from his childhood seemed by
his teachable disposition and humility of soul to have inherited the
spirit of St Vincent Ferrer ; when he was fifteen he set off on his
own on a pilgrimage to Compostela, and had to be fetched back by

a ruse. He then wanted to take the religious habit among the Dominicans. His father opposed his inclination on account of his age and other reasons, and the prior of that order at Valencia could not but pay regard to his remonstrance. The next prior was the celebrated Father John Mico, who had been brought up a shepherd in the mountains. He gave the habit to young Bertrand when he was eighteen and conducted the novice through his time of probation to profession and sacerdotal ordination, which was given to him by the Archbishop of Valencia, St Thomas of Villanova, in 1547. The fervour with which he sang his first Mass never cooled. He prepared himself to offer that adorable sacrifice by spending always some hours in prayer and penance, by which and by confession he endeavoured to purify his soul from the least stain, to correct the least irregularities, and to cleanse away all the poison of self-love. The ardour of his love, the impression of which appeared in his countenance, and the tears which he shed at the altar, inspired with devotion all that heard his Mass. He was made master of novices five years after profession, and discharged that office for periods which totalled thirty years. He was very severe and strict, but both by his example and words taught them sincerely and perfectly to renounce the world and their own will, to conceive an entire distrust of themselves, and by a spirit of prayer closely to unite their souls to God. St Louis Bertrand was not particularly learned, though a painstaking student, and he was somewhat lacking in humour, a characteristic not uncommon among Spaniards. Nor did his talents at first appear promising for the pulpit; nevertheless he overcame all difficulties and his discourses produced very great results, for they were animated with charity and breathed a spirit of sincere religion and humility. In 1557 a pestilence raged in Valencia and the saint knew no danger and spared no pains in comforting and assisting the sick and burying the dead. He about this time made the acquaintance of St Teresa, who wrote and asked his advice about her projected convent of reformed Carmelites. St Louis replied : " The matter about which you ask my advice is of such great importance to our Lord's service that I wished to recommend it to Him in my poor prayers and at the holy Sacrifice : that is why I have been so long in replying. Now I bid you, in the name of the same Lord, arm yourself with courage to undertake so great an enterprise. He will help and support you in it and I assure you, as from Him, that before fifty years are out your order will be one of the most famous in the Church, who keeps you in her holy protection."

St Louis, who prayed for martyrdom and cheerfully exposed his life for his brethren during the plague, obtained of his superiors leave to preach the gospel to the savages in America, a most painful and dangerous mission. He embarked at Seville in 1562, with another friar of his order, and landed at Cartagena in New Granada (Colombia) where there was a convent of his order. Without allowing himself any rest after the fatigues of his journey, he prepared to open his mission. During the course of his journeys he often lay in the open air, on the ground or on pieces of wood, which formed rather a rack than a bed, and he often suffered the utmost severities of hunger and other hardships. St Louis spoke only Spanish, and had to use an interpreter, but the gifts of tongues, of prophecy, and of miracles were conferred by Heaven on this apostle, the bull of his canonisation tells us. In the isthmus of Panama and the province of Cartagena, in the space of three years, he converted to Christ and baptised many thousand souls. The baptismal registers of Tubera, in St Louis's own handwriting, show that all the inhabitants of that place were converted, and he had a like success at Cipacoa. The people of Paluato were more difficult, and the prayers, tears, and mortifications which the saint offered up for them seemed at that time to be lost; but afterwards they produced a more plentiful harvest. The next mission which the saint undertook was among the inhabitants of the mountains of Santa Marta, who received him as an angel sent from Heaven. He is said to have baptised there about fifteen thousand persons;* and also a tribe of fifteen hundred Indians who, having changed their minds, had followed him thither from Paluato, were baptised by him and his companions. He visited the Caribs of the Leeward Islands (whom Alban Butler considers "the most brutal, barbarous, and unteachable people of the human race"—certainly they tried to poison St Louis), San Thomé in the Virgin Islands, and San Vincente in the Windwards, and then returned to Colombia to gain more souls for the Church. Heaven protected him more than once from attempts made upon his life by poison and other ways. He foretold many things to come, and was pierced to the quick to see the avarice and cruelty of the Spanish adventurers in the Indies and not to be able to find any means of putting a stop to those evils. He was desirous to seek redress in Spain, and about that time he was

---

* These wholesale baptisms of natives who could not possibly have an adequate idea of the Faith and its obligations are tributes to the apostolic zeal rather than to the prudence of such great saints as St Louis Bertrand and St Francis of Solano. They were often a source of embarrassment to their successors. When Father de Victoria, O.P., took over the vast diocese of Tucuman in 1581 he found there five secular priests and a few regulars, *not one of whom could speak any of the local languages.*

recalled thither, thus ending a marvellous mission of six years for which he well merits his title of Apostle of New Granada.

St Louis arrived at Seville in 1569, whence he returned to Valencia, and was appointed successively prior of two convents of his order. He wonderfully revived in them the primitive spirit of their founder St Dominic, and preached the divine word during eleven years without intermission in several dioceses in Spain. He trained up many excellent preachers, who succeeded him in the ministry of the word. The first lesson he gave them was that humble and fervent prayer must always be the principal preparation of the preacher : for words without works never have the power to touch or change hearts. The two last years of his life he was afflicted with painful illness and frequent fevers, under which it was his constant prayer, with St Augustine, " Here cut, here burn, here spare not, that I may find mercy for eternity." Under his infirmities he continued his penitential austerities and apostolic labours. In 1580 he preached the Lent at Xativa, and went thence to preach in the cathedral at Valencia, where he was carried from the pulpit to his bed, from which he never rose again. Amidst the grief of all about him he appeared cheerful at the approach of death. The Archbishop of Valencia attended him during his illness and waited on him with his own hands, till St Louis gave up his soul to God amidst his prayers, in company with all the brethren of his convent, on October 9, 1581, being fifty-five years old. St Louis Bertrand, who is the principal patron of Colombia, was canonised by Pope Clement X in 1671.

Those apostolic pastors who converted so many souls to Christ were men filled with His spirit, who regarded nothing but His glory, and lived for Him alone, as Christ on earth lived entirely to the glory of His Father, to whom He offered Himself and His kingdom. Whoever becomes His minister must in like manner have no aim or intention but to advance the divine honour. For this he must be dead to the world, that is to all desire of honours, pleasure, riches, or any earthly goods whatever. Such an one sees nothing in this world which he hopes for or desires and nothing that he much fears. He seeks no terms with it while he is engaged in the cause of his Master ; and no threats or terrors from its persecution can damp his courage in defending the honour of God or cool his zeal for the salvation of souls.

A very full and devout *Life of St Lewis Bertrand* was published by Father Bertrand Wilberforce, O.P., in 1882. The book has been translated into German and French, and seemingly also into Spanish. As Father Wilberforce tells us, his narrative is founded on the biography of the saint, printed in 1582–3, almost immediately after his death, by Father V. J. Antist, O.P., his intimate friend and disciple. A Latin version of this, made from the Spanish original, is included in the *Acta Sanctorum*, October, vol. v, and it is there supplemented by a still longer biography which was compiled and published in 1623 by Father B. Aviñone who was familiar with the evidence given in the process of beatification and had come to Rome as procurator of the cause. There were several other Lives printed in Spain and Italy during the seventeenth and eighteenth centuries, but it does not seem that any new material of notable importance has so far been brought to light. Immense enthusiasm was aroused in Valencia when the formal decree of beatification was issued in 1608. A book describing these *Fiestas* was compiled by G. de Aguilar in 1608 and a modern edition of it was brought out in 1914. Moreover, another small work by V. Gomez, dealing with the *Sermones y Fiestas* which marked the same occasion, appeared in 1609. Copies of both are in the British Museum.

BD. JOHN LEONARDI, Conf.

FOUNDER OF THE CLERKS REGULAR OF THE MOTHER OF GOD

A.D. 1609

John Leonardi was a young assistant to an apothecary in the city of Lucca in the middle of the sixteenth century. He was of a religious disposition, became a member of a confraternity founded by Blessed John Colombini, and after a time began to study privately with the object of receiving holy orders. After he had been ordained he was very active in the works of the ministry, especially in hospitals and prisons, and he attracted several young laymen to assist him. Their headquarters was at the church of Our Lady *della Rosa* in Lucca, and they lived in common in a house near by. It was a time when the Council of Trent and the ravages of Protestantism had filled serious Catholics with a passion for reform, and John Leonardi and his followers, several of whom were studying for the priesthood, soon projected a new congregation of secular priests. When this scheme was spread abroad it at once provoked powerful opposition in the Lucchesan republic. This opposition was political, and rather difficult to understand, but was formidable enough to keep the founder an exile from Lucca for practically the rest of his life except when he was able to visit there under special papal protection. In 1580 he secretly acquired the church of Santa Maria Cortelandini (or Nera) for the use of his followers, who three years later were recognised officially by the Bishop of Lucca, with the approval of Pope Gregory XIII, as an association of secular priests with simple vows (they were granted their present name and solemn vows in 1621). Blessed John received the encouragement and help

of St Philip Neri and St Joseph Calasanctius, and his fathers
became so great a power for good in Italy that their congregation
was confirmed by Clement VIII in 1595. This pope had a very
great regard for the character and capabilities of Blessed John, and
appointed him commissary apostolic to superintend the reform of
the monks of Vallumbrosa and Monte Vergine. He obtained from
Clement the church of Santa Maria in Portico, and Cardinal Baronius
was made cardinal protector of the congregation. His zeal for the
institution of foreign missions is referred to by the Roman Martyrology, but the Clerks Regular of the Mother of God have had only
one house outside of Italy ; by the deliberate policy of their founder
they never had more than fifteen churches, and they form to-day
only a very tiny congregation.

John Leonardi died on October 9, 1609, and was beatified in
1861. Pope Leo XIII ordered his feast to be observed by the clergy
of Rome, an honour extended to no other *beati* who were not popes.

Apart from the documents printed in the process of beatification, more
than one Life of this *beato* has been published. See, for example, L.
Marracci, *Vita del Padre Giovanni Leonardi, Lucchese,* 1673, and, at the
time of the beatification, A. Bianchini, *Vita del Beato Giovanni Leonardi,*
1861. His cause is frequently referred to by Prosper Lambertini (Benedict
XIV) in Bk. II of his great work, *De Beatificazione, etc.*

OCTOBER 10

ST FRANCIS BORGIA, Conf.

A.D. 1572

THE family of de Borja was one of the most noble and distinguished of the kingdom of Aragon, but it was not till the fifteenth century that it became known outside Spain, when from 1455 to 1458 Alphonsus Borgia was Pope under the name of Callistus III. At the end of that century there was another Borgia pope, Alexander VI, who at the time of his elevation to the papacy was the father of four children. As a provision for his son, Peter, he bought the dukedom of Gandia in Spain, and on Peter's death bestowed it upon another son, John. John was murdered soon after his marriage, and his son, the third duke of Gandia, married the daughter of a natural son of King Ferdinand V of Aragon. Of this union was born at Gandia in the year 1510 Francisco de Borja y Aragon, now known to us as St Francis Borgia, great-grandson of a pope and of a king and cousin of the Emperor Charles V. As a child Francis was an apt pupil and of such a pious disposition that his mother had to remind him that he was destined for a secular career and that even a good Christian could be a soldier. When he was ten years old his mother fell dangerously ill, and Francis, shutting himself up in his room, prayed for her with many tears and took a sharp discipline ; this was the first time he used that mortification which he afterwards frequently made a part of his penance. But the Duchess died and the boy was plunged in a grief more than passing ; her words and example had always been a great spur to virtue, and he took care never to forget them. At that time Spain was filled with tumult and insurrections of the *comuneros* against the regency. The rebels, taking advantage of the absence of the young king, Charles V, plundered the houses of the nobility in Valencia, and made themselves masters of the town of Gandia. The Duke fled with his whole family, Francis and his tutor barely escaping the hands of the mob. He was taken to Saragossa and there left by his father in the care of the archbishop, John of Aragon, who was his uncle. He made up a household for his nephew, and provided him with masters in grammar, music, and

124

fencing, which he had begun to learn at Gandia. The young Francis found himself in not very edifying surroundings, but two sermons which he heard from an Hieronymite friar, who was his confessor and a learned and spiritual man, one on the Last Judgement, the other on the Passion, made strong impressions on his mind. When he was twelve he was sent to Tordesillas, to be taken into the service of the Infanta Catherine, who was soon after to be married to John III, King of Portugal. When this marriage took place in 1525 the Duke of Gandia, who had views for his son in Spain, recalled him, and the Archbishop of Saragossa resumed the care of his education. Francis was then fifteen years old, and after he had finished rhetoric studied philosophy two years with great application,* and by the time he was eighteen had a strong inclination for the religious life. This did not suit his father and uncle at all, and to divert his thoughts they made arrangements that he should be received at the imperial court. At this time occurred an incident of which the significance was not seen till long afterwards. At Alcalá de Henarez Francis was impressed by the appearance of a man whom he saw being taken to the prison of the Inquisition. That man was Ignatius Loyola.

At Valladolid Francis entered whole-heartedly into court life, for he considered his duty to his prince as his duty to God ; and though he willingly accepted every mark of Charles's regard for him, he was careful to refer himself, his actions, and whatever he received purely to the divine honour. He was exact in regulating both his personal time and the principal duties of his household. Hours were appointed for everyone to go every day to Mass, for evening prayers, for recreation and meals. He heard sermons as often as possible, and went to confession almost every Sunday and on all great festivals, and took care to spend well those days which are particularly set apart for the divine service. It is from the manner in which a Christian passes them that we may form an idea of his general practice and sense of religion. St Francis delighted chiefly in the company of the most virtuous, but was courteous to all and never spoke ill of anyone, or suffered others to do so in his presence.

* Here Alban Butler delivers a brief disquisition on humane studies, in which he says, " Many so learn these sciences as to put on in their thoughts and expressions a scholastic garb which they cannot lay aside, so that their minds may be said to be cast in Gothic moulds. . . . Nothing is more horrid than a mere scholar, that is, a pedant who appears in the world to have reaped from his studies scarce any other advantage than to be rendered by them absolutely unfit for civilised society." The association of " scholastic gard," gothic, and unfitness for civilised society show him a true child of the eighteenth century.

He avoided all ambition, gallantry, luxury, and gaming : vices which are often fashionable in courts. He not only never gambled, but did not like to see others play, saying that a man commonly loses by it four things, his money, his time, the devotion of his heart to God, and his conscience. One of his servants discovered that on occasions when he would be exposed to temptations of sensuality he wore a hair-shirt. In him it appeared that there is no readier way to gain the esteem of men without seeking it than by the practice of Christian virtue, and his personal charm and vivacity, his skill in music and in the bull-ring, added to his popularity. And he was a handsome young man ; " a young Apollo," " another Narcissus," say his biographers. His own predilection was hawking : " I acknowledge," he said, " that I received particular graces from God when out in the country." The Empress had great esteem for Francis and fixed her eye on him to marry Eleanor de Castro, a Portuguese lady who had been educated with her and whom she had brought with her out of Portugal. The Emperor was well pleased with the proposal, and made a settlement with the Duke of Gandia, who at first refused his consent : he aimed higher. But Charles won him over, and at the marriage made Francis marquis of Lombay and master of the horse to the Empress, and having had experience of his wisdom and fidelity admitted him into his privy council. The Marquis, to rid himself of the importunities of those who followed more dangerous diversions, developed his talent for music, for he played on several instruments and sang very well ; he made settings for songs and composed cantatas which were sung in some churches in Spain and called after his title. He learned mathematics, especially the branches which are most useful for the art of fortifying towns and the military art in general. The Emperor made him his companion in the disastrous expedition which he undertook against France into Provence in 1536, whence he despatched him to the Empress to carry her news of his health and affairs.

A series of deaths at this time made a strong impression and had lasting influence on Francis. The first was that of his friend, the poet Garcilaso de la Vega, who was killed during the Provence campaign. Then in 1537 was taken his grandmother, Doña Maria Henriquez, who, widowed at nineteen, had become a Poor Clare at thirty-four. Her doctor had declared that if she embraced so severe a manner of life she could not live one year ; nevertheless she survived for thirty-three. Francis used afterwards to say that from the time that his grandmother went to Heaven he found his soul animated with new strength and courage to devote himself more perfectly to the divine service. On his return to Toledo the Emperor made Francis viceroy of Catalonia, and created him knight commander of the military Order of St James, the most honourable in Spain. Barcelona was the residence of his government, and no sooner had he taken possession of his post than he changed the face of the province. The highways were cleared of robbers, against whose bands the Viceroy marched in person, and the defences of the city improved. He carefully watched the judges, obliging them to administer justice impartially and to despatch lawsuits with reasonable speed. He set up schools and seminaries for youths, and assisted debtors and all distressed persons with extraordinary charity : he was at once the judge, the father, and the protector of the people. He afterwards said that " it was when I was viceroy of Catalonia that God prepared me to be general of the Society of Jesus. I then learned to decide important questions, to settle rival claims, to see both sides of an affair, in a way I could not otherwise have done." He was already a different man ; " he saw with other eyes and heard with other ears than before : he spoke with another tongue, because his heart also was not the same." Several hours a day were devoted to prayer without any prejudice to public affairs or neglect of his family. He added to every hour of the Divine Office a meditation on a station of our Saviour's passion, so as to accompany Him every day from the garden to the sepulchre. When he was obliged to assist at public entertainments or functions his mind was often so absorbed in God that if he was afterwards asked about them, he could give no account of what had passed or been said. He entertained in a suitable manner the lords who visited him and the officers that attended him ; but dining with this company he ate very little and slowly, and talked a lot so that no one would notice. His watching, disciplines, and other austerities were very severe. By this rigorous way of living he who before was fat became so lean that his servant found his clothes grown too big for him within a year. He had formerly been accustomed to communicate once a month. After he had altered his manner of living he confessed once every week and communicated in public on all great festivals and privately every Sunday.* This was the life of the Viceroy when Father Antony Araoz, the first professed Jesuit after the ten that were concerned in the foundation of that order, came to preach at Barcelona. By

* Weekly communion was so rare at this time that the example of St Francis Borgia caused great excitement and precipitated a controversy among the theologians of Spain. The general view, contrary to the practice of the first Christians, was that it was presumptuous in a layman, concerned in the affairs of the world, to receive the Body of the Lord so often !

his means Francis became acquainted with this new society and the character of its founder, to whom he wrote to ask whether so frequent communion as once a week was to be commended. St Ignatius, who was then at Rome, answered him that frequent communion is the best means to cure the disorders of our souls and to raise them to perfect virtue, and advised him to continue therein.

In 1543 St Francis became duke of Gandia by the death of his father, whereupon the Emperor Charles accepted the resignation of his post, and he retired with his family to his estates at Gandia, following on the refusal of the King of Portugal to recognise him as master of the household to Prince Philip of Spain, who was about to marry the king's daughter. This was a definite check to the public career of Francis Borgia and he proceeded to interest himself in more personal affairs. He fortified Gandia that it might not be exposed to the Moors and pirates from Barbary, built a convent for the Dominicans at Lombay, and repaired the hospital. The Bishop of Carthagena wrote to a friend at this time, " During my recent stay at Gandia I found Don Francis to be a model duke and a perfect Christian gentleman ; humble, truly good, a man of God in every sense of the term. . . . How carefully his children are brought up ! How thoroughly his dependents are looked after ! How great is his pleasure in the company of priests and religious ! . . ." This happy and peaceful life at Gandia was brought suddenly to an end by the death in 1546 of Doña Eleanor. For seventeen years she had been his beloved and faithful companion, and when she lay ill it took all Francis's determination to pray that not his will but God's should be done in her regard. They had had eight children, of whom the youngest was eight at his mother's death ; the five boys all had distinguished careers in the imperial service, two of the girls married, and the third became a Poor Clare. Very shortly after Eleanor's death, Blessed Peter Faber, St Ignatius's first associate in founding his order, came to Gandia. He was then leaving Spain to go into Italy, and was ordered by St Ignatius to call upon the Duke of Gandia on his way. Francis made a retreat under his direction according to the spiritual exercises of St Ignatius, and arranged with him the preliminaries for the foundation there of a Jesuit college. Blessed Peter (who died in Rome three months later) laid the first stone of the building, to which Pope and Emperor gave the status of a university. Francis was now determined to enter a religious order, but for some time wavered as to which one : he was undecided between the contemplative Carthusians and the active Franciscans, and then was moved towards the Society of Jesus by the opposition which it was meeting and by its cutting him off from the danger of ecclesiastical dignities. He asked the opinion of his confessor and other experienced men, and finally sent his petition for admittance to St Ignatius at Rome. He received his request with great joy ; but in his answer advised the duke to defer the execution of his design till he had settled his children and finished the foundations he had begun, telling him in the meantime to study a regular course of theology at Gandia, and to take the degree of doctor in that faculty ; he was, moreover, " to take every precaution to prevent this astonishing piece of news from being prematurely divulged " (it was not astonishing to Ignatius : he had prophesied it some years before). Francis punctually obeyed but was troubled in the following year by being summoned to assist at the *cortes* of Aragon. He therefore wrote to St Ignatius and as a consequence was allowed to make the first vows of the Society before private witnesses in the chapel of the college at Gandia. Ignatius had obtained a brief from the Pope, by which he was allowed to spend four years in the world after he should have made his first vows, in consideration of the family duties which held him. Three years was in fact enough to see his children properly established and Gandia put in charge of the eldest, Charles, and on August 31, 1550, St Francis Borgia set out for Rome. He was yet only forty years old.

When he arrived in Rome Francis would not stay anywhere but at the Jesuit residence. St Ignatius waited to receive him at the door, and the Duke, throwing himself at his feet, begged his blessing and honoured him as his father and superior. After paying his homage to Pope Julius III and receiving and returning the visits of all the great men at Rome, he fulfilled his devotions for the Jubilee indulgence. Then, four months after his arrival, he left Rome, went back to Spain, and retired to a hermitage at Oñate, near Loyola. Here he received the Emperor's permission to make over his titles and estates to his son Charles, whereupon he shaved his head and beard, assumed the clerical dress, and was ordained priest in Whitsun week, 1551. " A duke turned Jesuit " was the sensation of the day, and when Francis celebrated his first public Mass, for assistance at which the Pope granted a plenary indulgence, the crowd at Vergara was so great that the altar had to be set up in the open air. At Oñate the object of all this admiration was set by his superiors to serve the cook, fetch water, and carry wood ; he made the fire and swept the kitchen ; and when he waited at table he fell on his knees to beg pardon of the fathers and brothers for having served them with such clumsiness. Directly after his ordination he was allowed to preach throughout Guipuzcoa, and he went through the villages with a bell, calling the children to catechism, teaching them their prayers and the Christian doctrine, and instructing and preaching to all ranks of society. But within the house the superior treated Father Francis with such severity as he deemed the previous exalted position of his subject required. The saint undoubtedly suffered much during this time, but the only signs of impatience he ever gave were when he was treated otherwise than as a religious. Once he got a gash in his head, and the doctor who dressed it apologised, " I am afraid, my lord, that I cannot help hurting your grace." " You can't hurt me more," was the reply, " than you are doing by your unseemly manner of addressing me." St Francis had always practised corporal mortifications, which after his " conversion " became excessive ; they were now curbed by religious obedience, but he was ingenious in the devising of physical discomforts. In after years he was of the opinion that he had been imprudent in his ways of mortifying his body, especially before he became a Jesuit. He left Oñate for several months to preach in other parts of Spain to which he was invited. Much success everywhere attended his labours ; many persons desired to regulate their affairs and their consciences by his advice, and he was one of the first to recognise the greatness of the Carmelite nun of Avila, Teresa. After doing wonders in Castile and Andalusia, he seemed to surpass himself in Portugal, especially at Evora and Lisbon, and in 1554 St Ignatius made him commissary general of the Society in Spain. Then was added to his charge the care of the missions to the Indies. Upon renouncing the world he signed his letters " Francis the Sinner," calling this his only title, till St Ignatius ordered him to omit it, as a singularity. Twice there was talk of his being made a cardinal, which Julius III wished to do, and on the second occasion in order to relieve his fears St Ignatius directed that he should take his solemn vows, which bound him to refuse such preferments. He used to say that he hoped the Society of Jesus would prosper for God's glory on three things, prayer and the sacraments, the opposition of the world, and perfect obedience. On those things flourished the soul of Francis Borgia.

During his years as commissary general St Francis Borgia was practically the founder of the Society in Spain, establishing in a short time new houses and colleges at over a dozen places. But he did not neglect the immediate care of those whom he had left behind him in the world. He soothed and made sweet the last moments of the Queen Dowager, Joanna, who fifty years before had gone mad at the death of her husband and had shown a special aversion from the clergy. In the next year, soon after the death of St Ignatius, his old friend the Emperor Charles V abdicated his rule, and sent for

St Francis to visit him in his place of retirement at Yuste. Charles had been prepossessed against the Society of Jesus and expressed his surprise that Francis should have preferred it to so many older orders. The saint removed his prejudices, and said, for the motives which had determined him in his choice, that God had called him to a state in which the active and contemplative life are joined together, and in which he was freed from the danger of being raised to dignities of which he had had enough in the world. He added that if the Society was a new order the fervour of those engaged in it answered that objection. After the death of the Emperor in 1558 St Francis went into Portugal, where he was very popular. During his absence Philip II came to rule in Spain and, turning against his former friend, listened to the calumnies which jealousy was raising against St Francis. He remained on the work of the Society in Portugal for two years, and was then summoned to Rome by Pope Pius IV, at the instance of the Jesuit general, Father Laynez.

St Francis was most warmly received in Rome and among those who regularly attended his sermons were Cardinal Charles Borromeo and Cardinal Ghislieri, afterwards St Pius V. Becoming acquainted with the work of the headquarters of the Jesuits, he fulfilled offices in the Society, and on the death of Father Laynez in 1565 was elected general. During his generalate of seven years he promoted the work of the Society in all parts of the world with such success that he might be called a second founder, and the zeal with which he propagated the missions and animated the labourers in planting the gospel in remote countries entitles him to a great share in the conversion of those countries to the faith. He was not less active in directing his religious brethren in Europe for the reformation of the manners of Christians. St Francis's first care as general was to establish a properly regulated novitiate in Rome and to provide for the same in the provinces. When he first came to the city fifteen years before he had shown a strong interest in the project of the Roman college, and had given a large sum of money therefor. He now built a church for the use of the students, and concerned himself personally in the direction of the college and the arrangement of its curriculum. In effect he was the founder of this college, but he always refused the title, which is given to Pope Gregory XIII who re-established it as the Gregorian University. St Francis also built the church of Sant' Andrea on the Quirinal, with the adjoining residence, to house the novitiate, contributed towards the Gesù, and enlarged and improved the German college which was intended to send missioners to all those northern lands which had been infected by Protestantism. Pope St Pius V had confidence in the Society of Jesus and a great trust and admiration for its general, so that St Francis could proceed freely with all the projects he had at heart. He founded colleges in Piedmont, provided for the extension of the Society across the Alps and in his own Spain and Portugal, and established the province of Poland. He used his influence with the French court to obtain a more favourable reception for the Jesuits in France, where he was able to set up eight colleges. And he was far from neglecting the foreign missions. Those of the East Indies and the Far East were reformed and those of the Americas begun. Among the visitors that he sent out was Blessed Ignatius Azevedo, who with his thirty-nine Jesuit companions was martyred by Huguenot privateers while on his way to Brazil in 1570. St Francis published a new edition of the rules of the Society and drew up regulations and directions for those members who were engaged in special work of various kinds. The work he himself got through in seven years was amazing, and he never allowed it to distract him from the end to which it was directed or to affect adversely his own interior life. Father Verjus, S.J., wrote, a century later, " It may be truly said that the Society owes to St Francis Borgia its characteristic form and true perfection. For if St Ignatius planned the building and laid the foundations, Father Laynez built the walls and his successor St Francis roofed it and fitted up the inside, thus finishing the great work of which the design had been revealed to St Ignatius by God." Nor was St Francis so immersed in the responsibilities of his office that he had no time to spare for matters outside. This was shown when in 1566 a pestilence made great havoc in Rome, on which occasion St Francis procured both from the Pope and magistrates plentiful alms for the relief of the poor, and commissioned the fathers of his order, two and two, to attend the sick in all parts of the city, with imminent danger of their own lives.

In the year 1571 the Pope sent his nephew, Cardinal Bonelli, on an embassy to Spain, Portugal, and France, and St Francis accompanied him. Though politically not a great success, it was a personal triumph for the Jesuit. Everywhere crowds clamoured " to see the saint " and to hear him preach, old animosities were forgotten, and King Philip received him as gladly as did his people. But the fatigues entailed were too much for St Francis. He had been for some time in bad health ; his infirmities, inclination to retirement, and a deep sense of the weight of his post had made him try to procure a discharge from it in 1570, but this his brethren would not listen to. During this legation his weakness increased so much that when he arrived at Ferrara on his return the Duke, who was his cousin, sent him from thence to Rome in a litter. He lived for two

days only after his arrival, during which he refused any official visits.
By his brother Don Thomas he sent his blessing to all his children
and grandchildren, but their names had to be rehearsed to him, for
his memory was failing. The fathers of the Society begged he would
name his successor and allow them the satisfaction of making his
picture : but he would do neither. When he had lost his speech,
a painter was, with peculiar insensibility, introduced to his bedside.
The saint saw him, expressed his displeasure with his dying hands
and eyes, and turned away his face so that nothing could be done.
He died at the midnight of September 30–October 1, 1572. The
process of his canonisation was begun in 1607 at the instance of his
grandson, the Duke of Lerma, whose own granddaughter had been
healed at the intercession of Francis. His body was translated to
Madrid ten years later, and in 1670 the canonisation was achieved.
His feast was fixed for this day by Pope Innocent XI in 1684.
St Francis Borgia is one of the patron saints of Portugal and is
invoked against earthquakes.

The greatness of this saint appeared not in the honours and
applause which he often received, but in the humility which he took
care to nourish in his heart, so that he looked upon humiliations as
his greatest gain and honour. From the time that he began to give
himself totally to the divine service he learned the importance and
difficulty of attaining to this perfect humility, and he tried unremit-
tingly to humble himself beneath all creatures in the divine presence
and within himself. Amidst the honours and respect that were
shown him at Valladolid, his companion, Father Bustamente, noticed
that he was not only mortified and quiet but more than ordinarily
self-effacing, for which he asked the reason. " I considered," said
St Francis, " in my morning meditation that Hell is my due. I
think that all men and even dumb creatures ought to cry out after
me, ' Hell is your place.' " By this reflection he humbled his soul.
He one day told the novices that in meditating on the actions of
Christ he had for six years always placed himself in spirit at the feet
of Judas ; but then he realised that Christ had washed the feet even
of that traitor, so that he thenceforth felt unworthy to approach even
him.

An immense amount of material is now available concerning the life
of St Francis Borgia. But most of this, printed in five special volumes of
the *Monumenta Historica Societatis Jesu* (1894–1911), has only been brought
to light in modern times. There are over one thousand letters of the saint
published *in extenso*, together with a spiritual diary of his later years, and
a number of miscellaneous documents relating to his family. Alban Butler,
whose account is in the main reproduced above, had not access, of course,
to these materials, but they have been fully utilized by Père Suau, *Histoire*

de S. François de Borgia, Paris, 1910, and by Otto Karrer, *Der heilige Franz von Borja*, Freiburg im Breisgau, 1921. Butler had to be content with such earlier biographies as those of D. Vasquez, S.J. (1585), still in MS. but reproduced in substance by Father J. E. Nieremberg in 1644, and P. de Ribadeneira, S.J., *Vida del P. Francisco de Borja* (1598). Both Vasquez and Ribadeneira were contemporaries and friends of the saint, but for fear of giving scandal much was suppressed, more particularly concerning Francis Borgia's efforts as a secular to contend with grave abuses in the administration of justice by the grandees and magistrats of Spain. On the other hand, in these early biographies, and most conspicuously of all in that of Cardinal de Cienfuegos, S.J., the tone is one of extravagant panegyric, and fictitious anecdotes and marvels are accepted without any examination. The story, for example, that Francis, on viewing the corpse of the Empress Isabella, exclaimed : " Never more will I serve a master who can die," is devoid of all historical foundation (Suau, p. 68 ; Karrer, p. 281). An excellent shorter Life of the saint by Père Suau has appeared in the series *Les Saints* (1905), and in English Miss A. M. Clarke published *The Life of St Francis Borgia* in the Quarterly Series, but the writer had to depend entirely upon the older biographies. A very complete bibliography is supplied by Karrer, pp. xi–xvi.

ST GEREON AND HIS COMPS., MARTS.

A.D. 287 (?)

In the Roman Martyrology there is entered on this day : " At Cologne, the passion of St Gereon the Martyr and his 318 Companions, who in the persecution of Maximian patiently gave their necks to the sword for the true religion. In the territory of the same city, the passion of St Victor and his fellow-martyrs. At Bonn in Germany, the passion of the holy martyrs Cassius and Florentius with many others." The early medieval martyrologists refer to a number of martyrs near Cologne who were traditionally supposed to have been members of separated detachments of the Theban Legion (September 22), but it was not until the beginning of the thirteenth century that one Helinand, a Cistercian monk of Froimont, ventured to supply a *passio* for them. He averred that St Gereon and 318 others suffered at Cologne, St Victor and 330 more at Xanten, SS. Cassius, Florentius, and an unnamed number at Bonn. His forces being thus reduced, Maximian sent for reinforcements from North Africa, and when it was found that these also were Christians another massacre followed. The Roman Martyrology refers to these as 300 in number on October 15. Helinand says, absurdly enough, that the Empress St Helen found the relics of these martyrs and built churches to shelter them at Cologne and Bonn. There was a further finding of relics of the dead, at Cologne in 1121 and Xanten in 1284 ; these were hastily assumed to belong to the martyred Theban legionaries and were accordingly enshrined and venerated as such. Whoever these martyrs of the Rhine were, they had nothing to do with those of Agaunum and there is no reason to suppose that the relics found were authentic.

That there were a band of martyrs whose sepulture was venerated at Cologne seems to be established by a fragmentary epitaph of the fifth century in which a certain Rudufula seems to be described as " *sociata martyribus,*" *i.e.* buried in the neighbourhood of the martyrs. Gregory of Tours further tells us that at Cologne " there was a basilica built in the place where fifty men of the sacred Theban legion had been put to death for Christ." He adds that, on account of the rich mosaics with which it was adorned, they were styled " the golden martyrs." It has been suggested that these *martyres aurei* may through some misconception have given rise to the idea of martyrs from Africa (*Mauri*) ; but the whole matter is very uncertain. The name Gereon is not mentioned by Gregory, but it occurs in the Berne text of the *Hieronymianum* (see Delehaye's commentary, pp. 547–8, 550 and 557) and in Bede's Martyrology. *Cf.* also Zilliken, *Der Kölnische Festkalender* (1901), pp. 104–107, and Rathgen, *Die Kunst-denkmäler des Rheinprovinz,* vol. i, pp. 1–102.

SS. EULAMPIUS AND EULAMPIA, MARTS.

c. A.D. 310

These two martyrs probably suffered by the sword at Nicomedia under Gallienus. Their unreliable *acta* relate that Eulampius was a youth among the Christians who fled from persecution in the city and took refuge in caves. He was sent into the town to buy food and, seeing the decree against Christians posted up, he stopped to read it. When a soldier spoke to him he was seized with panic, and took to his heels. Suspicion was thus aroused, he was pursued, caught, and brought before the prefect in chains. This magistrate reproved the guards for their harshness, ordered the bonds of Eulampius to be removed, and began to question him. When he had learned his name and honourable status the prefect suggested he should sacrifice to one or other of the gods, but this Eulampius stoutly refused to do, retorting that the gods were only idols. This angered the prefect, who had the boy beaten and, when he showed himself yet more defiant, hung on the rack. Thereupon the sister of Eulampius, Eulampia, ran out from the crowd and embraced him, so she too was arrested. Both were then tortured in various ways but suffered no harm, coming unscathed even out of a bath of boiling oil (referred to in the Roman Martyrology). This marvel and the constancy of the martyrs moved two hundred of the bystanders to confess Christ, and they were all beheaded together.

The Greek text of this *passio* with a full discussion will be found in the *Acta Sanctorum*, October, vol. v. Another redaction is printed in Migne, P. G., vol. cxv, cc. 1053–1065.

ST MAHARSAPOR, Mart.
A.D. 421

This martyr was a Persian of noble birth, even more distinguished by his virtue and his zeal for the Christian faith. On this account the persecution was no sooner begun by King Yezdegerd, precipitated by the destruction by St Abda of Susa of a Mazdæan temple, than Maharsapor was seized, the first of many, together with Nerses and Sabutaka. The two latter after divers tortures finished their martyrdom by the order and sentence of a judge who had been raised to that dignity from a slave. By this inhuman magistrate Maharsapor also was often examined and put to the torture; after which he was left to languish three years in prison in stench and darkness. Then the same judge again examined the confessor and, finding him steadfast and invincible in confessing Christ, he condemned him to be thrown into a pit, there to perish with hunger. Several days after this sentence had been executed, officers and soldiers opened the pit and found the martyr's body, without life indeed but in light and on his knees, as if he had been at prayer, in which attitude the saint, triumphing by such a death over his enemies, had breathed out his soul. St Maharsapor suffered in October in the year of our Lord 421, the second of Bahram V.

Père Peeters transliterates the name of this martyr as Mihrsabor. His *passio* may be found in Assemani, *Acta Martyrum Orientalium*, vol. i, pp. 234–236; but the Syriac text has also been more critically edited by Bedjan, *Acta Martyrum et Sanctorum*, vol. ii, no. 10. St Mihrsabor is not mentioned in the Martyrologium of Rabban Sliba, but the name has been inserted in the margin of the MS.; see the *Analecta Bollandiana*, vol. xxvii (1908), p. 115.

ST CERBONIUS, Bp. of Populonium, Conf.
c. A.D. 575

When St Regulus and other bishops were driven out of Africa by the Vandals at the beginning of the sixth century, Cerbonius came with Regulus to Populonium (Piombino in Tuscany), and in the year 544 was made bishop of the place. St Gregory in his *Dialogues* says that because he had given shelter to some Roman soldiers Cerbonius was ordered by Totila, king of the invading Ostrogoths, to be exposed to a bear ; but the animal would do him no worse harm than to lick his feet. Thereupon the Bishop was let go free but sent into exile on Elba, where he died some thirty years later. His body was brought back to Piombino for burial and he is venerated as the patron of the town and of the diocese of Massa Marittima. A late and worthless Life of St Cerbonius asserts that he was summoned before Pope Vigilius for insisting on celebrating Mass at dawn on Sundays, so that many in the city were unable to be present. But because of the marvels which attended his journey to Rome the Pope and his clergy came out to meet him as a saint, and sent him back with honour to his see. The Roman Martyrology also mentions another St Cerbonius to-day, a bishop in Verona of whom nothing is known. The feast of Cerbonius of Populonium is kept by the Canons Regular of the Lateran because he lived the common life with his clergy.

Two redactions are known of the legendary life of St Cerbonius ; one is printed in the *Acta Sanctorum*, October, vol. v, the other in Ughelli ; *Italia Sacra*, vol. iii, pp. 703–709. An Italian Life based on these materials was published at Lucca by A. Brandeglio in 1706.

ST PAULINUS, ABP. OF YORK, CONF.

A.D. 644

St Paulinus is celebrated in the Roman Martyrology and in those of our country as the apostle of the largest and at that time the most powerful of the kingdoms of the English. St Augustine having asked Rome for more missionaries, St Gregory the Great in 601 sent him Mellitus, Justus, Paulinus and others, together with the *pallium*, sacred vessels, altar-cloths and other ornaments for churches, vestments for priests, relics of the apostles and martyrs, and many books, decreeing by letter that when the northern countries should receive the faith, York should be appointed a metropolitical see in like manner with London (Canterbury). St Paulinus, who like the others was a monk of St Andrew's on the Cœlian, employed himself in Kent with great zeal for twenty-four years, until Edwin, the powerful king of Northumbria, demanded in marriage Ethelburga, sister of Edbald, King of Kent. When the pagan Edwin promised entire liberty and protection with regard to her religion, and expressed his

own favourable dispositions towards it, the princess was sent. No
one being judged more proper to be her guardian and to undertake
this new harvest than Paulinus, he was ordained bishop by St Justus,
Archbishop of Canterbury, on July 25, 625, and accompanied the
young queen to her husband. It was a continual affliction to his
heart to live in the midst of a people who were strangers to the true
worship of God, and all his preaching and endeavours to make Him
known and served by them were at first unsuccessful. But his
prayers were at length heard. King Edwin was brought over to the
faith in a manner that will be related in his Life (October 12), but
he desired the concurrence of the chief men of his kingdom. A
great assembly was called in which the pagan high priest himself
condemned the worship of idols, and liberty was given for any to
embrace the Christian faith. The King was baptised by St Paulinus
at York at Easter in 627, in a church of wood, raised in haste while
the king was a catechumen. Edwin afterwards began one of stone,
which was finished by St Oswald, intended for the cathedral of
St Paulinus, whose see was now fixed at York. The king's two
sons by his first wife and many of the nobles and people followed
Edwin's example, and, churches and fonts not being yet built for
the crowds that flocked to receive baptism, St Paulinus, when among
the Deiri, baptised in the river Swale, near Catterick. Edwin's
residence among the Bernicians was at Yeavering in Glendale, and
in that country St Paulinus baptised the people in the river Glen or
Bowent. He once spent thirty-six days in this place, instructing
and baptising the people day and night without intermission. The
name Pallingsburn is said to preserve the memory of one of these
baptisings ("Paulinus's Brook"), and tradition associates him also
with Dewsbury, Easingwold, and elsewhere. The apostolate of
St Paulinus was chiefly in the south of Northumbria, and he crossed
the Humber and preached the faith to the inhabitants of Lindsey.
Here he baptised Blecca, the Saxon governor of Lincoln, and there
built a church of stone, in which after the death of St Justus he
consecrated St Honorius as archbishop of Canterbury. Assisted by
his deacon James he baptised a great number of people in the river
Trent at Southwell, as St Bede heard, through the abbot Deda, from
one of the neophytes on that occasion. From the same source he
learned that St Paulinus was "a tall man, stooping a little, with
black hair, thin face, and narrow aquiline nose, venerable and majestic
in appearance." Pope Honorius I sent the *pallium* to St Paulinus as
the northern metropolitan in Britain, and in his letter of congratula-
tion to King Edwin upon his conversion he wrote, "We send *pallia*
to the metropolitans Honorius and Paulinus, that whenever it shall

please God to call either of them out of this world the other may
ordain a successor for him by virtue of this letter." St Paulinus,
however, never wore that *pallium* in his cathedral, and when the
letter reached England Edwin was dead. Some months before it
was written the pagan Mercians, under Penda and reinforced by
the Christian Britons from Wales, invaded Northumbria, and in
resisting them at the battle of Hatfield Chase Edwin was slain, with
his son Osfrid, whom he had by a former wife and who had been
christened with him. Much of the work of Paulinus in Northumbria
was undone and, leaving the deacon James in charge of the church
of York, he conducted Queen St Ethelburga with her two
children and Edwin's grandson by Osfrid into Kent by sea. There
she founded a nunnery at Lyming, where she took the veil. The
party was well received by King Edbald and St Honorius, and
arrangements were made to send the two boys to the court of King
Dagobert in France, where both died young ; the girl, Eanfleda,
married King Oswy and was venerated as a saint. As the see of
Rochester was at that time vacant, St Paulinus was asked to administer it, which he did for ten years, "until he departed to Heaven
with the glorious fruits of his labours." He was probably at least
sixty when he came south with St Ethelburga, and it was out of
the question that he should return to the confusion and turmoil of
Northumbria. St Bede says that his *locum tenens*, the faithful James,
was a holy man who, by long teaching and baptising there, "rescued
much prey from the power of the old Enemy of mankind " ; when
peace came again to his church " he began to teach many to sing
according to the manner of the Romans." St Paulinus died on
October 10, 644, at Rochester, leaving his *pallium* to the cathedral
and a golden cross and chalice he had brought from York to Christ
Church at Canterbury. His feast is observed in several English
dioceses. The Roman Martyrology mentions to-day another ST
PAULINUS, a bishop of Capua who was driven from his see by the
Saracens and died about 843. He is said to have been an English-
man, who was promoted to the episcopate while passing through
Capua on a pilgrimage to Jerusalem.

The active and the contemplative, mutually assisting each other,
must have their parts in the life of every Christian, but in particular
of such as are called to the ecclesiastical state. Every pastor owes
to God the homage of continual praise, and to his people the suffrage
of his sacrifices and supplication in their behalf. How diligently
soever he acquits himself of his external duties towards them he fails
essentially if he ceases to recommend to God their public and private
spiritual necessities, for he is appointed a mediator betwixt them

and God. Moreover, recollection and meditation are the very soul of an ecclesiastical spirit. A life of habitual dissipation strikes not at particular duties only but destroys the very essence and spirit of this state; disqualifies a person for all its functions and leaves him a stranger to the spirit of all its sacred obligations. The most essential preparation and requisite of this state is a spirit of prayer; without this a person is no more than the shadow of a pastor, or like a body without a soul to animate it, and can never deserve the name of priest or religious man.

Our main authority is Bede's *Historia Ecclesiastica* (see Plummer's edition and notes). Not much that is reliable can be gleaned from Alcuin's versified chronicle, or from Simeon of Durham and the other writers included in Raine's *Historians of the Church of York* (Rolls Series). Canon Burton's excellent account in the *Catholic Encyclopedia* is accompanied by a good bibliography. For archæological details such works as G. Baldwin Brown, *The Arts in Early England* (2nd edition), and Sir Henry Howorth, *The Golden Age of the Early English Church*, are serviceable. The widespread *cultus* of St Paulinus is proved by the insertion of his name in so many calendars (see Stanton's *Menology*, p. 485), as well as by the stone crosses in the north of England which tradition connects with him.

ST DANIEL AND HIS SIX COMPS., MARTS.

A.D. 1227

Five Franciscan missionaries having glorified God by martyrdom in Morocco in the year 1220, as has been related under January 16, seven years later six other friars of the same order received permission from their vicar general, Elias of Cortona, to go to Africa with the same object of announcing Christ to the Mohammedans. Their names were Samuel, Angelo, Leo, Domnus, Nicholas, and Hugolino. On their way through Spain they were joined by Brother Daniel, minister provincial of Calabria, who became the superior of the band. On September 20, 1227, they reached Morocco, and spent ten days in preparation for their mission at a village near Ceuta which was inhabited by European merchants and their dependents. On Saturday, October 2, they made their confessions and washed one another's feet, spent the night in prayer, and early on Sunday morning entered the Mohammedan city of Ceuta and began to preach in the streets. Their appearance provoked an uproar, they were badly hustled, and eventually taken before the *cadi*. When he saw their rough clothes and uncovered shaven heads he took them to be mad, and ordered that they be confined till it was decided what to do with them. While they were imprisoned, freely exposed to the insults and ill-treatment of the fanatical Moors, St Daniel on their behalf wrote a letter to the Christians of the village in which they had stayed, saying what had happened to them and adding, " Blessed be God, the Father of mercies, who comforts us in all our tribulations ! " The following Sunday, it having been ascertained that they were missionaries and not madmen, the seven friars were invited to renounce their faith, first corporately and then individually in private. Neither threats nor bribes could move them, they continued to affirm Christ and to deny Mohammed, so they were ordered to be put to death. Each one of the martyrs went up to Brother Daniel, knelt for his blessing, and asked permission to give his life for Christ ; and the next day they were all beheaded outside the walls of Ceuta. Their bodies were mangled by the infuriated people, but the local Christians managed to rescue and bury them. Later on the relics were carried into Spain, and in 1516 these seven martyrs were canonised by Pope Leo X.

These martyrs are commemorated in the Roman Martyrology on October 10, but in the *Acta Sanctorum* an account is given of them on October 13 (vol. vi), which seems to be the day they actually suffered. Nothing material has yet been added to the two texts printed by the Bollandists, *i.e.* a letter of a certain Friar Marianus a Janua, and a brief *passio* of later date. See *Analecta Franciscana*, vol. iii, pp. 32–33 and 613–616 ; A. Lopez, *La Provincia de España, O.M.—Apuntes historico-criticas* (1915), pp. 61–65 and 329–330 ; and a not very critical essay of D. Zangari, *I sette Frati Minori martirizzati a Çeuta*, 1926. An English account is furnished in P. Léon, *Auréole séraphique* (Eng. trans.), vol. iii, pp. 296–299.

OCTOBER 11

THE MOTHERHOOD OF OUR LADY

THE celebration on this day throughout the Western Church of a feast in honour of the Motherhood of the Blessed Virgin Mary, Mother of God, was enjoined by Pope Pius XI in the encyclical, *Lux Veritatis*, published on December 25, 1931, in view of the fifteenth centenary of the Council of Ephesus.

In the third lesson of the second nocturn of the office of the new feast mention is made of the chancel arch in the basilica of St Mary Major, which Pope Xystus III (432–440) had decorated with mosaics shortly after the council, and which has been restored in modern times by the care of Pope Pius XI himself. This, we are taught, remains as a striking monument of the proclamation of Our Lady's incomparable privilege as Mother of God. But in the institution of the present festival, the Pope, as his encyclical explains, had also other objects in view.

" One thing in particular," he says, " and that indeed one of great importance, we specially desire that all should pray for, under the auspices of our heavenly Queen. That is, that she, who is loved and worshipped with such ardent piety by the separated peoples of the East, would not suffer them to wander and be unhappily ever led away from the unity of the Church, and therefore from her Son, whose vicar on earth We are. May they return to the common Father, whose judgement all the Fathers of the synod of Ephesus most dutifully received, and whom they all saluted with concordant acclamations as the guardian of the faith ; may they all return to Us, who have indeed a fatherly affection for them all, and who gladly make Our own those most loving words which Cyril used, when he earnestly exhorted Nestorius that ' the peace of the churches may be preserved, and that the bond of love and of concord among the priests of God may remain indissoluble.' "

Further, the Pope continues :

" We may well regard it as a happy omen, that it has fallen to Us to celebrate this fifteenth centenary : to Us, we say, who have defended the dignity and the sanctity of chaste wedlock against encroaching fallacies of every kind (encyclical, *Casti Connubii*), and who have both solemnly vindicated the sacred rights of the Catholic Church over the education of youth, and have declared and explained the manner in which it should be imparted, and the principles to which it should conform (encyclical, *Divini illius Magistri*). For the precepts which We have set forth, concerning both these matters, have in the office of the divine Maternity, and in the family of Nazareth, an excellent example, proposed for the initiation of all. As Our predecessor, Leo XIII of happy memory, says : ' Fathers of families indeed have in Joseph a glorious pattern of vigilance and paternal prudence ; mothers have in the most holy Virgin, Mother of God, a remarkable example of love and modesty and submission of mind, as well as of perfect faith ; while the children of a family have in Jesus, who was subject to them, a divine model of obedience, which they may admire and worship and imitate.'

" But in a more special manner it is fitting that those mothers of this our age who, being weary, whether of offspring or of the marriage bond, leave degraded and neglected the office they have undertaken, may look up to Mary and meditate intently on her who has raised this grave duty of motherhood to such high nobility. For in this way there is hope that they may be led by the help of grace from the heavenly Queen, to feel shame for the dishonour done to the great sacrament of matrimony, and may happily be stirred up to follow after the wondrous praise of her virtues by every effort in their power.

" If all these things prosper according to Our purpose, that is to say, if the life of the family, the beginning and the foundation of all human society, is recalled to this most worthy model of holiness, without doubt We shall at length be able to meet the formidable crisis of evils confronting Us, with an effective remedy. In this way it will come to pass that ' the peace of God which passeth all understanding ' may keep the hearts and minds of all, and that the much-desired Kingdom of Christ, minds and forces being joined together, may be everywhere established."

The text of the encyclical, *Lux Veritatis*, is printed in the *Acta Apostolicæ Sedis*, vol. xxiii (1931), pp. 493-517. Celebrations in honour of the Maternity of the Blessed Virgin were observed locally in many countries long before the present century, but there was no general usage in the matter and the dates selected for this commemoration differed widely.

The earliest records of a feast of the Maternity B.V.M. seem to be connected with Portugal and with the Portuguese overseas dominions. It was conceded to the clergy of Portugal in 1751, but rapidly spread to other countries, *e.g.* to Venice and to Poland. See Holweck, *Calendarium Festorum Dei et Dei Matris* (1925), pp. 368, 148, etc.

SS. TARACHUS, PROBUS, AND ANDRONICUS, MARTS.

A.D. 304

Their *acta*, for long thought to be authentic, but judged by Père Delehaye to be a combination of a few facts with a lot of purely imaginative detail, state that Tarachus was a Roman born in Isauria, an ex-soldier, sixty-five years old ; Probus was born at Side in Pamphylia ; and Andronicus belonged to one of the principal families of the city of Ephesus. Being apprehended at Pompeiopolis in Cilicia during the persecution under Diocletian and Maximian, they were presented to Flavius Clemens Numerianus Maximus, governor of the province, upon his arrival in that city, and by his order were conducted to Tarsus, the metropolis. Maximus being arrived there, and seated on his tribunal, Demetrius the centurion brought them before him, saying they were the persons who had been presented to him at Pompeiopolis for professing the religion of the Christians and disobeying the command of the Emperors. Maximus addressed himself first to Tarachus, observing that he began with him because he was well on in years, and asked his name. Tarachus replied : " I am a Christian."

MAXIMUS : Speak not of your impiety but tell me your name.

TARACHUS : I am a Christian.

MAXIMUS : Strike him upon the mouth, and bid him not answer one thing for another.

TARACHUS : I tell you my true name. If you would know that which my parents gave me, it is Tarachus ; when I bore arms I went by the name of Victor.

MAXIMUS : What is your profession and country ?

TARACHUS : I am of a Roman family, and was born at Claudiopolis in Isauria. I was a soldier, but left the service on account of my religion.

MAXIMUS : Your impiety rendered you unworthy to bear arms, but how did you get your discharge ?

TARACHUS : I asked it of my captain, Publius, and he gave it me.

MAXIMUS : In consideration of your grey hairs, I will get you the favour and friendship of the Emperors, if you will obey their orders. Sacrifice to the gods, as the Emperors themselves do all the world over.

TARACHUS : They are deceived by the Devil in so doing.

MAXIMUS : Break his jaws for saying the Emperors are deceived.

TARACHUS : I repeat it. As men, they are deluded.

MAXIMUS : Sacrifice to our gods and renounce your folly.

TARACHUS : I cannot renounce the law of God.

MAXIMUS : Is there any law, fellow, but that which we obey ?

TARACHUS : There is, and you transgress it by worshipping stocks and stones, the work of men's hands.

MAXIMUS : Strike him on the face. Abandon your folly.

TARACHUS : What you call folly is the salvation of my soul, and I will never leave it.

MAXIMUS : But I will make you leave it, and force you to be wise.

TARACHUS : Do what you please with my body ; it is entirely in your power.

Then Maximus said : " Strip him and beat him," and Tarachus, when beaten, said : " You have now made me truly wise. I am strengthened by your blows and my confidence in God and in Jesus Christ is increased."

MAXIMUS : How can you deny a plurality of gods, when according to your own confession you serve two gods ? Did you not give the name of God to someone named Christ ?

TARACHUS : I did. For this is the Son of the living God ; He is the hope of the Christians and the author of salvation to such as suffer for His sake.

MAXIMUS : Stop this idle talk ; come here and sacrifice.

TARACHUS : I am no idle talker. Thus have I been brought up, and I cannot forsake the truth.

Demetrius the centurion said : " Poor man, I pity you. Be advised by me ; sacrifice and save yourself." But Tarachus told him to keep his advice to himself, whereupon Maximus ordered that he be taken back to prison in chains, and the next prisoner brought forward. Of him he asked, " What is your name ? "

PROBUS : My chief and most honourable name is Christian ; but the name I go by in the world is Probus.

MAXIMUS : Of what country and birth are you ?

PROBUS : My father was of Thrace. I am a plebeian, born at Side in Pamphylia, and I profess Christianity.

MAXIMUS : That will do you no good. Sacrifice to the gods, and enjoy my friendship.

PROBUS : I want nothing of that kind. I was formerly possessed of a considerable estate, but I relinquished it to serve the living God through Jesus Christ.

MAXIMUS : Strip him to the waist and lash him with ox's sinews.

Demetrius the centurion said, whilst they were beating him : " Spare yourself, my friend. See how your blood runs in streams."

PROBUS : Do what you will with my body. Your torments are sweet to me.

MAXIMUS : Is your obstinate folly incurable ? What can you hope for.

PROBUS : I am wiser than you are, because I do not worship devils.

MAXIMUS : Turn him, and strike him on the belly.

PROBUS : Lord, assist Thy servant.

MAXIMUS : Ask him at every stroke where is his helper ?

PROBUS : He helps me, and will help me ; for I take so little notice of your torments that I do not obey you.

MAXIMUS : Look, fool, at your mangled body ; the ground is covered with blood.

PROBUS : The more my body suffers for Jesus Christ, the more my soul is strengthened.

Thereupon Maximus ordered him to the stocks and called up the third man, who said his name was Andronicus and that he was a patrician of Ephesus. He also refused to sacrifice, defied the judge, and ignored the good-natured hints of Demetrius. So he too was remanded to prison, and so ended the first examination. The second was held by Maximus at Mopsuestia, and the *acta* give *in extenso* similar interrogations and answers, the prisoners being submitted to various tortures. Andronicus draws attention to the fact that the wounds of his previous scourging are perfectly healed, and Maximus abuses the guards. "Rascals and traitors," he says. "Did I not strictly forbid you to let anyone see them or dress their wounds ? Yet see here ! " Pegasus the jailor replied, " I swear by your greatness that no one has applied anything whatever to his wounds, or even had admittance to him. He has been kept in chains in the inner part of the prison on purpose. If you catch me in a lie, I'll forfeit my head."

MAXIMUS : How comes it then that there is nothing to be seen of his wounds ?

PEGASUS : I swear by your high birth that I do not know how they have been healed.

ANDRONICUS : Foolish man, the physician that has healed me is no less powerful than He is tender. You know Him not. He cures, not by the application of medicines, but by His word alone. Though He dwells in Heaven, He is present everywhere. But you know Him not.

MAXIMUS : This silly talk will not help you. Sacrifice, or you are a lost man.

ANDRONICUS : I will not change my answers. I am not a child to be wheedled or frightened.

The third examination was held at Anazarbus. In it Tarachus

146

answered first, with his usual constancy, saying to all threats that a speedy death would finish his victory and complete his happiness, and that tortures would procure him the greater recompense. When Maximus had him stretched on the rack he said : " I could plead the rescript of Diocletian which forbids judges to put military men to the rack. But I waive my privilege, lest you should suspect me of cowardice." Maximus had Probus also tortured, and ordered some of the wine and meat that had been offered on the altars of the pagan gods to be forced down his throat. " There ! " he exclaimed. " Now you see that after suffering torments rather than sacrifice, you have nevertheless partaken of a sacrifice."

PROBUS : You have done no great feat in making me taste these accursed offerings against my will.

MAXIMUS : No matter ; it is done. Promise now to do it voluntarily and you shall be released.

PROBUS : God forbid that I should yield. If you should force into me all the offerings of all your altars, I should be in no way defiled. For God sees the violence which I suffer.

Maximus then again pressed Andronicus to comply, asserting that his two companions had at length sacrificed to the gods and to the Emperors themselves. The martyr replied : " This is truly the part of a worshipper of the god of lies, and by this imposture I know that the men are like the gods whom they serve. May God judge you, O worker of iniquity." He was then treated in the same way as Probus, and, remaining unmoved, all three were sentenced to the wild beasts. Maximus sent for Terentianus, who had the care of the games and spectacles, and gave him orders to hold a public show the next day. In the morning a great multitude of people flocked to the amphitheatre, which was a mile distant from the town of Anazarbus. The author of the *acta* gives a circumstantial account of what followed, which he says he and two fellow-Christians watched from outside, coming " as near as we could on a hill behind, and concealing ourselves by piling stones before us as high as our breasts, that we might not be known or observed." No sooner were the martyrs led down than a deep silence followed at the sight of such pitiable objects, and the people began openly to murmur against the governor for his barbarous cruelty. Many even left the circus, which provoked the governor, and he ordered soldiers to guard all the ways to stop any from departing. A bear, a lioness, and other animals were in turn loosed on the three Christians, but they all refused to harm them, fawning around them and licking their wounds. Maximus was furious, had the keepers beaten, and called for the gladiators to dispatch the martyrs with their swords, which they did. He commanded the bodies to be mixed up with those of the gladiators who had been slain and also to be guarded that night by six soldiers, lest the Christians should carry them off. The night was very dark, and a violent storm of thunder and rain dispersed the guards. The searchers distinguished the three bodies by a miraculous star or ray of light which streamed on them, and they carried them on their backs and hid them in a cave on the neighbouring mountains. The Christians of Anazarbus, says the writer, sent this relation to the church of Iconium, desiring that it might be communicated to the faithful of Pisidia and Pamphylia for their encouragement.

The heroism of the martyrs consists not only in the constancy and invincible courage with which they chose to die rather than to sin against God, but also in the patience with which they bore all their sufferings. In our daily and hourly trials we have continual opportunities of exercising this virtue. If we fail even in small things and so show ourselves strangers to the Christian spirit, can we assume without blushing at ourselves the sacred name of disciples of Christ?

The *Acta Sanctorum*, October, vol. v, with Ruinart furnish Latin and Greek texts of the *passio*. Other recensions exist, and a Syriac version has been edited by Bedjan. There is also a panegyric by Severus of Antioch printed in the *Patrologia Orientalis*, vol. xx, pp. 277–295. Harnack (*Die Chronologie der altchrist. Litteratur*, vol. ii, 1904, pp. 479–480) in noticing these *acta*, gives reasons for thinking that they cannot be regarded as a transcript of any official document, but he seems to form a slightly better opinion of them than Delehaye, *Les Légendes hagiographiques* (1927), p. 114.

ST NECTARIUS, Abp. of Constantinople, Conf.

A.D. 397

When St Gregory Nazianzen resigned the see of Constantinople almost as soon as he was appointed in the year 381 he was succeeded by this Nectarius, a native of Tarsus in Cilicia and *prætor* of the imperial city. The peculiar and doubtful story of his election is as follows. While the second œcumenical council was in progress at Constantinople Nectarius, who was about to visit his home, called on Diodorus, Bishop of Tarsus, to ask if he could carry any letters for him. Greatly impressed by his looks and manner, Diodorus recommended him to the Bishop of Antioch as successor to St Gregory. He laughed at the idea, but the name of Nectarius was nevertheless added to the list of candidates presented to the Emperor. Theodosius chose Nectarius, who was a friend of his, much to everybody's astonishment, for he was not even yet baptised (he is also said to have been married, with one son). However, the choice was ratified by the council, Nectarius was duly baptised and ordained, and being so inexperienced he chose as an adviser Cyriacus, Bishop of Adana, his countryman. On leaving Constantinople St Gregory Nazianzen wrote to the bishops : " You may have a throne and a lordly place then since you think that is the important thing. Rejoice, lift yourselves up, claim the title of patriarch, let broad lands be subject to you," and the council gave some justification for the rebuke ; for soon after the appointment of Nectarius it passed a canon giving Constantinople rank next after Rome. For this reason St Nectarius is often called the first patriarch of the city, though it was long before the Holy See recognised the precedence accorded against its judgement.

His episcopate lasted for sixteen years, but little is known of it or him. He consistently opposed the Arian heretics, with the result that, when in 388 there was a rumour that the Emperor had died in Italy, they burnt his house over his head. St Nectarius is principally remembered for having abolished in his diocese the office of priest-penitentiary and with it the custom of public confession as a part of penance, on account of an open scandal that had occurred. He died on September 27, 397, and was followed in his see by St John Chrysostom. St Nectarius figures in the Greek *Menaion* but not in the Roman Martyrology ; the Byzantines of Constantinople keep his feast to-day together with his brother Arsacius (*d.* 406), Atticus (*d.* 425), and Sisinnius I (*d.* 427), who all occupied the see, the claim to sanctity for the first of whom at least is very doubtful.

The more important passages of the church historians which bear upon the life and activities of Nectarius have been brought together in the *Acta Sanctorum*, October, vol. v. Regarding the abolition of the office of priest-penitentiary a convenient summary will be found in the *Dictionnaire de Théologie*, vol. xii, cc. 796–798.

ST CANICE, OR KENNETH, ABBOT AND CONF.

A.D. 599

This great disciple of St Cadoc and St Columba is a famous saint both in Ireland and Scotland, but in the traditions about him here is little upon which much reliance can be placed. He was an Irishman by birth (he is also called Cainneach and Kenny), the son of a bard named Lugaidh, born at Glengiven in Derry about the year 515. When a youth he went over into Wales and became a monk under St Cadoc at Llancarfan, where he was ordained. His master's particular affection and the favour which he showed him earned for Canice the jealousy of some of his brethren ; Baring-Gould and Fisher identify him with the St Macmoil (his mother's name was Maul) for whom Cadoc built a church in Gwent, on Cefn Mamoel, near Bedwellty. After an alleged visit to Rome St Canice went back to Ireland and came to study at the school of St Finnian at Clonard, whence he went with St Kieran, St Comgall, and St Columba to St Mobhi at Glasnevin. For some time he preached in Ireland and made several monastic foundations, and about the year 560 made his first visit to Scotland, being one of the four holy founders of monasteries to visit Iona. There are many traces of him in place-name and legend in that country, notably at Cambus-kenneth below Stirling and at Kilchainnech on Iona itself. He went with St Columba on his mission to the Pictish King Brude at Inverness, and with the sign of the cross paralysed Brude's hand when he threatened the monks with his sword. He converted numerous pagans and was bound in close friendship with St Columba, who on one occasion, when he was in great danger at sea, said to his companions, " Don't be afraid ! God will listen to Kenneth, who is running to church with only one shoe on to pray for us." At the same time Canice in Ireland was aware of his friend's peril and jumped up from a meal to go to the church.

The best known of St Canice's foundations in Ireland was the monastery at Aghaboe in Ossory, but he probably also had a see at Kilkenny, whose old cathedral was dedicated in his honour. A lost work on the gospels, called *Glas Cainneach*, " the Chain of Canice," was attributed to him. His zeal in preaching the gospel and practising Christian perfection have ranked him amongst the most glorious saints whose virtue has enlightened both Ireland and Scotland, and his feast is observed in both countries ; throughout the land in one and in the dioceses of Saint-Andrews and of Argyll in the other.

There is a Latin biography which has been edited by C. Plummer, mainly from the *codex Salmonticensis*, in his *Vitæ Sanctorum Hiberniæ*, vol. i, pp. 152–169. Consult also Forbes, *Kalendars of Scottish Saints*, pp. 295–297. St Cainneach's intercourse with other Irish saints is noted in Kenney, *The Sources for the Early History of Ireland*, vol. i, pp. 409, etc. and see the gloss on the *Felire* of Œngus, p. 223.

ST ETHELBURGA, ABBESS OF BARKING, VIRG.

c. A.D. 678

Ethelburga is said to have been born at Stallington in Lindsey, and she was the sister of St Erconwald, of whom it is said they were " bound together by a common love, one in heart and one in soul." Fired doubtless by the example of her brother, St Ethelburga determined to become a nun, and nothing could shake her resolution, for the world loses all its influence upon a mind which is wholly taken up with the great truths of faith and eternal salvation. A soul which is truly penetrated with them listens to no considerations in the choice of a state of life but to those which virtue and piety suggest ; and, supported by those principles which religion inspires, whether she is placed in the world or in the cloister, whether in wealth or poverty, amid honours or in obscurity, equally carries all her desires to their proper end, acquits herself of every duty of her state, and acts up to the dignity of her vocation. This makes saints who live in the world the best rulers, the best subjects, the best parents, the best neighbours, the most dutiful children, and the most diligent and faithful workmen or servants. The same principle renders them in a cloister the most humble, the most obedient, the most devout, and the most careful of monastic discipline. St Erconwald, before he became bishop of London, founded for himself a monastery at Chertsey and another for both monks and nuns at Barking in Essex. Over this he set Ethelburga as abbess, and as there were then very few nunneries in England and she and her sisters were quite inexperienced, St Hildilid (Hildelitha) was fetched from a French abbey to train her. We are told there was somewhat of a competition in austerity between the two saints, and Ethelburga, when the rule of the house was entrusted to her, by her example and spirit sweetly led on all the other nuns in the path of virtue and Christian perfection. " She behaved in all respects as became the sister of such a brother, living according to the rule, devoutly, and orderly, providing for those under her, as was also manifested by heavenly miracles," of which St Bede relates several.

When an epidemic carried off some of the monks they were buried in the ground adjoining the church, and a discussion arose among the nuns as to where they should be buried when their time came, in the same part of the churchyard or another part. They could come to no decision, till one morning after Matins they were praying by the graves of the dead brothers, when suddenly a great light (which from Bede's description would certainly seem to have been summer lightning) fell first upon them and then upon another side of the church ; which light they understood " was intended to show the place in which their bodies were to rest and await the day of resurrection." St Bede tells a touching story of a little boy of three years old, who was being brought up in the monastery and who died calling for one of the nuns, Edith, who shortly followed him ; and of another nun who, dying at midnight, asked for the candle to be put out, exclaiming, " I know you think I am mad, but I am not. I see this room so filled with light that your candle there looks dark to me." And when they left it, she said, " Very well ; let it burn. But it is not my light, for my light will come to me at day-break." And at the dawn she died. St Ethelburga herself seems to have survived this visitation, only to die shortly after, her approaching end being foreseen in a vision by a nun called Theorigitha, who for nine years had been an invalid ; and Ethelburga's life " is known to have been such that no person who knew her ought to question but that the heavenly kingdom was opened to her directly she left this world," says Bede. Three years later St Theorigitha herself was dying, and had lost the use of her tongue. Suddenly she spoke and said, " Your coming is a great joy to me. You are welcome," and began to talk with an invisible person about how much longer she had to live. The bystanders asked who she was talking to, and were told, " With my most dear mother, Ethelburga." The feast of St Ethelburga is observed in the diocese of Brentwood on this the day of her death.

There does not seem much to add to the account given in Bede, *Historia Ecclesiastica*, Bk. iv (see Plummer's edition and notes) ; but the Bollandists have reprinted the short biography of Capgrave. Traces of liturgical *cultus* survive both in medieval calendars (noted in Stanton, *Menology*, p. 486), and in certain antiphons, etc. (Hardy, *Materials*, vol. i, p. 385).

ST AGILBERT, Bp. of Paris, Conf.

c. A.D. 685

When Coinwalch, King of the West Saxons, had received the Christian faith and baptism at the court of Anna, King of the East Angles, and been restored to his dominions, there came into Wessex a certain bishop called Agilbert. He was a Frank and had been a monk of Jouarre, but had been living in Ireland for a long time engaged in the study of the Scriptures. His object in coming to Wessex was to preach to the people and convert the King (whose irregularities had made him notorious), and Cœinwalch, impressed by his learning and zeal, asked him to stay there as bishop of the West Saxons. To this St Agilbert agreed, and he showed himself an indefatigable pastor and missionary, extending his labours far beyond the borders of Wessex. In the year 663 he was in Northumbria, where he was known personally to the king, Aldfrid, and to St Wilfrid, then abbot of Ripon, and at the King's request he ordained Wilfrid priest. It was then decided to hold a council to decide the controversy between Roman and Celtic customs, and St Agilbert stayed on to assist at the Synod of Whitby in the following year. At this assembly he was looked on as leader of the Roman party and was called on by King Oswy to be the first to reply to the Irish St Colman of Lindisfarne. St Agilbert asked to be excused and named St Wilfrid to answer, because " he can explain our opinion better in English than I can by an interpreter."

This language difficulty was shortly after a cause of serious trouble to Agilbert. After he had been bishop of the West Saxons for fifteen years or so, King Coinwalch, " who," says St Bede, " understood no tongue but that of the Saxons, grew weary of that bishop's barbarous speech." He therefore divided his kingdom into two dioceses, and appointed to that which included the royal city of Winchester an English bishop named Wini. Agilbert was very vexed that the King should have done this without first consulting him (as he well might be) and, resigning his see, he returned to France. In 668 he was made bishop of Paris. Wini in the meantime had become bishop of London by simony, Wessex was without a bishop again and the prey of its enemies, so Coinwalch asked St Agilbert to come back. He replied that he could not leave the see and flock of his own city, but sent instead his nephew Eleutherius, " whom he thought worthy to be made a bishop "; he was consecrated by St Theodore of Canterbury. All that is known of St Agilbert's French episcopate is that he was sent, with St Regulus of Reims, on a mission to Duke Martin of Laon, unwilling tools of that treacherous mayor of the palace, Ebroin, and that he consecrated St Wilfrid bishop as is narrated when treating of that saint. St Agilbert died about the year 685 and was buried at the abbey of Jouarre, where he had been a simple monk.

Here again Bede (see Plummer's text and notes) is our main authority, but we hear of Agilbert also in the *Liber Historiæ Francorum* and in the continuation of Fredegarius. *Cf.* Duchesne, *Fastes épiscopaux*, vol. ii, p. 468.

ST GUMMARUS, OR GOMER, CONF.

c. A.D. 774

Gummarus was a son of the lord of Emblehem, a village near Lier in Brabant, where he was born about the year 717. He served at the court of Pepin, where from a spirit of religion he was faithful in every duty and an enemy to vanity, ambition, and dissimulation ; as well as exact and fervent in all exercises of devotion and beneficent and liberal in works of mercy. Pepin, though absorbed by ambition, was a lover of uprightness and virtue, and being acquainted with the probity of Gummarus raised him to a high post. This king proposed a match between him and a lady of good birth named Gwinmaria, and the marriage was solemnised with their mutual consent. This marriage, which seemed unhappy in the eyes of the world, was directed by God to perfect the virtue of His servant and exalt him to the glory of the saints. For Gwinmaria was most extravagant and perverse in her ways, haughty, capricious, and altogether unteachable. Life became from that time a train of continual trials for Gummarus. We are prepared for evil treatment from rivals or enemies, but when those from whom we have reason to expect help and support seem to have no other satisfaction but to wound and persecute us it is one of the severest of trials ; and one under which it is hard for the firmest mind to maintain its ground without sometimes failing in the duties of charity, patience, and meekness.

This was the heroic virtue which Gummarus practised for several years, endeavouring by all means which prudence and charity could suggest to encourage his wife to ways more agreeable to reason and religion. He was called upon by King Pepin to attend him in his wars, first in Lombardy, afterwards in Saxony, and then in Aquitaine, and he was absent eight years. Returning home, he found his wife had thrown all things into disorder and confusion, and that few among his servants, vassals, or tenants had escaped her oppression. She was so mean that she even refused beer to the reapers at harvest. Gummarus made to every one of them full restitution and satisfaction ; and Gwinmaria was at length so far overcome by his patience and kindness as to be ashamed of her past conduct, and to seem penitent. This change, however, was only exterior, and her wilfulness broke out again worse than ever. Gummarus tried to reclaim her : but at length he gave up the attempt and obtained her consent to live a retired life in a cell near his own house. With St Rumold he is said to have founded the abbey at Lier which afterwards bore his name. St Gummarus started on a pilgrimage to Rome, but got

no further than Nivesdonck, where he built himself a hermitage and
lived alone for some years. He is named on this day in the Roman
Martyrology, and is still venerated at Lier.

There is both a prose Latin Life of Gummarus and a metrical synopsis ;
for which see the *Acta Sanctorum*, October, vol. v. A very full discussion
of the subject has also been printed in Flemish by P. G. Deckers, *Leven en
eerdienst van den h. ridder Gummarus* (1872).

ST BRUNO THE GREAT, Abp. of Cologne, Conf.
A.D. 965

Of the saints bearing the name of Bruno the founder of the
Carthusians would seem most to deserve the epithet " the Great,"
but traditionally it is given to the powerful prince-bishop who, eighty
years before his namesake was born in his episcopal city of Cologne,
co-operated so conspicuously with his own brother, the Emperor
Otto I (also called " the Great "), in the religious and social building-
up of Germany and the Empire. This Bruno was the youngest son
of the five children of the Emperor Henry the Fowler and his wife
St Matilda ; he was born in the year 925 and from early years showed
that he shared the good dispositions of his parents. When only four
he was sent to the cathedral-school at Utrecht, where he acquired
a keen love of learning from the bishop, Baldericus : Prudentius
was said to be his favourite bedside book, and later on he learned
Greek from some Byzantines at the imperial court. He was called
thither by his brother Otto when he was fourteen, and in spite of
his extreme youth he was given rapid preferment. In 940 he was
made the Emperor's confidential secretary, with the title of chancellor, and soon after was ordained deacon and given the abbeys of
Lorsch and Corvey. This irregular proceeding had a happy result
in that he restored a stricter Benedictine observance in both of them.
Bruno was ordained priest when he was twenty-five, and in the
following year went with Otto into Italy as archchancellor of
the Empire, in which office he used all his power to bring about
the Emperor's ideal of a close union between Church and State. The
time was at hand when he would be in an even more favourable
position to forward this unity. In the year 953 the archbishopric
of Cologne became vacant, and Bruno was appointed to it.

Throughout the twelve years of his episcopate St Bruno played
a leading part in imperial politics, in which ecclesiastical affairs were
inextricably mixed up, but not for a moment did he slacken his
attention to the spiritual requirements of the people and the purely

religious responsibilities of his office. In the first place he set a high example of personal goodness and devotion, and kept clergy and laity on their mettle by frequent visitations. Sound learning and the monastic spirit were the means by which a high standard of pastoral care and spiritual life were to be maintained ; his cathedral-school was staffed by the best professors he could find, and he founded the abbey of St Pantaleon at Cologne. Nor was St Bruno's solicitude confined to his own diocese : he used his influence and authority to spread his reforms throughout the kingdom, and at the same time as he became archbishop this authority was further notably extended by the action of the Emperor. While Otto was absent in Italy the Duke of Lorraine, his son-in-law Conrad the Red, had risen in rebellion with the help of the Magyars ; whereupon Otto deposed Conrad and put St Bruno in his place, with two counts to help him in the administration of the province. The duchy was not made appurtenant to the bishopric, but this appointment of Bruno was the beginning of the temporal power formerly exercised by the archbishops of Cologne ; they were princes of the Holy Roman Empire. St Bruno was as capable a statesman as he was a good man. He had peculiar aptitude in settling the numerous political disputes of the Lorrainers which came under his cognizance, and he made German influence supreme over them. In this unifying task his highly trained and apostolic clergy played a large part, and such was the number and quality of the bishops that he appointed that St Bruno was called " the bishop-maker." The recognition of his worth and ability reached its climax in 961 when, the Emperor going to Rome to be crowned by Pope John XII, he was appointed with his half-brother William, Archbishop of Mainz, co-regent of the Empire and guardian of their nephew, the infant King of the Romans, during his father's absence.

Four years later, on October 11, 965, Bruno the Great died at Reims while on his way to Compiègne to compose a quarrel between his nephews ; he was only forty years old. His body was buried in the church of St Pantaleon at Cologne and his immemorial *cultus* in that diocese and Tournai was confirmed by the Holy See in 1870.

The Life of St Bruno by his devoted disciple Ruotger is reckoned one of the most reliable and satisfactory of medieval biographies. It may be read in the *Acta Sanctorum*, October, vol. v, or in Pertz, *M. G. H.*, *Scriptores*, vol. iv, pp. 224–275. It was written within three or four years of Bruno's death. For a careful study of this work see H. Schrörs' series of papers in the *Annalen d. histor. Vereins f. d. Niederrhein*, 1910, 1911 and 1917. *Cf.* also Hauck, *Kirchengeschichte Deutschlands*, vol. iii, pp. 41 *seq.*

ST JOHN OF BRIDLINGTON, Conf.

A.D. 1379

Though it has been often said that St Thomas of Hereford was the last English saint of the Middle Ages to be formally canonised, there is a bull of Pope Boniface IX that seems to be a valid canonisation of John of Bridlington at the beginning of the fifteenth century and his feast is now again celebrated in the diocese of Middlesbrough and by the Canons Regular of the Lateran. He was surnamed Thwing, from the place of his birth near Bridlington, on the coast of Yorkshire, and the little which is known of his life presents nothing of unusual interest. He was well brought up, and at about the age of seventeen went for two years to study at Oxford. When he returned from the university, finding all occupation distasteful which took off his mind from God, he took the religious habit in the monastery of regular canons of St Augustine at Bridlington. In this solitude it was his great study to know himself and God : to discover and to wipe away with tears of sorrow all the imperfections of his soul and to purge his affections from whatever could defile or distort them, that he might offer to God a continual sacrifice of obedience, love, and praise with a perfect purity of heart. Thus he prepared his soul to let in those heavenly beams which are always streaming from God upon minds fitted to receive them ; and he advanced daily in the victory over himself and in the experimental knowledge of spiritual things. He was successively precentor, cellarer, and prior of his monastery. This last charge he had averted by his protests the first time he was chosen ; but upon a second vacancy his brethren obliged him to take up the office. In discharging it he relieved the necessities of all persons in distress, to whom he looked upon everything as due that by frugality and prudent economy could be spared from the requirements of his community. His application to prayer showed how much his conduct was regulated by the spirit of God, and a great spiritual prudence, peace of mind, and meekness of temper were the fruits of his virtue. When he had been seventeen years prior and had earned a universal esteem and reverence, he was called to God on October 10, 1379. Many miracles wrought through his intercession are mentioned by the author of his Life, and by Thomas of Walsingham, who testifies that by order of Pope Boniface IX, Richard Scrope, the greatly venerated archbishop of York, assisted by the Bishops of Durham and Carlisle, performed the ceremony of the translation of his relics to a more worthy shrine. This took place on March 11, 1404. The nave of the priory church in which St Robert Thwing presided is now the Anglican parish church of Bridlington.

See the *Acta Sanctorum*, October, vol. v, where a Life by one Hugh, himself a canon regular, is printed. There is also a shorter summary by Capgrave in his *Nova Legenda Angliae*. *Cf.* the *Dict. Nat. Biog.*, vol. xxix, p. 451, and Stanton's *Menology*, pp. 481–482. But most important of all is the article of Father Paul Grosjean, S.J., in the *Analecta Bollandiana*, vol. liii (1935), pp. 101–129. He has gathered up much new material, while expressing his indebtedness to the booklet, *St John of Bridlington* (1924) and other papers by J. S. Purvis. Mr. Purvis has published the text of the canonisation document from the Lateran *Recesta*.

BD. JAMES OF ULM, CONF.

A.D. 1491

The Griesingers were a respectable family of Ulm in Germany, where Blessed James was born in the year 1407. He left home when he was twenty-five and went to Italy where, after devoutly visiting the holy places of Rome, he earned his living for nine years. He was first a soldier in the service of Alfonso II at Naples, but the licence of military life shocked and frightened him, and when he found that his comrades took no notice of his better example and words he left the army and became secretary to a wealthy lawyer at Capua. He did his work so well that when, at the end of five years, he wanted to leave his master refused to let him go. So James slipped away and made for Germany, but when he got so far as Bologna he was induced again to enlist as a soldier. In that city he used often to go to the church of St Dominic, and presently he was moved to offer himself as a lay brother to the friars there. He was accepted, and for fifty years he was a model of regular observance and Christian virtue. His prior on one occasion wished to display the lay brother's prompt obedience for the edification of a visiting prelate. He called for Brother James and gave him a letter, saying it was to be taken to Paris at once. The journey ordered was a long, toilsome, and dangerous one, but James just pocketed the letter and asked permission first to go to his cell to get his hat and stick.

The works of the Friars Preachers hold a remarkable place in the history of Christian art, and Blessed James, like his fellow-Dominican William of Marcillat, was a master of the art of painting on glass. On such work he was principally engaged, and a large window in the church of St Petronius at Bologna was made by him. He prepared himself for his work by assiduous prayer : every day he assisted at Matins, and was the first in choir, then he said the first part of his lay-brother's office of *Paters*, visited all the altars in the church, and served two Masses. While at prayer he was often rapt in ecstasy and a number of miracles were attributed to him both before and after death. Blessed James died on October 11, 1491, being eighty-four years old to a day, and was beatified by Pope Leo XII in 1825.

A biographical memoir written by Father Ambrosino of Saracino, a contemporary, has been translated from Italian into Latin in the *Acta Sanctorum*, October, vol. v. See also H. Wilms, *Jakob Griesinger* (1922) in German, and Procter, *Dominican Saints*, pp. 287–291.

ST ALEXANDER SAULI, Bp. of Pavia, Conf.

A.D. 1593

It is recorded of Alexander Sauli that when he was a youth he one day burst into a crowd of people who were watching the antics of some acrobats and tumblers, and, waving a crucifix before the astonished eyes of audience and performers, he warned them solemnly against the dangers of frivolous amusements and pleasure seeking. After allowance due to youth for the lack of proportion, this incident may be seen as prophetic of Alexander's career, of which the chief business was the restoration to order of Christians who had grown slack, feeble, and worse in the enervating atmosphere of the mid-sixteenth century. He was born at Milan of a good Genoese family in 1534, and after a good education became a Barnabite clerk regular at the age of seventeen. He was sent for his studies to their college at Pavia, to which he presented a library and for the enlargement of which he paid out of his own pocket. After his ordination to the priesthood in 1556 he taught philosophy and theology at the university, and was soon made theologian to the bishop, Hippolytus Rossi, at the same time rapidly making a reputation as a preacher. He was so successful at Pavia that St Charles Borromeo invited him to preach in the cathedral of Milan, and St Charles and Cardinal Sfondrati (afterwards Pope Gregory XIV) were present. The burning words of the young Barnabite moved them to tears, and both became his penitents, Father Sauli continuing to direct and advise the archbishop for many years. In 1567 he was elected provost general of his congregation and, though only thirty-three years old, was sufficiently self-confident to withstand both Pope St Pius V and St Charles. Cardinal Borromeo was the protector of the small remnant of Humiliati friars and had a commission to reform them, for they had become both wealthy and, in many individual cases, wicked. It seemed to him, and the Pope agreed, that it would be a good thing if these friars were united to the newly founded and zealous Barnabite congregation. But St Alexander, though willing to do all he might for the improvement of the Humiliati, did not feel called on to agree to any proceeding that might have a detrimental effect on his own spiritual children, and St Charles had to withdraw his proposal.

St Alexander had now shown himself unmistakenly to be the firm and zealous sort of priest required by St Pius's reforming activities, and in 1569 he was appointed bishop of Aleria in Corsica. He protested, in vain this time, was consecrated by St Charles, and proceeded to his diocese. It presented a formidable task. The clergy were ignorant and debased, the people barbarous and with hardly the rudiments of religion : the island was overrun with brigands and family *vendette* were continual and ruthless. He took three clerks regular to help him and, when he had established himself at Tallona (his see city was a ruin), he summoned a synod at which he announced the reforms he proposed to carry out. He then proceeded to a visitation of the diocese, during which the new ways were inaugurated with considerable and necessary severity. He governed the unruly diocese for twenty years, and brought it to such a flourishing state that he was called the apostle of Corsica. In his third synod he promulgated the decrees of the Council of Trent, and his insistence on the observance of these did more than anything else for the restoration of religion. He had to cope not only with sullen opposition from within but with violence from without, from the raids of Corsairs from the Barbary coast : three times on their account he had to move his residence and seminary, but eventually established his cathedral and chapter at Cervione.

During his episcopate St Alexander Sauli had frequent occasion to visit Rome, where he became a close friend of St Philip Neri, who held him up as an example of a model bishop. He wrote a number of pastoral and catechetical works, and was a capable canonist : during the last year of his life he defended the right of the bishops of Pavia to wear the *pallium* as against Gaspar Visconti who had followed St Charles as archbishop of Milan. St Alexander's success in Corsica caused him to be offered the sees of Tortona and Genoa, but he refused all preferment until Gregory XIV insisted on transferring him to Pavia. This was in 1592, but he died in the following year while on a visitation at Calozza in that diocese. During his life St Alexander had displayed the gift of prophecy, and the calming of storms and other miracles were attributed to his intercession. These were continued after his death, and in 1742 he was beatified by Pope Benedict XIV. His canonisation took place in 1904, and his relics are venerated in the cathedral of Pavia.

A Latin Life by J. A. Gabutius, who was a contemporary, is printed in the *Acta Sanctorum*, October, vol. v. The canonisation of the saint in 1904 gave rise to the publication of much important material in the *Rivista di Scienze Soriche* for 1905, and again in the vols. for 1907 and 1908. Padre Orazio Premoli was responsible for the more valuable part of these contributions, and he is also the author of an excellent work on the Barnabites, *Storia dei Barnabiti*, 2 vols., 1914 and 1922. Another full but less well-documented account of St Alexander Sauli is that of Padre F. T. Moltedo (1904), and there is also a French Life by A. Dubois (1904). On the saint's writings consult G. Boffito, *Scrittori Barnabiti* (1933–4).

OCTOBER 12

ST MAXIMILIAN, Bp. of Lorch, Mart.

A.D. 284

MAXIMILIAN was an apostle of that part of the Empire formerly called Noricum, between Styria and Bavaria, where he founded the church of Lorch near Passau, and was martyred during the second half of the third century. Further particulars depend on *acta* written so late as the thirteenth century and are quite unreliable. These state that he was born at Cilli in Styria, and at the age of seven was entrusted to a priest named Oranius to be educated. His parents were wealthy folk, and when he grew up he gave away his inheritance in charity and undertook a pilgrimage to Rome. Pope St Sixtus II sent him back to be a missionary in Noricum and he established his episcopal see at Lorch. Maximilian survived the persecutions under Valerian and Aurelian and ministered with great success among the pagans for over twenty years, making large numbers of conversions. But under Numerian the prefect of Noricum, Evalisius, published an edict of persecution, in consequence of which St Maximilian was called on to sacrifice to the gods. He refused and was beheaded outside the walls of Cilli, at a spot still shown. There have been several translations of his relics, the first recorded of which was by St Rupert to Bischofshofen in the beginning of the eighth century.

The legend is printed in the *Acta Sanctorum*, October, vol. vi, with the usual prolegomena. See also Ratzinger, *Forschungen z. bayr. Gesch.* (1898), pp. 325 *seq.*, and J. Zeiller, *Les Origines chrétiennes dans les Provinces Danubiennes* (1914).

SS. FELIX and CYPRIAN, Bps.
AND MANY OTHER MARTYRS

c. A.D. 484

The second entry in the Roman Martyrology to-day runs : " In Africa, the passion of 4966 holy confessors and martyrs in the Vandal persecution under the Arian king, Hunneric, some of whom were

bishops of the churches of God and some priests and deacons, with
the multitudes of the faithful associated with them. They were
driven into exile in a horrible desert for defending Catholic truth.
Many of them were cruelly treated by the Moors, being compelled
to run by the points of spears and struck with stones ; others were
dragged like corpses, with their legs tied together, over rough and
stony ground, and torn limb from limb ; all of them, being tortured
in various ways, at the last achieved martyrdom. Among them were
those distinguished priests of the Lord, the bishops Felix and
Cyprian." The persecution of orthodox Christians by the Arian
Vandals thus summarised is described at length by Victor Vitensis,
an African bishop who was contemporary and an eye-witness. Soon
after the death of King Genseric, Hunneric ordered a general persecution of the orthodox and exiled them by hundreds into the
Libyan desert, where they perished under conditions of the greatest
barbarity. Numbers of them were concentrated in a small building,
where they were visited by Bishop Victor, who found prisoners and
prison in a state reminiscent of the notorious " black hole " of
Calcutta. When at length the order was brought to lead the Catholics
into the wilderness, they came out singing psalms and amid the
lamentations of their fellow-Christians. Some even, including women
with children, voluntarily followed the confessors to exile and death.
St Felix, the bishop of Abbir, was very old and half paralysed, and
it was represented to Hunneric that he might just as well be left to
die at home. But the brutal king replied that if he could not ride
a horse he could be tied to a yoke of oxen and dragged. Eventually
the old man made the terrible journey tied across the back of a
mule. Many even of the young and strong did not reach their
destination : stones were thrown at them and they were pricked
with spears to make them keep up, till they collapsed by the wayside
and perished of thirst and exhaustion. St Cyprian, another bishop,
expended all his time, energy, and property in caring for the confessors and encouraging them, till he too was apprehended and sent
into banishment, where he died a martyr from the hardships he
endured.

We know, practically speaking, no more of these martyrs than is told us
by Victor of Vita. His text is quoted and discussed in the *Acta Sanctorum*,
October, vol. vi. It is curious that no identifiable notice of the group
seems to occur in the ancient calendar of Carthage or in the *Hieronymianum*.

ST EDWIN, King of Northumbria, Mart.

A.D. 633

The school of adversity prepared this prince for great achievements, as necessity often makes men industrious whilst affluence and prosperity ruin others. Edwin was son of Ælla, King of Deira, but at his father's death was deprived of his kingdom by Ethelfrid, King of the Bernicians, who united all the Northumbrians in one monarchy. Edwin fled eventually to Redwald, King of the East Angles, who by threats and promises was secretly brought to a resolution to deliver him into the hands of his enemy. The young prince was informed of his danger by a friend, but he refused to go wandering from refuge to refuge any more. It is said that as he sat very melancholy one night before the house, a stranger promised him the restoration of his kingdom if he promised to do what should be taught him for his own life and salvation. Edwin made this promise, and the stranger, laying his hand upon his head, bade him remember that sign. Shortly after Redwald was diverted from his treacherous intention by the persuasion of his wife, and defeated and slew Ethelfrid, who was marching against him, on the east side of the river Idle in Nottinghamshire. By this victory in 616 Edwin was put in possession of the whole kingdom of Northumbria, after being an exile for nearly thirty years ; he received the title of *bretwalda* and had a certain lordship over the other English kings. When his first wife died, he asked in 625 for the hand of Ethelburga, daughter of Edbald, King of Kent, and was informed that " it is not lawful to marry a Christian maiden to a pagan husband." However, he gave an assurance that she should be free in her religion, and that he would look into it himself, and thereupon the marriage was allowed, St Paulinus being sent north as chaplain to the Queen and bishop for his converts. At Easter in 626 an assassin named Eumer, sent by Cuichelm, King of the West Saxons, attempted to stab King Edwin with a dagger. He would have certainly killed him if Lilla, his favourite minister, had not, for want of a buckler, interposed his own body and so saved the King's life with the loss of his own. At the same time Queen Ethelburga gave birth to a daughter, and when the King gave thanks to his gods for her preservation St Paulinus told him it was the effect of the prayers of his queen and her bishop to the true God that she had had an easy and safe delivery. The King seemed pleased with this idea and was prevailed upon to consent that his daughter who was just born should be consecrated to God. She was baptised with twelve others on Whitsunday, and called Eanfleda, and they were the first-fruits of the Northumbrians. Edwin moreover promised Paulinus that if God made him victorious over those who had conspired to take away his life he would himself become a Christian. He assembled his army, marched against the King of the West Saxons, vanquished him in the field, and either slew or took prisoners all those who had plotted against him. From this time he no more worshipped idols, but listened to the instructions of St Paulinus, and being, as St Bede says, a man of unusual wisdom, " sat much alone by himself, silent of tongue, deliberating in his heart how he should act and to which religion he should adhere." Pope Boniface V sent him an encouraging letter, and a silver looking-glass and an ivory comb to the queen, admonishing her to press him upon that subject. Paulinus continued to instruct him and to pray for his conversion but without visible effect, till one day the bishop came and, laying his hand upon his head, asked him if he remembered that sign. The king, trembling, would have thrown himself at his feet ; but Paulinus, raising him up, said affectionately, " You see that God has delivered you from your enemies ; and He offers you His everlasting kingdom. Take care on your side to perform your promise, by receiving His faith and keeping His commandments." Edwin answered he would invite his chief counsellors to do the same with him, to which the bishop consented ; and the king having assembled his nobles he asked their advice. Coifi the chief priest spoke first, declaring that by experience it was manifest their gods had no power : " No one has worshipped them more diligently than I, but others are more preferred and more prosperous than I am. If our gods were any good they would favour me, who have been more careful to serve them ! " Another said that the short moment of this life is of no weight, if put in the balance with eternity : " like the swift flight of a sparrow through the warmed room where we sit and sup in winter when there is snow without. It flies in at one door and out at the other, into the dark and cold from which it has just emerged." Others spoke to the like effect, and then St Paulinus addressed the assembly. Coifi applauded his discourse and advised the king to command fire to be set to the temples and altars of their false gods. The king asked him who should first profane them. Coifi answered that he himself, who had been the foremost in their worship, ought to do it for an example to others. Then he asked to be furnished with arms and a horse ; for according to their belief it was not lawful for the high priest to bear arms or to ride on a horse, but only on a mare. Mounted on the king's own horse, with a sword by his side and a spear in his hand, he rode to the temple, which he profaned by casting his spear into it. " And the people beholding it, thought he was mad." Where this took place, says Bede, is shown not far from York, to the east beyond the Derwent, and is called Godmundingham, that is now Goodmanham, a mile from Market Weighton.

King Edwin was baptised at York at Easter in the year 627, on the site of the present York Minster, in the wooden church of St Peter which he had caused to be built. He afterwards began a large church of stone, which was finished by his successor, St Oswald. St Paulinus baptised among others four sons, one daughter, and one grandson of the king; and both nobles and people flocked in crowds to be instructed and to receive the sacrament of Baptism. People being converted in such large numbers there were necessarily many who were unworthy of or dishonest in their new profession, but many more became changed people, whose first thought now was to serve God in this world and enjoy Him for ever in the next. And of these the holy Edwin was himself a shining example, being as zealous to spread the truth as to practise it. His old protector, Redwald, King of the East Angles, had received baptism in Kent, but was seduced by his wife and false teachers, and joined the worship of his ancient gods and that of Jesus Christ, erecting, Samaritan-like, two altars in the same temple. His son and successor, Earpwald, was prevailed upon by St Edwin to embrace with his whole heart the faith of Christ with many of his people, and so return was made for what Edwin owed to the might of his father's arms. St Edwin imposed tribute on the north Welsh chieftains and took possession of the island of Môn, since called Anglesey; and in the north consolidated his kingdom to the Pentland Hills, where the fortress of Edinburgh preserves his name and memory. He provided that on the main highways brass cups should be chained to stakes by the best springs for the convenience of travellers, nor dare any man touch them for any purpose but that for which they were put there. "There was then," says St Bede in a well-known passage, "such perfect peace in Britain, wheresoever the rule of King Edwin extended, that, as is still proverbially said, a woman with her new-born babe might walk throughout the island from sea to sea unharmed."

This good king had reigned seventeen years over the English and the Britons, of which he had spent the last six in the service of Christ, when the Welsh chief Cadwallon marched in arms against him with Penda of Mercia, a pagan. King Edwin met them at Hatfield Chase (?) on October 12, 633, and in the ensuing battle in defence of his Christian state he was slain, together with his son Osfrid.

St Edwin was certainly venerated in England as a martyr, but though his claims to sanctity are far more obvious than those of some other royal saints, English and other, he has had no liturgical *cultus* so far as is known. His relics were held in veneration, the head at York Minster, the remainder at Whitby ; Speed says that churches were dedicated in his honour in London and at Brene in Somerset ; and Pope Gregory XIII permitted him to be represented among the English saints on the walls of the chapel of the *Venerabile* at Rome.

The *Anglo-Saxon Chronicle* and other early sources add little or nothing to the account in Bede's *Historia Ecclesiastica*. See Plummer's text and notes, and consult further the bibliography given above under St Paulinus, October 10.

ST WILFRID, Bp. OF YORK, CONF.

A.D. 709

St Wilfrid stands out prominently among the early ecclesiastics of the Church in England as an upholder of the Holy See of Rome, who worked hard and successfully to bring and keep the English Church into closer touch with that centre of unity, and suffered much for his loyalty. In a joint pastoral of the English bishops in 1893 they said of him : " It is to St Wilfrid and to his brave and untiring appeals to the Apostolic See that this country owes its salvation from internal schism, and the stability of an ecclesiastical organisation which was to be proof against many a storm in days to come." He was born in 634, son of a Northumbrian thegn ; Ripon claims to be his birthplace, but without producing any evidence of the honour. His mother died when he was a child, and the unkindness of his stepmother made him seek the court of Oswy, King of Northumbria, when he was thirteen. He was befriended by Queen Eanfleda, who in the following year sent him to the monastery of Lindisfarne that he might be trained in the study of the sacred sciences, in which he showed application, penetration, and maturity of judgement beyond his years. A desire of greater improvement than he could attain to in that house, where he perceived the Celtic discipline that was practised to be imperfect, gave rise to a project of travelling into France and Italy. He made some stay at Canterbury, where he studied the Roman discipline under St Honorius, and learned the psalter according to the Roman version, instead of that which he had used before. In 654 St Bennet Biscop, his countryman, passed through Kent on his first journey to Rome ; and St Wilfrid, who had set out with the same object, crossed the

sea with him. At Lyons Wilfrid was detained a whole year by
St Annemundus, archbishop of that city, who took so great a liking
to him that he offered him his niece in marriage, and promised to
procure him a considerable position ; but the youth continued steadfast in the resolution he had taken to devote himself to God, and
proceeded on his journey the year following. At Rome he visited
every day the tombs of the martyrs, and put himself under Boniface
the archdeacon, a pious and learned man ; he was secretary to Pope
St Martin, and took much delight in instructing young Wilfrid. He
carefully explained to him the four gospels, the right calculation of
Easter (against the erroneous practice of the Britons and Irish), and
the other rules of ecclesiastical discipline. He presented him to the
Pope, who gave him his special blessing, by the imposition of his
hands and a prayer. After this, Wilfrid returned to Lyons to the
archbishop, whom he reverenced as his father. He stayed three
years there and received the ecclesiastical tonsure after the Roman
manner, thus adopting an outward and visible sign of his dissent
from Celtic customs. St Annemundus desired to make him his heir,
but his own life was suddenly cut short by murder, and Wilfrid
himself was spared only because he was a foreigner. After he had
interred his spiritual father he returned to England, where Aldfrid,
natural son of Oswy, hearing that Wilfrid had been instructed in
the discipline of the Roman Church, sent for him. After he had talked
with him concerning the customs of that church, he asked Wilfrid
to instruct him and his people accordingly. This St Wilfrid consented to, and the prince entered into an intimate friendship with
him. Aldfrid had recently founded a monastery at Ripon and peopled
it with monks from Melrose, among whom was St Cuthbert. These
he now required to abandon their Celtic usages, whereupon the
abbot Eata, Cuthbert, and others, elected to return to Melrose. So
St Wilfrid was made abbot of Ripon, and shortly after he was
ordained priest by St Agilbert, the Frankish bishop of the West
Saxons. Wilfrid used all his influence to win over the clergy of the
north to Roman ways. The principal trouble was that they followed
an erroneous calculation of Easter ; and King Oswy and his Queen
Eanfleda, who came from Kent, sometimes kept Lent and Easter at
different times in the same court. The Scots and Britons were not
schismatics herein, for this difference between them and the Universal Church had not proceeded to a breach of communion. But
to put an end to this dispute, in 664 a conference was held in the
monastery of St Hilda at Streaneshalch, now Whitby, before Oswy
and Aldfrid. Colman, Bishop of Lindisfarne, brought thither his
Scottish clergy, and was supported by St Cedd, Bishop of the East

Saxons, and the abbess St Hilda ; on the other side Bishop Agilbert
had with him Agatho, a priest from Paris, Romanus, the Queen's
chaplain, the abbot Wilfrid, and the deacon James, last surviving
disciple of St Paulinus. Colman alleged the example of his predecessors and of St Columba himself, and claimed that practice to
have been established in Asia by St John the Evangelist : which
assertion it would have been a difficult task to prove, as Alban Butler
gently observes. Agilbert, pleading himself unpractised in English,
asked St Wilfrid to reply for him, and he accordingly pointed out
to the assembly at some length that Colman and his followers would
be at fault did they refuse to follow the instructions of the Apostolic
See. St Wilfrid concluded his persuasive speech (preserved for us
by St Bede) by quoting our Lord's commission to Peter : " Thou
art Peter. . . ." Oswy asked Colman if it were true that these words
were spoken. " It is true," answered Colman. Then said the King,
" Can you show any such power given to your Columba ? "
" None."—" Do you all," asked Oswy, " on both sides admit that
our Lord said this particularly to Peter, and that the Lord gave him
the keys of the kingdom of Heaven ? " They replied : " We do."
" Then," he concluded, " I declare that I will not oppose this keeper
of the gate of Heaven, and that I will obey his orders to the utmost
of my power lest he shut that gate against me." This resolution of
the King was approved by the whole assembly.* St Cedd declared
upon the spot that he embraced the Roman discipline. But Colman
said he could not accept the decision, at variance with the practice
of the monks of Iona, and retired to them with his Scottish priests,
and taking the relics of St Aidan. Tuda was consecrated bishop
of the Northumbrians in his room, but soon after died, and Aldfrid
desired to have his own priest, Wilfrid, placed in the episcopal see.
Wilfrid looked on the nonconforming northern bishops as schismatics, and so went to France to receive consecration at the hands
of his old friend Agilbert, who had returned to his native country,
where the bishopric of Paris was given him. Agilbert joyfully

---

* The form of the tonsure was also discussed ; the Celtic monks shaved
the part of the head in front of a line drawn over the crown from ear to ear.
There was also supposed to be something the matter with the way they
baptised. The synod of Whitby marked the end of the paschal controversy
in the West, but as in other like disputes there was more than matters of
discipline at stake. St Wilfrid definitely led the churches of the British
Isles towards closer dependence on Rome. Had both " Celts " and
" Romans " previously shown more of the Roman tolerance, as expressed
in Pope St Gregory's famous letter of instruction to St Augustine of
Canterbury, the acerbities and damage of their controversy would have
been considerably less.

received Wilfrid, and with other bishops performed the ceremony of his ordination with great solemnity at Compiègne. He was then in his thirtieth year. For some reason St Wilfrid did not come back at once, and when he did was delayed by bad weather. In the meantime King Oswy had got impatient, sent St Chad, Abbot of Lastingham, south, where he was consecrated by Wini, Bishop of the West Saxons, and then appointed him to be bishop at Lindisfarne. Wilfrid on his return to England would not dispute the election of St Chad ; but retired to Ripon, which monastery he made his residence for the next three years. He was often called into Mercia by King Wulfere to ordain deacons and priests, and to perform other episcopal functions, and at the invitation of King Egbert he went to Kent for the same purpose. On his return he brought with him a monk named Stephen Eddius, who became his friend and biographer and assisted the saint to introduce the Rule of St Benedict, first at Ripon and then elsewhere in the north. In 669 St Theodore of Tarsus, the newly appointed archbishop of Canterbury, in his visitation found the election of St Chad to have been irregular, and removed him, and at the same time put St Wilfrid in possession of the see of York. Wilfrid consecrated the great church of St Peter which he had built at Ripon in 670, and afterwards that of St Andrew at Hexham, and several others. Being a man of persuasive oratory and strict virtue, he everywhere promoted religion with great success. With the help of Eddius, who had been precentor at Canterbury, he established in all the churches of the north the use of Roman chant, he restored the cathedral at York, and discharged all his episcopal duties in a most exemplary way. He made visitations of his large diocese on foot, and was deeply beloved and respected by all his people—but not by his prince, Egfrid, who had succeeded Oswy. Egfrid had in 659 married St Etheldreda, daughter of King Anna of the East Angles. For ten years she refused to consummate her marriage with him, and when he had appealed to St Wilfrid he had taken Etheldreda's part and helped her to leave her husband's house and become a nun at Coldingham. In these circumstances Egfrid, not without reason, thought he had a grievance against the bishop, and had no intention of letting his resentment remain inactive. When therefore there was indication that St Theodore wanted as metropolitan to subdivide the great diocese of the Northumbrians, he encouraged the project, and moreover slandered St Wilfrid's administration and demanded his deposition. Theodore appears to have listened to Egfrid, the diocese of York was divided into four, and Theodore consecrated three bishops in Wilfrid's own cathedral. Wilfrid protested, and before the King and his council

appealed to the judgement of the Holy See—the first example of
such an appeal in the history of the Church in England. Dreading
a disturbance or schism, he raised no clamour but, being too well
versed in the canons not to see the irregularity and nullity of many
steps that had been taken against him, embarked for Rome. Being
driven by contrary winds at sea upon the coast of Friesland, during
that winter and the following spring he stayed there and converted
and baptised many. Thus he opened that harvest which St Willibrord and others afterwards cultivated. In the meanwhile his enemies
sent a message to Theodericus, King of Neustria, to intercept him,
but the mayor of the palace, Ebroin, in his zeal detained Winfrid,
Bishop of the Mercians, by mistake. Then he sent letters to the
King of Friesland, promising him a bushel of gold if he would send
him Bishop Wilfrid or his head. The King read the letters publicly
before Wilfrid, the messengers, and his own officers, and, tearing
them to pieces, threw them into the fire.

Next summer Wilfrid travelled through Austrasia, where King
Dagobert II entertained him most honourably, and entreated him
to fill the vacant bishopric of Strasburg. Upon his refusal, this
prince sent Adeodatus, Bishop of Toul, to accompany him to Rome,
where he arrived late in the year 679. He found Pope St Agatho
already apprised of what had passed in England by a monk whom
Theodore had despatched on his side with letters. To discuss this
cause the Pope assembled a synod in the Lateran basilica, at which
the appellant and the defendant's representative were heard in person. The synod decided that Wilfrid was to be restored to his
undivided see, and that he himself should choose coadjutors to
assist him in its government. St Wilfrid stayed over four months
at Rome, and assisted at the Lateran council of one hundred and
twenty-five bishops, in which he with the rest condemned the Monothelite heresy. When he arrived in England, he went to King Egfrid
and showed him the sealed decress of the Pope. The prince cried
out that they had been obtained by bribery, and commanded Wilfrid
to be taken to prison, where he was detained nine months. They
took from him everything but the clothes which he wore, and sent
his attendants away, some one way and some another. Queen Ermenburga (St Etheldreda's successor) took away his case of relics, which
she hung up in her room and carried about with her when she went
out. The Bishop's guards heard him singing in his dark dungeon,
and beheld a light which terrified them ; and the saint having cured
the governor's wife with holy water, he refused to guard him any
longer, and the King ordered him to be removed to another prison.
At length the Queen was seized with a sickness in a monastery, the

abbess whereof (who was St Ebba, the King's aunt) represented to her the injustice done to St Wilfrid ; whereupon he was set at liberty by the frightened Egfrid, his relics restored, and his companions sent back to him.

St Wilfrid fled to Mercia for safety, but was driven thence into Wessex, and from there, by Ermenburga's sister, into Sussex. Here he was among the still pagan South Saxons, but their King Ethelwalch, who had been lately baptised in Mercia, received him with open arms. The saint by his preaching converted nearly the whole nation. At his coming the country was oppressed with a dreadful famine and drought, but on the day on which St Wilfrid first administered baptism with great solemnity to a number of the nobility and people, abundant rain fell. The saint also taught the people to fish, which was a great boon to them, for hitherto they had known only how to catch eels. The Bishop's men collected a number of eel-nets and adapted them for sea-fishing ; in their first venture they caught three hundred fish, of which the saint gave one hundred to the poor and as many to those of whom they had borrowed the nets, keeping the rest for their own use. The King gave him land of eighty-seven families at Selsey, whereon he established a monastery ; this place became an episcopal see, which was afterwards removed to Chichester. St Wilfrid chiefly resided in the peninsula of Selsey, and conducted his missions from thence for five years till, upon the death of King Egfrid, St Theodore, who was very old and ill, sent to him requesting that he would meet him at London with St Erconwald, bishop of that city. He confessed to them all the actions of his life, and said to St Wilfrid : " The greatest remorse that I feel is that I consented to deprive you of your see without any fault committed on your part. I confess this crime to God and St Peter, and I take them to witness that I will do all that lies in my power to make amends for my fault and to reconcile you to all the kings and lords who are my friends. I shall not live to the end of this year, and I wish to establish you in my lifetime archbishop of my see." St Wilfrid replied : " May God and St Peter pardon all our differences ; I will always pray for you. Send letters to your friends that they may restore to me my diocese, according to the decree of the Holy See. The choice of a successor in your see will be afterwards considered in a proper assembly." Accordingly, St Theodore wrote to Egfrid's successor, Aldfrid, to Ethelred, King of the Mercians, to St Elfleda, who had succeeded St Hilda in the abbey of Whitby, and others. Aldfrid recalled the Bishop towards the end of the year 686, and restored to him his monastery of Hexham, and soon after that of Ripon and the episcopal see of York ; St Bosa of York, St Cuthbert of Lindisfarne, and St John of Beverley at Hexham relinquishing their sees to him. These bishops were holy men, well qualified for their ministry, and in simplicity had taken upon themselves a charge which their immediate superiors imposed upon them. St Wilfrid after his restoration reduced Hexham and Ripon to their original condition of abbeys, but after a time King Aldfrid wanted a new bishopric erected at Ripon. Wilfrid opposed the project, and was obliged once more to fly, five years after he had been restored. He retired to Ethelred of Mercia, who received him most graciously, and entreated him to take upon himself the care of the vacant see of Lichfield, which he administered for some years. The new archbishop of Canterbury, Brihtwold, was not sympathetic to St Wilfrid, and in 703 he called a synod which decreed, at the instigation of Aldfrid, that Wilfrid should resign his bishopric and retire to his abbey of Ripon. He vindicated all he had done for the Church in the north in an impassioned speech, and again appealed to the Holy See. The synod broke up, and he started on his third journey to Rome. He was in his seventieth year.

St Wilfrid's opponents also sent representatives to Rome and nearly seventy sessions were held over a period of four months to examine the cause. The synod was naturally impressed by the previous judgement of Pope St Agatho, and Pope John VI honourably acquitted the saint, who had in everything proceeded according to the canons. His very enemies had always acknowledged his life to be irreproachable, and a bishop cannot be deposed unless a canonical fault be proved against him. If it was necessary to divide his bishopric, this was not to be done without his concurrence and reserving to him his own see, and by the authority not of some small consistory, but at least of a provincial council. Moreover, this persecution was raised by court envy, jealousy, and resentment. St Wilfrid, being the best skilled in sacred learning and in the canons of the Church in all Britain, as St Theodore on his death-bed acknowledged him to be, was too great a disciplinarian for some at court. How pure his views were, and how remote from avarice and ambition, appeared from his charity toward his persecutors, the modesty with which he maintained the rights of his see and the discipline of the Church, and the disinterestedness with which he refused the bishopric of the Mercians and excused himself when St Theodore desired to make him his coadjutor in the metropolitical see of Canterbury. It is noteworthy too that, so far as is known, he never claimed the metropolitan jurisdiction for the see of York and the *pallium* for himself, which had been granted to St Paulinus. St Wilfrid met at Rome with that protection and approval which were due to his heroic virtue. Pope John VI in 704 sent letters to the Kings of Mercia and Northumbria in favour of the persecuted Bishop, charging Archbishop Brihtwold to call a synod which should do him justice : in default of which he ordered the parties to make their personal appearance at Rome. St Wilfrid on his return was taken dangerously ill at Meaux in France, when, as St Bede relates, he was assured by a heavenly vision that Christ, through the intercession of His mother Mary, and at the prayers of his friends, had prolonged his life four years. When he landed in England, Brihtwold promised him restoration to his former see, and Ethelred, the late king of Mercia, then abbot of Bardney, received him with joy and warmly recommended him to his nephew Coenred, to whom he had resigned his crown. Aldfrid still made difficulties ; but he died in 705, and in his last sickness repented of the injustice he had done to St Wilfrid, as his sister St Elfleda gave testimony. His restitution, therefore, was agreed to by the whole kingdom under Osred who, being only eight years old, succeeded his father. St Wilfrid, having vindicated the canons and the authority of the Holy See, now gracefully consented, at a synod held on the river Nidd, to a compromise : he took possession of the diocese of Hexham, but chiefly resided in his monastery of Ripon, leaving York to St John of Beverley. " On that day," writes Eddius, " all the bishops kissed and embraced one another, and, having broken bread, communicated. Then, giving thanks to the God of all this happiness, they returned to their own places in the peace of Christ." In 709 St Wilfrid made a visitation of the monasteries in Mercia of which he had been the founder, and he died at one of these, at Oundle in Northamptonshire, having divided his goods between his monasteries, churches, and the former companions of his exile. His body was buried in his church of St Peter at Ripon, but the subsequent history of it is a matter of dispute. Eadmer says that the greatest part of his remains was translated to Canterbury in the time of St Odo, enshrined by Lanfranc, and deposited on the north side of the altar by St Anselm, the day of which translation became his principal festival. These relics have been said by some to be still beneath the pavement, near the tomb of Cardinal Pole. But the church of Ripon maintained that these were the relics of Wilfrid II (*d. c.* 732), taken by mistake, and continued to venerate his shrine at Ripon throughout the Middle Ages.

True virtue is always of a piece with itself, is always governed by the same principle, and always steers the same course. In prosperity it is humble, modest, and equable ; in adversity, magnanimous and equally active and brave. To suffer from good men is often the severest of trials : but from whatever quarter persecution comes, it is our duty not to sink under it but, sincerely humbling ourselves before both God and man, to be undaunted, considering that on one side it is the part of cowards only to be weak or to despair ; and on the other, that it is arrogance and pride to fall into impatience, or to repay injuries with revenge, insults, or ill will. St Wilfrid saw the clouds gather and burst over his head, yet was undismayed, and never reviled his persecutors. By his friend and biographer Eddius he was described as " courteous to everybody, active in body, a quick walker, eager for every good work, never cast down." He is named in the Roman Martyrology and his feast is kept in several dioceses of England, the prayer of his office being taken from the old office of the church of York.

For many years past the career of St Wilfrid has been a fruitful source of Anglican controversy. For materials, we have, beside the copious account given in Bede, a full biography by Wilfrid's companion and disciple Eddius as well as the somewhat turgid poem of Fridegodus (*c.* 945) which was sponsored by Odo, Archbishop of Canterbury, and finally some other sources of much later date, the principal of which is the Life, or Lives, by Eadmer. These biographical documents may most conveniently be consulted in the first volume of Raine's *Historians of the Church of York* (Rolls Series). To discuss the disputed episodes in the series of St Wilfrid's many conflicts would be impossible here. The account given above, which is substantially that of Butler, is at least supported by the statements of Bede and Eddius, and though there is some ground for suspecting the latter of a partiality which led him to suppress incidents which he deemed derogatory to his hero, there is no proof forthcoming that he was an unscrupulous falsifier of history. The Anglican position may be gathered from Dr. William Bright, *Chapters of Early English Church History*, and in a more extreme form from G. Forrest Browne, *Theodore and Wilfrith*. See also B. W. Wells in *The English Historical Review*, vol. vi (1891), pp. 535–550. Dr. T. Hodgkin in his *History of England to the Norman Conquest* more impartially avers that " the life of Wilfrid with all its strange vicissitudes of triumph and disgrace is confessedly one of the most difficult problems in early Anglo-Saxon history," but further on he tells us : " With justice he (Wilfrid) exclaimed again and again, ' What are the crimes of which you accuse me ? ' They had, it would seem, no crimes to allege against him." Neither does Dr. Hodgkin hesitate to describe him as " the brave old man " and " the greatest ecclesiastic " of Northumbria. The *Life of St Wilfrid*, by F. W. Faber, published under Newman's editorship in 1844, caused a great outcry on account of its undisguisedly Roman sympathies. Some startling extracts were cited, years later, by Faber's biographer (pp. 224–225). His conversion followed quickly. He took the name of Wilfrid in confirmation, dedicated in honour of St Wilfrid the church he built at Cotton, and chose for himself the name of Brother Wilfrid in the congregation which he founded, the members of which were for the short time of its duration known as " Wilfridians."

ST SERAPHINO, Conf.

A.D. 1604

The life of St Seraphino was of that uneventfulness which one associates with the vocation of a lay brother, though spiritually he attained great heights and numerous miracles are related of him. He was born at Montegranaro in 1540, of very humble parentage, and like many another saint he began to earn his living as a shepherd boy. When he was left an orphan he was taken into the service of his elder brother, a bricklayer and a harsh master. Young Seraphino was treated rather brutally by him, and when he was sixteen he ran away and became a lay brother with the Capuchins. He had always been very devout and good, and now he progressed rapidly on the path of heroic sanctity. Every night he spent three hours in prayer before the Blessed Sacrament, and did not go to bed again after Matins ; he won sinners by his kindness and moving words, and was beloved by all the poor. Had his superiors allowed, he would have emulated St Francis and gone to work among the infidels ; but he unmurmuringly accepted God's will that he should live and die in obscurity at home. The decree of his canonisation (published by Pope Clement XIII in 1767) records two of his miracles : namely, that when on a pilgrimage to Loreto he passed the river Potenza in flood not merely unharmed but quite dry, and that when he was reproved for his reckless generosity to the poor the vegetables which he had cut for them overnight in the friary garden were grown up again the next day. With the sign of the cross he cured the sick and he received the gifts of discernment of spirits and reading the future, so that he was consulted by both civil and ecclesiastical dignitaries. St Seraphino died at Ascoli Piceno on October 12, 1604 ; his shrine is in the Capuchin church of that town and famous for miracles.

The story of St Seraphino told in some detail is included in the *Annales Ordinis Capuccini* (1639) by Z. Boverio. This has been reprinted in the *Acta Sanctorum*, October, vol. vi, and with it the full text of the bull of canonisation. There are other Lives by C. de Harenberg (1642), P. B. Joannini (1709) and Cardinal Svampa (1904). Further bibliographical details may be gleaned from Giuseppe da Fermo, *Gli Scrittori Cappuccini delle Marche* (1928).

OCTOBER 13

ST EDWARD THE CONFESSOR, King of England

A.D. 1066

AFTER the neglect, quarrelling, and oppression of the reigns of the two Danish sovereigns Harold Harefoot and Hartha-canute, the people of England gladly welcomed the repre-sentative of the old English line of kings, known in history as Edward the Confessor. "All men took him as was his right," and, for the peace and relief that prevailed during his reign, he was undoubtedly one of the most popular of English sovereigns, though his significance was much exaggerated later by the Normans, whose friend and patron he had been. And the noble qualities for which Edward is venerated as a saint belonged to him rather as a man than as a king ; he was devout, gentle, and peace-loving but with hardly sufficient force to stand up to some of the strong characters by whom he was sur-rounded. On the other hand he was not feeble and pietistic, as is now sometimes alleged : he was handicapped by lack of physical strength, but had a quiet determination which enabled him to cope successfully with opposing influences. Edward was the son of Ethel-red the Redeless by his Norman wife Emma, and during the Danish supremacy was sent to Normandy for safety, with his brother Alfred, when he was ten years old. They came to England in 1036 but Alfred was seized, mutilated, and murdered by the brutality of Harold Harefoot, and so Edward did not set foot again in his native land until he was called to be king in 1042 : he was then forty years old and more Norman than English. Two years later he married Edith, the daughter of his chief minister, Earl Godwin : a beautiful and religious girl, " whose mind was a school of all the liberal arts." It is traditionally claimed as an aspect of Edward's sanctity that, for love of God and greater perfection, he lived with his wife in absolute continence. The fact is not certain, nor, if it be so, is his motive certain either. William of Malmesbury, a hundred years later, says that the continency of the King and his wife was notorious, but adds, " I have not been able to discover whether he acted thus from dislike of her family or out of pure regard for chastity." The chronicler Roger of Wendover says the same thing, but thinks that Edward was certainly unwilling " to beget successors of a traitor stock." The difficulty common to so many of these cases again arises, namely : Why did he marry at all ?

After his coronation Edward took severe measures to restrain his mother, who in second wedlock had married Canute and was suspected of being privy to the murder of Alfred, and took other steps to ensure his peaceful occupancy of the throne ; one of them was doubtless his marriage, for he knew that security was threatened less by Danish influence than by the ambition of Earl Godwin. Godwin for his part was the chief opponent of that Norman influence which had its centre at the royal court and made itself felt in appointments to bishoprics and baronies as well as in lesser matters. After a series of " incidents," things came to a crisis and Godwin and his family were banished ; even his daughter, Edward's queen, was confined to a convent for a time. In the same year, 1051, William of Normandy visited the English court, and it can hardly be doubted that Edward then offered him the succession to the crown : the Norman conquest began, not at the battle of Hastings, but at the accession of St Edward. It was not many months before Godwin returned, and as both sides were averse from a civil war the King restored him, and the council " outlawed all Frenchmen that aforetime disregarded the law, gave unjust judgements, and counselled ill counsel in the land." The Norman archbishop of Canterbury and bishop of Hereford fled overseas " in a crazy ship." Nothing is more praised at this time than the " laws and customs of good King Edward " and the realm's freedom from war. The only serious fighting was between Harold of Wessex (Godwin's son) and Gruffydd ap Llywelyn in the Welsh Marches, and the expeditions under Earl Siward sent by St Edward to assist Malcolm III of Scotland against the usurper Macbeth. The King's religious and just administration caused him to reign in the hearts of his people. The love, harmony, and agreement between him and the great council of the nation produced such a happiness as to be the measure of the people's desires in all succeeding reigns ; the law and government of King Edward being petitioned and strenuously contended for by English and Norman barons. Not the least popular of his acts was the remission of *danegeld*, a tax which had been levied originally to buy off the Danes, and which the Danish kings continued to collect to pay their fleet ! The amount of the tax in hand collected in his reign was handed over by Edward to the poor.

William of Malmesbury gives a personal picture of St Edward, in which he says that he was " a man by choice devoted to God, living the life of an angel in the administration of his kingdom, and therefore directed by Him. . . . He was so gentle that he would not say a word of reproach to the meanest person." He was generous to the poor and strangers, especially if they were from abroad, and a great encourager of monks. His favourite diversions were hunting and hawking, at which he would go out for days on end, but even then never omitted to be present at Mass every morning. In appearance he was tall and well built, with a ruddy face and white hair and beard.

St Edward during his exile in Normandy had made a vow to perform a pilgrimage to St Peter's tomb at Rome if God should be pleased to put an end to the misfortunes of his family. When he was settled on the throne he held a council, in which he declared the obligation he lay under. The assembly commended his devotion, but represented that the kingdom would be left exposed to domestic divisions and to foreign enemies. The King was moved by their entreaties and reasons, and consented that the matter should be referred to Pope St Leo IX. He, considering the impossibility of the King's leaving his dominions, dispensed his vow upon condition that by way of commutation he should give to the poor the sum he would have expended in his journey and should build or repair and endow a monastery in honour of St Peter. King Edward selected for his benefaction an abbey in London, first mentioned in a charter of King Offa in 785. This monastery was called Thorney, and, being destroyed by the Danes, was restored by King Edgar. St Edward repaired and endowed it in a magnificent manner out of his own patrimony, and obtained of Pope Nicholas II ample exemptions and privileges for it in 1059. From its situation it had come to be called West Minster in distinction from the minster of St Paul in the east of the city. The new monastery was designed to house seventy monks, and, though the abbey was finally dissolved and its church made collegiate and a " royal peculiar " by Queen Elizabeth, the ancient community is now organically and legally represented by the monks of St Lawrence's Abbey at Ampleforth. The present church called Westminster Abbey, on the site of St Edward's building, was built in the thirteenth century and later.

The last year of St Edward's life was disturbed by troubles between the Northumbrians and their earl, Tostig Godwinsson, whom eventually the King was constrained to banish. At the end of the year, when the nobles of the realm were gathered at the royal court for the feast of Christmas, the new choir of Westminster abbey-church was consecrated with great solemnity, on Holy Innocents' day, 1065. St Edward was ill before the ceremony began, and immediately after took to his bed. He died a week later,* and was buried in Westminster Abbey. In 1161 he was canonised, and two years later his incorrupt body was translated to a shrine in the choir by St Thomas Becket, on October 13, the day now fixed for his feast; the day of his death, January 5, is also mentioned in the Roman Martyrology. There was a further translation, in the thirteenth century, to a shrine behind the high altar, and there the body of the Confessor still lies, the only relics of a saint (except those of the unidentified St Candida at Whitchurch Canonicorum in Dorsetshire) remaining *in situ* after the violence and impiety of the Protestant reformers. St Edward the Confessor was the first English sovereign to exercise the power of " touching for the King's Evil " (scrofula and allied affections), as was done subsequently by many others, and cures apparently obtained. Alban Butler states that, " Since the revolution [of 1688] only Queen Anne has touched for this distemper," but Cardinal Henry Stuart (*de iure* King Henry IX ; died 1807) also did so. St Edward is the principal patron of the city of Westminster and a lesser patron of the archdiocese ; his feast is kept by the whole Western Church and was formerly a holiday of obligation in England.

A collection of *Lives of St Edward the Confessor* was edited for the Rolls Series by H. R. Luard in 1858. This, besides a Norman-French poem and a Latin poem both of late date, includes an anonymous *Vita Æduuardi Regis* which is generally believed to have been written shortly after the King's death. Another Life by Osbert of Clare was compiled about 1141, and the latter document has been edited in the *Analecta*

---

* Alban Butler refers to his giving a ring to the Abbot of Westminster, with the legend relating thereto and the fanciful derivation of the name of Havering-atte-Bower in Essex. At the time that the church of Havering was about to be consecrated, Edward, riding that way, alighted, to be present at the consecration. During the procession a fair old man came to the king and begged alms of him, in the name of God and St John the Evangelist. The king having nothing else to give, as his almoner was not at hand, took a ring from his finger and gave it to the poor man. Some years afterwards two English pilgrims, having lost their way as they were travelling in the Holy Land, " were succoured and put in the right way by an old man," who at parting told them he was John the Evangelist, adding, as the legend proceeds, " Say ye unto Edwarde your Kying that I grete hym well by the token that he gaaf to me this Ryng wyth his own handes at the halowyng of my Chirche, whych Rynge ye shall deliver to hym agayn : and say ye to hym, that he dyspose his goodes, for wythin six monethes he shall be in the joye of Heven wyth me, where he shall have his rewarde for his chastitie and his good lyvinge." At their return home, the two pilgrims waited upon the king, who was then at this Bower, and delivered to him the message and the ring ; from which circumstance this place is said to have received the name of Have-Ring.

Bollandiana (vol. xli, 1923, pp. 5–131) by M. Marc Bloch, who argues at length that the anonymous Life is not older than the twelfth century— between 1103 and 1120. On this see *The Month*, May 1923, pp. 448–451. Yet another biography has for its reputed author St Ælred of Rievaulx, and it has been more than once printed among his works. Besides this we have many briefer notices, *e.g.* in the *Anglo-Saxon Chronicle*, and in such writers as William of Malmesbury and Henry of Huntingdon. The reign of Edward the Confessor is also, of course, discussed in numberless modern histories (notably in E. A. Freeman's *Norman Conquest*, vol. ii), often in a tone the reverse of sympathetic. On the King's connection with Westminster, see Flete's *History of Westminster Abbey*, edited by Dean Armitage Robinson (1909). As for the Confessor's reputation as a law-giver, it must be remembered, as F. Liebermann has shown in his *Gesetze der Angelsachsen*, that the code which at a later time was current under his name was not formulated until fifty years after the Conquest and cannot be traced to any enactments for which he was personally responsible.

SS. FAUSTUS, JANUARIUS, AND MARTIAL, Marts.

A.D. 304

These saints are called by Prudentius "the Three Crowns of Cordova," in which city they with undaunted constancy confessed Jesus Christ before a judge named Eugenius, in the year 304. First Faustus, then Januarius, and lastly Martial, who was the youngest, was hoisted on to the instrument of torture called the "little horse." Whilst they were thus tormented together Faustus said, "How happy is this union in our sufferings, which will unite us in our crowns!" Eugenius charged the executioners to keep on increasing their pains till they should adore the gods. Faustus hearing these orders cried out, "There is one only God, who created us all." The judge commanded his nose, ears, eye-lids and under-lip to be cut off, and the teeth to be beaten out of his jaws. At the cutting of each part, the martyr gave thanks to God. Januarius was then treated in the same manner, and all the while Martial prayed earnestly for constancy as he lay on the rack. The judge pressed him to comply with the imperial edicts, but he resolutely answered, "Jesus Christ is my comfort. Him I will always praise with the same joy with which my companions have confessed His name in their torments. There is one only God, Father, Son, and Holy Ghost, to whom homage and praise are due." The three martyrs were condemned to be burnt alive and cheerfully finished their martyrdom by fire at Cordova in Spain, in the reign of Diocletian.

Here again, as so frequently happens, we have a *passio* which is historically worthless, though the fact of the martyrdom and the locality where it occurred cannot be doubted, the names of the martyrs are perpetuated in inscriptions of the fifth or sixth century, and also by an entry on this day in the *Hieronymianum*. See on all this Père Delehaye's commentary (p. 554) and *cf.* his *Origines du Culte des Martyrs*, pp. 415–416. The *passio* has been printed by Ruinart as well as in the *Acta Sanctorum*, October, vol. vi, but its details are quite untrustworthy.

ST COMGAN, ABBOT AND CONF.

EIGHTH CENTURY

The diocese of Aberdeen to-day keeps the feast of the holy abbot Comgan. He was the brother of St Kentigern, their father being Kelly, Prince of Leinster, an ancestor of the O'Kellys of Rathdown. Comgan succeeded to the authority of his father, which he wielded wisely throughout the province, until he was attacked by neighbouring rulers, defeated in battle, and wounded. He was forced to fly and, taking with him his sister and her children (of whom one became the abbot St Felan), he crossed over to Scotland. He settled in Lochalsh, opposite Skye, in Argyllshire, and with seven men who had accompanied him made a monastic settlement there. St Comgan lived an austere life for many years, and after his death was buried on Iona by his nephew Felan, who also built a church in his honour. This was the first of several which, in various forms, Cowan, Coan, etc., still testify to the veneration in which the memory of St Comgan was formerly held in Scotland.

The lessons in the Aberdeen Breviary are reprinted in the *Acta Sanctorum*, October, vol. vi, in default of better material. A. P. Forbes in his *Kalendars of Scottish Saints* (pp. 310–311) finds little to add, but he supplies a list of churches believed to have been dedicated in honour of St Comgan.

ST GERALD OF AURILLAC, CONF.

A.D. 909

This nobleman was born in 855, a time when the art of war was a necessary part of a gentleman's education; but a lingering illness kept him a long time at home, during which he took so much delight in studies, prayer, and meditation, that he could never be drawn into the tumult of secular life. He became count of Aurillac after the death of his parents, and he gave a great part of the revenue of his estate to the poor; he went modestly clad, in a manner suitable to the austere life he led ; and kept always a very frugal table. He got up every morning at two o'clock, even on journeys, said the first part of the Divine Office, and then heard Mass ; he divided the whole day according to a rule, devoting a great part of it to prayer and reading. St Gerald made a pilgrimage to Rome, and after his return founded at Aurillac a church under the invocation of St Peter, in the place of that of St Clement which his father had built there, together with a Benedictine abbey, which he peopled with monks from Vabres. The monastery afterwards attained considerable fame. St Gerald had some thoughts of himself taking the monastic habit, but was dissuaded by the advice of St Gausbert, Bishop of Cahors, who assured him that he would be much more useful in the world. For the last seven years of his life he was afflicted with blindness ; he died at Cézenac in Quercy in 909 and was buried at the abbey of Aurillac. St Gerald is accounted patron saint of Upper Auvergne.

St Gerald of Aurillac lived a holy life " in the world " at a time of considerable degeneracy and disorder. The example shows us that for any to impute their want of a Christian spirit and virtue to the circumstances of their state or situation is a false and foolish pretence : a proof of which is that, if these were changed, they would still remain the same persons. The fault lies altogether in our own lack of right will. One who is truly in earnest makes dangers and difficulties a motive of greater vigilance, and even converts them into means of sanctification. Temperance may be practised, the spirit of true religion acquired, and all virtues exercised even in an heroic degree, where a desire and resolution does not fall short. From obstacles and contradictions themselves the greatest advantages may be reaped : by them patience, humility, and charity are perfected, and the soul is continually awaked, and quickened into a lively sense of her duty to God.

Although Butler has dealt rather summarily with the story of St Gerald, his Life, in the longer recension, printed in the *Acta Sanctorum*, October, vol. vi, is one of the freshest and most attractive character-sketches which have survived from the period in which he lived. He was the contemporary of another great layman, our own King Alfred, and he was more fortunate than the Anglo-Saxon monarch, in that he had for his biographer the famous St Odo, Abbot of Cluny. The question of the authorship of the Life and its relation to the shorter recension has been convincingly treated by Père Albert Poncelet in the *Analecta Bollandiana*, vol. xiv (1895), pp. 88–107. See also E. Sackur, *Die Cluniacenser*, who shares Poncelet's views, though perhaps upon inadequate data.

ST COLOMAN, Mart.

A.D. 1012

In the beginning of the eleventh century the neighbouring nations of Austria, Moravia, and Bohemia were engaged against each other in dissensions and wars. Coloman, a Scot or Irishman who was going on a penitential pilgrimage to Jerusalem, arrived by the Danube from the enemy's country at Stockerau, a town six miles above Vienna. The inhabitants, persuading themselves that he was a spy, tortured him various ways, because, not knowing their language, he could not give a satisfactory account of himself, and at length hanged him on October 13, in 1012. His patience under unjust sufferings were taken as a proof of the sanctity of Coloman, which was confirmed by the incorruption of his body, which was said to be the occasion of many miracles. Three years after his death his body was translated to the abbey of Melk, where it still reposes. After a time St Coloman came to be venerated as a minor patron of Austria, and a quite imaginary royal Scottish ancestry was invented for him. He is the titular of many churches in Austria, Hungary, and Bavaria, and is invoked for the help and healing of horses and horned cattle. On his feast the blessing of these animals takes place at Hohenschwangau, near Füssen. St Coloman is also appealed to by the plague-stricken and by girls who want husbands.

The *vita*, attributed to Erchenfried, Abbot of Meik, has been printed in the *Acta Sanctorum*, October, vol. vi, and has also been edited for Pertz, *M. G. H. Scriptores*, vol. iv, pp. 675–677. See further Gougaud, *Gælic Pioneers* (1923), pp. 143–145 and the *Lexikon für Theologie und Kirche*, vol. vi, c. 95. It must be admitted that there is no evidence that St Coloman was in a strict sense martyred, and there has never been any formal canonization. On the folk-lore aspects of the case see Bächtold-Stäubli, *Handwörterbuch des Deutschen Aberglaubens*, vol. ii, pp. 95–99 and Künstle, *Ikonographie*, vol. ii, pp. 383–384.

ST MAURICE, Abbot of Carnoët, Conf.

A.D. 1191

This holy monk, who is venerated in the Cistercian Order and throughout Cornouailles, was a native of the district of Loudéac in Britanny, and though his parents were of a modest state they contrived to send him to Paris to be educated. He showed considerable ability and a distinguished career was open to him, but he was keenly conscious of the special dangers of life in the world to one of learning and sensibility and he became a monk at the Cistercian abbey of Langonet in his own country. He was then about twenty-five years old, the Cistercian reform was in its first fervour, and so whole-heartedly did he throw himself into the life that he surpassed all his fellows and was elected abbot, it is said, only three years after profession. His reputation for prudence and wisdom was not con-fined to his own monastery : he was called on to decide a difficult dispute between the chapter of Nantes and the Benedictines of Quimperlé, and the Duke of Britanny, Conan IV, frequently con-sulted him. It was with the encouragement of St Maurice that Conan undertook to found a new Cistercian monastery and chose the forest of Carnoët for its site, which in accordance with monastic tradition was one which required to be broken into cultivation. Maurice was appointed the first abbot and undertook the new estab-lishment with twelve monks from Langonet. Before it was com-pletely achieved Duke Conan died, but St Maurice carried it through under the patronage of his daughter Constance, and had governed Carnoët for nearly fifteen years when he died, on September 29, 1191. St Maurice was never formally canonised, although the process was begun, but he has always had a *cultus* in his order and in the dioceses of Quimper and Saint-Brieuc, and Pope Clement XI permitted the Cistercians to observe his feast liturgically.

There is a longer Latin Life which has been printed by Dom Plaine in the *Studien und Mittheilungen Ben. u Cist. Ord.*, vol. vii (1886), part 1, pp. 380–393, and another more contracted in part 2 *ibid.*, pp. 157–164. A popular account with illustrations was published by L. Le Cam, *Saint Maurice, Abbé de Langonnet*, 1924. This Abbot Maurice seems to be identical with the St Mawes of whose history Canon Doble has written a brief sketch.

BD. MAGDALEN PANATTIERI, Virg.

A.D. 1503

Many have seen in the dress of the Order of Preachers the emblem *par excellence* of loving-kindness and devotion to one's neighbour, and, in the days when such a course of action was common, many assumed the habit of the Dominican third order and lived in their homes a life of usefulness and charity in accordance with that dress. St Catherine of Siena is the outstanding example ; Blessed Magdalen Panattieri is another. She was born and spent all her life in the little town of Trino-Vercellese in the marquisate of Montferrat, between Piedmont and Lombardy, and before she was twenty bound herself by a vow of celibacy and became a Dominican tertiary, with the consent of her parents, in a local chapter of widows and maidens who engaged themselves in works of devotion and benevolence under the direction of the friars, who had a convent in the town. The life of Blessed Magdalen was notably lacking in eventfulness, and she seems to have been spared all external contradiction and persecution, soon becoming a force in her town of Trino. Her care for the poor and young children (in whose favour she seems several times to have acted miraculously) paved the way for her work for the conversion of sinners ; she prayed and suffered for them and supplemented her austerities with exhortation and reprimands, especially against the sin of usury. She was a veritable Preacheress and was appointed to give conferences to the women and children of the town in a building called the chapel of the Marquis, adjoining the Dominican church ; soon the men also, and priests and religious as well, attended and the young novices were taken to hear and profit by her words. She was looked up to as the mother of the town.

By her efforts the Dominicans were inspired to undertake a more strict observance, and in 1490 Blessed Sebastian Maggi came from Milan to inaugurate it at her suggestion. These same friars were involved in a lawsuit with a Milanese councillor, who used his power so oppressively that he was excommunicated from Rome. In the resulting disorder a young man named Bartholomew Perduto publicly slapped Blessed Magdalen in the face, and she turned her other cheek and invited him to smack that also, which made him yet more angry. The people of Trino did not fail to attach significance to the fact that Bartholomew came to a violent end before the year was out, and that the Milanese was stricken with disease and died miserably : but to the gentle and forgiving Magdalen these unhappy deaths were an occasion only of sorrow. She seems to have foreseen the calamities that overtook northern Italy during the invasions of the sixteenth century and made several covert references to them ; it was afterwards noticed and attributed to her prayers that, when all around was rapine and desolation, Trino was for no obvious reason spared ; but not always, for in 1639 the town was bombarded by the Spaniards and Neapolitans and the relics of Blessed Magdalen destroyed.

When she knew that she was dying she sent for all her tertiary sisters, and many others pressed into her room. She made her last loving exhortation to them, promising to intercede for them all in eternity, adding, " I could not be happy in Heaven if you were not there too." Then, fortified by a vision of our Lord and His Mother and several other saints, she peacefully made an end, while the bystanders were singing the thirtieth psalm. From before the day of her death, October 13, 1503, the grateful people of Trino had venerated Blessed Magdalen Panattieri as a saint, a *cultus* that was confirmed by Pope Leo XII.

In the *Auctarium* for October, published as an appendix to the *Acta Sanctorum*, the Bollandists have given a full account of this *beata*, reprinting the Life compiled by Marchese in his *Sagro Diario Domenicano*, vol. v. See also J. A. Iricus, *Rerum Patriæ Tridinensis Libri tres* (1745), and M. C. de Ganay, *Les Bienheureuses Dominicaines* (1924), pp. 355–368. There are other Lives in Italian by S. M. Vallaro (1903) and by G. Cereghino (1927), and a summary in Procter, *Lives of the Dominican Saints*, pp. 291–294.

OCTOBER 14

ST CALLISTUS I, Pope and Mart.

c. A.D. 222

IT is unfortunate that most of our knowledge of this pope is derived from works written by the unorthodox antipope Hippolytus and by Tertullian after he had joined a schismatic sect, who were actuated by a bitter animosity against him. The account of his early life given by Hippolytus is doubtless founded on facts, but facts which the writer was presenting as unfavourably as possible. Callistus when a young man was a slave of Carpophorus, a Christian in the imperial household, who made him manager of a bank in which the Christian brethren and widows deposited their savings. Callistus lost their money, whether by his own fault, through carelessness or bad speculation or misappropriation is not known; but he fled from Rome. At Porto he went on board ship, but finding himself closely pursued by his master he tried to escape by jumping into the sea. He was caught and sentenced to a slave's punishment at the mill. He was released at the intercession of the Christians in order that he might try and recover some of the lost money, and he tried in vain to collect some debts owing by Jewish moneylenders. Callistus very imprudently followed them with his importunities into the synagogue, from whence they dragged him before the prefect Fuscianus and charged him with brawling during their religious services. Carpophorus gave evidence against him, declaring untruly that Callistus was not a Christian, but the magistrate sent him to join other Christians in the mines of Sardinia after he had been scourged. When these confessors were released at the instance of Marcia, the mistress of the Emperor Commodus, the name of Callistus was omitted from the list supplied by Pope St Victor, but he nevertheless persuaded the official in charge to add him to it and he returned to Rome with the others. Pope Victor would not betray the fact of his irregular release, but instead made him an allowance and sent him to Antium. Callistus is next heard of nine or ten years later, on the accession of St Zephyrinus as bishop of Rome. By his condemnation to the mines he had become free from his master Carpophorus, and he had evidently made up for what may have been discreditable in the earlier part of his career, for the new pope at once recalled him to Rome. He was made superintendent of the public Christian burying-place on the Appian Way, one of the oldest and most famous of the catacombs of Rome, still known by his name, San Callisto. In a part of it known as the papal crypt all the popes from Zephyrinus to Eutychian were buried, except Cornelius who lay near by, and Callistus himself. He extended and unified the cemetery, bringing the isolated private plots into communal possession, the first property in land held by the Church. He was the trusted friend and adviser of St Zephyrinus, and in encouraging him to oppose the unorthodoxy of Hippolytus earned his enmity. Hippolytus abuses Callistus in most unmeasured terms and complains bitterly that he had called him a ditheist. But although he accuses him of being leader of a " school " within the Church, it was Callistus who on the death of Zephyrinus was elected to succeed by the clergy and people of Rome.

A momentous act of his short pontificate increased the anger of Hippolytus and incurred that of Tertullian, whose treatise *de Pudicitia* is supposed to be directed against it : " I hear that a most peremptory edict has been published. The bishop of bishops, which means a supreme pontiff, proclaims : I remit the crimes of adultery and fornication to those who have done penance." Orthodox Christianity knows of no sins that are unforgivable or that permanently cut off the sinner from the communion of the Church provided he be truly penitent. Hippolytus and Tertullian were rigorists who, among others throughout the history of Christianity, were led by their rigorism into exaggeration and error and estrangement from the spirit of Christ. St Callistus saw the danger and declared against it, and we find Hippolytus complaining that the Pope had received those whom Hippolytus had excommunicated (from his own sect !), that he had ruled that commission of mortal sin was not in itself sufficient reason for deposing a bishop, that he had allowed clergy and even bishops to contract second marriages, and that he recognised as legitimate marriages between patrician ladies and plebeian men or slaves, contrary to Roman civil law : matters of discipline, for his action in which, and for his opposition to his own theological views, the presbyter Hippolytus calls the pope Callistus a heretic. But he no longer speaks against his personal character. As well as those of Hippolytus, St Callistus condemned the errors of Sabellius, whose followers saw in the Blessed Trinity simply the three different relations of God to mankind, as creator, incarnate redeemer, and sanctifier.

The Emperor Alexander Severus, in whose reign St Callistus

died, had a Christian mother and was himself not unfavourable to Christians, but it is nevertheless likely that the tradition which makes Callistus a martyr is correct, though his *acta* are spurious. These state that in consequence of an allegation of arson against the Christians, the consul Palmatius sent to arrest Callistus, who hid in the house of Pontian in the quarter called Ravenna, *i.e.* the Trastevere. Here he was found and thrown out of an upper window by the mob, who then flung his body down a well. Asterius the priest buried him in the cemetery on the Aurelian Way, where a few months before St Calepodius, martyr in a popular outbreak, had been buried by Callistus. It is supposed to be in the Trastevere that Callistus had built a chapel on a piece of ground which had been adjudged to him by the Emperor as against some inn-keepers : Alexander declaring that any religious rites were better than a tavern. This is probably the church of San Callisto, near Santa Maria-in-Trastevere, which has been known since the year 352, and it has a well, the one, it is said, into which his body was thrown. The cemetery of Calepodius, at about the third milestone on the Aurelian Way, has also been discovered, but the relics of St Callistus were translated therefrom to Santa Maria-in-Trastevere by Pope St Julius I.

In the assured faith of the resurrection of the body, the saints in all ages were careful to treat their dead with religious respect, and to give them decent burial. The commendations which our Lord bestowed on the woman who poured precious ointments upon Him a little before his death, and the devotion of those who took so much care of His funeral, recommended this office of charity ; and the practice of the primitive Christians in this respect was most remarkable. Julian the Apostate, writing to a pontiff of the idolaters, tells him to notice three things by which he thought Christianity had gained most upon the world, namely, " Their kindness and charity to strangers, their care for the burial of their dead, and the dignity of their carriage." Their care of the dead did not consist in any extravagant pomp, in which the pagans far outdid them, but in a religious gravity and respect, which was most expressive of their firm hope of a future resurrection ; they regarded the mortal remains of their dead as precious in the eyes of God, who watches over them, regarding them as relics to be raised one day in the brightest glory and made shining in the heavenly Jerusalem.

Very little can be learnt concerning the life of this pope from the *Liber Pontificalis* (Ed. Duchesne, vol. i, pp. 141–142), or from the quite worthless *passio* (printed in the *Acta Sanctorum*, October, vol. vi). A considerable literature, however, has gathered round those acts of his pontificate which have been mentioned above. It must suffice to indicate two or three notable authorities such as Duchesne, *Histoire ancienne de l'Eglise*, vol. i, pp. 292–325 ; A. d'Alès, *L'Édit de Calliste* (1914) ; and P. Galtier in the *Revue d'Histoire Ecclésiastique*, vol. xxiii (1927), pp. 465–488. A fuller bibliography may be found in J. P. Kirsch, *Kirchengeschichte*, vol. i (1930), pp. 797–799. On the burial and catacomb of St Callistus consult Delehaye's Commentary on the *Hieronymianum*, pp. 555–556, and Leclercq in the *Dictionnaire d'Archéol.*, etc., vol. ii, cc. 1657–1754.

ST JUSTUS, Bp. of Lyons, Conf.

c. A.D. 390

Was born in the Vivarais, of the family of the Counts of Tournon, and whilst he served the church of Vienne as deacon he was advanced to the see of Lyons. He showed by the whole tenour of his conduct that he feared nothing but God, hoped for nothing but from God, and regarded not the flattery or presents but the needs of those that approached him. His zeal made him severe in reproving everything that deserved reproof, and his attachment to discipline and good order was displayed at the Synod of Valence in the year 374. A council of Western prelates being assembled at Aquileia in 381, St Justus of Lyons with two other bishops from Gaul assisted at it. The chief affairs there debated regarded the Arians, and St Ambrose, who was present, procured the deposition of two Arian bishops. He had a particular respect for St Justus, as appears from two letters which he addressed to him concerning certain questions of holy Scripture.

It happened a little before this council that at Lyons a madman, who had stabbed some persons in the street, took sanctuary in the great church ; and St Justus, in order to appease the mob, delivered him into the hands of the magistrate's officer upon a promise that the prisoner's life should be spared. Notwithstanding this he was despatched by the populace. The good bishop was apprehensive that he had been accessory to his death and was by that irregular and disqualified for the ministry of the altar. Having long desired to serve God in retirement, it is said that he made use of this as a pretext to resign the pastoral charge. The opposition of his flock seemed an obstacle, but his journey to the council afforded him an opportunity. On his return he stole from his friends in the night at Torrente, and at Marseilles took ship with a lector of his church, named Viator, and sailed to Alexandria. Concealing his identity, he lived unknown in a monastery in Egypt, surpassing the whole community in the fervour of his penance. He was discovered by one who came from Gaul to visit the monasteries in the Thebaid, and the church of Lyons sent a priest called Antiochus to urge him in the name of the clergy and people to return ; but he was not to be prevailed upon. Antiochus (who succeeded Justus in his see and is himself venerated as a saint, on October 15) determined to bear him company in his solitude, and the saint shortly after died in his arms about the year 390. His body was soon after translated to Lyons and buried in the church of the Machabees which afterwards bore his name. His minister St Viator survived him only a few weeks, and is named in the Roman Martyrology on October 21, and the translation of their bodies together on September 2.

Alban Butler states that the village of Saint Just in Cornwall takes its name from Justus of Lyons. This seems to be a guess, and a bad one. Saint Just-in-Roseland was probably founded by St Jestin, a Cornishman and the son of Geraint ab Erbyn. On the 18th of this month the Roman Martyrology mentions another St Justus, said to have been a boy of nine, martyred near Beauvais in 287. He was formerly very famous and is a lesser patron of the abbey of Einsiedeln.

An early Latin Life of St Justus is printed in the *Acta Sanctorum*, September, vol. i (under September 2), and there seems no reason to doubt that it is in the main reliable. The fact that Justus is mentioned on five different days in the *Hieronymianum* (see Delehaye's commentary, pp. 566–567) may be taken as satisfactory proof of the interest which his *cultus* inspired. Sidonius Apollinaris in a letter gives a description of the enthusiasm with which crowds flocked to the shrine on his feast-day. Consult also Duchesne, *Fastes Épiscopaux*, vol. ii, p. 162 ; Coville, *Recherches sur l'histoire de Lyon* (1928), pp. 441–445 ; and Leclercq, *Dictionnaire d'Archéol.*, etc., vol. x, cc. 191–193.

ST MANECHILDIS, Virg.

c. A.D. 490

Sigmarus, *comes* in the Perthois, and his wife Lintrudis had six daughters, all of whom are venerated as saints in different parts of Champagne ; they were Lintrudis, Amata (Amée), Pusinna, Hoildis, Menna, and Manechildis (Ménéhould), who was the youngest. After living together at home for many years they all received the veil of consecrated virgins from St Alpinus, Bishop of Châlons, and thenceforward the virtue and recollection of their daily life was redoubled. Manechildis in particular gave herself to all sorts of spiritual and temporal good works ; she would accompany her father on his visits to Château-sur-Aisne (now called Sainte-Ménéhould), one of the limits of his jurisdiction, in order to tend the sick of that place where, on account of its situation, malarial fevers were endemic. A tradition of Laneuville-au-Pont says that she also used to stay there, and on the Côte-à-Vignes is a spring said to have been produced miraculously by the saint to quench the thirst of the people who came to her in large numbers when she was at her cell on the side of the mountain. After the death of her parents St Manechildis left her home and sisters to live as a solitary at Bienville on the Marne, and here she died amid the lamentations of the poor and sick whom she had tended, about the year 490.

There seems to be little or nothing to add to the account of the Bollandists who print and comment upon a very short and unconvincing Latin text which cannot be dated. There is no mention of this saint in the *Hieronymianum*.

ST ANGADRISMA, Virg. and Abbess

c. A.D. 695

Angadrisma (Angadrème), daughter of Count Robert of Renty, a high official at the court of Clotaire III, was brought up under the eye of St Omer, in whose diocese of Thérouanne she lived, and of her cousin St Lambert of Lyons, who during her youth was a monk at Fontenelle. It was probably his influence and example that helped her to her resolution to become a nun, although her father had promised her in marriage to St Ansbert, the young lord of Chaussy. It is said that, in order to overcome Count Robert's wishes, Angadrisma asked God to make her so physically repulsive as to put marriage out of the question, and that she was accordingly visited with a leprosy or other incurable disease of the skin. Be that as it may, Ansbert married someone else (later in life he was abbot of Fontenelle and then archbishop of Rouen) and Angadrisma received the religious habit from the hands of St Ouen, on which occasion her disease disappeared, leaving her more beautiful than ever. She was an exemplary nun in the convent to which St Ouen had assigned her, and was later transferred to a Benedictine monastery called Oroër des Vierges, near Beauvais, of which she became abbess. The prudence of her direction and holiness of life were rewarded by the gift of miracles, in one of which she is said to have stopped an outbreak of fire which threatened to devastate the whole house by opposing to it the relics of St Ebrulfus (Evroult), which were kept in the church. She died when over eighty years of age, after having humbly asked the forgiveness of her offences from the community to whom she had endeared herself by her government for thirty years. In addition to her principal feast to-day the diocese of Beauvais (of which city she is principal patron) observes a feast of the Patronage of St Angadrisma on June 27. This commemorates the successful defence of the city when it was besieged by an army of Burgundians in 1472 : at a critical moment the relics of the saint were taken up to the ramparts, and the defenders, calling for her intercession and encouraged by a girl who led them armed with an axe, finally beat their enemies off. Similar deliverances, from the fury of the English during the Hundred Years' War, were attributed to the intercession of this saint.

In the notice of this saint which appears in the *Acta Sanctorum*, October, vol. vi, the text of the Latin Life from which Mabillon quoted (*Act. SS. O.S.B.*, vol. ii, pp. 1016–1018) has not been printed at length. See also Vacandard, *Vie de S. Ouen*, pp. 191, 192, 204 ; and, for further references, the *Dict. d'Hist. et de Géog. ecclés.*, vol. iii, cc. 3–4.

ST BURCHARD, Bp. of Würzburg, Conf.

c. A.D. 754

After the death of his parents the priest Burchard left his home in Wessex to be a missionary in Germany, and offered his services to his fellow-countryman St Boniface sometime after the year 732. Before long St Boniface consecrated St Burchard as the first bishop of Würzburg in Franconia, where St Kilian had preached the word of life and suffered martyrdom about fifty years before. This whole country profited by his apostolic labours for five or six years, and then he visited Rome to report to the Holy See the progress of his diocese. Soon after he was appointed by Pepin the Short to go with St Fulrad, Abbot of Saint-Denis, to lay before Pope St Zachary the question of the succession to the throne of the Franks, and brought back a reply favourable to the ambitions of Pepin. Burchard obtained from the Pope permission to venerate St Kilian and translated his relics to the cathedral of St Saviour, to which he attached a Benedictine monastery ; he also founded the abbey of St Andrew in Würzburg, which afterwards bore his own name. Excessive fatigues having exhausted his strength, with the consent of King Pepin and the approbation of St Lullus (St Boniface having gone to preach in Friesland) he resigned his bishopric to a monk of Fritzlar about 753. Retiring to Hohenburg (Homburg on Maine), he spent the remaining part of his life there with six fervent monks. He died on February 9, 754, and was buried near the relics of St Kilian. Hugh, Bishop of Würzburg, made a solemn translation of his relics, and October 14, the day on which this ceremony was performed, has ever since been his principal festival.

Two medieval Latin Lives are preserved to us, and, strange to say, the second, though two or three centuries later and abounding in fictitious incidents, preserves more data of historical value than the other. The former is printed in the *Acta Sanctorum*, October, vol. vi ; the latter, which seems to have been written by Engelhard, who later became abbot of the monastery of St Burchard, has been well edited in a brochure, *Vita sancti Burkardi* (1911), by F. J. Bendel, who has enriched the text with an introduction and commentary in German. Several articles dealing with St Burchard have been published by Bendel and others in the *Archiv. des hist. Vereins d. Unterfranken*, notably a paper upon the death of the saint in vol. lxviii (1930), pp. 377–385.

ST DOMINIC LORICATUS, Conf.

A.D. 1060

The severity with which this young man condemned himself to penance for a crime which was not his own is a reproach to those who, after offending God with full knowledge and through malice, expect pardon without considering the conditions which true repentance requires. Dominic's parents aspired to an ecclesiastical state for their son, and he was promoted to priest's orders while under the canonical age, the dispensation being obtained by his father from the bishop by means of a bribe. When the young priest came to the knowledge of this crime, condemned by the divine law and punished with severe penalties and censures by the canons of the Church, he was struck with remorse and could not, it is said, be induced again to approach the altar to say Mass or exercise any other sacerdotal function. In Umbria at this time, amidst the Apennine mountains, a holy man called John of Montefeltro led a most austere life as a hermit, with whom in eighteen different cells lived as many fervent disciples who had put themselves under his direction. Dominic repaired to this superior, and begged with great humility to be admitted into the company of these anchorites. He obtained his request, and by the extraordinary austerity of his penance gave proof how deep the spirit of sorrow was with which his heart was pierced. After some years he changed his abode in 1044, retiring to the hermitage of Fonte Avellano, which St Peter Damian then governed according to the Rule of St Benedict. The abbot, who had been long accustomed to meet with examples of heroic penance, was astonished at the fervour of this new penitent. Dominic wore next his skin a rough iron coat of mail (from which he was surnamed *Loricatus, i.e.* "the Mailed"), and which he never put off except to receive the discipline or because of necessity; he further burdened his limbs with chains. The physical mortifications of St Dominic Loricatus were altogether extraordinary. The earlier penitential discipline of the Church having by that time fallen into desuetude, it had become a practice of many penitents to substitute voluntary flagellation, counting stripes self-inflicted whilst the person recited thirty psalms as equal to one year of canonical penance. Thus the whole psalter, accompanied with about fifteen thousand stripes, was esteemed equivalent to five years of canonical penance. Dominic was indefatigable in this penitential practice, which was entirely "unofficial" and drew its chief merit from the spirit of compunction from which it sprang. He is said to have habitually gained in this fashion one hundred years of indulgence in a week, and in a Lent one thousand years, hardly remitting his psalms or his discipline day or night, till he fell asleep with fatigue. He ate as little as was allowed, and if in sickness he was induced to mix a little wine with water, he would never continue this custom after he had recovered his health, even in old age. When he had loaded himself with his cuirass and chains and iron rings he would make numerous prostrations or stand with arms extended cross-wise, until the weight dragging on his limbs proved too much for him. And these practices he continued up to his death, which occurred a year after he had been appointed prior of a hermitage founded by St Peter Damian at Frontale, near San Severino. The last night of his life St Dominic recited Matins and Lauds with his brethren, and expired whilst they sung Prime, on October 14, 1060.

Little or nothing is known of this saint beyond what we learn from St Peter Damian. All that is of value has been gathered up in the article devoted to St Dominic in the *Acta Sanctorum*, October, vol. vi.

OCTOBER 15

ST TERESA, VIRG.

A.D. 1582

ST TERESA, one of the greatest, most attractive, and widely appreciated women whom the world has ever known, and the only one to whom the title Doctor of the Church is popularly, though not officially, applied, speaks thus of her own parents : " The having of virtuous parents and such as live in the fear of God, together with those favours which I received from His divine Majesty, had been able to have made me good, if I had not been so very wicked. My father delighted in reading good books, and used to have them in Spanish that so his children might also read them. . . . He was a man of much charity towards poor people, and compassion towards the sick. He was a man of much truth. My mother was also enriched with many virtues, and she passed through this life of hers with grievous sickness. . . . She was of a most sweet disposition and much understanding." The one was Don Alonso Sanchez de Capeda, the other Doña Beatrice Davila y Ahumada, his second wife, who bore him nine children ; there were three children by his first marriage, and of this large family St Teresa says, " all, through the goodness of God, were like our parents in being virtuous, except myself." She was born at Avila in Castile on March 28, 1515, and when only seven took great pleasure in the lives of the saints and other pious books, in which she spent much time with a brother called Rodrigo, who was near the same age. They were much impressed by the thought of eternity, and they used to repeat often together, " For ever, for ever, for ever," admiring the victories of the saints and the everlasting glory which they possess ; " For ever they shall see God." The martyrs seemed to them to have bought Heaven very cheaply by their torments, and after many conferences together on this subject they resolved to go into the country of the Moors, in hopes of dying for their faith. They set out secretly, praying as they went that God would inspire them with His love that they might lay down their lives for Christ. But when they had got as far as Adaja they were met by an uncle, and brought back to their frightened mother, who reprimanded them; whereupon Rodrigo laid all the blame on his sister. Teresa and the same little brother then wanted to become hermits at home, and built themselves hermitages with piles of stones in the garden, but could never finish them. Teresa sought to be much alone, and had in her room a picture of our Saviour discoursing with the Samaritan woman at the well, before which she often repeated the words, " Lord, give me of that water that I may not thirst," meaning that of His grace and love. Her mother died when she was fourteen, and " as soon as I began to understand how great a loss I had sustained by losing her, I was very much afflicted; and so I went before an image of our Blessed Lady and besought her with many tears that she would vouchsafe to be my mother." Teresa adds that she did this with great simplicity, and that she was later indebted to our Lady's intercession for deliverance from great danger. Here she refers to nothing worse than a brief period of somewhat relaxed fervour, due to her liking for tales of chivalry, which she had inherited from Doña Beatrice. Visits from a certain girl-cousin about this time encouraged the interest, and Teresa and Rodrigo began to spend many hours reading romances and trying to write them themselves. " These tales," she says in the *Autobiography*, " did not fail to cool my good desires, and were the cause of my falling insensibly into other defects. I was so enchanted that I could not be content if I had not some new tale in my hands. I began to imitate the fashions, to take delight in being well dressed, to have great care of my hands, to make use of perfumes, and to affect all the vain trimmings which my position in the world allowed." The change in Teresa was sufficiently notice-able to disturb the mind of her father and, not being able to forbid this vain relative his house, he placed his daughter, who was then fifteen years of age, in a convent of Augustinian nuns in Avila where many young women of her rank were educated. Teresa found separa-tion from her companions grievous; but from the precautions which her father had taken she realised that her danger had been greater than she imagined.

After a year and a half spent in this convent, Teresa fell danger-ously sick, and her father took her home. When she had recovered, she went to her eldest sister in the country, and calling to see an uncle, her father's brother, stayed with him for some time. His name was Peter Sanchez de Cepeda, a widower, and a very prudent and pious man. He gave several books to Teresa to read, and his speech was most commonly of God and of the vanity of the world. When she returned to her father's house she began for some time to deliberate with herself seriously about undertaking the religious life, in regard to which she was moved both by emotional attraction and repulsion. It was by the reading of a book that she was enabled to make up her mind and to fix her will, and this book was, very characteristically, the Letters of St Jerome, whose realism and fire found an answering echo in her Castilian spirit. She told her father that she wished to become a nun, but he would by no means give his consent : after his death she might dispose of herself as she pleased. Fearing from former experience she might again relapse, though she felt a severe interior conflict in leaving her father, she went secretly to the convent of the Incarnation of the Carmelite nuns outside the walls of Avila, where her great friend, Sister Jane Suarez, lived. " I remember . . . that whilst I was going out of my father's house, I believe the sharpness of sense will not be greater in the very instant or agony of my death than it was then. . . . There was no such love of God in me at that time as was able to quench that love which I bore to my father and my friends." She was then twenty years old and, the step being taken, Don Alonso ceased to oppose it. A year later she was professed. An illness, which seized her before her profession, increased very much after it, and her father got her removed out of her convent, in which the law of inclosure was not then established. Sister Jane Suarez bore her company, and she remained partly at her sister's in the country and partly at Bazeda almost a year, in the hands of certain physicians. Their treatment only made her worse (she seems to have been suffering from malignant malaria), and she could take no rest either day or night. She was also oppressed with a profound sadness of mind. Her father after this caused her to be brought to his own house, where the doctors gave her up and she got worse and worse. At length she lay nearly four days in a trance or coma, during which time it was expected that every moment would be her last. Under these afflictions she was helped by the prayer which she had then begun to use. When she was taken into the country her devout uncle Peter put into her hands a little book of Father Francis de Osuna, called the *Third Spiritual Alphabet*, treating of the prayer of recollection and quiet. Taking this book for her guide she applied herself to mental prayer according to the manner prescribed in it, and progressed towards the prayer of quiet (in which the soul rests in the divine contemplation, so as to forget all earthly things) and sometimes, though not for a longer space than an *Ave Maria* at a time, she was granted prayer of union, in which all the powers of the soul are absorbed in God. However, for want of an experienced instructor she made little solid progress and was not able to hold any discourse in her understanding or to meditate without a book without her mind being immediately distracted. After three years' suffering she was restored to her health.

Her prudence and charity and, not least, her personal charm, gained her the esteem of all that knew her, and an affectionate and grateful disposition inclined her freely to return the civilities which others showed her. Finding herself a success in society, she began to take delight in it, and lost that love of retirement which is the soul of a religious or interior life. By an irregular custom of her convent quite common in Spain in those days, visitors of all kinds were freely received and mixed with, so giving opportunity to this inclination, and Teresa spent much time in conversing with seculars in the parlour of the monastery, and she contracted an intimacy with one whose company was particularly dangerous to her. She began to neglect mental prayer, and persuaded herself that this was a part of humility, as her dissipated life rendered her unworthy to converse so much or so familiarly with God. She also said to herself that there could be no danger of sin in what so many others, more virtuous than she, did. One day whilst she was talking with an acquaintance she seemed to see our Lord, who represented Himself to the eyes of her soul as testifying that her conduct displeased Him. She took this for the effect of imagination, and still persuaded herself that there could be no harm in so much exterior conversation and that no damage resulted from it. Her father had been induced by her, when she first learned the use of mental prayer, to apply himself earnestly to it, and he often called to see her and to converse with her on spiritual things. He thought she still practised mental prayer as she had formerly done, when in fact she had lived a year or more without it and in that state of dissipation. Finding her father's mistake, she disabused him, telling him she no longer used mental prayer, for which she alleged the infirmities to which she was subject. But she adds, " This reason of bodily weakness was not a sufficient cause to make me give over so good a thing, which requires not corporal strength, but only love and custom. In the midst of sickness the best of prayer may be made; and it is a mistake to think that it can only be made in solitude." Her father looked upon her excuse as just, and pitied her because she had enough to do to attend the choir. Soon after her father died, and his confessor, a Dominican friar, pointed out to Teresa the dangerous state she was in. At his instance she returned to the practice of private prayer and never again abandoned it. But she had not yet the courage to follow God perfectly, or entirely to renounce dissipating her time and gifts. During all these years of wavering and yet of gradually increasing strength and growing purpose, St Teresa tells us she never tired of listening to sermons, " however bad they were " ; but in prayer her thoughts were " more busied about desiring that the hour resolved to be spent in prayer might come quickly to an end, still listening when the clock would strike, than upon better things." Becoming more and more convinced of her own unworthiness, she had recourse to the two great penitents, St Mary Magdalen and St Augustine, and with them were associated two events decisive in fixing her will upon the pursuit of religious perfection. One was the reading of St Augustine's *Confessions :* the other was a movement to penitence before a picture of our suffering Lord, in which " I felt St Mary Magdalen come to my assistance . . . . from that day I have gone on improving much ever since in my spiritual life."

After she had finally withdrawn herself from the pleasures of social intercourse and other occasions of dissipation and faults (which she exceedingly exaggerated), St Teresa was favoured by God very frequently with the prayer of quiet, and also with that of union, which latter sometimes continued a long time with great increase of heavenly joy and love, and God began to visit her with intellectual visions and interior locutions. The warning of certain women who had been miserably duped by imagination and the Devil much impressed her and, though she was persuaded her favours were from God, she was perplexed with these fears and consulted so many persons that, though binding them to secrecy, the affair was divulged abroad, to her mortification and confusion. One person to whom she spoke was a gentleman of the town named Francis de Salsedo, a married man who was an example of virtue to the whole country. He introduced to her Dr. Daza, a learned and virtuous priest, who, after an examination from what she declared of herself, judged her to be deluded by the Devil, saying that such divine favours were not consistent with a life so full of imperfections as she claimed hers to be. Teresa was alarmed and not satisfied, and Don Francis (to whom the saint says she owed her salvation and her comfort) bade her not be discouraged. He recommended that she should consult one of the fathers of the newly formed Society of Jesus. A father of the Society visited her, to whom she made a general confession in which, with her sins, she gave him an account of all the particulars through the course of her whole life relating to her manner of prayer and her extraordinary favours. The father assured her these were divine graces, but told her she had neglected to lay the true founda-tion of an interior life by the practice of a universal self-denial and mortification. On his advice, though he judged her experiences in prayer to be from God, she endeavoured for two months to resist and reject them. But her resistance was in vain. St Francis Borgia, at that time commissary general of the Jesuits in Spain, coming to Avila, he spoke with Teresa and assured her without hesitation that the Spirit of God was the author of her prayer. He commended her resistance for a trial during the two months past, but advised her not to resist any elevation if our Lord was pleased to visit her so in prayer, provided it was quite unsought by herself. Another Jesuit, Father Balthasar Alvarez, pointed out certain habits contrary to her perfect sanctification, especially in her remaining still too desirous of the satisfaction of pleasant, witty, and learned conversation. He told her she would do well to beg of God that He would direct her to do what was most pleasing to Him, and for that purpose to recite every day the *Veni Creator Spiritus.* She did so, and one day whilst she was reciting that hymn she was seized with a rapture, in which she heard these words spoken to her within her soul, " I will not have you hold conversation with men, but with angels." The saint afterwards had frequent experience of such interior speeches and explains how they are even more distinct and clear than those which men hear with their bodily ears, and how they are also operative, producing in the soul the strongest impressions and sentiments of virtue, and filling her with an assurance of their truth, with joy and with peace. Whilst Father Balthasar Alvarez was her director she suffered grievous persecutions for three years and, during two of them, extreme desolation of soul intermixed with gleams of spiritual comfort and enlightenment. It was her desire that all her heavenly communications should be kept secret, but they became a common subject in conversation and she was censured and ridiculed as deluded or an hypocrite. A confessor whom St Teresa went to during the absence of Father Balthasar told her that her prayer was an illusion, and commanded her when she saw any vision, to make the sign of the cross and to repel it as if it were an evil spirit. She assures us that these visions and raptures carried with them their own evidence and demonstration, so that whilst they continued it was impossible for her to harbour the least doubt but they were from God. Nevertheless, she knew them to be subordinate to the ordinary means which God has established to conduct our souls to Him, and therefore in simplicity she obeyed this order of her confessor. Pope Gregory XV in the bull of canonisation commends her obedience as the test of her spirit and of her visions : " She was wont to say that she might be deceived in discerning visions and revelations, but could not in obeying superiors."

Father Balthasar Alvarez, who was a good man but exceedingly timorous, durst not oppose the tide of disapproval, though he continued to hear her confessions. In 1557 St Peter of Alcantara, of the Franciscans of the Observance, came to Avila, and of course visited the famous, or notorious, Carmelite. Few saints have been more experienced in an interior life, or better versed in the supernatural gifts of prayer than he was, and he discovered in Teresa most certain marks of the graces of the Holy Ghost. He expressed great compassion for her sufferings from the contradictions and slanders of even good men and learned doctors, and publicly declared that, except the truths of faith, nothing appeared to him more evident than that her soul was conducted by the Spirit of God; but he foretold that she was not come to an end of her persecutions and sufferings. If the various proofs by which it pleased God to try Teresa served only to purify her virtue, the heavenly communications with which she was favoured served continually to humble and fortify her soul, to give her a strong disrelish of the things of this life, and to fire her with the desire of possessing God. In raptures she was sometimes lifted in the air, of which she gives a careful description, and adds that God " seems not content with drawing the soul to Himself, but He must needs draw up the very body too, even whilst it is mortal and compounded of so unclean a clay as we have made it by our sins." During these raptures or ecstasies the greatness and goodness of God, the excess of His love, the sweetness of His service, and such great truths are placed in a great light and made sensibly manifest to the soul; all which she understands with a clearness which can be in no way expressed. The contempt of this world and the desire of Heaven with which these visions inspired her could not be declared. " Hence also," she says, " I lost the fear of death, of which I had formerly a great apprehension." During this time took place such extraordinary manifestations as spiritual espousals, mystical marriage, and the piercing (*transverberatio*) of the saint's heart. Of this last she gives the following account : " I saw an angel very near me, towards my left side, in a corporal form (which is not usual with me ; for though angels are often represented to me, it is only by the intellectual vision). This angel appeared rather little than big, and very beautiful ; his face was so shining that he seemed to be one of those highest angels called seraphim, who appear to be all on fire with divine love. He had in his hand a long golden dart, and at the end of the point methought there was a little fire : and I conceived that he thrust it several times through my heart after such a manner that it passed through my very bowels ; and when he drew it out, methought it pulled them out with it and left me wholly on fire with a great love of God." She says that this caused great pain in her soul, which also affected her body ; but it was accompanied with exceeding great delight, and whilst it continued she was like one transported, not caring to see or speak but only to burn and be consumed with that pain, which was a greater happiness to her than any that can be found in created things. The saint's desire to die that she might be speedily united to God was tempered by her desire to suffer for His love, and she writes, " It seems to me there is no reason why I should live but only to suffer, and accordingly this is the thing which I beg with most affection of God. Sometimes I say to Him with my whole heart : Lord, either to die or to suffer ; I beg no other thing for myself." After the death of St Teresa her heart was found to bear a long and deep mark, as it were a scar, and her response to this remarkable happening was in the following year (1560) to make a vow that she would in everything do always that which seemed to be the most perfect and best pleasing to God. To bind oneself by vow to such an undertaking is an action so humanly rash that it can only be justified by the successful keeping of it. St Teresa kept her vow.

The account which this saint has given in her *Autobiography* of these visions, revelations, and raptures carries with it the intrinsic marks of evidence. It is not possible attentively to peruse it, and not be convinced of the sincerity of the author by the genuine simplicity of the style, scrupulous nicety, and fear of exaggerating the least circumstance, characteristics which appear in all her writings. Her doctrine is called by the Church, in the prayer of her festival, *cœlestis*, " heavenly." It is conformable to the spirit of the saints, and in it secret places of the soul are laid open. The most elusive matters, which experience alone can teach but no words utter, are explained with greater perspicuity than the subject seems capable of bearing ; and this was done by a relatively uneducated woman, in the straightforward vernacular of Castile, which she had learnt " in her mother's womb," the rough tongue of the soldiers and dames of Avila ; a woman who wrote alone, without the assistance of books, without study or acquired abilities, who entered upon the recital of divine things with humility and reluctance, submitting everything without reserve to the judgement of her confessor, and much more to that of the Church, and complaining that by this task she was hindered from spinning. She undertook to write about herself only out of obedience to her Dominican confessor : " Obedience is put to the test in different commands," she said. It is well known that there is nothing more difficult than for a man to speak at length of himself without showing self-complacency and symptoms of secret self-love and pride, even in a studied attempt to suppress them, by colouring or passing over his own failures or weakness, and in displaying covertly his own talents and advantages. And nothing seems a clearer proof how perfectly St Teresa was dead to herself by sincere humility than the artless manner in which she constantly, and not on certain occasions only, speaks of herself with depreciation. In her writings she everywhere speaks with respect of her persecutors, and, putting the best construction on their words and actions, represents them always as good servants of God and her true friends. When she was attacked at Seville and someone asked her how she could hold her peace, she answered with a smile, " No music is so pleasing to my ears. They have reason for what they say, and speak the truth." Her patience under sickness, provocation and disappointment; her firm confidence in God and in her crucified Redeemer under all storms and difficulties; and her undaunted courage in bearing incredible hardship and persecution and dangers are a practical commentary on the words. She remained so long imperfect in virtue, and was slow in completing the victory over herself, because for some time she was not persevering and unwearying in prayer. The necessity of the spirit of prayer, the way it is practised, and the nature of its fruits are set out incomparably in her own writings. These works were written during the years in which she was actively engaged in the most difficult business of founding convents of reformed Carmelite nuns and thus, quite apart from their nature and contents, are significant of St Teresa's vigour, industry, and power of recollection. She wrote the *Way of Perfection* for the direction of her nuns, and the book of *Foundations* for their edification and encouragement, but the *Interior Castle* may be said to have been written for the instruction of the Church. In it she is a doctor of the spiritual life. " She lays bare in her writings," says the over-critical Abbé Baillet, " the most impenetrable secrets of true wisdom in what we call mystical theology, of which God has given the key to a very small number of favoured servants. This may somewhat diminish our surprise that an unlearned woman should have expounded what the greatest doctors never attained, because God employs in His works what instruments He wills, and we may say that the Holy Ghost had the principal share in the works of St Teresa."

The Carmelite nuns, and indeed those of other orders as well, were very much relaxed from their early austerity and enthusiasm in sixteenth-century Spain. We have seen how the parlour at Avila was a sort of social centre for the ladies and gentlemen of the town, and that the nuns went out of their enclosure on the slightest pretext; those who wanted an easy and sheltered life without responsibilities could find it in a convent. The size of the communities was both a cause and an effect of this mitigation ; there were 180 nuns in the convent at Avila, and the result afterwards wrung from St Teresa the cry, " Experience has taught me what a house full of women is like. God preserve us from such a state ! " This state of things was taken for granted, there was no rebuking consciousness among religious at large that the nature of their daily life fell far short of what was required by their profession according to the mind of their founders, so that when a Carmelite of the Incarnation house at Avila began to talk of the possibility of the foundation of a small community bound to a more perfect way of life the idea struck St Teresa not as a very natural one but as an inspiration from Heaven. She determined to undertake the establishment of such a reformed convent, and received a promise of immediate help from a wealthy widow, Doña Guiomar de Ulloa. The project was approved by St Peter of Alcantara, St Louis Bertrand, and the Bishop of Avila, and the saint procured the licence and approbation of Father Angelo de Salazar, provincial of the Carmelites ; but no sooner had the project taken shape than he was obliged by the objections which were raised against it to recall his licence. A storm fell upon Teresa through the violent opposition which was made by all her fellow-nuns, the nobility, the magistrates, and the people. Father Ybañez, a Dominican, secretly encouraged her, and assisted Doña Guiomar to pursue the enterprise, together with Doña Juana de Ahumada, a married sister of the saint, who began with her husband to build a new convent at Avila in 1561, but in such a manner that the world took it for a house intended for herself and her family. Their son Gonzalez, a little child, was crushed by a wall which fell upon him while playing around this building, and he was carried without giving any signs of life to Teresa, who, taking him in her arms, prayed to God and after some minutes restored him perfectly sound to his mother, as was proved in the process of the saint's canonisation. The child used afterwards often to tell his aunt that it was her duty to secure his salvation by her prayers, seeing it was owing to her that he was not long ago in Heaven. Another apparently strong wall of this house falling in the night as soon as it was finished, many were discouraged and Teresa's brother-in-law was refusing to pay the men who had built it ; but she assured him that it was the mischief of evil spirits and directed that the workmen should be paid. Countess Louisa de la Cerda, sister of the Duke of Medina Celi, being in the deepest affliction for the loss of her husband, prevailed upon the provincial of the Carmelites to send an order to Teresa to come to her at Toledo, for the goodness and sympathy of the saint were already noised abroad above the din of local controversy. She stayed

in her house for six months, making new friends and working quietly
for the accomplishment of her plans.　She here modified none of
her usual mortifications and devotions, and her provincial no sooner
released her from the obedience which he had imposed on her, and
left it to her choice, either to go or stay, than she returned to her
monastery of the Incarnation at Avila.　The same evening that she
arrived the Pope's brief for the erection of her new convent was
brought thither.　St Peter of Alcantara, Don Francis de Salsedo,
and Dr. Daza had persuaded the bishop to concur, and the new
monastery of Saint Joseph was established by his authority, and on
St Bartholomew's day in 1562 was made subject to him, the Blessed
Sacrament being placed in the chapel and the saint's niece and three
other novices taking the habit.　Hereupon great excitement broke
out in the town.　That very afternoon the prioress of the Incarnation
sent for Teresa from St Joseph's, and she went in some trepidation,
" thinking they would certainly put me in prison."　She had to give
an explanation of her conduct before the prioress and Father Angelo,
the provincial, in which, she admits, they had a certain case against
her.　However, Father Angelo promised she should return to
St Joseph's when the popular excitement had died down.　The
people of Avila looked on the new foundation as uncalled for, were
nervous of suspicious novelties, and feared that an unendowed convent would be too heavy a burden on the town.　The mayor and
magistrates would have had the new monastery demolished, had not
Father Bañez, a learned Dominican, dissuaded them from so hasty
a resolution.　Amidst slanders and persecution the saint remained
calm, recommending to God His own work, and was comforted by our
Lord in a vision.　In the meantime Don Francis de Salsedo and other
friends of the new establishment deputed a priest named Gonzalez
de Aranda to go before the King's council to plead for the convent,
the two Dominicans, Ybañez and Bañez, reasoned with the bishop
and the provincial, the public clamour abated, and at the end of four
months Father Angelo, the provincial, sent Teresa to the new convent, whither she was followed by four fervent nuns from the old
house.　One of these was chosen prioress, but the bishop soon after
obliged Teresa to take upon herself that charge.　Strict enclosure
was established with almost perpetual silence, and the most austere
poverty, at first without any settled revenues ; the nuns wore habits
of coarse serge, sandals instead of shoes (whence they are called
" discalced "), and were bound to perpetual abstinence.　At first
St Teresa would not admit more than thirteen nuns to a community,
but in those which should be founded with revenues, and not to
subsist solely on alms, she afterwards allowed twenty-one to be

received. The prior general of the Carmelites, John Baptist Rubeo of Ravenna, who resided at Rome, came into Spain and to Avila in 1567, and was charmed with the conversation and sanctity of the foundress and with the wise regulations of the house. He gave St Teresa full authority to found other convents upon the same plan, in spite of the fact that St Joseph's had been established without his knowledge or leave, and she even received from him a licence for the foundation of two houses of reformed friars (" Contemplative Carmelites ") in Castile. St Teresa passed five years in her convent of St Joseph with thirteen fervent nuns, whom she discreetly exercised in every sort of religious observance, being herself the first and most diligent, not only at prayer but also in spinning, sweeping the house, or any other work. " I think that they were the most quiet years of my life," she writes. " I there enjoyed the tranquillity and calmness which my soul has often since longed for. . . . His divine Majesty sent us what was necessary without asking, and if at any time we were in want (which was very seldom) the joy of these holy souls was so much the greater." She is not content with vague generalities, but records such enticing details as of the nun who obediently planted the cucumber horizontally and of the water which was piped into the house from a source that the plumbers said was too low. In August 1567, she went to Medina del Campo and, having conquered many difficulties, founded there a second convent. The Countess de la Cerda earnestly desired to found a convent of this order at her town of Malagon, and Teresa went to see her about it, incidentally paying a visit to Madrid which the saint describes as " boring." When this convent was safely launched she went to Valladolid, and there founded another nunnery. St Teresa made her next foundation at Toledo. She met great obstacles, and had no more than four or five ducats when she began. But she said, " Teresa and this money are indeed nothing : but God, Teresa, and these ducats suffice." Here a young woman who had gained a reputation of virtue petitioned to be admitted to the habit, and added : " I will bring with me my Bible."—" What ! " said the saint, " your Bible ? Do not come to us. We are poor women who know nothing but how to spin, and to do as we are told." At Medina del Campo she had met with two Carmelite friars who were desirous to embrace her reform, Antony-of-Jesus (de Heredia), then prior there, and John-of-the-Cross. As soon, therefore, as an opportunity offered itself, she founded a convent for men at a village called Duruelo, in 1568, and in 1569 a second at Pastrana, both in extreme poverty and austerity. After these two foundations St Teresa left to St John-of-the-Cross the care of all other foundations that should be made for men. At Pastrana she also established a convent for nuns. When Don Ruy Gomez de Silva, who had founded these convents at Pastrana, died his widow wished to make her religious profession in this nunnery, but claimed many exemptions and would still maintain the dignity of princess. Teresa, finding she could not be brought to the humility of her profession, ordered the nuns, lest relaxations should be introduced, to leave that house to her and retire to a new convent in Segovia. In 1570 St Teresa founded a convent at Salamanca where with another nun she took possession of a house which had been occupied by some students, who had had "little or no regard for cleanliness." It was a large, rambling, and eerie place, and when night fell the other nun became very nervous. As they lay down on their piles of straw ("the first furniture I provided when I founded monasteries, for having this I reckoned I had beds"), St Teresa asked her what she was looking about at. "I was wondering," was the reply, "were I to die here now what you would do alone with a corpse?" St Teresa admits the remark startled her, for, though she did not fear dead bodies, they always caused her "a pain at her heart." But she only replied, "I will think about that when it happens, sister. For the present, let us go to sleep." In July of this year she had a revelation while at prayer of the martyrdom at sea of Blessed Ignatius Azevedo and his thirty-nine companions of the Society of Jesus, among whom was her own relative Francis Perez Godoy. She had a clear vision as it were both to her eyes and ears of what took place and she at once told it in detail to Father Balthazar Alvarez. When the news of the massacre reached Spain a month later he recognised the minute accuracy of the account already given to him by St Teresa.

At this time Pope St Pius V appointed visitors apostolic to inquire into relaxations in religious orders with a view to reform, and he named a well-known Dominican, Peter Fernandez, to be visitor to the Carmelites of Castile. At Avila he not surprisingly found great fault with the convent of the Incarnation and to remedy its abuses he sent for St Teresa, who had formerly consulted him in her doubts, and told her she was to take charge of it as prioress. It was doubly distasteful to her to be separated from her own daughters and to be put from outside at the head of a house which opposed her activities with jealousy and warmth. The nuns at first refused to obey her; some of them went into hysterics at the very idea. She told them that she came not to coerce or instruct but to serve and to learn from the least among them. "My mothers and sisters, our Lord has sent me to this house by the voice of obedience, to fill an office of which I was far from thinking and for which I am quite unfitted. . . . I come solely to serve you. . . . Do not fear my rule. Though I have lived among and exercised authority over those Carmelites who are discalced, by God's mercy I know how to rule those who are not of their number." Having by such sweetness and modesty won the sympathy and affection of the community, she had less difficulty in establishing discipline according to its rules. Too frequent callers were forbidden (to the annoyance of certain gentlemen of Avila), the finances of the house were put in order, and a more truly claustra spirit reigned—a characteristically Teresian performance. At the end of the three years of her office the nuns much desired to detain her, but she was appointed prioress of her own convent of St Joseph in the same town. When making a foundation at Veas St Teresa met for the first time Father Jerome Gratian, and was easily persuaded by him to extend her activities to Seville; he had just preached the Lent there, and was himself a friar of the reform. With the exception of the first, no one of her convents was so hard to establish as this. Among the difficulties was a disappointed novice who delated the new nuns to the Inquisition as *Illuminati*, and worse.

The Carmelite friars in Italy had, in the meantime, become afraid of the progress of the Spanish reform lest, as one of their number said, they should one day be compelled to set about reforming themselves, a fear which was shared by their mitigated brethren in Spain. The prior general, Father Rubeo, who had hitherto favoured St Teresa, now sided with the objectors and upheld a general chapter at Placentia which passed several decrees gravely restricting the reform. The new nuncio apostolic, Philip de Sega, dismissed Father Gratian from his office of visitor to the Discalced Carmelites, and St John-of-the-Cross was imprisoned in a monastery; St Teresa herself was told to choose one of her convents to which to retire and to abstain from further foundations. While recommending her undertaking with many tears to God for the honour of His divine name, she did not disdain to avail herself of the help of her friends in the world. These interested the king, Philip II, on her behalf, and he, on the information of certain Dominican friars of great reputation, warmly espoused her cause and that of her establishments. The nuncio, Mgr. de Sega, was called before him and sternly rebuked for his activities against the discalced friars and nuns, and in 1580 an order was obtained at Rome to exempt the Reformed from the jurisdiction of the mitigated Carmelites, so that each should have their own provincials. Father Gratian was elected for the Reformed. "The separation has given me one of the greatest pleasures and consolations I could receive in this life, for the order has had to endure more troubles, persecutions, and trials in twenty-five years than I have space to tell. Now we are all at peace, Calced and Discalced, having no one to disturb us in the service of our Lord."

St Teresa was certainly a person endowed with great natural talents. The sweetness of her temperament, the affectionate tenderness of her heart, and the liveliness of her wit and imagination, poised by an uncommon maturity of judgement and what we should now call psychological insight, gained the respect of all and the love of most. It was no mere flight of fancy which caused the seventeenth-century poet Crashaw (who himself died a canon of Loreto) to refer both to " the eagle " and to " the dove " in St Teresa. She stood up when need be to high authorities, ecclesiastical and civil, and would not bow her head under the blows of the world. It was no hysterical defiance when she bade the prior provincial, Father Angelo, " Beware of fighting against the Holy Ghost " ; it was no authoritarian conceit that made her merciless to a prioress who had made herself unfit for her duties by her austerities. It is as the dove that she writes to her erring nephew, " God's mercy is great in that you have been enabled to make so good a choice and to marry so soon, for you began to be dissipated when you were so young that we might have had much sorrow on your account. From that you see how much I love you." She took charge of this young man's illegitimate daughter, and of his sister, who was seven years old : " We ought always to have a child of this age among us." Her wit and " forthrightness " were sublimely good-tempered, even when she used them, as sword or hammer, to drive in a rebuke. When an indiscreet man praised the beauty of her bare feet she laughed and told him to have a good look at them for he would never see them again. " You know what a number of women are when they get together," or " My children, these are just women's fads," she would say when her subjects were fussy and tiresome. In criticising an essay by her good friend Francis de Salcedo she was quick to point out that " Señor de Salcedo keeps on repeating throughout his paper : ' As St Paul says,' ' As the Holy Ghost says,' and ends up by declaring he has written nothing but nonsense. I shall denounce him to the Inquisition." The quality of St Teresa is seen very clearly in her selection of novices for the new foundations. Her first requirement, even before any promise of a considerable degree of piety, was intelligence. A person can train herself to piety, but more hardly to intelligence, by which quality she meant neither cleverness nor imagination, but a power of good judgement. " An intelligent mind is simple and submissive ; it sees its faults and allows itself to be guided. A mind that is deficient and narrow never sees its faults, even when shown them. It is always pleased with itself and never learns to do right." " Even though our Lord should give this young girl devotion and teach her contemplation, if she has no sense she never will come to have any, and instead of being of use to the community she will be a burden." " May God preserve us from stupid nuns ! " This was her good hard Spanish realism ; nobody was ever less sentimental.

By the time of the definite separation between the two observances of the Carmelite Order in 1580 St Teresa was sixty-five years old and quite broken in health. During her last two years she saw her final foundations, making them sixteen in all, at Soria, Granada, and Burgos. The second of these carried the reform into Portugal, and was made actually by the Venerable Anne-of-Jesus. A cruel trial was reserved for her last days. The will of her uncle Don Lorenzo, whose daughter was prioress at Valladolid, was in dispute and St Teresa was drawn unwillingly into the proceedings. A lawyer was rude to her in person, and to him she said, " Sir, may God return to you the courtesy you have shown to me." But before the conduct of her niece she was speechless and impotent : for the prioress of Valladolid, hitherto an irreproachable religious, showed her aunt the door of the convent of which she was foundress and general superior and told her never more to return to it. St Teresa wrote to Mother Mary-of-St-Joseph, " I beseech you and your daughters not to wish or pray for me to live longer. Ask on the contrary that I may go to my eternal rest, for I can be of no more use to you." The last foundation, at Burgos, was made under difficulties, and when it was achieved in July 1582 St Teresa wished to return to Avila, but was induced to set out for Alva de Tormez, where the Duchess Maria Henriquez was expecting her. Blessed Anne-of-St-Bartholomew describes the journey, not properly prepared for and the foundress so ill that she fainted on the road ; one night they could get no food but a few figs, and when they arrived at Alva St Teresa went straight to bed. Three days later she said to Blessed Anne, " At last, my daughter, the hour of death has come." She received the last sacraments from Father Antony de Heredia, who asked her where she wished to be buried. She only answered, " Is it for me to say ? Will they deny me a little ground for my body here ? " When the Blessed Sacrament was brought in she sat up in bed, helpless though she was, and exclaimed, " O my Lord, now is the time that we may see each other ! " Apparently in wonder at the things her Saviour was showing her, St Teresa-of-Jesus died in the arms of Blessed Anne at nine in the evening of October 4, 1582. The very next day the Gregorian reform of the kalendar came into force and ten days were dropped, so that it was accounted October 15, the date on which her feast was ultimately fixed. Her body was buried at Alva, till in 1585 by a decree of a provincial chapter of the Discalced Carmelites it was secretly removed to Avila. In the following year the Duke of Alva got an order from Rome that it should be returned to Alva de Tormez, and there it remains.

Although the history of St Teresa in the *Acta Sanctorum* occupies almost the whole of a very stout folio volume (October, vol. vii), and although it was compiled by Father Van der Moere less than a century ago, its contents have to a considerable extent been superseded by better edited texts and by fresh material which has since then come to light. Amongst the most important sources of all must always be reckoned the *Autobiography* and the *Book of Foundations*. Both these have been printed in a photographic facsimile from St Teresa's own autograph (1873 and 1880). For scholarly use all her work and correspondence have now been critically edited in Spanish by Padre Silverio, C.D., and occupy nine volumes ; the first six of which, containing the *Obras*, were printed between 1915 and 1919, while the last three, constituting the *Epistolario* (of about 450 letters recognised as authentic) appeared in 1922–1924. Nearly all this material, though often translated from less accurate texts, had previously been accessible both in French and in English ; Mr. David Lewis, Father Benedict Zimmerman, C.D., and the Benedictine nuns of Stanbrook having in this matter rendered great service to English readers. For our knowledge of the character and activities of St Teresa we are also much indebted to her early biographers, notably to three who all knew her intimately in her later years. The first of these was Father Francisco de Ribera, S.J. The Life he wrote was printed in 1590, but the best edition is that edited and copiously annotated by Father Jaime Pons, S.J. (Barcelona, 1908). Another biography was published (1599) by Diego de Yepes, who was also keenly interested in the sufferings of the English Catholics and who afterwards became Bishop of Tarragona. The third was written by St Teresa's chaplain, Julian of Avila, but, the manuscript having been lost sight of, it was only discovered and printed in 1881. Besides these, much information is obtainable from the writings and letters of such prominent friends of the Saint as Father Jerome Gracian, D.C., Blessed Anne-of-St-Bartholomew, and many others.

An English translation of the Autobiography by " W.M." was printed at Antwerp as early as 1611 ; but better from a literary point of view is Sir Tobie Mathew's version, which appeared in 1623 under the title of *The Flaming Heart ; or, The Life of the Glorious St Teresa*. A fuller account, which included some of the saint's writings, began to appear (1669) in more than one volume and was due to Abraham Woodhead. In more modern times we have the *Life and Letters of St Theresa*, 3 vols., by Father Coleridge ; G. Cunninghame Graham, *Santa Teresa* ; D. Lewis and Benedict Zimmerman, *The Life of St Teresa written by herself*, with notes and introduction ; Lady Lovat, *Life of St Teresa* (in substance a translation from the Carmelite French Life) ; H. H. Colville, *Saint Teresa of Spain* ; and J. J. Burke, *St Teresa of Jesus* (noteworthy for its illustrations of the saint's various foundations). To give a catalogue of the shorter biographies, or of those published in French, Spanish, and Italian, would be an endless task. Reference, however, ought to be made to the admirable study by Dr. R. Hoornaert, *Sainte Térèse Écrivain* (Eng. trans. 1931), and to G. Echegoyen, *L'Amour et les Sources térèsiennes* (1922).

ST LEONARD OF VANDŒUVRE, ABBOT AND CONF.

c. A.D. 570

In a footnote to his account of St Leonard of Noblac Alban Butler refers to his contemporary and namesake of Vandœuvre, who introduced monastic life into the valley of the Sarthe. He is supposed to have belonged to the neighbourhood of Tongres and, wandering into Maine in search of solitude, he came to Vandœuvre on the banks of the river and settled at where is now Saint-Léonard-des-Bois. He was befriended by St Innocent, Bishop of Le Mans and a great encourager of monks, and soon Leonard had a number of followers who put themselves under his direction. Eventually they were formed into a community, a monastery was built, and St Leonard was recognized as its founder and abbot. There were some who were ill-disposed towards the new monastery, and these reported to King Clotaire I that Leonard was persuading the king's subjects to alienate their goods and withdraw themselves from their allegiance, claiming plenary authority over them himself. Clotaire sent commissioners to inquire into the matter, and at the very moment of their arrival they witnessed a young nobleman abandon his estate to his relatives and to the poor and receive the monastic habit. The commissioners pointed out to St Leonard that in this way the King was being deprived of the services of valuable men-at-arms. St Leonard answered them by saying that he only taught people to put into practice the words of our Lord Himself, that all things and all earthly ties should be given up to follow Him. The envoys had nothing to say to this and went back to report to Clotaire, who in time withdrew his opposition and even became a patron of St Leonard and his abbey. Among the friends of this saint were St Germanus of Paris and Innocent's successor at Le Mans St Domnolus, in whose arms Leonard died at a great age about the year 570. Some hundred years later his relics were translated to the abbey of Corbigny where they were treasured until their destruction by the Huguenots in 1562.

In the *Acta Sanctorum*, October, vol. vii, a short Life of this saint is printed with the usual commentary. See also the *Dict. Christ. Biog.*, vol. iii, pp. 686–687.

ST THECLA, VIRG. AND ABBESS

c. A.D. 790

St Thecla, whom the Roman Martyrology names to-day, was one of the nuns sent by St Tetta, abbess of Wimborne, into Germany to help in the mission of St Boniface by their prayers and influence. She probably went at the same time as her kinswoman St Lioba, under whom she certainly was for a time at the abbey of Bischofsheim, until St Boniface made her abbess at Ochsenfürt. At the death of St Hadeloga, foundress and first abbess of the nunnery of Kitzingen on the Main, St Thecla was called to preside over that house as well, which she did for many years with conspicuous devotion and holiness. The name Thecla does not appear in the extant list of abbesses of Kitzingen, but it would seem that she is referred to under the name of Heilga, that is, " the Saint." During the Peasants' War of the sixteenth century the relics of St Thecla and her predecessors in the abbey church were shamefully abused and scattered from their shrines.

Both to her spiritual children and to the rough German women among whom they lived the holy abbess ever gave an example of humility, gentleness, and charity. Humility consists in this : that when others humiliate us, we humble ourselves still more ; when others accuse us, we accuse ourselves ; when we are given lowly tasks, we admit that they are what we deserve ; when we are ignored, we do not complain. A religious, or any other person, cannot give a more evident indication of pride than a vain self-confidence in the undertaking of anything or an immodest thrusting forward of one's own opinions. Saint Chantal said that she would have her lips pierced and joined together if thereby the mouths of her religious might be always shut against the least word that would offend against humility. Our aim should be so unwearingly to practise this virtue that it becomes as it were the natural and constant frame of our souls, which no provocation can disturb.

The Bollandists in the *Acta Sanctorum*, October, vol. vii, have brought together a few scattered references to this abbess.

ST EUTHYMIUS THE THESSALONIAN, ABBOT AND CONF.

A.D. 886

This holy monk, venerated principally in Russia, was a Galatian, born at Opso, near Ancyra. He is called " the Thessalonian " because he was eventually buried at Salonika, or " the New," apparently to distinguish him from St Euthymius the Great who lived four hundred years earlier. Euthymius was one of three children in a family of good position, and at his baptism received the name of Nicetas. His father died when the boy was seven and he was brought up by his mother and two sisters. At an early age he married, and had a daughter Anastasia, but when he was still only eighteen, in the year 842, he left his wife and child (in circumstances that, as reported, look curiously like desertion) and entered a *laura* on Mount Olympus in Bithynia. For a time he put himself under the direction of St Joannicius, who was then a monk there, and afterwards of one John, who clothed him in the monastic habit and gave him the name of Euthymius. When he had trained him for a time, John sent him to lead the common life in the monastery of Possidinion, where Euthymius showed himself an exemplary monk and advanced rapidly in the ways of holiness.

When the patriarch of Constantinople, St Ignatius, was driven from his see and Photius intruded in 858, the monks of Possidinion were divided in their allegiance. The abbot Nicholas was loyal to Ignatius and was deposed from his office ; Euthymius followed him and determined to seek a less troubled life in the solitudes of Mount Athos. Before leaving Olympus he asked for and received the " great habit," the outward sign of the highest degree in monasticism to which the Eastern monk can aspire, from an old monk named Theodore. Euthymius was accompanied by one companion, but he was frightened away by the rigours of Athos, and Euthymius sought the company of a hermit already established there, one Joseph. He was a good and straightforward soul, in spite of the fact that he was an Armenian (says the biographer of St Euthymius), and soon the two hermits were engaged in a sort of competitive trial of asceticism. First they fasted for forty days on nothing but vegetables. Then Euthymius suggested that they should stop in their cells for three years, going outside only to gather their nuts and herbs, never speaking to the other hermits and only rarely to one another. At the end of the first year Joseph gave it up, but Euthymius persevered to the end of the period, and when he came out of his seclusion was warmly congratulated by the other brethren. Later he was at Salonika, visiting the tomb of the monk Theodore, who before his death had made a vain attempt to join his disciple on Athos. While in Salonika St Euthymius lived for a time in a tower, from whence he could preach to the crowds who came to him and use his power of exorcism over those who were possessed, while keeping something of the solitude which he loved. Before leaving the city he was ordained deacon. So many visitors came to him on Mount Athos that he fled with two other monks to the small island of Saint Eustratius ; when they were driven out of here by sea-rovers Euthymius rejoined his old friend Joseph and remained with him.

Some time after the death of Joseph St Euthymius was told in a vision that he had contended as a solitary long enough ; he was to move once more, this time to a mountain called Peristera on the east of Salonika. There he would find the ruins of a monastery dedicated in honour of St Andrew, now used for folding sheep : he was to restore and re-people it. Taking with him two monks, Ignatius and Ephrem, he went straight to the place and found as it had been said. At once he set about rebuilding the church and, with the enthusiastic help of the Thessalonians, it was finished, it is said, by 863, less than five years from his leaving Mount Olympus. Dwellings were also made for the monks, who rapidly increased in number and fervour, and St Euthymius was their abbot for fourteen years. Then he paid a visit to his home at Opso and gained there a number of recruits, both male and female, among them his sister Epiphania. Another monastery was built for the women and Epiphania put in charge, with the name of Euthymia. When both houses were thoroughly established St Euthymius handed them over to the Metropolitan of Salonika and went to pass the rest of his days in the solitude of Athos once more. When he knew that death was at hand he summoned his fellow-hermits to celebrate with him the feast of the translation of his patron St Euthymius the Great ; then, having said farewell to them, he departed with the monk George to Holy Island, where five months later he died peacefully on October 15 in the year 886.

The Life of St Euthymius was written by one of his monks at Peristera, Basil by name, who became metropolitan of Salonika. He narrates several miracles of his master, of some of which he was himself a witness and even a beneficiary, and as an example of the saint's gift of prophecy he tells how, while he was in retreat after having been shorn a monk, Euthymius came to him and said, " Though I am utterly unworthy to receive enlightenment from on high, nevertheless, as I am responsible for your direction, God has shown me that love of learning will draw you from the monastery and you will be made an archbishop."—" And later," says Basil, " the call of ambition made me choose the noisy and troubled life of a town before the peace of solitude."

The name of this St Euthymius does not seem to occur in the synaxaries, and, except for a reference under October 15 in Martinov's *Annus ecclesiasticus græco-slavicus*, his existence was hardly known in the West until Père Louis Petit published the Greek text of the Life in the *Revue de l'Orient chrétien*, vol. vi (1903), pp. 155–205 and 503–536. The Life, with the Greek Office for the feast, was also published separately in 1904. The reference to the ' hollow tower ' which he occupied at Salonika shows, as Père Delehaye points out (*Les Saints Stylites*, pp. cxxix–cxxx), that Euthymius was at one time a ' stylite.' See also E. von Dobschütz in the *Byzantinische Zeitschrift*, vol. xviii (1909), pp. 715–716.

OCTOBER 16

ST HEDWIG, Widow

A.D. 1243

HEDWIG (Jadwiga), one of the greatly venerated saints of Poland, was of Moravian descent, daughter of Berthold of Andechs, Duke of Croatia and Dalmatia. She was born at Andechs in Bavaria about the year 1174, one of eight children, and through her sister Gertrude was aunt to St Elizabeth of Hungary. She was placed when very young in the monastery of Hitzingen in Franconia, and taken thence when twelve years old to marry Henry, Duke of Silesia, who was then eighteen and head of the royal Polish family of Piast; but his mother was a German and he was of strong German sympathies. They had seven children, of whom only one, Gertrude, survived her mother, and she became abbess of Trebnitz. Her husband succeeded to his father's dukedom in 1202, and he at once, at Hedwig's persuasion, and upon her yielding into his hands her whole dowry for this purpose, founded the great monastery of Cistercian nuns at Trebnitz, three miles from Breslau, the capital of Silesia. He settled on it the town of Trebnitz, and other estates, endowing it for the maintenance of one thousand persons, of which, in the first foundation, one hundred were nuns; the rest were young women who were to be educated and afterwards provided with competent portions to marry advantageously, or if they were inclined to a monastic state they were at liberty to profess it in this or any other nunnery. This building was begun in 1203, and was carried on fifteen years without interruption, during which time all malefactors in Silesia, instead of other punishments, were condemned to work at it. This was the first convent of women in Silesia, and the first of a large number of monastic establishments by the foundation of which the Duke and Duchess both aided the religious life of their people and spread a Germanic culture over their territories. Among them were houses of Augustinian canons, Cistercian monks, Dominican and Franciscan friars. Henry established the hospital of the Holy Ghost in Breslau and Hedwig one for female lepers at Neumarkt, in which they took a close personal interest. After the birth of her last child Hedwig

218

engaged her husband to agree to a mutual vow of her perpetual continence, which they made before the Bishop of Breslau ; from which time they lived to a considerable extent in different places. Her husband faithfully kept this vow for the thirty years that he lived afterwards, during which time he never wore gold, silver, or purple, and never shaved his beard, from which he was surnamed Henry the Bearded.

Their children were the occasions of a good deal of trouble for them. Gertrude was betrothed to Otto of Wittelsbach, but in 1208 he murdered King Philip of Swabia, whereupon the engagement was broken off and Gertrude later became a nun at Trebnitz. In 1212 Duke Henry made a partition of his duchies between his sons Henry and Conrad, but on terms dissatisfying to Conrad, who was nevertheless his favourite. St Hedwig supported the cause of Henry, which was that of the elder. The two brothers with their factions came to an open rupture, and, notwithstanding their mother's efforts to reconcile them, a battle was fought, in which Henry entirely routed his younger brother's army. Conrad fled, and died soon after from a hunting accident. This was one of those crosses by which the Duchess learned more bitterly to deplore the miseries and blindness of the world, and more perfectly to disengage her heart from its slavery. Whether in prosperity or adversity her whole comfort was in God, and she practised even in her palace greater austerities than many religious in their cloisters. The simplicity which she observed in her dress, even whilst she lived with her husband, showed that she regarded ducal state but lightly. St Hedwig after her separation from her husband carried her love of humility and penance much further in this respect, and wore only clothes of plain grey stuff. Her desire of advancing in perfection made her fix her principal residence near Trebnitz monastery, often retiring into that austere house, where she slept in the dormitory and complied with all the exercises of the community. She wore the same cloak and tunic summer and winter, and underneath a hair-shift, with sleeves of white serge that it might not be seen. With going to church barefoot over ice and snow her feet were often blistered and chilblained, but she carried shoes under her arms, to put on if she met anyone. An abbot once gave her a new pair, insisting that she should wear them, which she promised to do. When he met her some time after she was still unshod, and he asked what had become of them. Hedwig produced them from under her cloak, brand-new. " I always wear them there," she said. After Compline she prolonged her prayers in the church till very late, and from Matins till break of day. Her daughter-in-law testified to the interior joy with which she was often overwhelmed during prayer and the raptures with which she was sometimes favoured, as did Herbold, her confessor, and other observers.

In 1227 Henry the Bearded and Duke Ladislaus of Sandomir met at Gonsawa to plan defence against the Duke of Greater Poland and Swatopluk of Pomerania. They were unexpectedly attacked by Swatopluk, Henry was surprised in a bath, and was seriously wounded, barely escaping with his life. St Hedwig hurried to Gonsawa to nurse him, but he was soon in the field again, fighting with Conrad of Masovia for the territories of Ladislaus, who had been killed. Henry was successful and established himself at Cracow, but he was again surprised, this time while hearing Mass, and was carried off by Conrad to Plock. The faithful Hedwig followed, and induced the two Dukes to come to terms, her two granddaughters being promised in marriage to Conrad's sons. Thus the intervention of Duke Henry's forces was rendered unnecessary, to the great joy of St Hedwig, who could never hear of the effusion of Christian blood without doing all in her power to prevent it. In 1237 the nobles elected a child, Boleslaus V, overlord of Poland, and Henry was appointed regent, but he died in the following year, being succeeded by his son Henry, called " the Good." When the news was brought the nuns at Trebnitz shed many tears. Hedwig was the only person with dry eyes, and comforted the rest : " Would you oppose the will of God ? Our lives are His. Our will is whatever He is pleased to ordain, whether our own death or that of our friends." The serenity of mind and features with which she urged the duty of resignation to the divine will showed still more than her words how perfectly faith and hope triumphed in her soul. From that time she put on the religious habit at Trebnitz, but she did not take the corresponding vows, in order that she might be free to administer her own property in her own way for the relief of the suffering. St Hedwig once got to know a poor old washerwoman who could not say the Our Father, and was very slow at learning it. Hedwig went on patiently teaching her for ten weeks, and even had her into her own room to sleep, so that at every spare moment they could go through it together, until the woman could both repeat and understand it.

In 1240 the Mongol Tartars swept through Ruthenia and Poland. Duke Henry II led his army against them in the plain of Liegnitz, and a great battle was fought near Wahlstatt, in which, it is said, the Tartars used a sort of poison-gas, for " a thick and nauseating smoke, issuing from long copper tubes shaped like serpents, stupefied the Polish forces." In the course of the battle Henry was killed, and his death was known to St Hedwig three days before the news was brought to her. "I have lost my son," she told her companion Dermudis. "He has gone from me like a bird in flight, and I shall never see him again in this life." When the messenger arrived, it was she, the old woman, who comforted the younger ones, Henry's wife Anne and his sister Gertrude. She concealed her grief and controlled her tears : "God has dealt with my son as it has pleased Him. We ought to have no other will than His. I thank Thee, O my God, for having given me such a son, who always loved and honoured me, and never gave me the least pain. To see him alive was my great desire, yet I feel a still greater joy in seeing him by such a death deserve to be for ever united to Thee in the kingdom of Thy glory. O my God, with my whole heart, I commend his soul to Thee." The example of her own faith and hope was honoured by God with the gift of miracles. A nun of Trebnitz who was blind recovered her sight by the blessing of the saint with the sign of the cross, and her biographer gives an account of several other miraculous cures wrought by her and of several predictions, especially of her own death. In her last sickness she insisted on being anointed before any others could be persuaded that she was in danger. She died in October 1243, and was buried at Trebnitz. St Hedwig was canonised by Pope Clement IV in 1267 and is the patron saint of Silesia.

The control and recollection of St Hedwig in the loss of her husband and children were not due to insensibility or the lack of those affections proper to human beings. The affections of good people are the more tender as their charity is more compassionate and more extensive. But a lively consciousness of eternity and of the nothingness of temporal things makes them see this life as a moment, and set no value on anything in it except inasmuch as God, His love and will, and our immortal glory may be concerned in it. Louis of Granada tells us in the Life of Blessed John Avila that the Marchioness of Pliego, when she saw her eldest son delight in nothing but retirement and devotion, used to say that no other pleasure in this world can equal that of a mother who sees her children virtuous. He mentions another lady, likewise a spiritual daughter of that holy man, who when she lost her beloved son said she was not able to express her joy for having sent so dear a saint before her to Heaven. If our grief at such times is ungoverned it may be because our faith is weak, so that it makes but slight impression on our souls.

There is a Latin Life or legend of St Hedwig which seems to have been compiled towards the close of the thirteenth century by an unknown writer who claims to have based his narrative in the main upon memoirs provided by a Cistercian, Brother Engelbert of Leubus. There is a shorter as well as a longer form of the story, which is printed in the *Acta Sanctorum*, October, vol. viii, as well as elsewhere. A MS. copy written in the year 1353 and preserved at Schlackenwert is of great interest on account of the miniatures with which it is decorated. They have often been reproduced, as for example in the book of H. Riesch, *Die hl. Hedwig* (1926). There are several Lives of the Saint in German, *e.g.* by F. H. Görlich (1854), F. Becker (1872), E. Promnitz (1926), K. and F. Metzger (1927), and a few in French, notably that by G. Bazin (1886). See also G. Morin in the *Revue Bénédictine*, vol. vii (1890), pp. 465–469.

SS. MARTINIAN AND OTHERS, MARTS., AND MAXIMA, VIRG.
A.D. 458

After referring to the passion of 270 martyrs who suffered together in Africa, the Roman Martyrology records the martyrdom in the same country of SS. Martinian and Saturian and their two brothers. " Who, in the time of the Vandal persecution under the Arian King Genseric, were the servants of a certain Vandal and were converted to the faith of Christ by their fellow-servant, the holy maiden Maxima. For their constancy in the Catholic faith they were first beaten with knotted whips, which bit to their very bones, by their heretical master. Then, when they had suffered such things for a long time and always appeared unhurt on the next day, they were forced into exile, where they converted many barbarians to the faith of Christ and obtained from the Roman Pontiff a priest and other ministers who baptised them. Then lastly they were made to pass over thorny places in the woods, with their feet bound together and tied to the backs of moving chariots. Maxima, however, after triumphing in several contests, was set free by the power of God and made a good and peaceful end in a monastery, the mother of many virgins."

Victor Vitensis in his history of the Vandal persecution gives an account of these confessors. Martinian, he says, was an armourer, and his master wanted to marry him to Maxima. She dare not refuse, though she had made a vow of virginity, but Martinian respected her vow and they all ran away to a monastery, from whence they were brought back and savagely beaten because they would not receive Arian baptism. On the death of their master they were given by his widow to another Vandal, who released Maxima and sent the three men to a Moorish chief. It was here that they made converts and sent for a priest (not to Rome but to the nearest Roman town), and in consequence Genseric ordered them to be dragged to death. Their feast is observed in the province of Algiers.

This group of martyrs is dealt with in the *Acta Sanctorum* for October, vol. vii, part 2. The only evidence of value is that of Victor of Vita.

ST GALL, Conf.
A.D. 641 OR 645

Among the eminent disciples which St Columbanus left to be imitators of his heroic life, none seems to have been more famous than St Gall. He was born in Ireland soon after the middle of the sixth century, of parents who were conspicuous both for their piety and their rank. By them he was offered to God and by their care educated in the great monastery of Bangor under the direction of the holy abbots St Comgall and St Columbanus. Studies, especially of sacred learning, flourished in this house, and St Gall was well versed in grammar, poetry, and the holy Scriptures, and was ordained priest there, according to some accounts. When St Columbanus left Ireland St Gall was one of those twelve who accompanied him into France, where they were courteously received by Guntramnus, the King of Burgundy. St Columbanus, assisted by the liberality of that prince, founded the monastery of Anegray and two years afterwards that of Luxeuil. St Gall lived here for twenty years, but the only incident recorded of that period is that, being sent to fish in one river, he went to another. On his return with an empty basket he was reproved for his disobedience, whereupon he went to the right river and made a big catch. In the year 610, at the instigation of Queen Brunehild, St Columbanus was driven thence by King Theodoric, whom he had reproved for his lust. St Gall shared his exile, and, after they had in vain tried to return to Ireland, they eventually found themselves in Austrasia, and preached around Tuggan, on Lake Zürich. The people did not receive their new teachers gladly, and they soon left " that stiff-necked and thankless crowd, lest in trying to fertilize their sterile hearts they should waste efforts that might be beneficial to well-disposed minds," as St Gall's biographer says. Then one Willemar, priest of Arbon near the lake of Constance, afforded them a retreat. The servants of God built themselves cells near Bregenz, converted many idolaters who had a temple near that place, and at the end of one of his sermons Gall broke their brazen statues and threw them into the lake. The bold action made as many enemies as it did converts, but they stayed there for two years, made a garden and planted fruit, and St Gall, who was evidently a keen fisherman, occupied his spare time in knotting nets and fishing the lake. But the people who remained obstinate persecuted the monks and slew two of them; Gunzo, governor of the country, also declared himself their enemy, and on King Theodoric becoming master of Austrasia

St Columbanus decided to retire into Italy. St Gall was unwilling to be separated from him, but was prevented from bearing him company by sickness. St Columbanus, however, says one legend, did not believe Gall was so ill as all that and thought he was malingering, wherefore he imposed on him never again to say Mass during his (Columbanus's) lifetime. This unjust sentence St Gall obeyed. After his master and brethren had departed, Gall packed up his nets and went off by boat to stay with Willimar at Arbon, where he soon recovered his health. Then, directed by the deacon Hiltibod, he selected a suitable spot by the river Steinach (that it had a good fishing-pool is expressly mentioned ; also that they had trouble with water-sprites therein), and settled down there to be a hermit. He soon had disciples, who lived under his direction according to the Rule of St Columbanus, and the fame of Gall's holiness continued to grow year by year until his death, on October 16, about 630, at Arbon, whither he had gone to preach to the people at the earnest entreaty of the priest Willimar.

St Gall's biographers give several more particulars of his life, some of doubtful authenticity, others certainly mistaken. The week after he established himself with the deacon Hiltibod he had to go, very unwillingly, to the Duke Gunzo, whose demoniac daughter had been exorcised in vain by two bishops. Gall was successful, and the evil spirit went out of the girl in the form of a black bird issuing from her mouth. King Sigebert, the betrothed of this Fridiburga, offered Gall a bishopric in thankfulness, but he refused it on the ground that he was still suspended from celebrating Mass, and moreover induced Fridiburga to become a nun at Metz instead of marrying the King. However, this did not abate Sigebert's good-will,* and it was afterwards claimed, erroneously, by the abbey of St Gall that the King had given their land to Gall's community and exempted it from the jurisdiction of the Bishop of Constance. This see was again offered to the saint, who again refused but nominated one of his own disciples, the deacon John, at whose consecration he preached. St Gall learned in a vision of the death of St Columbanus at Bobbio, whose monks at his direction sent Gall their dead abbot's pastoral staff as a token of his forgiveness in not accompanying his master into Italy. At the death of St Eustace, whom St Columbanus had left abbot of Luxeuil, the monks chose St Gall ; but that house was then grown rich in lands and possessions, and the humble servant of God understood too well the advantages of holy poverty

---

* When he had himself handed his bride over to be the bride of Christ, he " went out of the church," says Walafrid Strabo, " and wept secretly for his beloved."

in a penitential life to suffer himself to be robbed of it. The charge of a numerous community also alarmed him : for he was aware how difficult a matter it is to maintain a true spirit of perfection in multitudes ; and the lukewarmness of one monk would have been to him a subject of perpetual trembling, not only for that soul, but also for his own and for the whole community from the contagion of such an example. Instead he continued to be taken up in the apostolic labours of the ministry. He only left his cell to preach and instruct, chiefly the wildest and most abandoned among the inhabitants in the mountainous parts of the country : and returning to his hermitage he there often spent whole nights and days in prayer and contemplation before God.

Walafrid Strabo adds to his Life of the saint a second book, of nearly equal length, relating the miracles which took place in connection with his tomb and relics. The same writer remarks that St Gall had " plenty of practical sense " and he was certainly a principal missionary of Switzerland (his feast is kept there as well as in Ireland), but his own fame has been exceeded by that of the monastery bearing his name which grew up on the site of his hermitage on the Steinach, where is now the town of Saint-Gall in the *canton* of the same name. In the eighth century it was reorganised by St Otmar under the Rule of St Benedict, and during the Middle Ages it rendered incalculable service to learning, literature, music, and other arts ; its library and *scriptorium* were among the most famous of western Europe. It was secularised after the Revolution, but happily a large part of the library remains, adjoining the rebuilt abbey church, now the cathedral of the Bishop of Saint-Gall.

Much painstaking research has been spent upon the history of St Gall. Apart from the casual references which occur in the Life of St Columbanus by Jonas, we have three main documents dealing with St Gall in particular. The first, unfortunately preserved only in a fragmentary state, was written about a century after the saint's death, the second by Abbot Wetting dates from the early years of the ninth century, and the third by Walafrid Strabo must be another twenty years or so later. All three have been edited by Bruno Krusch in *M. G₁H. Scrip. rer. Meroving.*, vol. iv, pp. 251–337. There is also a metrical Life by Notker. See further J. F. Kenney, *The Sources for the Early History of Ireland*, vol. i, pp. 206–208 ; Gougaud, *Christianity in Celtic Lands*, pp. 140–144 ; and M. Joynt, *The Life of St Gall* (1927).

ST MOMMOLINUS, Bp. of Noyon, Conf.

c. A.D. 686

He was a native of the territory of Constance, and became a monk at Luxeuil. He was sent with SS. Bertram and Bertinus to St Omer among the Morini in Artois, and was appointed superior whilst they lived about eight years in their first habitation, called the Old Monastery (now Saint-Mommolin). Here he laboured tirelessly with his brethren for the conversion of the heathen, and removed with them to the New Monastery, St Peter's, on Sithiu. Upon the death of St Eligius, in 659 or so, he was consecrated bishop of Noyon and Tournai, and constituted Bertram abbot of the monastery of St Quentin, which he erected in that town. This abbey afterwards became a famous collegiate church. St Mommolinus governed his extensive see for twenty-six years ; his name occurs in the subscriptions to the Testament of St Amandus and to several charters of that age. His body was interred in the church of the Apostles and was then enshrined in the cathedral of Noyon.

There are two short Latin Lives of this saint, the more important of the two being printed in the *Acta Sanctorum*, October, vol. vii, part 2. See also Van der Essen, *Étude critique sur les Vitæ des Saints méroving.* (1907), pp. 375–384.

ST BERCHARIUS, MART.

A.D. 696

When St Nivard, Archbishop of Reims, was travelling in Aquitaine, some time just before the middle of the seventh century, he made the acquaintance of the parents of young Bercharius and, much impressed by the boy's openness and promise, urged them to do their best to have him educated for the priesthood. This they did, and in due course he was ordained and became a monk at Luxeuil. When St Nivard founded the monastery of Hautvilliers St Bercharius, now experienced and tested in the monastic life, was its first abbot. From it he established several " stations " in the forest of Der and eventually a new monastery in the same place, called thence Moutier-en-Der. He also founded a convent of women, known as Puellemoutier, of which the first six nuns are said to have been slaves whom the abbot had ransomed. Towards the end of his life St Bercharius made a pilgrimage to Rome and Jerusalem, and, on his return laden with relics, he retired to Moutier-en-Der. He had a premonition of his violent end, for at his last visit to the nuns of Pellemoutier he told them that they would not see him again. There was in his monastery a young monk named Daguin, whom Bercharius had brought up from tender years but who was by no means a satisfactory religious. For some misdemeanour the abbot imposed a sharp penance on this Daguin who, furious at the continual reproofs that he brought on himself, slipped into the cell of Bercharius and stabbed him while he slept. Seized with remorse and fear immediately after, he rushed to the church and rang the bell, which brought the community running to the abbot's cell, where they found him dying. When someone went to see who had rung the bell, Daguin was found and miserably confessed his guilt. He was brought before St Bercharius, who freely forgave him, imposing the obligation of going to Rome to be absolved and receive his penance at the tomb of St Peter. St Bercharius lingered for two days and died on March 27, about the year 696. He is sometimes represented in art with a barrel. This has reference to a story told of him at Luxeuil, that, being called by the abbot while he was drawing wine or beer, he hurried off obediently but without turning off the tap. When he returned the liquid had not overflowed but was standing up in a column above the jug.

A Latin Life of this ' martyr ' was written by Abbot Adso a hundred years after his death. It has been printed both by Mabillon and in the *Acta Sanctorum*, October, vol. vii, part 2.

ST LULLUS, Bp. of Mainz, Conf.

A.D. 786

He was an Englishman, probably a native of the kingdom of the West Saxons. The foundation of his education was laid in the monastery of Malmesbury, where he remained as a young man and was ordained deacon. Hearing the call of the foreign missions when he was about twenty years old, he passed into Germany, and was received with great joy by St Boniface, who is thought to have been related to him. He made him his archdeacon and employed him in preaching the gospel to idolaters. From this time Lullus shared with that great saint the labours of his apostleship, and the persecutions which were raised against him. Three years later St Boniface promoted him to priest's orders and in 751 sent him to Rome to consult Pope St Zachary on certain matters which he did not care to commit to writing. Upon his return, St Boniface selected him for his successor, and wrote to Fulrad, abbot of St Denis, entreating him to procure the consent of King Pepin. This being obtained, Lullus was consecrated as coadjutor, and when Boniface departed on his last missionary journey into Frisia St Lullus took over the government of the see of Mainz.

It is generally believed that the mission of St Lullus to the Holy

See had been to obtain exemption from episcopal jurisdiction for St Boniface's abbey of Fulda (where, in accordance with his wish, Lullus had buried the body of the martyr, to the discontent of Mainz and Utrecht). A long dispute now began concerning this exemption between Lullus, as bishop of Mainz, and St Sturmius, abbot of Fulda, in the course of which the abbot was deposed in favour of a nominee of the bishop. But King Pepin intervened and recognised the independence of Fulda, whereupon Sturmius was restored and St Lullus refounded the monastery of Hersfeld, where he enshrined the relics of St Wigbert. He was a most energetic pastor, and during the space of thirty years that he governed the diocese of Mainz he assisted at several councils in France and elsewhere.

It appears by the letters which were addressed to him from Rome, France and England to consult him upon difficult points of doctrine and discipline that St Lullus had a great reputation for learning. His answers to these are lost, and only nine of his letters are published, among those of St Boniface. The contents are interesting. In the fourth, we notice his zeal to procure good books from foreign countries, by which means they were dispersed in all parts of his diocese, and in the others we meet with examples of his firm attachment to his friends, his pastoral vigilance, and his zeal for the observance of the canons. One is an episcopal mandate to order prayers, fasts, and Masses, "those which are prescribed to be said against tempests," to obtain of God that the rains might cease which were then ruining the harvest. St Lullus announces in the same the death of the Pope (Paul I or Stephen III), for whom he orders the accustomed prayers to be said. Cuthbert, abbot of Wearmouth, in a letter to St Lullus mentions that he had ordered ninety Masses to be said for their deceased brethren in Germany, for they sent to each other the names of those that died among them, as also appears from several letters of St Boniface, *e.g.*, in one to the abbot of Monte Cassino and several to his brethren in England. Towards the end of his life St Lullus retired to his abbey at Hersfeld, where he died.

The main authority for the history of St Lullus is the Life by Lambert, Abbot of Hersfeld, though this, written two centuries after the death of Lullus, is not very reliable. This document is printed in the *Acta Sanctorum*, October, vol. vii, part 2, but the best text is that edited among the works of Lambert by Holder-Egger (1894), pp. 307–340. Similarly the letters of Lullus should be consulted in the edition of M. Tangl, *Bonifatiusbriefe* (1915). See also H. Hahn, *Bonifaz and Lul* (1883); Hauck, *Kirchengeschichte Deutschlands*, vols. i and ii; and M. Stimming, *Mainzer Urkundenbuch* (1923), vol. i.

ST ANASTASIUS OF CLUNY, Conf.

A.D. 1085

This Anastasius was a native of Venice and a man of considerable learning who, by the middle of the eleventh century, was a monk at Mont-Saint-Michel. The abbot there was not a satisfactory person —he was accused of simony—and Anastasius eventually left the monastery in order to live as a hermit at Tombelaine in Normandy. About the year 1066 St Hugh of Cluny passed that way on a journey, met St Anastasius, and induced him to return and join the community at Cluny. After seven years there he was ordered by Pope St Gregory VII to go into Spain, either to preach to the Moors or, more likely, to help in inducing the Spaniards to give up their Mozarabic liturgy for the Roman, an undertaking begun by Cardinal Hugh of Remiremont (rather inappropriately called *Candidus*), who was then legate in France and Spain. St Anastasius was soon back at Cluny, where he lived quietly for another seven years, and then went to be a hermit in the neighbourhood of Toulouse. Here he preached to the people of the countryside (and is said to have shared his solitude with Hugh of Remiremont, who had been deposed and excommunicated for repeated acts of simony) and lived in contemplation until he was recalled to his monastery in 1085. On his way he died and was buried at Doydes.

His Life by a certain Galterius is printed by Mabillon and in the *Acta Sanctorum*, October, vol. vii, part 2. He is supposed to have been the author of an ' Epistle to Geraldus ' on the Real Presence. See *Dictionnaire de Théologie*, vol. i, c. 1166.

ST BERTRAND, Bp. of Comminges, Conf.

A.D. 1123

In its more than a thousand years of existence before it was suppressed the see of Comminges (now included in Toulouse) was governed by several men well known in history, but no one of them is more famed locally than St Bertrand, who was bishop for fifty years in the eleventh–twelfth century. His father was the lord of l'Ile Jourdain and his mother came of the family of the Counts of Toulouse. Bertrand is said to have been brought up in a monastery, though it cannot have been the Cistercian abbey of Escale-Dieu, for that was not established till after his death. At first he had no other aim than to be a military lord like his father, but after a time he turned to the ecclesiastical state, received a canonry at Toulouse, and became archdeacon. He was known by all for his good works, a man of chastity, humility, and mercifulness, and it was remarked that he owed his dignities neither to requests nor bribes. In 1073 he was called to govern the diocese of Comminges, and having rebuilt both the temporal and spiritual fortifications of his episcopal city he proceeded to a thorough reformation of the whole diocese, establishing a community of canons regular at Comminges as an example for the secular clergy. His zeal was not always acceptable. When he went to preach in the Vallée d'Azun he met with a very hostile reception, and it required all his efforts to calm the people and bring them to a better frame of mind. However, they afterwards were so sorry for the way they had received their bishop that they promised to give in perpetuity to the see of Comminges all the butter that was made in Azun every year during the week before Whit-sunday. This tribute was rendered, not always willingly, up to the time of the Revolution. St Bertrand several times had to face violent opposition even out of his own territory : in 1100 he was at the synod at Poitiers when King Philip I was excommunicated and the synodal fathers were stoned at the instigation of the Count of Poitiers, and at the consecration of the cemetery of St Mary at Auch, when the aggrieved monks of Saint-Orens tried to set fire to the church and kill the prelates present.

A number of miracles are related of St Bertrand, one of which gave rise to the " Great Pardon " or Jubilee at his church in Comminges. In a feud between the Counts of Comminges and Bigorre, Bertrand's diocese was overrun by the troops of Sanchez of Olcia, who carried off all the cattle they could lay their hands on. To save his people from ruin the Bishop implored Sanchez to restore the booty, but he refused unless he was paid its value. " All right," said St Bertrand. " Bring them back. I'll pay you before you are dead." Some time after Bertrand himself was dead, Sanchez was captured and imprisoned by the Moors in Spain and was threatened with deportation to Africa. One night he had a vision in his dungeon of Bertrand, who said he had come to redeem his promise and led him out of prison to a spot near his home at Olcia, where the vision passed, after recommending Sanchez to make a visit of thanksgiving every year to his tomb at Comminges. The appearing of St Bertrand is commemorated locally on May 2 every year, and Pope Clement V, who had been bishop of Comminges, granted a plenary indulgence to be gained at the then cathedral church of St Bertrand, from May 1 to 3, every year that the feast of the finding of the Holy Cross falls on a Friday. St Bertrand was canonised by Pope

Alexander III only a few years after his death, at the instance of his nephew, the Archbishop of Auch.

On October 23 is commemorated BLESSED BERTRAND, Cistercian abbot of Grandselve for twenty years, who died on July 11, 1149.

In the *Acta Sanctorum*, October, vol. vii, part 2, is printed a Life said to be the work of Vitalis, a notary of Auch, who was a contemporary.

ST GERARD MAJELLA, CONF.

A.D. 1755

St Gerard, said Pope Pius IX, " was a perfect model for those of his own condition, the lay brothers " ; Leo XIII referred to him as " one of those angelic youths whom God has given to the world as models to men " ; and in his short life of twenty-nine years he became the most famous wonder-worker of the eighteenth century. He was born at Muro, fifty miles south of Naples, the son of a tailor. His mother testified after his death : " My child's only happiness was in church, on his knees before the Blessed Sacrament. He would stop there till he forgot it was dinner-time. In the house he prayed all day. He was born for Heaven." At the age of ten he was allowed to receive holy Communion every other day, which at a time when the influence of Jansenism was yet not purged away argues that his confessor was sensible of what manner of child Gerard was. When his father died he was taken away from school and apprenticed to a tailor, Martin Pannuto, a worthy man who understood and respected his apprentice. Not so his journeyman, a rough fellow who ill-treated young Gerard and was only exasperated by the boy's patience. When he had learned his trade, which he did very efficiently, he offered himself to the local Capuchins, of whom his uncle was a member, but they refused him as too young and delicate. He then became a servant in the household of the Bishop of Lacedogna, who had confirmed him when he was fourteen. Humanly speaking this was an unfortunate experience, for this prelate was a man of ungovernable temper who treated Gerard with a very great lack of consideration and kindness. Nevertheless he served him faithfully and uncomplainingly till the bishop died in 1745, when he returned home to Muro and set up as a tailor on his own. Already his life was one of heroic sanctity. He lived with his mother and three sisters, and one-third of his earnings he handed over to her, another third was given in alms to the poor, and the rest in stipends for Masses for the souls in Purgatory. He had already begun to discipline himself with severity and several hours of the night were passed in prayer in the cathedral.

When Gerard was twenty-three a mission was given in Muro by some fathers of the newly founded Congregation of the Most Holy Redeemer. He offered himself to them as a lay brother, but again his delicate appearance was against him and his mother and sisters were not at all anxious to let him go. But he persisted, and at length Father Cafaro sent him to the house of which he was rector at Iliceto, with the written message : " I send you a useless brother." When Father Cafaro returned thither he found he had been mistaken in his judgement, and at once admitted Gerard to the habit. Working first in the garden and then in the sacristy he was so industrious, punctual, and self-effacing that it was said of him, " Either he is a fool or a great saint." St Alphonsus Liguori, founder of the Redemptorists, knew which he was and deliberately shortened his novitiate for him. Brother Gerard was professed in 1752, adding to the usual vows one always to do that which should seem the more pleasing to God. Father Tannoja, who wrote the Lives both of St Gerard and of St Alphonsus and who was healed by Gerard's intercession after his death, tells us that when Gerard was a novice he one day saw him praying before the Tabernacle. Suddenly he cried aloud, " O Lord, let me go, I pray Thee ! I have work that I *must* do." Surely one of the most moving stories in the whole of hagiology. During his three years as a professed lay brother Gerard was engaged as the community tailor and infirmarian, in begging for the house, and in accompanying the fathers on their missions and retreats because of his gift of reading souls. There are over twenty examples of his having brought secret sinners to repentance by revealing their own wickedness to themselves. This was the period, too, of the principal supernatural phenomena : ecstatic flight (he is said to have been carried through the air a distance of half a mile), " bilocation," and power over inanimate nature and the lower animals are recorded of him, as well as prophecy and infused knowledge. In his ecstasies an appeal to his obedience was the only force that could recall him to his surroundings before the appointed time. At Naples he knew of the murder of the Archpriest of Muro at the time it happened fifty miles away, and on several occasions he was apprised of and correctly acted on the mental wishes of persons at a distance. He read the bad conscience of the secretary of the Archbishop of Conza with such accuracy, that the man completely changed his life and was reconciled to his wife, so that all Rome was talking of it. But it is for the phenomenon called bilocation that St Gerard is most famous in this connection.

He was alleged to have been with a sick man in a cottage at Caposele at the same time as he talked with a friend in the monastery at the same place. Father Tannoja states, among other examples, that he was seen at Muro on a day when he certainly did not leave Caposele. Once the rector looked for him in his cell and he was apparently not there, so when he saw him in the church he asked where he had been. " In my cell," was the reply. " What do you mean ? " asked the rector, " I have been there twice to look for you." Pressed, Gerard explained that as he was in retreat he had asked God to make him invisible, lest he be disturbed. " I forgive you this time," said the rector. " But don't make such prayers again."*

It is not, however, for these marvels that St Gerard Majella is canonised and revered ; they were simply an effect of his surpassing holiness which God in His wisdom could have withheld, without abating thereby one jot of that goodness, charity, and devotion which made him that model which Pius and Leo declared him to be. One of the most surprising results of his reputation was that he was allowed to be, in effect, the spiritual director of several communities of nuns—an activity not usually associated with lay brothers. He interviewed individuals and gave community conferences at the *grille*, and wrote letters of advice to superiors, religious, and priests. Some of these are extant. There is nothing remarkable in them : plain, straightforward statements of a Christian's duty in whatsoever state it has pleased God to call him ; urging gentleness to a prioress, vigilance to a novice, tranquillity to a parish priest, utter conformity with the divine will to all. In 1753 the young divines at Iliceto went on an expedition to the shrine of St Michael at Monte Gargano. They had the equivalent of twelve shillings all told to cover their expenses, but they also had St Gerard with them, and he saw to it that they wanted nothing the whole time ; their nine days' holiday was a succession of marvels. But just a year later he was brought under suspicion, and underwent a terrible trial. A young woman whom he had befriended, Neria Caggiano, who was of wanton conduct, accused Gerard of lechery and he was sent for by St Alphonsus at Nocera. Believing it to be in accordance with his vow to do the more perfect thing, he did not deny the charge, and thereby placed his superior in a quandary, for it was difficult to believe that Gerard was really guilty. So he was forbidden to receive Holy Communion

---

* Examples of bilocation, when proved, are usually explained either by the imagination of the beholder being impressed miraculously by the image of a person not physically present, or by the production by God of a real external image of an absent person, or by the person being seen through all the intervening space as though he were present.

or to have any dealings with the outside world. "There is a God in Heaven. He will provide," said Gerard. For some weeks suspicion rested on him, and then Neria and her accomplice voluntarily confessed that they had lied and trumped-up the charge. St Alphonsus asked St Gerard why he had not protested his innocence. "Father," he replied, "does not our rule forbid us to excuse ourselves?" A provision which, of course, was never intended to apply to circumstances such as these. Soon after this St Gerard was sent with Father Margotta to Naples, where his reputation and miracles caused the Redemptorist house to be beset day and night by people who wanted to see him; so at the end of four months he was removed to the house at Caposele and made porter there.

This was a job after his own heart, and "our house at this time," wrote Father Tannoja, "was besieged with beggars. Brother Gerard had the same concern for their good that a mother has for her children. He had the knack of always sending them away satisfied, and neither their unreasonableness nor cunning dodges ever made him lose patience." During the hard winter of that year two hundred men, women, and children came daily to the door and received food, clothes, and firing; nobody but the porter knew where it all came from. In the spring he went again to Naples where, and at Calitri, Father Margotta's home, he performed several miracles of healing. On returning to Caposele he was put in charge of the new buildings, and one Friday when there was not a penny in the house wherewith to pay the workmen his prayers brought an unexpected sum of money, sufficient for their immediate needs. He spent the summer questing for funds for these buildings, but the effort in the south Italian heat was too much for him, and in July and August his consumption made rapid advance. He was a week in bed at Oliveto, where he cured (or as he put it, "gave effect to obedience") a lay brother who had been sent to look after him and was himself taken ill, and then dragged himself back to Caposele. He was able to get up from bed again only for a few days in September, and his last weeks were a compound of physical suffering and spiritual ecstasy, in which his gifts of infused knowledge and prevision seemed more powerful than ever before. He died on the day and at the hour he had foretold, just before the midnight of October 15–16, in the year 1755. St Gerard Majella was beatified by Pope Leo XIII in 1893 and canonised by Pius X in 1904. Among those who gave evidence in the process in 1843 was an aged man who remembered Brother Gerard visiting Melfi: "We children used to flock round him and he used to talk to us about the love of God. 'We understand each other, don't we?' he would say, 'Everything for the good God!'

... Once I saw him take off his shoes and stockings and give them to a beggar. But the most wonderful thing about him was his zeal for the conversion of sinners." On account of a miracle which took place in answer to his prayers at Senerchia, St Gerard is invoked in Italy by women in labour.

Apart from the testimonies collected in the process of beatification, the best authority for the story of St Gerard is the biography by Father Tannoja. This was translated into English for the Oratorian Series and was printed in the volume *Lives of the Companions of St Alphonsus* (1649), pp. 243–453. Besides this we have in English : O. Vassall-Phillips, *Life of Blessed Gerard Majella* (1893, 4th Edn., 1914) ; Saint-Omer, *Life, Virtues and Miracles of St Gerard Majella* (1907) ; and another sketch by J. Magnier (1905). The best German biography is that by Father Dilgskron, C.SS.R. ; the seventh edition appeared in 1923, and it is said to have been translated into English.

OCTOBER 17

ST MARGARET-MARY ALACOQUE, Virg.

A.D. 1690

IN the *Revelations of St. Gertrude* we are told that, in a vision granted to St Gertrude the Great on December 27, she asked St John the Divine why he had written nothing concerning the sweetness he had experienced when he rested his head on the breast of Jesus Christ at the Last Supper. And St John is said to have replied, " My mission was to make a simple statement to the infant Church concerning the uncreated Word of God the Father, sufficient to feed the intelligence of the whole human race until the end of the world, without, however, anyone being able fully to understand it. But to speak of the sweetness of the beatings of His heart was reserved for later times, that the world, when growing old and tepid in the love of God, should regain its fervour by hearing of such things." It would seem that these " later times " began in the seventeenth century, when, at any rate in France, love of God had gone cold, on the one hand because of widespread rebellion and sinfulness, on the other because of the numbing influence of Jansenism, which presented God as not loving all mankind alike. And accordingly there flourished, between 1625 and 1690, three saints, John Eudes, Claude de la Colombière, and Margaret-Mary Alacoque, who between them brought and taught to the Church, in the form that we have had it ever since, devotion to our divine Lord in His sacred Heart, " the symbol of that boundless love which moved the Word to take flesh, to institute the Holy Eucharist, to take our sins upon Himself, and, dying on the cross, to offer Himself as a victim and a sacrifice to the eternal Father."

The third and most prominent of these " saints of the Sacred Heart " was born in 1647 at Janots, the eastern quarter of L'hautecour, a small town in Burgundy. Her father, Claude Alacoque, was a notary of some distinction, whose wife, Philiberte Lamyn, bore him seven children, of whom Margaret was the fifth. She was a devout and good little girl, with a horror of " being naughty." When she was four she " made a vow of chastity," though she admitted afterwards that, as one would expect at that age, she knew not what either a vow or chastity was. When she was about eight her father died and she was sent to school with the Urbanist Poor Clares at Charolles ; she was at once attracted by what she could see and understand of the life of the nuns, and they on their side were so impressed by Margaret's piety that she was allowed to make her first Communion when she was nine. Two years later she was afflicted by a painful rheumatic affection that kept her to her bed till she was fifteen, and in the course of it she was taken back to her home at L'hautecour. Her father's house was now occupied by several other members of the family as well, and one sister and her husband had taken all domestic and business authority out of the hands of the widow Alacoque. She and Margaret were treated almost as servants, and she recovered from her sickness only to be confronted by this persecution of her mother. " At this time," she writes in her autobiography, " all my desire was to seek happiness and comfort in the Blessed Sacrament, but as I lived some way from the church I could not go without the leave of these persons, and sometimes one would give and another refuse her consent." They would say it was a pretext to meet some boy or other, and Margaret would go and hide herself in a corner of the garden, and stop there crying and praying for the rest of the day, without food or drink unless somebody from the village took pity on her. " The heaviest of my crosses was my powerlessness to lighten those laid upon my mother. . . . I always went in my troubles to the Blessed Virgin and our dear Lord and Master."

From the energy with which Margaret reproaches herself for worldliness, faithlessness, and resistance to grace, it may reasonably be gathered that she was not averse from a reasonable participation in those opportunities for gaiety and amusement that came her way, and when her mother and other relatives wanted her to marry she considered the proposal not unfavourably for some time. In her uncertainty she inflicted cruel austerities on herself in punishment for her faults, and brought the further dislike of her relations upon herself by collecting neglected village children into the house or garden and giving them lessons. When she was twenty, more pressure was brought to bear on her to marry, but now, fortified by a vision of our Lord, she made up her mind once for all what she would do and firmly refused. An opportunity was given her by an uncle, whose daughter was an Ursuline, to join that order, but she declined, having her attention already fixed on the Visitandines. Not till she was twenty-two did she receive the sacrament of Confirmation (it was then that she took the name of Mary), and thus armed she was able to withstand the final opposition of her family. Her brother Chrysostom furnished her dowry, and in June 1671 she entered the Visitation convent at Paray-le-Monial, which had been indicated to her by an interior voice.

As a novice Margaret-Mary was humble, obedient, simple, and frank, and she edified the community, testified a fellow-novice, " by her charity to her sisters, to whom she never uttered an irritating word, and by her patience under the sharp reproofs, scorn, and ridicule to which she was often submitted." But her novitiate was not an easy one. A Visitation nun must not " be extraordinary except by being ordinary," and already God was leading Margaret-Mary by extraordinary paths. For example, she was quite unable to practice discursive meditation : " No matter how much I tried to follow the method taught me, I invariably had to return to my divine Master's way [*i.e.* ' prayer of simplicity '], although I did my best to give it up." In due course she was professed, and on that occasion our Lord was pleased to accept her as His spouse, " but in a way that she felt herself incapable of describing." From that time " my divine Master urged me incessantly to ask for humiliations and mortifications," and they came unsought when she was appointed to assist in the infirmary. The infirmarian, Sister Catherine Augustine Marest, was temperamentally very different from her assistant : active, energetic, efficient, while Margaret-Mary was quiet, slow, and clumsy. The result she summed up in her own words : " God alone knows what I had to suffer there, as much through my impulsive and sensitive disposition as from my fellow-creatures and the Devil." But, granted that Sister Marest was too vigorous in her methods, she on her side probably had something to suffer too. During these two and a half years our Lord continually made Himself sensibly present to Margaret-Mary, often as crowned with thorns, and on December 27, 1673, her devotion to His sacred passion was rewarded with the first of the great revelations.

She was kneeling alone at the *grille* before the Blessed Sacrament exposed on the altar, and all at once she felt herself, as she says, " invested " by the divine Presence, and heard our Lord inviting her to take the place which St John (it was his feast) had occupied at the Last Supper. He then went on speaking, " in so plain and effective a manner as to leave no room for doubt, such were the results that this grace produced in me, who am always afraid of deceiving myself about what I assert to take place interiorly." He told her that the love of His heart must needs spread and manifest itself to men by means of her, and that He would reveal the treasures of its graces through her, His chosen instrument and the disciple of His sacred heart. Then it was as though our Lord took her heart

and put it within His own, returning it burning with divine love
into her breast. During a period of eighteen months our Lord continued to appear to Margaret-Mary at intervals, explaining and
amplifying the first revelation. He told her that His heart was to
be honoured under the form of a heart of flesh, represented in a way
now familiar to Catholics throughout the world, and that, in consideration of the coldness and rebuffs given to Him by mankind in
return for all His eagerness to do them good, she should make up for
their ingratitude so far as she was able. This was to be done by
frequent loving communion, especially on the first Friday of each
month and by an hour's vigil every Thursday night in memory of
His agony and desertion in Gethsemane—practices which Catholics
have made their own in the devotions of the Nine Fridays and the
Holy Hour. After a long interval a final revelation was made within
the octave of Corpus Christi in 1675, when our Lord said to St
Margaret-Mary, " Behold the heart which has so much loved men
that it has spared nothing, even exhausting and consuming itself in
testimony of its love. Instead of gratitude I receive from most only
indifference, by irreverence and sacrilege and the coldness and scorn
that men have for Me in the Sacrament of love." Then He asked
that a feast of reparation be instituted for the Friday after the octave
of Corpus Christi (now the feast of the Sacred Heart). Thus through
His chosen instrument, a young nun whom He Himself called " a
very abyss of unworthiness and ignorance," God made known to the
world His will concerning the reparation due for human ingratitude
towards His goodness and mercy, by worship of the heart of flesh
of His Son, considered as united to His divinity and as the symbol
of His love in dying for our redemption.*

Our Lord had told St Margaret-Mary that she was to " do
nothing without the approval of those who guide you, in order that,
having the authority of obedience, you may not be misled by Satan,
who has no power over those who are obedient." When she carried
the matter to her superior, Mother de Saumaise, she " mortified and
humiliated her with all her might, and allowed her to do none of the
things that our Lord had asked of her, treating contemptuously all
that the poor sister had said." " This," adds St Margaret-Mary,
" consoled me very much and I withdrew in great peace." But she
was seriously over-wrought by all that had happened, was taken ill,
and her life was in grave danger. Mother de Saumaise was looking

* It is interesting to note that just before this time Thomas Goodwin,
Independent (Congregationalist) chaplain to Oliver Cromwell, wrote a book
entitled *The Heart of Christ in Heaven towards Sinners on Earth.* It has
remarkable affinities with the teaching of Blessed Claude de la Colombière.

for a sign to guide her in dealing with Sister Alacoque, and said to her, "If God cures you, I shall take it as a proof that all you experience comes from Him, and I will allow you to do what our Lord wishes in honour of His sacred heart." St Margaret-Mary prayed accordingly, she at once recovered, and Mother de Saumaise fulfilled her promise. But there was a minority in the community definitely hostile to their sister and her spiritual experiences, and the superior ordered her to set them out for the opinion of certain theologians. These men lacked experience in such matters, diagnosed them as delusions, and recommended that the visionary should take more food. Our Lord, however, had promised that an understanding director should come to St Margaret-Mary, and when Blessed Claude de la Colombière arrived as confessor extraordinary to the nuns she knew at once that he was the man. He did not stay at Paray long, but long enough to be convinced of the genuineness of St Margaret-Mary's experiences, to gain a deep respect and affection for her, and sincerely to adopt the teaching of the Sacred Heart while confirming the saint herself in it. Soon after Blessed Claude had left for England ("where," he complained, "there are no Daughters of Holy Mary, much less a Sister Alacoque"), Margaret-Mary underwent probably the most distressing trial of her life. She was asked in vision to become the sacrificial victim for the shortcomings of the nuns of her community and for the ingratitude of some to the Sacred Heart. For long she demurred, asking that this chalice might pass from her. Then our Lord asked her again that she would do this thing, not merely interiorly but in public. She accepted, not in desperation or defiance, but in an agony of fear at what she felt bound to do because God had asked her—and had had to ask her twice. On that very same day, November 20, 1677, this young nun of only five years' standing, having first told her superior and been told by her to obey God's voice, "said and did what her Lord required of her"—knelt before her sisters in religion and told them in the name of Christ that she was appointed to be the victim for their failings. They did not all take it in the same spirit of utter humility and obedience, and on that occasion, she says, our Lord, "chose to favour me with a little sample of the grievous night of His own passion." It is a tradition at Paray that the next morning there were not enough priests available to hear all the nuns who wanted to go to confession, but unhappily there is reason to believe that for many years afterwards there were sisters who nursed resentment against St Margaret-Mary.

During the rule of Mother Greyfié, who succeeded Mother de Saumaise, St Margaret-Mary alternately received great graces and underwent great trials, both interiorly and from her fellow-creatures. She was tempted to despair, vainglory, and self-indulgence, and had a good deal of sickness. In 1681 Blessed Claude de la Colombière came to Paray for the good of his health, and died there in February of the following year, St Margaret-Mary having told him that it was not God's will that he should go to Vienne as his doctor wished. She is said to have been supernaturally assured that his soul was in Heaven, as she was from time to time regarding the state of others who were dead. Two years later Mother Mary Christina Melin, who had known Margaret-Mary during all her religious life, was elected superior at Paray and she appointed the saint as her assistant, with the approval of the chapter. From henceforth any remaining opposition ceased, or at least was silenced. The secret of her divine revelations was made known to the community in a rather dramatic (and for her embarrassing) way, being read out, presumably by accident, in the refectory in the course of a book written by Blessed Claude de la Colombière. But the ultimate triumph made no difference, one way or another, to St Margaret-Mary. One of the duties of the assistant superior was to sweep out the choir, and one day while she was doing it she was asked to go and lend a hand in the kitchen. Without brushing up the dust under her hand she went off, and when the nuns assembled for office the heap of dust was still there, in full view. That is the sort of thing that twelve years before had upset Sister Marest the infirmarian : she still lived and was to have Sister Alacoque to help her again, and doubtless she remembered it with a grim smile. St Margaret-Mary was also made mistress of the novices, with such success that professed nuns would ask leave to attend her conferences. Her secret being now known, she was less reticent in encouraging devotion to the Sacred Heart, and inculcated it among her novices, who privately observed the feast in 1685. In the following year the family of a dismissed novice caused trouble by denouncing the novice mistress as an impostor and unorthodox innovator, and for a time some of the old feeling was raised against her in the convent, but it soon subsided and on June 21 the whole house privately celebrated the feast so far as they were able. Two years later a chapel was built at Paray in honour of the Sacred Heart, and the devotion began to be accepted in other convents of the Visitandines, and to be propagated here and there throughout France.

While serving a second term as assistant superior St Margaret-Mary was taken ill in October 1690. " I shall not live," she said, " for I have nothing left to suffer," but the doctor did not think anything was very seriously wrong. A week later she asked for the last sacraments, saying, " I need nothing but God, and to lose myself in the heart of Jesus." The priest came and began to administer Extreme Unction ; at the fourth anointing, of the lips, she died. St Margaret-Mary Alacoque was beatified in 1864 and canonised by Pope Benedict XV in 1920.

In the very complete *Vie de Sainte Marguerite-Marie* by Père A. Hamon, S.J., of which the first edition appeared in 1907 and the fifth in 1923, nearly thirty pages are devoted to an ' étude des sources ' and to a full bibliography. It must suffice here to note, as most important of all, the autobiographical sketch which was written by the saint at the bidding of her director five years before her death, as well as 133 letters of hers and a number of notes and spiritual memoranda in her own handwriting. Besides these we have a valuable *mémoire* by her superior, Mère Greyfié, with other letters concerning her, and the depositions of the sisters at Paray-le-Monial, who were examined on oath with a view to her ultimate beatification. The first printed summary of what was then known of the saint's history was published in 1691 as an appendix which Père Croiset added to his little book on *Devotion to the Sacred Heart*. Upon this followed the very careful biography of Mgr Languet, Bishop of Soissons, which appeared in 1729. Since then we have a long succession of Lives, among which it will be sufficient to mention that of Mgr Bougaud (Eng. trans, 1890), that of Mgr Léon Gauthey (1890)—a fourth edition in three volumes appeared in 1915—and a short sketch by the Abbé Demimuid (1912), in the series ' Les Saints,' of which there is an English translation. There are many other short Lives in every European language. For the text of the saint's own writings reference is generally made to the *Vie et Œuvres* which was published by the Visitation nuns of Paray-le-Monial in 1876. See further the *Dictionnaire de Théologie*, vol. iii, cc. 320-351.

ST ANSTRUDIS, Virg. and Abbess

A.D. 688

She was the daughter of St Blandinus and St Salaberga, who founded the abbey of St John Baptist at Laon, in which Salaberga, with the consent of her husband, took the religious veil. Having refused a most favourable offer of marriage, Anstrudis faithfully walked in her steps, and after her death succeeded her in the abbacy. By a scrupulous observance of monastic discipline, a tender and affectionate care in conducting her sisters in the paths of Christian perfection, profuse charity to the poor, and constant application to prayer, she was a true model of sanctity. No exterior occupations were allowed to interrupt the union of her heart with God, and her watchings in prayer often kept her the whole night in church, except for a little rest on an uneasy bench before the church door. Her sanctity was proved and made perfect by afflictions in which her virtue was purified and tested as by fire. The saint's brother Baldwin was treacherously assassinated, and she herself was accused to Ebroin, mayor of the palace, of taking side against his interest. When he came to Laon with Theodericus III he burst into the convent and had the young abbess dragged before him, and would have led her to prison had he not been frightened off. The next day an attempt was made on the life of Anstrudis, but she escaped by clinging to the altar of the church. Attracted by her intrepid constancy and proved virtue and innocence, Blessed Pepin of Landen, when mayor of the palace, declared himself her protector. When Madelgarus, Bishop of Laon, tried to lay hands on the income of the convent, St Anstrudis lodged a complaint and Pepin sent his son Grimoald to deal straitly with the unjust prelate. The feast of St Anstrudis is observed at Soissons, where she is known as Ste Anstrude.

The Bollandists, following Mabillon, have printed a Life of this saint in the *Acta Sanctorum*, October, vol. vii, part 2. It purports to be of almost contemporary date, but Levison, in his critical edition, *M. G. H. Script. rer. Meroving.*, vol. vi, pp. 64 *seq.*, assigns it to the ninth century.

ST NOTHELM, Abp. of Canterbury, Conf.
c. A.D. 740

Nothelm, whom St Bede refers to as "a devout priest of the church of London," succeeded St Tatwin in the see of Canterbury in the year 734. Two years later he received the *pallium* from Pope St Gregory III. He was consulted by St Boniface from Germany and furnished him with a copy of the famous letter of instruction from Pope St Gregory I to St Augustine of Canterbury about how to deal with the English converts. But St Nothelm's name is principally remembered for his part in the composition of St Bede's *Ecclesiastical History*. In the preface thereto, addressed to the holy King Ceolwulf, Bede says that his chief aid and authority for his work had been the learned abbot Albinus at Canterbury, who transmitted to him " either by writing or by word of mouth of the same Nothelm, all that he thought worthy of memory that had been done in the province of Kent, or the adjacent parts, by the disciples of the blessed Pope Gregory [the Great], as he had learned them either from written records or the traditions of his ancestors. The said Nothelm afterwards went to Rome and, having with leave of the present Pope Gregory [III] searched into the archives of the Holy Roman Church, found there some letters of the blessed Pope Gregory and other popes. When he returned home he brought them to me, by the advice of the aforesaid most reverend father Albinus, to be inserted in my history. Thus . . . what was transacted in the church of Canterbury by the disciples of St Gregory or their successors, and under which kings they happened, has been conveyed to us by Nothelm through the industry of abbot Albinus. They also partly informed me by what bishops and under what kings the provinces of the East and West Saxons, as well as of the East Angles and the Northumbrians, received the faith of Christ." Nothelm also wrote some observations on St Bede's commentary on the books of Kings in the Bible, to which Bede replied in a personal letter.

St Nothelm died about the year 740 and was succeeded as archbishop by St Cuthbert, a monk of Lyminge in Kent whom he had consecrated as bishop of Hereford some four years earlier.

The saint is noticed in the *Acta Sanctorum*, October, vol. viii. We know little more than what Bede had told us. See Plummer's edition and notes.

BD. BALTHASAR OF CHIAVARI, CONF.

A.D. 1492

Balthasar Ravaschieri, of the house of the Counts of Lavagna, was born at Chiavari on the Gulf of Genoa about the year 1420. He gave up his secular position, joined the Friars Minor of the Observance, and in due course was professed and ordained. Blessed Balthasar was a friend and fellow-preacher with Blessed Bernardino of Feltre, and joined enthusiastically and successfully in his missions, but his activities were cut short by ill-health, especially attacks of gout. When he could not walk, or even stand up on his feet, he had himself carried on a stretcher into the church in order to assist at Mass and the choir offices and to hear the confessions of the faithful who came to him in crowds. He also used to be taken into the woods and left there for long periods of meditation and reading, and here he had a vision of our Lady and was miraculously sheltered from a heavy fall of snow. This double marvel was commemorated in the sixteenth century by an inscription cut in stone and in 1678 was recorded in the archives of the town of Chiavari. Blessed Balthasar died on October 17, 1492, at the friary of our Lady *del Campo* at Binasco, and was buried in a marble tomb which at once became the centre of a *cultus*. His relics were carried from place to place at times of public intercession ; and after several official translations were finally deposited in the cathedral of Bologna in 1812. In 1908 the Bishop of Pavia recognised the ancient and uninterrupted *cultus* of Blessed Balthasar, and in 1930 this was confirmed by the Holy See.

Who can consider the wonderful examples given by so many sons of St Francis of Assisi, and not cry out with our Redeemer, " I confess to Thee, Father, Lord of Heaven and earth, because Thou hast hid these things from the wise and prudent and hast revealed them to little ones. Yea, Father ; for so it hath seemed good in Thy sight." Thou resistest the proud, and hast dismissed them empty ; but Thou givest grace to the humble, delighting to communicate Thyself to those that are simple of heart, Thy little ones whose hearts are disengaged from earthly things. Thou art truly a hidden God, who dwellest in inaccessible light unknown to the world ; but Thou givest Thyself abundantly and lovingly to those who show forth in their hearts and bodies Jesus Christ crucified. This interior crucifixion of the heart, this simplicity and freedom of the affections, consists not in the exterior renunciation of the world (which is indeed often a help to it, or its effect) but in the spirit, and is compatible with the state and employment of every lawful condition in the world, as many saints have shown who, on thrones, in courts, in trades and professions, in commerce or in armies, learned to die to the world and themselves ; they used the things of this world as stewards only and as if they used them not, living as strangers and pilgrims on earth. For " a man may be in the world in two ways," as St Thomas remarks, " In one way by his bodily presence and in another way by the bent of his mind."

It is frankly admitted that though we have a certain amount of evidence regarding the later *cultus* of this *beato*, very little can be stated with certainty about the facts of his life. See the *Archivum Franciscanum Historicum*, vol. ii (1909), p. 523. What little is known has been gathered together in the small volume of Padre Bernardino da Carasco, *Il B. Baldassare Ravaschieri* (1908), of which a second edition appeared in 1930. The text of the decree of beatification is printed in the *Acta Apostolicæ Sedis*, vol. xxii (1930), pp. 171–174. It contains a slight historical summary.

BD. RICHARD GWYN, Mart.
Protomartyr of Wales

A.D. 1584

For forty years after the dissolution of the monasteries Wales remained a stronghold of the Catholic faith ; many of the great families and 90 per cent of the common people were faithful to it.

But soon after the missionary priests began to arrive from the continent, Queen Elizabeth and her ministers set themselves to stamp out the religion by cutting off the channels of sacramental grace and closing the mouths of those who should preach the word of God. In Wales the first victim of this campaign was a layman, Richard Gwyn (*alias* White). He was born at Llanidloes in Montgomeryshire in 1537, and was brought up a Protestant. On leaving St John's College, Cambridge, he went to Overton in Flintshire and opened a school. Some time after he became a Catholic, and his absence from Protestant worship drawing suspicion on himself, he left Overton with his family and conducted schools in several other places. In 1579, being in Wrexham, he was recognised by the vicar (an apostate), denounced, and arrested. He managed to escape. But in June 1580, the Privy Council directed the Protestant bishops to be more vigilant in their dealings with Catholic recusants, especially "all schoolmasters, public and private." Accordingly, in the very next month, Richard Gwyn was seized and brought before a magistrate, who sent him to Ruthin gaol. At the Michaelmas assizes he was offered his liberty if he would conform, and on refusal was returned to prison, to be kept in irons. At the May assizes he was ordered to be taken by force to the Protestant church, where he interrupted the proceedings by vigorously clanking his chains. He was then put in the stocks from 10 a.m. till 8 p.m., "vexed all the time with a rabble of ministers." One of them claimed that he had the power of the keys as much as St Peter ; but he also had a conspicuously red nose, and Gwyn retorted in exasperation, " There is this difference, namely, that whereas St Peter received the keys of the kingdom of Heaven you appear to have received those of the beer-cellar ! " He was indicted for brawling in church and fined the equivalent of £800, and brought up again in September and fined £1680 in modern money for not having attended church during the seven months he had been in gaol. The judge asked him what means he had to pay these absurd fines. " I have somewhat towards it," he replied. " How much ? " " Sixpence," said Gwyn. He appeared at three more assizes and was then sent with four others before the Council of the Marches, which had them tortured at Bewdley, Ludlow, and Bridgnorth to try and get the names of other Catholics.

In October 1584 Blessed Richard appeared at his eighth assizes, at Wrexham, with two others, Hughes and Morris, and was indicted for treason, in that he was alleged to have tried to reconcile one Lewis Gronow to the Church of Rome and to have maintained the supremacy of the Pope. He denied any knowledge of Gronow, and the man afterwards made a public declaration that his evidence and that of the other two witnesses was false and paid for at the instigation of the vicar of Wrexham and another zealot. The jury summoned had refused to appear, so another was impanelled on the spot. The members asked the judge whom they were to convict and whom to acquit! Accordingly Gwyn and Hughes were sentenced to death (Hughes was afterwards reprieved) and Morris released. Mrs. Gwyn was brought into court with her baby and warned not to imitate her husband. She rounded on the Sheriff. " If you lack blood," she said, " you may take my life as well as my husband's. If you will give the witnesses a little bribe they will give evidence against me too ! " Blessed Richard was executed on October 17, 1584, a wet day, at Wrexham (now the see of the Catholic diocese of Menevia, Mynyw). The crowd called for him to be allowed to die before disembowelling, but the Sheriff (himself an apostate) refused, and the martyr shrieked out in his agony, " O Duw gwyn, pa beth ydyw hwn ? " " Holy God, what is this ? " " An execution for the Queen's Majesty," said an official. " Iesu, trugarha wrthyf ! " " Jesus, have mercy on me ! " exclaimed Blessed Richard, and his head was struck off.

During his four years of imprisonment Gwyn wrote in Welsh a number of religious poems (not " carols," as they are generally called), calling on his countrymen to keep to " yr hen Fam," the old Mother Church, and describing with a bitterness that was unhappily excusable the new religion and its ministers. He was beatified in 1929.

It is under the name of White (a translation of the Welsh ' Gwyn ') that Bishop Challoner gives an account of this martyr—*Memoirs of Missionary Priests* (Ed. Pollen), pp. 102–105. See also Burton and Pollen, *Lives of the English Martyrs* (second series), vol. i, pp. 127–144 ; and *The Rambler*, 1860, pp. 223–248 and 366–388. For his poetical compositions in Welsh, consult the publications of the Catholic Record Society, vol. v, pp. 90–99.

THE URSULINE MARTYRS OF VALENCIENNES

A.D. 1794

Ursuline nuns established themselves at Valenciennes in the year 1654 ; nearly a hundred and forty years later, after devoting themselves throughout that time to the interests of their fellow-citizens by teaching their children and looking after the poor, their convent was suppressed under the Revolution and the nuns took refuge in the house of their order at Mons. When Valenciennes was occupied by the Austrians in 1793 they returned, reopened their school, and remained in the town after it had been recaptured by the French. In September 1794 they were arrested at the instance of Citizen Lacoste's commission, on the charge of being *émigrées* who had unlawfully returned and reopened their convent, and confined in the public prison. On October 17 five of them were brought up for trial, and on their stating openly that they had come back to Valenciennes to teach the Catholic faith they were sentenced to death. They were led to the guillotine in the great market-place amid the tears of their sisters. "Mother, you taught us to be valiant, and now we are going to be crowned you weep!" exclaimed Blessed Mary-Augustine (Mother Dejardin) to the mother superior. Five days later the superior herself, Blessed Mary-Clotilde (Mother Paillot) and the other five nuns suffered in the same place, among the last victims of the Revolution. "We die for the faith of the Catholic, Apostolic, and Roman Church," said Blessed Mary-Coltilde, and the truth of this statement was formally recognised by that same church when, in 1920, Pope Benedict XV solemnly beatified as martyrs the eleven Ursulines of Valenciennes. Among them were two, Blessed Lilvina (Lacroix) and Anne-Mary (Erraux), who had been professed Bridgettines, and one, Blessed Josephine (Leroux) who had been a Poor Clare ; they joined the Ursulines when their own communities were expelled.

As vice-postulator of the cause of the Valenciennes martyrs, the Abbé J. Loridan in his little volume *Les bienheureuses Ursulines de Valenciennes* (in the series ' Les Saints ') speaks with full authority and gives proof of exhaustive research. See also Wallon, *Les Representants du peuple, etc.*, vol. v, pp. 163–167 ; and H. Leclercq, *Les Martyrs*, vol. xii.

OCTOBER 18

ST LUKE THE EVANGELIST

FIRST CENTURY

ST PAUL, the apostle of the Gentiles, is the panegyrist of the Gentile evangelist when he refers to him as "the most dear physician" and a fellow-labourer with himself, and if further evidence were wanted it could be found in St Luke's own inspired writings. He was a Greek, a native of Antioch, the metropolis of Syria, and practised medicine. But nothing can be deduced from this as to his social status, for this art was at that time often managed by slaves who were trained up to it. Grotius conceives that St Luke perhaps had lived as servant in some patrician family, in quality of physician, till he obtained his freedom; after which he continued to follow his profession. This he seems to have done after his conversion to the faith, and even to the end of his life: the occasional practice of medicine, without being drawn aside by it from spiritual duties, being a charity very consistent with the ministry of the gospel. By a tradition of the early Middle Ages he is said to have been very skilful in painting. The Menology of the Emperor Basil II, compiled in 980, Metaphrastes, Nicephorus Callistus, and other late Greeks speak of his leaving many pictures of the infant Christ and the Blessed Virgin. Though most of the pictures attributed to St Luke can be traced to the Byzantines of the sixth century, Theodorus Lector, who wrote in the early part of that century, relates that a picture of our Lady painted by St Luke was sent from Jerusalem to the Empress St Pulcheria, who placed it in the church of the Hodegetria which she built at Contantinople. A very ancient inscription was found in a vault near the church of St Mary *in Via Lata* in Rome in which it is said of a picture of her discovered there, "One of the seven painted by St Luke." St Augustine, however, says distinctly that no likeness of our Lady was known in his day.

St Luke was a convert to the Christian religion, but whether direct from paganism or through Judaism is uncertain. Many Jews were settled at Antioch, chiefly such as were called Hellenists, who read the Bible in the Greek translation of the Septuagint. St Jerome

249

observes from Luke's writings that he was more skilled in Greek than in Aramaic; and that he was not a Jew by birth is shown both by his literary style and by St Paul's separation of him from those of the circumcision (Colossians iv 14); he was therefore not the Lucius mentioned in Romans xvi 21, who was related to St Paul. St Epiphanius makes him to have been a disciple of our Lord; but this contradicts St Luke's own words in the first four verses of his Gospel, and Tertullian positively affirms that he never was a disciple of Christ whilst He lived on earth. No sooner was he enlightened by the Holy Ghost and initiated in the school of Christ, than, as the Church says of him in the collect of his Mass, " He always bore in his body the mortification of the cross for the honour of the divine name." The first time in the history of the mission of St Paul that Luke speaks in his own name in the first person is when the apostle sailed from Troas into Macedonia (Acts xvi). Before this he had doubtless been for some time a disciple of St Paul, and from this time seems never to have left him, unless by his order for the service of the churches he had planted. It used to be held by many that St Luke wrote his Gospel during St Paul's two years of imprisonment at Caesarea (Acts xxiii–xxvi), a work he undertook, as he himself explains, that Christians might know the verity of those words in which they had been instructed: he was primarily a historian or recorder. And he indicates for us what were his sources: as many had written accounts of the things that had happened as they heard them from those " who from the beginning were eye-witnesses and ministers of the word," it seemed good to him also, " having diligently attained to all things from the beginning," to set them out in an ordered narrative. He delivered nothing but what he received immediately from persons present at and concerned in the things which he has left upon record, having a most authentic stock of credit and intelligence to proceed upon under the direction and influence of the Holy Ghost, from whose express revelation he received whatever he has delivered concerning all divine mysteries. Whether or not he wrote it during St Paul's imprisonment at Caesarea, the Gospel of St Luke was probably finished before the year 60. He mainly insists in his Gospel upon what relates to Christ's priestly office; for which reason the ancients, in accommodating the four symbolical representations mentioned in Ezechiel to the four evangelists, assigned the ox or calf to him as an emblem of sacrifice. It is only in the Gospel of St Luke that we have a full account of the annunciation of the mystery of the Incarnation to the Blessed Virgin, of her visit to St Elizabeth, and of the journeys to Jerusalem (ix 51; xix 28). He relates six miracles and eighteen parables not mentioned in the other Gospels.

It is an almost unanimous opinion that it was Luke who accompanied Titus to Corinth with St Paul's second letter to that church : the brother "whose praise is in the gospel through all the churches." When St Paul was sent to Rome in consequence of his appeal to Cæsar, St Luke was with him, shared the adventures of the voyage, and spent a good deal of Paul's two years' imprisonment with him. It was probably at this time he wrote the book called the *Acts of the Apostles* as an appendix to his Gospel, to prevent the false relations which some published by leaving an authentic account of the wonderful works of God in planting His Church and of some of the miracles by which He confirmed it. Having related some general transactions of the principal apostles in the first establishment of the Church, beginning at our Lord's ascension, he from the thirteenth chapter almost confines himself to the actions and miracles of St Paul, to most of which he had been privy and an eye-witness. He evidently continued to be the companion of St Paul after he was released from his confinement, for the apostle in his last imprisonment at Rome writes to Timothy that Luke alone was with him. Of what happened to him after St Paul's martyrdom we have no certain knowledge. A document of the early third century says that he was unmarried, wrote his Gospel in Achaia, and died at the age of eighty-four in Bithynia ; this last may be an error for Bœotia, for a later document, confirmed by St Paulinus of Nola, puts his death and burial at Thebes. St Epiphanius in the fourth century says that after the martyrdom of St Paul, St Luke preached in Italy, Gaul, Dalmatia, and Macedonia. By Gaul some understand Galatia. It is not known whether or not St Luke was a martyr ; probably not. The bones of St Andrew were translated from Patras in Achaia in 357 by order of the Emperor Constantius, and deposited in the church of the Apostles at Constantinople, together with those of St Luke ; but it is not stated and does not follow that his had previously reposed at Patras. When this church was repaired by order of Justinian, the masons found three wooden coffins in which, as the inscriptions averred, the bodies of St Luke, St Andrew, and St Timothy were interred. Baronius mentions that the head of St Luke was brought by St Gregory from Constantinople to Rome, and laid in the church of his monastery of St Andrew ; the Roman Martyrology, which puts Luke's death in Bithynia and says nothing of martyrdom, states that his relics are now at Padua, whither they are supposed to have been taken to the church of St Justina during the iconoclast troubles. St Luke is the patron of physicians, painters, and butchers.

Christ came not only to be our model by His example and our

redeemer by the sacrifice of His blood, but also to be our teacher by
His heavenly doctrine. He who from the beginning of the world
had inspired and opened the mouths of so many prophets, vouchsafed to become Himself our instructor, teaching us what we are to
believe and what we are to do that through His redemption we may
attain to everlasting life. With what earnestness and diligence, therefore, with what humble respect, we ought to listen to and meditate
upon the lessons which we read in His gospels or hear from the
mouth of His ministers, who announce to us His word in His name
and by His authority and commission. As by often iterating the
same action the nail is driven into the wood, so it is by repeated
reflection thereon that the divine word sinks deep into our hearts.
It cost the Son of God infinite humiliation and suffering to announce
it to us, and He has sent prophets, apostles, evangelists, and holy
ministers to preach the same for the sake of our souls. How intolerable then is our lukewarmness and carelessness in receiving it.

The erudition of the sixteenth and seventeenth centuries upon which
Butler's account of St Luke is based, took many things for granted which
are now seen to be more than doubtful. For a reliable appreciation of the
author of the third Gospel we must turn to the work of modern scholars,
for example to the admirable preface which Père Lagrange, O.P., has
prefixed to his book, *L'Évangile selon St Luc* (1921). Of a proper biography
there can of course be no question. Everything is uncertain beyond the
little we find recorded in the New Testament itself, but Harnack, writing
with the more persuasiveness as a non-Catholic at one time suspected of
rationalising tendencies, has very solidly demonstrated that Luke the
physician was the author both of the third Gospel and of the whole of
the Acts of the Apostles, despite the attempts which have been made, on
the basis of the so-called 'We' sections (*Wirstücke*) to prove that the
text of this last was a conflation of at least two different documents. (See
Harnack, *Lukas der Arzt*, and subsequent publications of his written in
support of the same thesis; all of which have been translated into English.)
Harnack even supposes the Gospel of St Luke to have been written before
St Paul's martyrdom (? before A.D. 67), but Lagrange does not follow him
in this. For the history of St Luke, the Latin and Greek preface to early
texts of the Gospel are worthy of being taken into consideration (see the
Revue Bénédictine, 1928, pp. 193 *seq.*, as also the short notice preserved in
the Muratorian canon. See further the preface to E. Jacquier's great
commentary, *Les Actes des Apôtres* (1926), and Theodore Zahn's *Die
Apostelgeschichte des Lukas* (1919–1921). On the portraits of our Lady
supposed to have been painted by St Luke, see the *Dictionnaire d'Archéol.*,
etc., vol. ix, c. 2614. In any case, St Augustine states, be it noted, that
nothing was known about the bodily appearance of the Blessed Virgin.

ST JUSTUS, Mart.

A.D. 287

" At Sinomovicus in the territory of Beauvais," says the Roman Martyrology, " the passion of St Justus the martyr who, while still a boy, was beheaded by the governor Rictiovarus during the persecution of Diocletian." This young martyr was formerly famous all over north-western Europe, and the church of Beauvais even had his name in the canon of the Mass and accorded his feast a proper preface ; but the extension of his *cultus* was in some measure due to confusion with other saints of the same name. His legend as it has come down to us is late and hardly trustworthy. According to it Justus lived with his parents at Auxerre, and when he was nine years old went with his father Justin to Amiens in order to ransom Justinian, Justin's brother, who was held a slave there. They called on his master, Lupus, who was ready to sell the slave if he could be identified, but when they were all paraded for inspection neither brother recognised the other. Whereupon Justus, who had never seen his uncle before, pointed out a man who was carrying a lamp, crying, " That is he ! " So it was, and Lupus handed him over. A soldier who had witnessed the occurrence reported to Rictiovarus that there were some Christian magicians in the town, and the governor sent four mounted men after them to bring them back, and if they would not come quietly they were to be killed on the spot. When the three Christians came to Sinomovicus (now Saint-Just-en-Chaussée), between Beauvais and Senlis, they sat down to eat by the side of a spring, when young Justus suddenly saw the four horsemen in the distance. Justin and Justinian at once hid themselves in a near-by cave, telling the boy to put the soldiers off if they came that way. When they rode up the pursuers saw Justus and asked him where were the two men they had seen with him and to what gods they were in the habit of sacrificing. He ignored one question and replied to the other that he was a Christian. At once one of the soldiers smote off his head, and was about to pick it up to carry it back to Rictiovarus when the dead body stood upright and a voice was heard saying, " Lord of Heaven and earth, receive my soul, for I am sinless ! " At this prodigy the soldiers fled from the place, and when Justin and his brother came out of the cave there was the body of St Justus with its head in its hands ; and it is fabled to have directed them to bury the trunk in the cave and to take the head home to his mother, " who, if she wants to see me again, must look for me in Heaven." A similar story is told of St Justin of

Louvre, venerated at Paris, for whom the " acts " of St Justus have been borrowed.

Although this legend is entirely fabulous, we may infer from the fact that it is preserved in four recensions that it must have enjoyed a certain popularity. See the *Acta Sanctorum*, October, vol. viii, and *Bib. Hagiograph. Latina*, nn. 4590–4594. There is no mention of this Justus in the *Hieronymianum*, and there seems grave reason to doubt whether Rictiovarus the persecutor, whose name occurs so frequently in the Roman Martyrology, ever existed.

ST GWEN, Mart.

c. A.D. 492

Bishop Challoner in his *Memorials of Ancient British Piety* notes under to-day's date the festival in Wales of St Gwendoline, abbess. This lady is not known to Welsh hagiology, and it seems likely that Challoner intended St Gwen or Gwenllian. She was a reputed daughter of King Brychan Brycheiniog, and married Llyr Merini, by whom she became the mother of Caradog Fraichfrâs, one of " King Arthur's knights " and the father of St Cadfarch, whose feast was kept at Penegoes in Cyfeiliog on October 24. St Gwen was murdered by the pagan Saxons at Talgarth in Breconshire about the year 492 and was there buried. The church at Talgarth is dedicated in her honour and an alleged relic of her hair was discovered under the chancel in 1873. This St Gwen is not the same St Gwen (Wenn, Blanche, Candida) whose feast is kept in Cornwall to-day. She was the maternal aunt of St David and mother of St Cybi by Selyf, Prince of Cornwall. Nothing more is known of her. A third St Gwen, famous in Brittany as " the Three-breasted " (Teirbron), is sometimes named on the third of this month and sometimes on March 3, with her sons SS. Winwaloe, Guethenoc, and Jacut and her second husband St Fragan. By her first husband she was the mother of St Cadfan, founder of Bardsey monastery.

These scattered references are a hopeless tangle. There seems to be no formal Life of any St Gwen, and Baring-Gould and Fisher, *Lives of the British Saints*, vol. iii, pp. 166–167, have done little to clear the matter up.

OCTOBER 19

ST PETER OF ALCANTARA, Conf.

A.D. 1562

CHRIST declares the spirit and practice of penitence to be the foundation of a Christian's spiritual life, and this great truth which in these latter ages is little understood even amongst the generality of those who call themselves Christians is set forth by the example of this saint to rebuke our sloth and silence our excuses. St Peter was born at Alcantara, a small town in the province of Estremadura in Spain in 1499. His father, Peter Gara- vita, was a lawyer and governor of that town; his mother was of good family; and both were persons eminent for their piety and personal merit in the world. Peter was sent to school locally, and had not finished his philosophy when his father died. By his step- father he was sent to Salamanca to study the canon law. During the year that he spent in that university he divided his time between the church, the hospital, the school, and his own room. In 1515 he was home on vacation and deliberated with himself about the choice of a state of life. On one side was represented to him the fortune and career which were open to him in the world; on the other, he considered the dangers of such a course and the happiness and spiritual satisfactions of holy retirement; and he felt in his soul a strong call to a religious state of life, in which he should have no other concern but that of serving God directly. Resolving therefore to embrace the rule of St Francis, in the sixteenth year of his age he took the habit of that order in the convent of Manjaretes, situated in the mountains which run between Castile and Portugal. An ardent spirit of penance determined his choice of this friary, for it was a house of Discalced Franciscans who, among the friars of the Regular Observance, aimed at a yet stricter observance. During his novitiate he had first the care of the sacristy, then of the refectory, and afterwards of the gate, all which offices he discharged without prejudice to his recollection, but not always with exactitude; he seems, indeed, to have been rather absent-minded. After having had the care of the refectory for half a year he was chidden by the superior for having never given the friars any fruit. To

255

which he answered that he had never seen any; he had never,
in fact, lifted his eyes to the ceiling, where the fruit was
hanging in bunches. In time he seemed by long habits of mortification to have lost the sense of taste, for when a little vinegar and salt
was thrown into a porringer of warm water, he took it for his usual
bean soup. He had no other bed than a rough skin laid on the floor,
on which he knelt a part of the night and slept sitting, leaning his
head against a wall. His watchings were the most difficult and
remarkable of all the austerities which he practised, and in consequence of them he has been regarded in after-ages as the patron
saint of night-watchmen. He inured himself gradually to them, that
they might not be prejudicial to his health.

A few years after his profession, Peter was sent to a remote convent near Belviso, where he built himself a cell with mud and wattles
at some distance from the rest, in which he could pray and practise
mortifications without being seen. About three years after, he was
sent by his provincial to Badajoz, to establish and be superior of a small
friary there, though he was at that time but twenty-two years old,
only five years professed, and not yet a priest. When the three years
of his guardianship were elapsed he received his provincial's command to prepare himself for holy orders, was promoted to the priesthood in 1524, and soon after employed in preaching. The ensuing
year he was made guardian of Robredillo and later of Placentia. In
all stations of superiority he set the strictest example by the literal
acceptance of evangelical counsels, as in the matter of having only
one coat. When his habit was being washed or mended he had to
seek a warm retired spot in the garden, and wait there with nothing
on. During this period he preached much throughout Estremadura
and, burning with the most ardent charity, he appeared in the pulpits
like a seraph sent by God to rouse sinners to a true spirit of penance
and to kindle in their breasts the fire of divine love. Great then was
the fruit which his sermons produced. Besides his natural talents
and learning he was enriched by God with an experimental and
infused knowledge and sense of spiritual things, which is never
acquired by study but is the fruit only of divine grace gained by an
eminent spirit of prayer and habits of virtue. His presence alone
seemed a powerful sermon, and it was said that he had but to show
himself to work conversions. He loved particularly to preach to the
poor and from the words of the Sapiential books and the prophets
of the Old Law. After a mission he would set up a large cross in
some conspicuous place, to remind the people of the truths he had
preached to them. The love of retirement was always St Peter's
predominant inclination, and he made petition to his superiors that

he might be placed in some remote convent, where he could give himself up to contemplation. Accordingly, he was sent to the convent of St Onuphrius at Lapa, situated in a solitary place, but at the same time he was commanded to take up the charge of guardian. In that house he composed his book on prayer, at the request of a gentleman who had often heard him speak on that subject. This famous treatise was justly esteemed a masterpiece by St Teresa, Louis of Granada, St Francis of Sales, Pope Gregory XV, and others, and has been translated into most European languages. St Peter was himself a proficient in the school of divine love, and his union with God was habitual. He said Mass with a devotion that astonished others, and often was seen to remain in prayer a whole hour with his arms stretched out. His ecstasies in prayer were frequent, sometimes of long continuance and accompanied by remarkable phenomena. The reputation of St Peter having reached the ears of John III, King of Portugal, he wished to consult him upon certain difficulties, and St Peter received an order from his provincial to go to him at Lisbon. King John was so well satisfied with his answers and advice and so much edified by his behaviour that he arranged for him to return again soon after. In these two visits the saint converted several great lords, and the Infanta Maria, the King's sister, wished to renounce the court, but from this St Peter dissuaded her. He allowed her to make a vow of virginity, on condition that she should continue at court and wear secular dress, her presence being necessary there. He encouraged her to found a hospital and a nunnery of Poor Clares at Lisbon, and both she and the King were extremely desirous to keep the saint with them. But though they had fitted up apartments like a cell, with an oratory, for him and allowed him liberty to give himself up wholly to contemplation according to his desire, yet he found the inconveniences too great and the palace not agreeable to his purpose. A quarrel having happened among the townsmen of Alcantara, he took this opportunity to leave Lisbon in order to reconcile those who were at variance. His presence and persuasion soon restored peace among the inhabitants.

St Peter was in 1538 chosen provincial of the Discalced Friars' province of St Gabriel, or of Estremadura. The age required for this office being forty years, he urged that he was only thirty-nine, but all were persuaded that his prudence and virtue were an overbalance. Whilst he discharged this office he drew up even more severe rules, which he wished the whole province to accept in a chapter which he held at Placentia for this purpose in 1540, but his ideas met with strong opposition. He therefore resigned, and went to Lisbon, to join Friar Martin-of-St-Mary, who interpreted the Rule of St Francis as an eremitical life, and was building his first hermitage upon a barren mountain called Arabida, at the mouth of the Tagus on the opposite bank to Lisbon. St Peter animated the fervour of these religious, and suggested many regulations which were adopted. They wore nothing on their feet, lay on bundles of vine-twigs or on the bare ground, never touched flesh or wine, and would have no library, in all of which things they went beyond the intentions of their founder St Francis. They broke their rest at midnight, when they said Matins together, after which they continued in prayer till break of day. Then they recited Prime, which was followed by one Mass only. After this, retiring to their cells they remained there till Terce. The time between Vespers and Compline was allotted for manual labour. Their cells were exceedingly poor and small; St Peter's was so little that he could neither stand up nor lie down in it at full length. A number of Spanish and Portuguese friars were attracted to this way of life, and with permission of the minister general other small communities were formed. That of Palhaes being appointed for the novitiate, St Peter was nominated guardian and charged with the direction of the novices. He had governed only two years when he was recalled into Spain. After the death of Father Martin in 1548 the friaries depending on him went into decline, and St Peter was allowed, at the request of Prince Louis, the King's brother, and of the Duke of Aveiro, to return to Portugal, when he raised the custody of Arabida to a more flourishing condition and founded a new convent near Lisbon. His reputation for sanctity drew so many eyes on him and gave so much interruption that he hastened back to Spain, hoping there to hide himself in some solitude, leaving Arabida in charge of Father John of Aquila.

St Peter was greatly distressed at the trials which the Church was then undergoing, and to oppose the weapons of prayer and penance to the effects of ill-living and false doctrine he in 1554 formed a design of establishing a reformed congregation of friars upon a yet stricter plan than before. His project was disapproved by the provincial of Estremadura, but welcomed by the Bishop of Coria, in whose diocese the saint, with one companion, made an essay of this manner of living in a small hermitage. A short time after he went to Rome, travelling barefoot all the way, to obtain the support of Pope Julius III. He got no encouragement from the minister general of the Observance, but eventually he prevailed on the Pope to put him under the minister general of the Conventuals and obtained a brief by which he was authorised to build a convent according to his plan. At his return a friend built such an one as he desired near Pedroso which is the beginning of this reformed institute of Franciscans, called of the observance of St Peter of Alcantara. The cells were exceedingly small, and one half of each was filled with a bed, consisting of three boards ; the church was of a piece with the rest. It was impossible for persons to forget their engagement in a penitential life while their habitations seemed rather to resemble graves than rooms. Among the supporters of this "reform" was a great friend of St Peter, the Count of Oropeza. Once when he bewailed the wickedness of the world, the saint replied, "The remedy is simple. You and I must first be what we ought to be : then we shall have cured what concerns ourselves. Let each one do the same, and all will be well. The trouble is that we all talk of reforming others without ever reforming ourselves." This gentleman built two similar friaries, and certain other houses received the new observance, so that St Peter became commissary general of the Reformed Conventuals of Spain. In the statutes which he drew up he orders that each cell should be only seven feet long, the infirmary thirteen, and the church twenty-four ; that the number of friars in a convent should never exceed eight ; that they should always go barefoot ; that they should employ three hours every day in mental prayer, and never receive any stipend for saying Mass ; and re-enacted the other extreme points of the observance of Arabida. In 1561 this new custody was erected into a province with the title of St Joseph, and Pope Pius IV removed it from the jurisdiction of the Conventuals to that of the Observants. These "Alcantarines" disappeared as a separate body when Pope Leo XIII united the different branches of the Observants in 1897. As is usual in affairs of this sort, the action of St Peter was not well received by those he had left, in this case, the province of St Gabriel. He was a hypocrite, traitor, disturber of peace, ambitious, and was sent for by the commissary general to be told so. "My fathers and brothers," he replied, "make allowance for the justice of my zeal in this matter, and if you are convinced it were better that it should not succeed, spare no pains to stop it." They did not spare them, but the "reform" nevertheless spread as we have just seen.

During the course of a visitation towards the year 1560, St Peter came to Avila, according to some in consequence of a direct instruction from Heaven. Here St Teresa, still at the Incarnation convent, was suffering exterior and interior trials from scruples and anxiety, for many told her that she was deluded by an evil spirit. A lady named Guiomar de Ulloa, an intimate friend of St Teresa, got leave of the provincial of the Carmelites that she might pass eight days in her house, and arranged that St Peter should there talk with her at leisure. From his own experience and knowledge in heavenly communications and raptures, he understood hers, cleared her perplexities, gave her strong assurances that her visions and prayer were from God, and spoke to her confessor in their favour. It is from St Teresa's autobiography that we learn much concerning St Peter's life and miraculous gifts, for he told her in confidence many things concerning the way in which he had lived for seven-and-forty years. " He told me," says she, " that, to the best of my remembrance, he had slept but one hour and a half in twenty-four hours for forty years together ; and that in the beginning it was the greatest and most troublesome mortification of all to overcome himself against sleep, and that for this he was obliged to be always either kneeling or standing. . . . In all these years he never put up his hood, however hot the sun or however heavy the rain ; nor did he ever wear anything upon his feet nor any other garment than his habit of thick coarse cloth (without anything next his skin) and this short and scanty and as straight as possible, with a cloak of the same over it. He told me that when the weather was extremely cold, he was wont to put off his mantle and to leave the door and the window of his cell open, that when he put it on again and shut his door his body might be somewhat refreshed with this additional warmth. It was usual with him to eat but once in three days, and he asked me why I wondered at it : for it was quite possible to one who had accustomed himself to it. One of his companions told me that sometimes he ate nothing at all for eight days. But that perhaps might be when he was in prayer : for he used to have great raptures and vehement transports of divine love, of which I was once an eye-witness. His poverty was as extreme as his mortification, even from his youth. . . . When I came to know him he was very old, and his body so shrivelled and weak that it seemed to be composed as it were of the roots and dried bark of a tree rather than flesh. He was very pleasant but spoke little unless questions were asked him ; and he answered in a few words, but in these he was worth hearing, for he had an excellent understanding." Though a person cannot perform such severe penance as this servant of God did, yet there are many other ways whereby we may tread the world under our feet, and our Lord will teach us these ways when He finds a mind that is receptive.

When St Teresa returned from Toledo to Avila in 1562 she found St Peter there, and in the midst of the business of making a visitation he spent much of the last months of his life and what strength remained to him in helping her to carry through the foundation of her first house of reformed Carmelites, and her success was in good measure due to his encouragement and advice, and to the use which he made of his influence with the Bishop of Avila and others.   On August 24 he was present with Father Peter Ybañez, O.P., and Father Balthasar Alvarez, S.J., when the first Mass was said in the chapel of the new convent of St Joseph.   In the troublous times which followed, when she had to return to the Incarnation convent, St Teresa was strengthened and comforted by several visions of St Peter of Alcantara, who was by then dead.   According to her testimony, quoted in the decree of his canonisation, it was St Peter who did more for her nascent reform than anyone else. That he approached things in a way that would appeal to her may be judged from the opening of his letter to her defending absolute poverty for the new foundation : " I confess I am surprised that you have called in learned men to solve a question which they are not competent to judge. Litigation and cases of conscience belong to canonists and theologians, but questions of the perfect life must be left to those who lead it.   To be able to deal with a matter one must know something about it, and it is not for a learned man to decide if you and I shall or shall not practise the evangelical counsels. . . . He who gives the counsel will provide the means. . . . The abuses in monasteries which have given up revenues arise from this —that poverty in them is endured rather than desired."   Two months after the opening of St Joseph's St Peter was seized with a mortal sickness in the house of the Count of Oropeza, and seeing that his last hour approached he was carried to the convent of Arenas, that he might die in the arms of his brethren.   In his last moments he exhorted his brethren to perseverance and to the constant love of holy poverty, and repeated those words of the psalmist, " I rejoiced at the things that were said to me : We shall go into the house of the Lord."   Then he rose upon his knees, and in that posture calmly died. St Teresa wrote : " Since his departure our Lord has been pleased to let me enjoy more of him than I did when he was alive ; he has given me advice and counsel in many things, and I have frequently seen him in great glory. . . . Our Lord told me once that men should ask nothing in the name of St Peter of Alcantara wherein He would not hear them. I have recommended many things to him that he might beg them of our Lord, and I have always found them granted."   St Peter of Alcantara was beatified by Pope Gregory XV in 1622 and canonised by Clement IX in 1669.

As compared with such mystics as St Teresa of Avila and St John of the Cross, the Life of St Peter of Alcantara seems only to have aroused languid interest. The earliest printed biography which we now possess did not appear until 1615, fifty-three years after the saint's death. It was written by Father John a Santa Maria and a Latin version of it is printed in the *Acta Sanctorum*, October, vol. viii. With this the Bollandists have coupled a somewhat longer Life by Father Laurentius of St Paul, first published in 1669. In 1667 Father Francis Marchese brought out a Life in Italian in which he claims to have made use of the depositions of witnesses in the process of canonisation. This has been translated into many languages, and an English version in two volumes was printed in the Oratorian Series in 1856.

SS. PTOLEMÆUS, LUCIUS, AND ANOTHER, MARTS.

c. A.D. 165

The Roman Martyrology mentions to-day these three martyrs, the circumstances of whose passion are known from the evidence of a contemporary, St Justin Martyr. A certain married woman of dissolute life was converted to Christianity, and in turn tried to reform her husband and to induce him to become a catechumen. Her efforts failed, and the blasphemies and immoralities of her husband becoming unsupportable, she obtained a judicial separation from him. He thereupon denounced her as a Christian, but the woman obtaining permission from the Emperor to reserve her defence, the charge was dropped and the man instead informed against her instructor in the faith, Ptolemæus, who had already been in trouble with the authorities. He was therefore arrested, and after being kept in prison for a long time was brought before the magistrate Urbicius. In reply to the question if he were a Christian, Ptolemæus said that he was, and without more ado was sentenced to death. Thereupon a Christian named Lucius who was present protested to Urbicius, saying, " How is it that this man can be condemned when he is guilty of no crime whatsoever ? Your judgement does no credit to our wise Emperor and the sacred senate." Urbicius turned on him and exclaimed, " You also seem to be one of these Christians," and when Lucius admitted that he was, he also was condemned. Another man, whose name is not recorded, then protested against the injustice, and he suffered with the others.

In the *Acta Sanctorum*, October, vol. viii, the extract is printed which Eusebius has quoted from St Justin's Apology. See also Urbain, *Ein Martyrologium der christlichen Gemeinde zu Rom*, but it should be read in the light of Père Delehaye's comments in the *Analecta Bollandiana*, vol. xxi (1902), pp. 89–93

ST VARUS AND HIS COMPS., MARTS., AND ST CLEOPATRA,
WIDOW

BEGINNING OF THE FOURTH CENTURY

The circumstances of the passion of St Varus, a soldier of the cohort of Tyana who suffered in Upper Egypt, are summarised thus by the Roman Martyrology : " Varus, a soldier, in the time of the Emperor Maximinus [according to the *acta* a mistake for Maximian], visited and fed seven holy monks while they were kept in prison, and when one of them died offered himself as a substitute in his place. And so, after suffering most cruel torments, he received the martyr's palm with them."

The mangled body of St Varus was secured by a Christian woman named Cleopatra, who hid it in a bale of wool and, so disguised, transported it to Adraha in Syria (Derâ'a, east of Lake Tiberias), where she lived. Here she gave it honourable burial and many Christians came to visit the martyr's tomb. When Cleopatra's son, John, was about to become a soldier in the imperial army, she determined to build a basilica in honour of Varus and to translate his body thereto, and at the same time to put her son and his fortunes under the particular patronage of this martyr who had himself been a soldier. She therefore sold a part of her property and built a noble church, and at its dedication she and John themselves carried the bones of St Varus to their new shrine under the altar. That same evening, when the bishop and clergy and other guests had dispersed, John was taken suddenly ill, and during the night he died in his mother's arms. Cleopatra had his body carried into the new church and laid before the altar, and she gave way to her grief and reviled the saint in whose honour she had done so much. She clung to the altar and called on God to restore to life her only child whose body lay there, and so she remained till the following night, when she sank into a deep sleep, exhausted by weeping and sorrow. While she slept she dreamed that St Varus appeared to her in glory, leading John by the hand, and that she laid hold of their feet in mute supplication. And Varus looked down on her and said, " Have I forgotten all the love you have shown for me ? Did I not pray to God that He would give health and advancement to your son ? And behold ! the prayer is answered. He has given him health for eternity and raised him to be among the hosts who follow the Lamb whithersoever He goeth." " I am satisfied," replied Cleopatra, " but I pray you that I also may be taken, that I may be with my son and you." But St Varus replied, " No. Leave your son with me, and wait awhile, and then we will fetch you." When Cleopatra awoke she did as she had been bidden in her dream and had the body of John laid beside that of Varus. And she lived a life of devotion and penitence until, when seven years were passed, she also was called to God, and her body was buried with John and Varus in the basilica which she had built.

The Roman Martyrology does not mention either St Cleopatra or her son, but they are referred to in the Greek *Menaion* under the date October 19.

There is a Greek *passio* which is edited in the *Acta Sanctorum*, October, vol. viii, but in the absence of early *cultus* this pathetic story must be regarded with great suspicion.

ST ETHBIN, Conf.

c. A.D. 580

His father dying when Ethbin was fifteen his mother entrusted him to the care of St Samson and herself retired from the world. Later St Ethbin also heard the call of God to a more perfect life and became a monk under Winwaloe, abbot of Taurac, about the year 554. He was one day walking with his master, when they saw a leper lying helpless at the side of the way. "What shall we do with this poor fellow?" asked Winwaloe. "Do as the apostles of Christ did. Bid him to rise up and walk," replied St Ethbin promptly. Winwaloe had faith both in his monk and in the power of God, and the sufferer was healed. When Taurac was destroyed by the Franks, Ethbin took refuge in Ireland, where he lived in a cabin in an unidentified spot called Nectan Wood for twenty years. And there he died, famous for his virtues and miracles. He is named in the Roman Martyrology.

We cannot put much trust in the short Life which has been printed in the *Acta Sanctorum*, October, vol. viii. See also Baring-Gould and Fisher, *Lives of the British Saints*, vol. ii, p. 466, and Duine, *St Samson* (1909).

ST AQUILINUS, Bp. of Evreux, Conf.

c. A.D. 695

Like many other Frankish saints of the Merovingian era Aquilinus spent years in courts and camps before entering the clerical state and attaining the episcopate. He was a native of Bayeux, born there

about the year 620, and married a lady of equal rank with his own.
He fought in the wars of Clovis II, and on returning from a campaign against the Visigoths met his wife at Chartres, and they there
determined to devote the rest of their days to the direct service of
God and His poor, he being then about forty years old. It is said
that during his absence his wife had made a vow of continence, and
that Aquilinus ratified her action and did the same. They went to
Evreux, where they lived quietly for ten years when, on the death of
St Æternus, said to have been martyred by heretics, St Aquilinus
was considered the most worthy to succeed to the see. He was
frightened of the distractions inseparable from the episcopate and
sought to live rather as a hermit than a bishop ; he had a cell built
near to his cathedral, whither he retired whenever opportunity offered
to spend long hours in prayer and penance on behalf of the flock
which he had been called on to govern. During his last years
St Aquilinus was deprived of his sight, but it made no difference to
his zeal, which God approved by the gift of miracles. He is mentioned in the Roman Martyrology and his Life was written by a
Benedictine called Hecelon in the eleventh or twelfth century.

There is a late biography which is printed in the *Acta Sanctorum*,
October, vol. viii. See also Mesnel, *Les Saints du diocèse d'Évreux*, part v
(1916) ; and Duchesne, *Fastes Épiscopaux*, vol. ii, p. 227.

ST FRIDESWIDE, Virg. and Abbess

c. A.D. 735

Frideswide, patron saint of Oxford and legendary foundress of
the city, was born about the year 650. Her father was Didan, a
South Mercian petty prince, and her mother's name was Safrida.
Her education was entrusted to the care of a virtuous governess
named Algiva, and in the early period of her life her inclinations led
her strongly to a religious state, for she had learned that " whatsoever is not God is nothing." Her father therefore founded for her
a monastery at the place which is now called Oxford. But Algar,
another Mercian prince, smitten with her beauty and not being able
to overcome her resolution, gave so far a loose rein to his passion
as to try to carry her off. St Frideswide thereupon fled down the
Isis with two companions to Abingdon or Benson, and concealed
herself for three years, using a pig's cote as her monastic cell. Algar
continued to pursue her and eventually, on her invoking the aid of
St Catherine and St Cæcilia, he was struck with blindness and only

recovered on his leaving the maiden in peace. From which circumstance it is said that the kings of England up to Henry II made a special point of avoiding Oxford ! On the way back to her monastery Frideswide met a young leper, who implored her in the name of God and His only-begotten Son to kiss him. Making the sign of the cross, she gently did so, and the man became clean. In order to live more perfectly to God in closer retirement, St Frideswide built herself a cell at Thornbury, near the town, where by the fervour of her penance and heavenly contemplation she advanced towards God and His kingdom. The fountain which the saint made use of at Binsey was said to have been obtained by her prayers, and was a place of pilgrimage in the Middle Ages. She died about the year 735, consoled in her last illness by a vision of her protectors, St Catherine and St Cæcilia ; her tomb was honoured with many miracles, and became one of the principal shrines of England.

The extant legend of St Frideswide dates only from four hundred years after her death, and little reliance can be put on it, but she undoubtedly founded a nunnery at Oxford in the eighth century. After various vicissitudes it was rebuilt and refounded in the early twelfth century for Canons Regular of St Augustine, and their theological school was probably the germ of the university. On February 11, 1180, the relics of St Frideswide were solemnly translated to a new shrine in the church of her name by Richard, Archbishop of Canterbury, in the presence of King Henry II ; and twice a year, at mid-Lent and on Ascension Day, it was visited ceremonially by the chancellor and members of the university. By permission of Pope Clement VII the priory of St Frideswide was dissolved by Cardinal Wolsey, who in 1525 founded Cardinal College on its site, the priory church becoming the college chapel. In 1546 the college was re-established by King Henry VIII as Christ Church (*Ædes Christi :* " the House "), and the church which had been St Frideswide's became, as well as college chapel, the cathedral of the new diocese of Oxford (and was so recognised by the Holy See on the reconciliation in Mary's reign). The relics of the saint had of course by this time been removed from their shrine, but apparently they were not scattered. For in the year 1561 a certain Protestant canon of Christ Church, named Calfhill, went to such trouble to desecrate them that it would seem he must have been insane with fanaticism. During the reign of Edward VI there had been buried in the church the body of an apostate nun, Catherine Cathie, who had been through a form of marriage with the apostate friar, Peter Martyr Vermigli. Calfhill had Catherine's remains dug up (they had been removed from the church under Mary), mixed them with the alleged relics of St Frideswide, and thus reinterred them in the church. In the following year an account of this performance was published in Latin (and another in German) which contained a number of pseudo-pious reflections on the text *Hic jacet religio cum superstitione :* " Here lies Religion with Superstition." It does not appear that these words were actually inscribed on the tomb or coffin, though that they were is asserted by several writers, including Alban Butler, whose pleasing comment is, " the obvious meaning of which [epitaph] would lead us to think these men endeavoured to extinguish and bury all religion."

St Frideswide is named in the Roman Martyrology, and her feast is observed in the archdiocese of Birmingham. She also enjoys a *cultus* at Borny in Artois (under the name of Frévise), where a local legend says she found shelter when eluding Algar. Certain relics preserved there are almost certainly spurious ; there is also a spring of water associated with her name, as at Bisney.

We admire in the saints the riches and happiness of which they were possessed in the inestimable treasure of the divine love. They attained to this grace by the exercise of contemplation and a spirit of prayer, and laid the foundation of this spiritual tower by humility and penance. It costs nothing for a man to say that he desires to love God ; but he lies to his own soul unless he strive to die to him-self. The senses must be restrained and taught to obey and the heart purged from inordinate attachments, before it can be moulded anew and rendered spiritual by pure and perfect love. This is the great work of divine grace in weak creatures : but the conditions are that humility and penance prepare the way and be the constant attendants of this love. It is always imperfect in our souls, if it is there at all ; and becomes yet more debased by a mixture of impure motives and the poison of self-love, not sufficiently vanquished because we neglect the means of grace. A sensual man cannot con-ceive those things which are of God.

The legend of St Frideswide has been transmitted in several varying texts (see the *Bibliotheca Hagiographica Latina*, nn. 3162–3169). The more important have been printed or summarized in the *Acta Sanctorum*, October, vol. viii, and have also been discussed by J. Parker, *The Early History of Oxford* (1885), pp. 95–101. *Cf.* also Hardy, *Descriptive Catalogue* (Rolls Series), vol. i, pp. 459–462 ; the *Dict. of Nat. Biog.*, vol. xx, pp. 275–276 ; Stanton's *Menology*, pp. 503–504 ; Baring-Gould and Fisher, *Lives of the British Saints*, vol. ii, pp. 484–487 ; and especially an article by Professor E. F. Jacob, in *The Times*, October 18, 1935, pp. 15–16. A summary of the legend was published by Father F. Goldie, *The Story of St Frideswide*, in 1881.

BD. THOMAS HÉLYE, Conf.

A.D. 1257

Around the district of Biville in Normandy, where he was born about the year 1187, Thomas Hélye is known as "the Wonder-worker" and enjoys a widespread popular *cultus* which was confirmed by Pope Pius IX in 1859. His parents seem to have been people of some local importance and, particularly to please his mother Matilda, Thomas was sent to school. When he was a young man he decided to put the fruits of this privilege at the disposal of other children, and he became a sort of village schoolmaster and catechist in his native place. The good results of his teaching reached the ears of the citizens of Cherbourg, the nearest town, and he was invited to go and instruct the children there, which he did until sickness drove him home again. When he was recovered he continued to live in his father's house, in a manner more like that of an austere monk than of a layman, and he soon became known to the Bishop of Coutances, who ordained him deacon. Thomas then undertook two pilgrimages, to Rome and to Compostela, before going to Paris to complete his studies ; after four years he was made priest. He increased his austerities, spending many hours of the night in prayer, that he might have the more time in the day for pastoral care and preaching, for which he had a great gift. His virtues and great influence brought him to the notice of the King, St Louis IX, who called him to be one of his chaplains. But the royal court, even of a St Louis, was not the place where this simple Norman priest could be happy and at his best, and before long he was allowed to return home. Thomas was then presented to the parochial benefice of Saint-Maurice, but he was by nature a missionary and, appointing a vicar for his cure, he took up his former work of preaching, catechising, visiting the sick and sinners, encouraging the poor and oppressed, exhorting the lukewarm and indifferent, wherever it seemed that God was calling him, not only in Coutances but in the neighbouring dioceses of Avranches, Bayeux, and Lisieux as well. In the midst of these missionary journeys Blessed Thomas was taken ill at the castle of Vauville in La Manche, and died there on October 19, 1257 : the first miracle after his death was the healing of the withered hand of his hostess.

The relics of Blessed Thomas Hélye have an interesting history. His body was buried in the cemetery of Biville ; in 1261 it was translated to a special chapel near the parish church, and later, probably in the sixteenth century, to the church itself. At the Revolution the church was profaned and the tomb of Blessed Thomas, left *in situ*, used as a desk, when M. Lemarié, vicar general of Coutances, determined to save the relics before it was too late. At 10.15 in the evening of July 13, 1794, he, with the parish priest and several of the faithful, penetrated secretly into the church and opened the shrine. The skeleton of the saint was found with nearly all the bones in place. It was quickly wrapped in linen and transferred to a wooden coffin, together with an affidavit of the proceedings, sealed up, and conveyed to the church at Virandeville, where it was hidden under an altar. The revolutionary authorities of Biville were unable to fix the responsibility for the "crime" and visited their annoyance on the "constitutional" *curé*, who was imprisoned for neglect of duty and for concealing the names of the delinquents, which he did not know. The relics were returned to their proper shrine in 1803, except the skull, which was brought back separately from Virandeville to Biville eight years later. There, nearly seven hundred years after the death of Blessed Thomas, they still rest.

There is a valuable medieval Life by a certain Clement, a contemporary, who was an actual witness of much that he records. Four years after the death of Blessed Thomas an investigation was held at which Clement assisted, and he quotes in his biography from the depositions made regarding the holy missionary's virtues and miracles. The text has been edited both in the *Acta Sanctorum*, October, vol. viii, and by L. Delisle in the *Mémoires de la Soc. Acad. de Cherbourg*, 1861, pp. 203–238. See also L. Couppey, *Vie du B. Thomas Hélye* (1903). There seems, however, as Père Van Ortroy has pointed out, no adequate evidence for the statement that Blessed Thomas was ever appointed chaplain to St Louis. *Cf.* the *Analecta Bollandiana*, vol. xxii (1903), p. 505.

BD. PHILIP HOWARD, EARL OF ARUNDEL AND SURREY, MART.

A.D. 1595

Thomas Howard, fourth Duke of Norfolk, was beheaded by order of Queen Elizabeth in 1572, and in consequence of the attainder his son Philip did not succeed to the dukedom of Norfolk; but he became Earl of Arundel and Surrey by right of his mother. His early education was partly under John Fox and partly under Dr. Gregory Martin, but Protestant influence predominated and he went to Cambridge for two years, where "he received no small detriment." At the age of twelve he had been married to Anne, daughter of Thomas, Lord Dacre of Gillesland. When he went to the court of Elizabeth, Philip suffered yet more detriment: he neglected his admirable wife, impoverished his estates, and earned the brief favour of the Queen. But in 1581 he was deeply impressed by hearing a disputation in the Tower of London between Blessed Edmund Campion and others and some Protestant divines ; he returned and became devoted to his wife, and in 1584 they were both reconciled to the Church by Father William Weston, S.J. Before this event they had begun to be under suspicion, and Philip was for a time imprisoned in his own house in London. After it, the manifest change in his way of life gave a further handle for the intrigues of his enemies, and he determined, with his family and his brother William, to fly to Flanders. Philip wrote a long letter to the Queen, explaining his conduct—he was come to the point " in which he must consent either to the certain destruction of his body or the manifest endangering of his soul "—and embarked in Sussex. But all his movements had been watched. He was captured at sea, brought back to London, and committed to the Tower. After twelve months, a charge of treason not being able to be substantiated, he was arraigned on lesser charges, vindictively fined £10,000, and sentenced to imprisonment during the royal pleasure. During the Armada scare he was again brought to trial, before his peers, for high treason in favouring the Queen's enemies. The evidence was partly fraudulent, partly worthless (extorted by fear of torture), but Philip was sentenced to death. The sentence was never executed, why, is not known. He was instead held a prisoner in the Tower for another six years, and he died there on October 19, 1595 (not without suspicion of poison). His dying request that he might see his wife and son, born after his imprisonment, was refused because he would not comply with a condition of attending Protestant worship, which would have also bought his release.

Blessed Philip Howard was thirty-eight years old at his death, and had been for ten years uninterruptedly in prison, wherein his patience and conduct were not merely exemplary but heroic. His conversion to the Faith had been whole-hearted, and he spent much of his time in writing and translating works of devotion. As if close confinement were not sufficient mortification, until his health failed he fasted three days a week, and got up every day for morning prayers at five o'clock. He was particularly penitent for the way he had treated his faithful wife. To Blessed Robert Southwell he wrote : " I call our Lord to witness that no sin grieves me anything so much as my offences to that party " ; and to her : " He that knows all things knows that which is past is a nail in my conscience and burden the greatest I feel there ; my will is to make satisfaction if my ability were able." His dying words to the harsh Lieutenant of the Tower reduced him to tears. He died " in a most sweet manner, without any sign of grief or groan, only turning his head a little aside, as one falling into a pleasing sleep." In a declaration prepared for his expected execution he wrote : " The Catholic and Roman faith which I hold is the only cause (as far as I can any way imagine) why either I have been thus long imprisoned or why I am now ready to be executed."

In the Beauchamp tower of the Tower of London may be seen two inscriptions cut in the wall by the hand of Blessed Philip in May and June 1587, and one referring to him after his death by another Catholic prisoner named Tucker. Philip Howard was beatified in 1929. His relics are at Arundel.

Volume xxi (1919) of the publications of the Catholic Record Society is entirely devoted to Blessed Philip Howard, Earl of Arundel, and these documents, taken in conjunction with the narrative printed in 1857 from the original manuscript under the title *Lives of Philip Howard, Earl of Arundel, and of Anne Dacres his wife,* afford a more perfect insight into the career and character of the Earl than is perhaps available in the case of any other of the Elizabethan martyrs. The biography of the Earl and Countess, as Father Newdigate has shown in *The Month* (March 1931, p. 247), was written in 1635, five years after Lady Arundel's death. The author was a Jesuit Father who acted as her chaplain but his name is not recorded. See also Stanton, *Menology,* pp. 505–507.

OCTOBER 20

ST JOHN CANTIUS, Conf.

A.D. 1473

JOHN CANTIUS (Jan z Kanty), a principal patron of the Latins of Poland and Galicia, was born in the Silesian town of Kenty in the year 1390, at a time when it was under the suzerainty of Bohemia. His parents, Stanislaus and Anne, were country folk of respectable position and, seeing that their son was as quick and intelligent as he was good, they sent him in due course to the University of Cracow. He took good degrees, was ordained priest, and appointed to a lectureship or chair in the university. He was known to lead a very strict life, and when he was warned to look after his health he replied by pointing out that the Fathers of the Desert were notably long-lived. There is a story told that once he was dining in hall, when a famished-looking beggar passed the door. John jumped up and carried out all his commons to the man ; when he returned to his seat he found his plate again full—miraculously. This was for long commemorated in the university by setting aside a special meal for a poor man every day ; when dinner was ready the vice-president would cry out in Latin, " A poor man is coming," to which the president replied, " Jesus Christ is coming," and the man was then served. But while he was yet alive John's success as a preacher and teacher raised up envy against him, and by intrigues he was prevented from taking part in the conference called by King Ladislaus in 1431 to discuss the teachings of the Hussites, and his rivals managed to get him removed and sent as parish priest to Olkusz. St John turned to his new work with single-hearted energy, but his parishioners did not like him and he himself was afraid of the responsibilities of his position. Nevertheless he persevered for eight years, and by the time he was recalled to Cracow had so far won his people's hearts that they accompanied him on part of the road with such grief that he said to them, " This sadness does not please God. If I have done any good for you in all these years, sing a song of joy."

St John's second appointment at the university was as professor of sacred Scripture, and he held it to the end of his life. He left such a reputation that his violet doctoral gown was for long used to vest each candidate at the conferring of degrees, but his fame was not at all confined to academic circles. He was a welcome guest at the tables of the nobility (once his shabby cassock caused the servants to refuse him admission, so he went away and changed it. During the meal a dish was upset over the new one. " No matter," he said, " my clothes deserve some dinner because to them I owe the pleasure of being here at all "), and he was known to all the poor in Cracow. His goods and money were always at their disposition, and time and again they literally " cleared him out." But his own needs were few ; he slept on the floor, never ate meat, and when he went to Rome (which he did four times) he walked all the way and carried his luggage on his back. He also made a pilgrimage to Jerusalem, where he invited martyrdom by preaching the gospel to the Mohammedans : perhaps his gentleness saved him, for he was never weary of telling his pupils to " fight all false opinions, but let your weapons be patience, sweetness, and love. Roughness is bad for your own soul and spoils the best cause." For a short time St John Cantius was tutor to the children of King Casimir IV and Queen Elizabeth, and so had a part in the formation of the young prince St Casimir, in whose honour the Polish church in London is dedicated. Several miracles were reported of St John, and when news got round the city that he was dying there was an outburst of sorrow. " Never mind about this prison which is decaying," he said to those who were looking after him, " but think of the soul that is going to leave it." He died on Christmas Eve, 1473, at the age of seventy-seven, and was buried in the university church of St Anne. St John Cantius was canonised by Pope Clement XIII in 1767, and his feast extended to the whole Western Church. He is the only confessor not a bishop who has different hymns for Matins, Lauds, and Vespers in the Roman Breviary.

The Bollandists in the *Acta Sanctorum*, October, vol. viii (1853), were unable to discover any satisfactory medieval account of St John Cantius, and they reproduced a biography published in 1628 by Adam of Opatow. This writer claims to have had access to materials preserved at Cracow, and in particular to have used notes compiled by a contemporary, Matthias of Miechow, who certainly drew up a record of miracles attributed to St John after his death. The latter document is also printed by the Bollandists. A note upon the place and date of birth of St John, by Father A. Arndt, will be found in the *Analecta Bollandiana*, vol. viii (1889), pp. 382–388. See also J. Bukowski and W. Wislocki in the *Sitzungs-Berichte* of the Academy of Cracow, 1890. A French Life of St John by E. Benoît was published in 1862. Lives in Polish are numerous.

ST CAPRASIUS, Mart.

c. A.D. 292 (?)

According to the legend of the church of Agen St Caprasius was the first bishop of that city, and when his flock dispersed and fled before the persecution of Maximian he followed them in their hiding-places to minister to them. But from his place of refuge on Mont-Saint-Vincent he was a witness of the passion of St Fides (October 6), and when he saw the marvels with which God surrounded her martyrdom he went down to the place where her body still lay on its pyre and confronted the prefect, Dacian. He had first been shown the will of God in his regard by a sensible sign, for, striking the rock where he stood and watched, a copious spring of water flowed therefrom. When asked his name he replied that he was a Christian and a bishop, and was called Caprasius. Dacian remarked on his good looks and youth and offered him rich rewards and the friendship of the Emperors if he would apostatise. Caprasius replied that he wanted to live in no other palace than that of Him whom he worshipped or to have any other riches than those that were imperishable. He was handed over to the torturers, and his constancy so impressed the bystanders that the prefect ordered him to prison. The next day Caprasius was sentenced to death and on his way to execution met his mother, who encouraged him to remain firm. Then he was joined by Alberta, sister of Fides, and by two young brothers called Primus and Felician, nor was the governor able to turn them from their determination to suffer with Caprasius. So they were all led to the temple of Diana, to give them a last opportunity to sacrifice to the false goddess, and when they refused were beheaded, Caprasius last of all. Then followed a wholesale massacre, for many pagans professed Christianity on the spot and were cut down by the soldiers or stoned by their neighbours.

This story is entirely fictitious, being an amplification and modification of another *passio* of St Caprasius, which in its turn is simply that of St Symphorian (August 22) with the necessary alterations of names and places; there is no mention in it of Caprasius being a bishop, though he was doubtless a real person. Alberta, Primus, and Felician, on the other hand, probably never existed, though the feasts of all of them are kept at Agen; the two last must be distinguished from the Roman martyrs of the same names on June 9. The Roman Martyrology gives a long entry to St Caprasius, but does not call him a bishop and makes no mention of his companions.

In the *Acta Sanctorum*, October, vol. viii, two or three variants are printed of that form of the *passio* in which the story of St Caprasius and St Faith are fused into one. See above, p. 75, under October 6. Mgr Duchesne, *Fastes Épiscopaux*, vol. ii, pp. 144–146, is inclined to date this amalgamation of the legends as late as the ninth century. See also Saltet, *Étude critique sur la Passion de Ste Foy et de St Caprais*, 1899.

ST ARTEMIUS, Mart.

A.D. 363

Cardinal Baronius inserted the name of St Artemius in the Roman Martyrology, following the example of the Eastern Church which had venerated him from time immemorial as " megalo-martyr," in spite of the fact that he was undoubtedly an Arian and that there is no record of his conversion to orthodoxy. He was a veteran of the army of Constantine the Great and in the year 356 was entrusted by Constantius with the task of translating the relics of St Andrew, St Luke, and St Timothy to Constantinople. Having done this satisfactorily he was made imperial prefect of Egypt, and in discharging this office he had to be a persecutor as well as a heretic. George the Cappadocian had been intruded upon the epis-copal throne of Alexandria by the Arian Emperor, St Athanasius had fled, and it was the duty of Artemius to find him, which he en-deavoured to do with great zeal among the monasteries and hermitages of the Egyptian deserts ; he also persecuted the faithful Catholics in general and several bishops were put to death or exiled under his administration. But Artemius was no less zealous against pagan-ism, destroying temples and images, so that when Julian the Apostate became emperor the persecutor was in turn persecuted. Many accusations against Artemius were made to the Emperor by the people of Alexandria, among others, that of breaking up idols ; he was accordingly deprived of his property and beheaded, probably at Alexandria and not at Antioch as the Roman Martyrology says. The *acta* of St Artemius say nothing about his Arianism and vio-lence ; as he has been venerated for so long by the Greeks it is possible that he abjured heresy and that all record of it is lost.

Whether the Artemius, whose healing shrine was a great centre of devotion at Constantinople, was identical with the Artemius, the prefect of Alexandria, put to death by Julian the Apostate, does not seem to be entirely clear. But the Greek Life, printed in the *Acta Sanctorum*, October vol. viii, which is based ultimately upon the Arian chronicler Philostorgius, quite definitely assumes this. The special interest of this alleged martyr lies in the miracles wrought at his shrine, the detailed record of which has been edited by A. Papadopoulos-Kerameus in his *Varia Græca Sacra* (1900), pp. 1–79. In these cures something analogous to the incubation, practised by the votaries of Æsculapius at Epidaurus and described by Aristides, seems to have been observed. See Delehaye, *Les Recueils Antiques des Miracles des Saints* (1925), pp. 32–38 ; and M. P. Maas, " Artemioskult in Constantinopel," in *Byzantinisch-Neugriechische Jahrbücher*, vol. i (1920), pp. 377 *seq.*

ST ACCA, BP. OF HEXHAM, CONF.

A.D. 742

In the household of St Bosa, who afterwards was made bishop of Deira (York), was brought up a young Northumbrian named Acca, who profited greatly from the instruction and example of his master. After a time he attached himself to St Wilfrid, whom he served faithfully throughout his troubled life and accompanied on his second journey to Rome in 692, where, says St Bede, Acca " learned many useful things about the government of Holy Church which he could not have learned in his own country." St Wilfrid confided to him the vision of St Michael, which he had at Meaux promising him a further four years of life, and when he was restored to the see of Hexham he made Acca abbot of the monastery of St Andrew there. St Wilfrid died in 709 and Acca succeeded to his bishopric. St Bede speaks very highly of him : " He was," he says, " a most active person and great in the sight of God and man . . . most orthodox in the profession of the Catholic faith and observant in the rules of ecclesiastical institution ; nor did he ever cease to be so till he received the reward of his religious devotion."

St Acca's activity was very varied. He decorated and enlarged his cathedral church and procured for it numerous relics of saints and martyrs, as well as vessels, lamps, and other furniture. He was learned in the holy Scriptures and formed a library in which he deposited the histories of the confessors whose deeds as well as whose relics he was diligent in gathering, and he was a munificent patron of scholars and students. He obtained from Kent the services of a celebrated cantor, Maban, who had been taught church chant according to the Roman manner by the successors of the monks sent to England by St Gregory. Both St Acca himself, who was a very good singer, and his clergy profited by the tuition of Maban for twelve years, learning many new chants and correcting those that were corrupt. In his encouragement of learning Acca caused Stephen Eddius to write the Life of his beloved master St Wilfrid, and also assisted St Bede, who dedicated some of his Biblical and other works to him.

In the year 732, for some reason now unknown, St Acca had to leave his diocese, and is said to have lived in exile at Withern in Galloway. But he was enabled to return to Hexham, where he died and was buried with great veneration in 742. There was a discovery of his relics, in consequence of a vision, three hundred years later, and they were solemnly translated to a new shrine; the miracles attributed to the saint were written down by St Aelred and by the chronicler Simeon of Durham.

For original sources we have Bede's *Ecclesiastical History*, and Richard of Hexham's *Brevis Annotatio*, but this last is little more than a careful compilation from Eddius and other earlier authorities. Raine's *Memorials of Hexham*, vol. i, pp. xxx–xxxv and 31–36, supplies nearly all the information obtainable, but consult also the *Acta Sanctorum*, October, vol. viii; Stanton's *Menology*, pp. 507–508; and A. S. Cook in *Transactions of the Connecticut Academy of Arts and Sciences*, vol. xxvi (1924), pp. 245–332. A letter of St Acca to Bede is preserved and has been printed in Bede's works and elsewhere.

ST ANDREW OF CRETE, Mart.

A.D. 766

This martyr is sometimes distinguished as " the Calybite " or " in Crisi " from the other St Andrew of Crete (July 4), who died some twenty years earlier. He was first a monk on his native island, but when he heard of the aggravated campaign under the Emperor Constantine Copronymus against the veneration of holy images he made his way to Constantinople to take part in the struggle. He was present at the palace of St Mamas when the Emperor himself was watching the torture of some orthodox Christians, and uttered a public and impassioned protest. He was dragged before the imperial throne, and when he had explained his action Constantine told him he was an idolater. St Andrew retorted by accusing the Emperor of heresy. He was set on and beaten by the bystanders and was carried, bruised and bleeding, to prison, calling out to Constantine, " See how powerless you are against faith ! " The next day he repeated his defence of images before the Emperor, who ordered him to be again scourged and then led through the streets as an example to the people. As he was being thus dragged along a fanatical iconoclast stabbed him through the foot with a fishing-spear, and at the Place of the Ox St Andrew fell dead from ill-usage and loss of blood. His body was thrown into a cesspit, but was retrieved by the orthodox, who buried it at a near-by place called Crisis, where the monastery of St Andrew was afterwards built.

Everything that has been and is and will be is known and present to God, and all the deeds that have been done by the help of His grace shine perpetually before His eyes. And it is His will that so much of these as can be recovered, from the divine works of Creation and the words and deeds of our incarnate Lord to the details of the lives of the blessed and of the passions of the martyrs, shall be written down to be known of men. He wishes to lead us by consideration of these things to the recognition and love of His glory and by recalling the memory of His faithful servants to remind us of the virtues and aims we should have ever before our eyes. God shows the martyrs particularly as examples of moral strength, types of true wisdom for all those whom He has called to eternal life.

The statement made by Theophanes (Confessor) that Andrew was at one time an anchorite seems to be erroneous. There are two apparently independent versions of the *passio*, both printed in the *Acta Sanctorum*, October, vol. viii. Pargoire in *Échos d'Orient*, vol. xiii (1910), pp. 84–86, maintains on good grounds that Andrew was martyred on November 20, 766.

OCTOBER 21

ST HILARION, Abbot and Conf.

c. A.D. 371

HILARION was born in a village called Tabatha, five miles to the south of Gaza, in the year 291, his parents being idolaters. He was sent by them to Alexandria to study, when by his progress in learning and his good temper and disposition he was beloved by all who knew him. Being brought to the knowledge of the Christian faith he was baptised when he was about fifteen, and having heard of St Antony, whose name was famous in Egypt, he went into the desert to see him. Moved by his example, he changed his dress and stayed with him two months, observing his manner of life. But Hilarion found the desert only less distracting than the town and, not being able to bear the concourse of those who resorted to St Antony to be healed of diseases or delivered from devils, and being desirous to begin to serve God, as Antony had done, in perfect solitude, he returned with certain monks into his own country. Upon his arrival, finding his father and mother both dead, he gave part of his goods to his brethren and the rest to the poor, reserving nothing for himself (for he was mindful of Ananias and Sapphira, says St Jerome). This happened about the year 307. He retired into the desert seven miles from Majuma, towards Egypt, between the seashore on one side and a swamp on the other. His friends warned him that the place was notorious for murders and robberies; but his answer was that he feared nothing but eternal death. He was a comely and even delicate youth, affected by the least excess of heat or cold, yet his whole clothing consisted only of a piece of sackcloth, a leather tunic which St Antony gave him, and an ordinary short cloak. He cut his hair only once a year, at Easter; never changed a tunic till it was worn out, and never washed the sackcloth which he had once put on, saying, " It is idle to look for cleanliness in a hair-shirt," which mortifications, comments Alban Butler, " the respect we owe to our neighbour makes unseasonable in the world."

For six years together his whole diet was fifteen figs a day, which he never took till sunset. When he felt the attacks of any temptation of the flesh he would say to his body, "I will see to it, thou ass, that thou shalt not kick. I will feed thee with straw instead of corn; and will load and weary thee till thou shalt think rather how to get a little bit to eat than of pleasure." He then cut off part of his scanty meal and sometimes fasted three or four days without eating, at the same time breaking up his ground that the labour might add to the hardship of fasting. His occupation was tilling the earth and, in imitation of the Egyptian monks, making baskets, whereby he provided himself with the necessaries of life. During the first four years of his penance he had no other shelter than a little arbour, which he made of reeds and rushes woven together. Afterwards he built himself a cell, which was still to be seen in St Jerome's time; it was four feet broad and five in height, and a little longer than his body, so that a person would have taken it for a tomb rather than a house. From the age of twenty-one he found that figs alone were insufficient to support life properly and permitted himself to eat as well vegetables, bread, and oil. But advancing age was not allowed to lessen his austerities. St Jerome remarks that slothful Christians too easily make old age, and every other pretence, a plea to be the more remiss in their penance; but fervour made St Hilarion contrive means to redouble his, the nearer the prospect of death grew and the shorter time remained for his preparation. St Hilarion underwent many grievous trials. Sometimes his soul was covered with a dark cloud and his heart was dry and oppressed with bitter anguish; but the deafer Heaven seemed to his cries on such occasions, the louder and the more earnestly he persevered in prayer. At other times his mind was haunted and his imagination filled with impure images or with the attractions of the theatre and circus. These painful assaults the hermit repulsed with prayer and hard labour, and after the departure of the vanquished enemy the saint found his soul filled with unspeakable peace, and in the joy of his heart sang to God hymns of praise and thanksgiving: "The horse and the rider He hath thrown into the sea. . . . Some trust in chariots and some in horses, but we will call upon the name of the Lord our God."

St Hilarion had spent twenty years in his desert when he wrought his first miracle. A certain married woman of Eleutheropolis (Beit Jibrin, near Hebron) was in despair for her barrenness, sought him out in his solitude, and prevailed upon him to pray that God would bless her with fruitfulness; and before the year's end she brought forth a son. Later, the prefect Elpidius and his wife Aristenata, returning from a visit to St Antony, arrived at Gaza, where their three children fell sick and their recovery was despaired of by the physicians. The mother addressed herself to Hilarion who, moved by her tears, went to Gaza to visit them. Upon his invoking the holy name of Jesus by their bedside, the children safely passed their crisis and soon after recovered. In consequence of his increasing fame many flocked to the saint, desiring to embrace a monastic life under his direction. Till that time neither Syria nor Palestine were acquainted with Christian monasticism, so that St Hilarion was the first founder of it in those countries as St Antony had been in Egypt. Among other miraculous happenings, St Hilarion is said to have helped a Christian citizen of Majuma, called Italicus, who kept horses to run in the circus against those of a *duumvir* of Gaza. Italicus, believing that his adversary had recourse to spells to stop his horses, came for aid to St Hilarion, by whose blessing his horses seemed to fly, while the others seemed fettered : upon seeing which the people cried out that the god of the *duumvir* was vanquished by Christ. From the model which he set a number of monasteries were founded all over Palestine, and St Hilarion visited them all on certain days before the vintage. In one of these visits, watching the pagans assembled in great numbers at Elusa, to the south of Beersheba, for the worship of their gods, he shed tears to God for them. Many of their sick had been cured by him, so he was well known to them and they came to ask his blessing. He received them with gentleness and humility, beseeching them to adore God rather than stones. His words had such effect that they would not suffer him to leave them till he had traced the ground for laying the foundation of a church, and till their priest, all dressed for his office as he was, had become a catechumen.

St Hilarion was informed by revelation in Palestine of the death of St Antony. He was then about sixty-five years old, and had been for two years much afflicted at the great number of bishops, priests, monks and other people, especially women, who crowded to him ; moreover the charge of his disciples was a great burden. " I have returned to the world," he said, " and received my reward in this life. All Palestine regards me, and I even possess a farm and household goods, under pretext of the brethren's needs." So he resolved to leave the country, and the people assembled to the number of ten thousand to stop him. He told them he would neither eat nor drink till they let him go ; and seeing him pass seven days without taking anything, they left him. He then chose forty monks who were able to walk without eating till after sunset, and with them he travelled into Egypt. On the fifth day he arrived at Pelusium, and in six days more at Babylon (Fostat or Old Cairo) in Egypt. Two days after he came to Aphroditopolis (Atfieh), where he applied to the deacon Barsanes, who used to let dromedaries to those who desired to visit St Antony. After travelling three more days in a waterless desert they came to St Antony's mountain, near the Red Sea, where they found two monks, Isaac and Pelusianus, who had been his disciples. St Hilarion walked all over the place with them. " Here it was," said they, " that he sang, here he prayed ; there he laboured and there he reposed when he was weary. He himself planted these vines, and these little trees ; he tilled this piece of ground with his own hands ; he dug this pond to water his garden, and he used this hoe to work with for several years." St Hilarion laid himself upon his bed, and kissed it as if it had been still warm. On the top of the mountain (to which the ascent was very difficult, twisting like a vine) they found two cells to which he often retired to avoid visitors and even his own disciples ; and near by was the garden where the power of Antony had made the wild asses respect his vegetables and young trees. St Hilarion asked to see the place where he was buried. They led him aside, but it is unknown whether they showed it him or no ; for they said that St Antony had given strict charge that his grave should be concealed, lest Pergamius, a very rich man in that country, should carry the body home and build a church for it.

St Hilarion returned to Aphroditopolis, and thence went with only two disciples into a neighbouring desert and gave himself with more earnestness than ever to abstinence and silence, saying that he then only began to serve Jesus Christ. It had not rained in the country for three years, ever since the death of St Antony, and the people addressed themselves to St Hilarion, whom they looked upon as St Antony's successor, imploring his prayers. The saint lifted up his hands and eyes to Heaven, and immediately obtained a plentiful downpour. Many labourers and herdsmen who were stung by serpents and insects were cured by anointing their wounds with oil which he had blessed and given them. Hilarion, finding himself too popular also in that place, departed secretly towards Alexandria, in order to reach a further desert. It not being his custom to stop in great cities, he turned aside from Alexandria into a ruined suburb, where several monks dwelt. He left this place the same evening, and when the monks pressed him to stay he told them that it was necessary for their security that he should leave. He showed the spirit of prophecy ; for that very night armed men arrived there in pursuit, to put him to death. When Julian the Apostate ascended the throne, the pagans of Gaza destroyed his monastery and obtained an order to kill him, in revenge for the many conversions he had made ; and they had sent this party into Egypt to carry out the sentence. The soldiers, finding themselves disappointed, exclaimed that he well deserved the character of a magician which he had at Gaza. The saint spent a year in an oasis of the western desert, and finding that he was too well known ever to lie concealed in Egypt determined to seek some remote island. He refused to return to his ruined monastery at Gaza, though Julian was now dead, and embarked with one companion for Sicily. He offered to pay for their passage with a copy of the gospels which he had written in his youth with his own hand ; but the master, seeing their whole stock consisted in that manuscript and the clothes on their backs, would not accept it, because, moreover, Hilarion by his prayers had delivered his son on board the vessel, who was possessed by a devil. From Cape Passaro they travelled twenty miles up the country and stopped in an unfrequented place ; here by gathering sticks he made every day a faggot, which he sent his disciple, Zananas, to sell at the next village in order to buy bread. St Hesychius, the saint's disciple, had sought him in the East and through Greece when, at Modon in Peloponnesus, he heard from a Jewish peddler that a prophet had appeared in Sicily who wrought many miracles. He arrived at Passaro and, inquiring for the holy man at the first village, found that everybody knew him : he was not more distinguished by his miracles than by his disinterestedness, for he could never be induced to accept anything, not even a morsel of bread, from anyone.

He found that St Hilarion wanted to go into some strange country where not even his language should be understood, and so Hesychius took him to Epidaurus in Dalmatia, near Ragusa. Miracles again defeated the saint's design of living unknown. St Jerome relates that a serpent of enormous size devoured both cattle and men, and that Hilarion, having prayed, induced this creature to come on to a pile of wood prepared on purpose ; then set fire to it so that it was burnt to ashes. He also tells us that when an earthquake happened in the year 366, the sea threatened to overwhelm the city of Epidaurus. The affrighted inhabitants brought Hilarion to the shore, as it were to oppose him as a strong wall against the waves. He made three crosses in the sand, then stretched forth his arms towards the sea which, rising up like a high mountain, returned back. St Hilarion, troubled over what he should do or whither he should turn, going alone over the world in his imagination, mourned that though his tongue was silent yet his miracles spake. At last he fled away in the night in a small vessel to the island of Cyprus. Arrived there, he settled at a place two miles from Paphos. He had not been there three weeks when such as suffered by unclean spirits in any part of the island began to cry out that Hilarion, the servant of Jesus

Christ, was come, and the inhabitants watched him that he might not leave them. Instead, he went to a solitary place twelve miles from the shore, pleasantly situated where there was water with fruit trees, though Hilarion never tasted the fruit. St Jerome mentions that though he lived so many years in Palestine Hilarion only once went up to visit the holy places at Jerusalem, and then stayed only one day. He went once that he might not seem to despise what the Church honours, but did not go oftener lest he should seem persuaded that God or His worship is confined to any particular place. In the eightieth year of his age, whilst Hesychius was absent, he wrote him a letter in the nature of a will and testament, in which he bequeathed to him all his riches, namely, his book of the gospels, a sackcloth, shirt, hood, and little cloak. Many persons came from Paphos to see him in his last sickness, among them St Epiphanius, Bishop of Salamis, who afterwards wrote his Life, and a woman named Constantia, whose son-in-law and daughter he had freed from death by anointing them with oil. He made them swear that as soon as he was dead they would bury him just as he was in his own garden. And now very little heat appeared in his body, nor did anything seem to remain in him of a living man except his understanding. But his eyes were still open, and he said to his soul, " Go forth ! What dost thou fear ? Go forth, my soul ! What dost thou doubt ? It is now near threescore and ten years that thou hast served Christ, and art thou afraid of death ? " He had scarcely spoken these words when he gave up the ghost, and was immediately buried as he had ordered.

If this saint trembled after an innocent, penitential, and holy life, because he considered how perfect the purity of a soul must be to stand before Him who is infinite goodness and infinite justice, how much ought tepid, slothful, and sinful Christians to fear ? Whilst love gives the saints an ardent desire of being united to God in the kingdom of love and peace, a holy fear of His justice checks and humbles in them all presumption. This fear must never sink into despondency, abjection, or despair, but rebuke our sloth, animate our fervour, and raise our courage ; it must be careful, not anxious or pusillanimous ; and, whilst we fear from whatever is in us, love and hope must fill our souls with peace and joy and with an entire confidence in the infinite mercy and goodness of God and the merits of our divine Redeemer.

The Life by St Jerome is our primary source and there is no reason to doubt that much of his information was derived from St Epiphanius who had had personal contact with Hilarion. The historian Sozomen also gives independent testimony, and there are other references elsewhere which have all been carefully collected in the *Acta Sanctorum*, October, vol. ix. A good deal has been written on the subject of recent years : see especially Zöckler, " Hilarion von Gaza " in *Neue Jahrbücher für deutsche Theologie*, vol. iii (1894), pp. 146–178 ; Delehaye, " Saints de Chypre " in *Analecta Bollandiana*, vol. xxvi (1907), pp. 241–242 ; Schiwietz, *Das Morgenländische Mönchtum*, vol. ii, pp. 95–126 ; and H. Leclercq, " Cénobitisme " in *Diction. d'Archéol.*, etc., vol. ii, cc. 3157–3158.

ST URSULA AND HER COMPS., VIRGS. AND MARTS.

THIRD CENTURY (?)

The feast of St Ursula and the maiden martyrs of Cologne is now treated with considerable reserve in the Roman liturgy (it was a project of Pope Benedict XIV to suppress it altogether). It is accorded only a commemoration, with no proper lesson at Matins ; the Martyrology ventures to say that they suffered at the hands of the Huns on account of their constancy in religion and chastity, but gives no particulars of numbers or other circumstances.

There is in the church of St Ursula at Cologne a stone bearing a Latin inscription, probably cut during the second half of the fourth century of our era. Its meaning is far from clear, but it seems certainly to record that one Clematius, a man of senatorial rank, rebuilt, in consequence of certain visions, a ruined basilica in honour of some virgins who had been martyred in that place. Nothing is said of the number, their names, or the time and circumstances of their passion. From this it may be inferred that some time or other some maidens were martyred at Cologne, and that they were sufficiently well known to have had a church built in their honour at least by the beginning of the fourth century. And this is all that can be said with reasonable certainty of the martyrs made famous by the great and ramified legend of St Ursula and her Eleven Thousand Virgins.

The earliest known form of that legend is a sermon preached at Cologne on their feast-day, probably between the years 731 and 834. The preacher says that there was then no authentic written account of their passion and nothing certainly known of them, and professes himself to give the local tradition : they were numerous, even thousands ; their leader was called Vinnosa (Pinnosa) ; and they suffered in the persecution of Maximian. He refers to the theory that the girls had come to Cologne in the wake of the Theban Legion, but himself inclines to the view that they were natives of Britain returning from a pilgrimage to Palestine. None of the classical martyrologies of this period mentions the martyrs, except that Usuardus records the virgins Martha and Saula with several companions at Cologne on October 20 (these are given separately from St Ursula in the present Roman Martyrology) and Wandalbert of Prüm refers to the thousands of virgins of Christ who suffered on the Rhine on October 21. The first mention of St Ursula, as one of eleven virgin-martyrs, occurs in a kalendar of the end of the ninth century, and other liturgical sources of about that time give the name as one of five, eight, or eleven, but in only one does Ursula come first. In the early years of the tenth century the number was beginning to be fixed at " eleven thousand," how or why is not known : the most favoured explanations are the abbreviation XI M.V (*undecim martyres virgines*) misunderstood as *undecim millia virginum* or a combination of the " eleven " of some documents with the " thousands " of others.

The legend as it took shape in Cologne at the latter part of the tenth century is as follows. Ursula, the daughter of a Christian king in Britain, was asked in marriage by the son of a pagan king. She, desiring to remain unwed, got a delay of three years, which time she spent on shipboard, sailing about the seas ; she had ten noble ladies-in-waiting, each of whom had a thousand companions, and they were accommodated in eleven vessels.* At the end of the period of grace contrary winds drove them into the mouth of the Rhine, they sailed up to Cologne and then on to Bâle, where they disembarked and went over the Alps to visit the tombs of the apostles at Rome. They returned by the same way to Cologne, where they were set upon and massacred for their Christianity by the heathen Huns, Ursula having refused to marry their chief. Then the barbarians were dispersed by angels, the citizens buried the martyrs, and a church was built in their honour by Clematius, who came there from the East. Another and parallel story, of Gaulish provenance, interesting to Englishmen but no less fanciful, is given in a later version by Geoffrey of Monmouth. He says that the Emperor Maximian (he means Magnus Clemens Maximus ; " Macsen Wledig "), having become master of Britain and Gaul (which Maximus did in 383), planted Armorica with British colonists and soldiers and put them under a prince called Cynan Meiriadog. Cynan appealed to the King of Cornwall, curiously named Dianotus, to send out women as wives for his settlers. Dianotus responded very handsomely by despatching his own daughter Ursula, with 11,000 maidens of noble birth and 60,000 young women of the meaner sort.

* There is a charming account of the mobilisation of this company in the *Golden Legend.*

Ursula was very beautiful and intended to be married to Cynan himself. But on its voyage to Brittany the fleet was scattered and blown north by a storm ; the women were cast away among strange islands and barbarous peoples, and suffered servitude and martyrdom at the hands of the Huns (and the Picts, adds Geoffrey).

The Cologne version represents the more or less official legend, the date 451 being assigned to the martyrdom, " when Attila and his Huns were retreating after their defeat in Gaul ; having captured Cologne, then a flourishing Christian city, the first victims of their fury were Ursula and her British followers " (lesson formerly read in England). But during the twelfth century it underwent incredible elaboration, chiefly by means of the " revelations " of Helentrudis, a nun of Heerse, near Paderborn, of St Elizabeth of Schönau, and of a Premonstratensian canon, Blessed Herman Joseph. It is not now questioned that these visionaries were deceived, but at the time they had the support of the " discovery " at Cologne in 1155 of numerous sham relics and forged inscriptions purporting to be the epitaphs of Pope St Cyriacus, St Marinus of Milan, St Papunius, King of Ireland, St Picmenius, King of England, and numerous other entirely imaginary people who were fabled to have suffered with St Ursula. The so-called revelations of Blessed Herman are even more surprising than those of St Elizabeth. They profess to solve several problems presented by the ever-expanding legend, including the presence of the bones of men, children, and even of babes among those of the martyrs. There is no doubt that the great finding of 1155 (there had been smaller ones previously) was due to the opening-up of a common burial-ground, and it is difficult to resist the conclusion that two Benedictine abbots of Deutz engineered an impious fraud in which St Elizabeth and Blessed Herman were inculpably implicated. There is a vast collection of these relics to this day in the church of St Ursula at Cologne, and portions of them have gone all over the world.

Through these mediæval activities numbers of names of individual Ursuline martyrs have gained currency and are found in local kalendars and martyrologies. Among them is St Cordula, named in the Roman Martyrology on the morrow. " She hid herself, being frightened by the sufferings and death of the others. But the next day she repented, gave herself up to the Huns, and was the last of all to receive the martyr's crown." This is a contribution of Helentrudis of Heerse to the legend.

The long dissertation of Father Victor de Buck which occupies 230 folio pages in the *Acta Sanctorum*, October, vol. ix (1858), was summarised by Cardinal Wiseman in an address which somehow seems to have escaped republication among his other writings. It may be read in a volume, *Essays on Religion and Literature*, edited by Manning (1865), where it bears the title " The Truth of Supposed Legends and Fables " (pp. 235–286) and is accompanied with a facsimile of the Clematius inscription. Father de Buck contributed much that was new and sound to the solution of the problem, reprinting most of the more vital texts, but his conclusions, more particularly his contention that the feast commemorates a great massacre of Christian virgins by the Huns in 451, have by no means been upheld by later research. The most important study of the subject which has since appeared is that of the eminently critical medievalist, W. Levison, *Das Werden der Ursula-Legende* (1928). He defends against all objections the authenticity of the Clematius inscription, but he agrees with other archæologists in regarding it as definitely anterior to the Hun inroad of 451. From its actual wording we learn that one Clematius, wishing to do honour to a group of martyred virgins, *restored* a small basilica, or *cella memorialis*, which, let us note, very possibly had been laid waste by the Franks *c.* 353. The martyrs seem to have been buried there, and Clematius laid a ban upon other interments in that spot. The language is quite inconsistent with the idea of a vast cemetery in which thousands of corpses had been heaped together. After the Clematius inscription, the *Sermo in natali*, and the brief liturgical notices referred to above, the most important document is the earliest *passio,* " Fuit tempore," which de Buck, not having seen the prologue, unfortunately disregarded. It was first printed in the *Analecta Ballandiana*, vol. iii (1884), pp. 5–20. From these origins the legend developed, but the evolution is too complicated and the literature too vast for more detailed notice. Consult, however, in particular, M. Coens in the *Analecta Bollandiana*, vol. xlvii (1929), pp. 80–110 ; Dom G. Morin in *Études, Textes, Découvertes* (1913), pp. 206–219, who sagaciously calls attention to Procopius, *De Bello Gothico*, iv, 20 ; T. F. Tout, *Historical Essays* (1907), pp. 17–56 ; Albert Poncelet in the *Catholic Encyclopedia*, vol. xv, pp. 225–228 ; H. Leclercq in *Diction. d'Archéol., etc.*, vol. iii, cc. 2172–2180 ; Baring-Gould and Fisher, *Lives of the British Saints*, vol. iv (1913), pp. 312–347 ; and Neuss, *Die Anfänge des Christentums im Rheinlande*, 2d Edition, 1933. One of the most recent contributions to the subject, dealing primarily with the representations of the legend in art, is that of Guy de Tervarent, *La Légende de Ste Ursule*, 2 vols. in 4°, 1931. Finally, as regards the statement that St Dunstan supplied the story which is recounted in the *passio* " Fuit tempore," it is a curious fact that St Dunstan seems to have received episcopal consecration on October 21, and also that some of the few saints named in the Ursula legend were honoured at an early date at Glastonbury and in the west of England. If Dunstan, as is now believed, was born in 910 and not in 925, some intercourse with Hoolfus, the envoy of the Emperor Otto, would have been by no means impossible.

ST MALCHUS, Conf.

END OF THE FOURTH CENTURY

For the story of St Malchus, who is mentioned to-day in the Roman Martyrology, we are indebted to St Jerome, who had it from the lips of the man himself. When he was in Antioch about the year 375 he visited Maronia, some thirty miles away, where his attention was attracted to a very devout old man whose name, he discovered, was Malchus (Melek). St Jerome was interested in what he heard about him, went to the old man for more information, and was told the following tale of his life. Malchus was born in Nisibis, the only son of his parents, who when he had reached the requisite age wanted him to marry. He, however, had already resolved to give himself wholly to God, so he ran away secretly and joined the hermits in the wilderness of Chalcis. Some years later he learned of the death of his father, and he went to his superior and told him that he wished to go home in order to comfort and look after his mother. The abbot was unsympathetic and represented the inclination to Malchus as a subtle temptation. Malchus pointed out to him that he was now entitled to some property and that with it he would enlarge the monastic buildings, but the abbot was an honest man who had made up his mind, and it was not altered by a consideration of that sort. He implored his young disciple to stay where he was, but Malchus was as persuaded of his duty as the abbot, and he started off without his permission.

Between Berea and Edessa the caravan to which Malchus had attached himself was attacked and plundered by Beduin, and Malchus and a young married woman were carried off by one of the marauding chiefs. They were carried on camels to the heart of the desert beyond the Euphrates, and Malchus was set to work as a sheep and goat herd at the encampment of the tribe. He was not unhappy, in spite of being among pagans and in a greater heat than that to which he was accustomed. " It seemed to me that my lot was very like that of holy Jacob, and I remembered Moses, both of whom had been shepherds in the wilderness. I lived on cheese and milk ; I prayed endlessly ; and I sang the psalms I had learned in the monastery." Then his master told him he was to marry his fellow-prisoner, but this Malchus would not do, for he knew she was married already. In spite of his expostulations arrangements were made for them to live together, and Malchus threatened the girl that he would kill himself. Whereupon she declared that she was quite indifferent to him and that she was prepared to live with him under a mere appearance of matrimony, and so satisfy their master. This they did, though neither of them found the arrangement satisfactory. " I loved the woman as a sister," declared Malchus to St Jerome, " but I never entirely trusted her as a sister."

One day Malchus was watching a crowd of ants at work in their heap and the thought came to him how like the sight was to that of a

busy and orderly monastery. The recollection of his past happiness
with the hermits was more than he could bear, and when he had
driven in his flocks he went and told his companion that he had
made up his mind to escape. She was anxious to find her real
husband and was willing enough to adventure with Malchus, so
they made their preparations secretly and ran away one night, carrying their provisions in two goatskins. By means of these skins, which
they inflated, they crossed the river in safety, but on the third day
they saw their master and another man of the tribe, on camels,
coming up with them. They hid themselves near the mouth of a
cave, and the chief, thinking he saw them go into the cave itself,
sent his man in to fetch them out. When he did not reappear, the
chief himself approached and went in, but neither did he come out
again. Instead there issued from the cave a great lioness with a cub
in her mouth, and she leaped off among the rocks, leaving the two
intruders dead on the floor of her den. Malchus and the woman
ran to the tethered camels on which the Arabs had come, mounted
them, and set off at a great pace.

After ten days' riding they came to a Roman station in Mesopotamia, where the governor Sabinian listened to their story and sent
them on to Edessa. From there St Malchus made his way to his
old monastery in Chalcis and eventually went to end his days in
Maronia, whither the aged sharer of his captivity accompanied him ;
she never found her husband, and spent the rest of her life in the
service of religion.

The text of St Jerome with a full commentary is printed in the *Acta
Sanctorum*, October, vol. ix.

ST FINTAN MUNNU, or MUNDUS, ABBOT AND CONF.

c. A.D. 635

An oriental austerity was an outstanding characteristic of the
early Irish monks, and St Fintan Munnu was reported to be of them
the most austere, and bodily sickness was added freely to his voluntary mortifications. For eighteen years he was a monk under St
Sinell at Cluain Inis, and then crossed to Iona with the object of
joining the community there. Irish accounts say that St Columba
was dead when Fintan arrived and that his successor, St Baithen,
sent him back, saying that Columba had prophesied that he should
found a monastery in his own country and be himself a father of
monks. The Scots tradition is that he lived on Iona for a time, and

returned home on St Columba's death in the year 597. In Scotland
Fintan is called St Mundus, and the Aberdeen Breviary calls him
abbot of Kilmun in Argyle, where an ancient burial-ground marks
the site of a former foundation ; he is also connected with Eilean-
munde, an island in Loch Leven. Somewhere about the beginning
of the seventh century St Fintan Munnu founded the monastery of
Taghmon in county Wexford, and while governing this abbey was
a zealous upholder of the Celtic method of computing Easter and
other local customs. At the synod held at Magh Lene in 630, and
others, he strongly opposed on this matter St Laserian and those
who wished to comply with the wish of Pope Honorius I that Ireland
should come into line with the rest of Christendom. The monastery
of Taghmon soon became famous, and there are references to its
founder in the Lives of St Canice, St Mochua McCronan, and
St Molua. The last two state that St Fintan was for some time a
leper, and there seems to have been a known rivalry between him
and St Molua : for when an angel who was supposed to visit Fintan
twice a week missed a day, and explained subsequently that he had
been detained by the necessity of receiving the soul of the recently
dead Molua into Heaven, Fintan is represented as being distinctly
" put out " about it ! His desire to emulate the merits of the Abbot
of Clonfert caused him to pray to be stricken with disease, that
by his patient bearing of it he should deserve a similar welcome
to the Celestial City.

Three Latin Lives of this saint are available (see Plummer, *Miscellanea
Hagiographica Hibernica*, p. 252). The longest has been printed in the
Acta Sanctorum, October, vol. ix, and the third has been edited by Plummer
from a MS. in Marsh's library (see *Vitæ Sanctorum Hiberniæ*, vol. ii,
pp. 226–239, and also the introduction, pp. 84 *seq.* J. F. Kenney, *Sources
for the Early History of Ireland*, i, p. 450, quotes with approval Plummer's
comment : " Speaking generally the historical element in this life is larger
than in some others, and we get an impression of Munnu as a real man
and not merely a peg to hang miracles on, a man of somewhat harsh and
hasty temper, but placable and conciliatory when the momentary irritation
was over." See also Forbes, *Kalendars of Scottish Saints*, pp. 414–416.

ST CONDEDUS, Conf.

END OF THE SEVENTH CENTURY

Condedus, called in French Condé or Condède, is said to have
been an Englishman who, wandering about in search of a place of
complete seclusion, came to France and settled down at a spot called
Fontaine-de-Saint-Valéry, on the Somme in the forest of Hardelot,

where there was still a hermitage up to the time of the Revolution. After some years he heard of the great reputation of the abbey of Fontenelle, which was at that time governed by St Lambert, and set out to visit it. He took boat down the Somme and landed in the Seine, where the inhabitants were so suspicious that they would not give him a shelter for the night, although the weather was very threatening. At last he found a woman who took pity on him, and we are told that her kindness was rewarded by a revelation of her guest's holiness. For the storm broke during the night, and when the good woman got up to cover her window she saw a great column of light reaching from the sleeping-place of Condedus to the sky above. That this was probably lightning or another phenomenon of the storm does not alter the significance that it had for the woman. It was in the year 673 about that St Condedus came to Fontenelle, and he asked to be admitted to the community. After being a monk for some time he asked leave to preach in the surrounding country, and the abbot assigned as his centre and residence an island called Belcinac, in the Seine near Candebec. King Thierry III visiting the place soon after, he made the acquaintance of the saint and was so pleased with him that he gave the island and the river banks for some distance on either side as endowment for the hermitage. St Condedus built two chapels thereon, to which people came from all around to get his direction and listen to his preaching. After his death he was buried on the island, but afterwards was translated to Fontenelle. To-day nothing is left of St Condedus on earth but vague legend: no church shows any relic of him; since the Benedictines were driven from Fontenelle in 1901 no church observes his feast; even Belcinac has disappeared, swallowed by the waters of the Seine.

A short Latin Life of St Condedus printed by Mabillon and in the *Acta Sanctorum*, October, vol. ix, has been re-edited by W. Levison in the *M. G. H. Scrip. rerum Meroving.*, vol. v, pp. 644–651. As the writer lived more than a century after the subject of his biography, the narrative cannot claim any great authority. Consult, on the other hand, Legris in the *Analecta Bollandiana*, vol. xvii (1898), pp. 282–287, and Vacandard, *St Ouen*, pp. 198–201. But Levison in the *Neues Archiv.*, vol. xxv, vindicates his own earlier conclusions.

BD. JAMES STREPAR, ABP. OF HALITCH, CONF.

A.D. 1409 OR 1411

The Friars Minor entered Poland not many years after their foundation and when they were well established extended their

preaching to the reconciliation of dissident Orthodox and the conversion of pagans in Lithuania and Ruthenia. Thus was inaugurated
the Latin church in Galicia and the Ukraine which was organised
into dioceses during the fourteenth century at the instance of King
Casimir the Great. Blessed James Strepar was a member of a noble
Polish family, born at Stramiecz in Galicia. He joined the Franciscans and became guardian of their friary at Lemberg, where he
played a conspicuous part in very troubled ecclesiastical affairs, the
city having been laid under an interdict by the Archbishop of Halitch.
He was a zealous defender of the mendicant friars, who were bitterly
attacked by the secular clergy, and at the same time organised the
Catholics against the very strong influence of the dissident Orthodox.
He worked among these in Red Russia for over ten years, making
great use of the Company of Christ's Itinerants, a sort of missionary
society of Franciscan and Dominican friars, and was put at the head
of the Franciscan mission to the schismatics and pagans in western
Russia ; the last named were still numerous, especially in Lithuania.
As a missionary preacher and organiser Blessed James had great
success, and was in 1392 called to govern the see of Halitch by Ladislaus II (Jagello), a convert who propagated Catholicism with great
energy in Poland and Lithuania. Blessed James was a tower of
strength to his prince. He had himself evangelised a considerable
part of his diocese, and was now in a position to consolidate his work.
He built numerous churches in remote districts and obtained experienced priests from Poland to take charge of them, founded religious
houses, and established hospitals and schools. Though a senator
of the realm as well as archbishop he sometimes carried out visitations on foot, and always wore the modest habit of his order at a time
when prelates not infrequently copied the ostentatious clothes of
lay lords. Blessed James governed his large diocese till his death at
Lemberg on June 1, about 1409. During his life he had been called
" protector of the kingdom " and the miracles at his tomb showed
that he was still mindful of his people. His *cultus* was confirmed by
Pope Pius VI in 1791 and his feast is kept in Poland on June 1, but
by the Franciscans to-day.

There is more than one Life in Polish, but only summaries seem to be
available in languages more generally known. See, however, Scrobiszewski,
Vitæ Episcoporum Halicensium (1628) ; Stadler, *Heiligen Lexikon*, vol. iii,
pp. 111 *seq.* ; Léon, *Auréole Séraphique* (Eng. trans.), vol. ii, pp. 312–315.
There is some doubt whether Blessed James died in 1409 or 1411.

BD. PETER OF TIFERNO, Conf.

A.D. 1445

Very few particulars of the life of this confessor have been preserved, in part no doubt owing to the destruction by fire of the archives of the friary of Cortona, where he spent the greater part of his life. He belonged to the family of the Cappucci and was born at Tiferno (Città di Castello) in the year 1390. When he was fifteen he received the Dominican habit and was sent to Cortona, where he was trained under the direction of Blessed Laurence of Ripafratta and in company of many other famous friars, including St Antoninus and Fra Angelico. Blessed Laurence recommended him to devote himself to contemplation rather than to activity, but the lessons of his office note that he was as ready to minister to those who required his services outside his monastery as within it. Several miracles are remembered of Blessed Peter. He once met a young man of bad character in the street, stopped him, and said, " What wickedness are you up to now ? How much longer are you going on adding sin to sin ? You have just twenty-four hours to live, and at this time to-morrow you'll have to give God an account of your sins." The man was frightened but took no more notice, till that night he had a bad accident ; Peter was sent for, and he received the sinner's humble penitence before he died. Blessed Peter used to preach holding a skull in his hands as a reminder to himself and his hearers, and so he is represented in pictures.

Information regarding Blessed Peter was certainly not widely disseminated. In the vast collection of names which figure in the book of G. Michele Piò, O.P., printed at Bologna in 1607, *Delle Vite degli Huomini Illustri di S. Domenico*, there is no mention of him. We have to fall back upon the lessons of the Dominican breviary, the *Année Dominicaine*, and such summaries as Procter, *Lives of the Dominican Saints*, pp. 294–297. Consult, however, Taurisano, *Catalogus Hagiographicus Ordinis Prædicatorum*.

OCTOBER 22

ST PHILIP, Bp. of Heraclea, and his Comps., Marts.

A.D. 304

PHILIP, a venerable old man, Bishop of Heraclea, the metropolis of Thrace, was a martyr of Christ in the persecution of Diocletian. Having discharged every duty of a faithful minister as deacon and priest in that city, he was raised to the episcopal dignity and governed that church with great virtue and prudence when it was shaken by persecution. To extend and perpetuate the work of God he trained up many disciples in sacred learning and solid piety. Two of the most eminent among them had the happiness to be companions of his martyrdom, namely, Severus, a priest, and Hermes, who was formerly the first magistrate of the city, but after he was engaged in the ministry earned his livelihood with his hands, and brought up his son to do the same. When Diocletian's first edicts against the Christians were issued, many advised the Bishop to leave the city ; but he would not stir, continuing to exhort the brethren to constancy and patience and to prepare them for the celebration of the feast of the Epiphany. Whilst he preached to them, Aristomachus, an officer of the town, came by the governor's order to seal up the door of the church. The Bishop said to him, " Do you imagine that God dwells within walls, and not rather in the hearts of men ? " and continued to hold his assembly outside. The next day officers came and set their seal upon the sacred vessels and books. The faithful who beheld this were much grieved ; but the Bishop, who stood leaning against the door of the church, encouraged them with burning words. Afterwards the governor, Bassus, finding Philip and many of his flock assembled before the church door, gave orders that they should be arrested and brought before him. When he was seated on his tribunal, he said to them, " Which of you is the teacher of the Christians ? " Philip replied, " I am." Bassus said, " You know that the Emperor has forbidden your assemblies. Give up to me the vessels of gold and silver which you use and the books which you read." The Bishop answered, " The vessels we will give you, for it is not by precious metal but by charity that God is honoured. But the sacred books it becomes neither you to demand nor me to surrender." The governor ordered executioners to be called into court, and commanded one among them to torture Philip, who bore his torments with invincible courage. Hermes told the governor that it was not in his power to destroy the word of God, even though he should take away all the writings in which the true doctrine is contained, and in reply Bassus had him scourged. After this he was taken with Publius, the governor's assistant, to the place where the sacred writings and plate were hid. Publius would have taken away some of the vessels, but being hindered by Hermes he gave him such a blow on the face that blood flowed. The governor was provoked at Publius for this action, and ordered the wound to be dressed. He distributed the vessels among his officers and, to please the infidels and terrify the Christians, ordered Philip and the other prisoners to be brought to the market-place, surrounded with guards, and the church roof to be stripped off. In the meantime soldiers burned the sacred writings, the flames mounting so high as to frighten the bystanders. This being told to Philip in the market-place, he spoke of the vengeance with which God threatens the wicked and told the people how their gods and temples had been often burned. Then a pagan priest appeared in the market-place with his ministers, who brought with them the necessary preparations for a sacrifice, and the governor Bassus came, followed by a multitude, some of whom pitied the suffering Christians ; others, especially the Jews, clamoured loudly against them. Bassus pressed the Bishop to sacrifice to the gods, to the Emperors, and to the fortune of the city. Pointing at a large and beautiful statue of Hercules, he bid him consider what veneration was due to that god. Then, turning to Hermes, he asked if he, at least, would sacrifice. "I will not," replied Hermes, "I am a Christian." Bassus asked, "If we can persuade Philip to offer sacrifice, will you follow his example ?" Hermes answered he would not ; neither could they persuade Philip. After many useless threats and pressing them to sacrifice at least to the Emperors, Bassus ordered them to be carried to prison. As they went along, some of the rabble pushed Philip and threw him down ; but he got up again with a smiling face, without showing the least indignation. Many admired his patience, and the martyrs entered the prison joyfully, singing a psalm of thanksgiving to God. A few days after they were allowed to stay at the house of one Pancras, near the prison, where many Christians and some new converts came to them to be instructed, and later were removed to a prison near the theatre, which had a door into that building, with a secret entry. They there received at night the crowds that came to visit them.

In the meantime, Bassus went out of office at the end of his term and Justin succeeded him. The Christians were much disappointed at this change : for Bassus often yielded to reason and his wife had for some time been a Christian herself ; but Justin was a violent man. Zoilus, the magistrate of the city, brought Philip before him, and Justin declared once more what was the Emperor's order, and pressed him to sacrifice. Philip answered, " I am a Christian, and cannot do what you require. Your business is to punish our refusal, not to force our compliance." Justin threatened him with torture, and the Bishop replied, " You may torment, but will not conquer me ; no power can induce me to sacrifice." He was told he would be dragged by the feet through the streets and thrown into prison to suffer anew. " God grant it may be so," was Philip's comment. Then Justin commanded the soldiers to tie his feet and drag him along. They dashed him against the stones so roughly that he was torn and bruised all over his body, and the Christians carried him in their arms when he was brought back to his dungeon. The persecutors had long been in quest of the priest Severus, who had hidden himself. Moved by the Holy Ghost, he at length surrendered and was committed to prison. Hermes was firm in his examination before Justin, and was treated in the same manner. The three martyrs were kept imprisoned in a bad place for seven months and then removed to Adrianople, where they were confined in a private house till the arrival of the governor. The next day, holding his court at the Baths, Justin had Philip brought before him and beaten till his bowels were exposed. His endurance astonished the executioners and Justin himself, who remanded him to prison. Hermes was next examined. All the officers of the court were favourable to him because, having been magistrate of Heraclea, he had obliged them all on several occasions, though he declared in his examination that he had been a Christian from his cradle. He persisted in this profession, and was sent back to prison, where the martyrs joyfully gave thanks to Jesus Christ for this beginning of their victory. Three days after this, Justin brought them again before his tribunal, and having in vain pressed Philip to obey the Emperors, said to Hermes, " If the approach of death makes this man think life not worth preserving, do not you be insensible to its blessings. Offer sacrifice." Hermes replied by denouncing idolatry, so that Justin, enraged, cried out, " You speak as if you wanted to make me a Christian." Having then consulted his assessor and others, he pronounced sentence : " We order

Philip and Hermes who, despising the commands of the Emperor, have rendered themselves unworthy of the name of Romans, to be burned, that others may learn to obey."

They went joyfully to the stake. Philip's feet were so sore that he could not walk, and had to be carried. Hermes also walked with much difficulty, and said to him, " Master, let us hasten to go to our Lord. Why should we be concerned about our feet, since we shall have no more use for them ? " Then he said to the crowds that followed, " The Lord revealed to me that I must suffer. While I was asleep, methought I saw a dove as white as snow, which rested on my head. Then it descended upon my breast and presented to me meat which was very sweet to the taste. I knew that it was the Lord that called me, and was pleased to honour me with martyrdom." Perhaps this delicious food means the Eucharist which the martyrs received before their passion. At the place of punishment, the executioners, according to custom, covered Philip's feet and legs with earth up to the knees ; and having tied his hands behind his back, nailed them to the stake. They likewise made Hermes go down into a ditch where, supporting himself on a stick because his feet trembled, he said smiling, " O demon, thou canst not suffer me even here." The executioners covered his feet with earth, but before they lighted the fire he called upon Velogius, a Christian, and said to him, " I implore you, by our Saviour Jesus Christ, tell my son Philip from me to restore whatever was committed to my charge, that I may incur no fault ; even the laws of this world ordain it. Tell him also, that he is young and must work for his living as he has seen me do ; and behave himself well to everybody." Then his hands were tied behind his back, and fire was set to the pile. The martyrs praised and gave thanks to God as long as they were able to speak. Their bodies were found entire : Philip having his hands stretched out as in prayer, Hermes with a clear countenance, only his ears a little blue. Justin ordered their bodies to be thrown into the Hebrus, but some citizens of Adrianople went in boats with nets, and fished them out whilst they were yet entire. Severus the priest, who had been left alone in prison, when he was informed of their martyrdom, rejoiced at their glory, and earnestly besought God not to think him unworthy to partake in it, since he had confessed His name with them. He was heard, and suffered martyrdom the day following. The order for burning the holy Scriptures and destroying the churches points out the time of their suffering to have been after the first edicts of Diocletian. The Roman Martyrology erroneously puts it in the time of Julian the Apostate, and adds the name of a St Eusebius who does not belong to this group. It also names on this day another ST PHILIP, Bishop of Fermo, who gave his life for the Faith under Valerian.

The martyrdom of SS. Philip, Hermes, and Severus may be counted among the best attested of the episodes of the Diocletian persecution. It is commemorated on this same day in the Syriac *breviarium* of the early fourth century. There is, moreover, a certain indirect confirmation in the reference made to it in the *passio* of Gurius and companions (see Gebhardt and Dobschütz in their edition of this last—*Texte und Untersuchungen*, vol. xxxvii, p. 6). The Latin text of the *acta* of Philip of Heraclea has been printed by Ruinart, and by the Bollandists, October, vol. ix. Dom Leclercq provides a French translation in *Les Martyrs*, vol. ii, pp. 238–257. *Cf.* also P. Franchi de' Cavalieri in *Studi e Testi*, no. 27, "Note Agiografiche," fascicule 5.

ST ABERCIUS, BP. OF HIEROPOLIS, CONF.

END OF THE SECOND CENTURY

There lived in Phrygia Salutaris during the second century a certain Abercius Marcellus, who was bishop of Hieropolis and who, while in his seventy-second year, made a visit to Rome. His homeward journey was taken through Syria and Mesopotamia, he visited Nisibis, and everywhere he went he met Christians, whose foreheads bore the shining seal of baptism and whose souls were nourished with the body and blood of Christ, the virgin-born, under the forms of bread and wine. Abercius when he returned home prepared a tomb for himself and had carved thereon an epitaph which, in symbolical and to the non-Christian baffling terms, briefly described the journey which had made so deep an impression on the Greek disciple of the all-seeing and universal Shepherd, who had gone to Rome " to contemplate majesty." About the year 193 St Abercius wrote a treatise against the Montanists, and must have died soon after.

A Greek hagiographer made use of the epitaph as the basis of an almost entirely fictitious account of the life of St Abercius. According to this ingenious narrative the Bishop made so many converts by his preaching and miracles that he deserved to be called " equal to the Apostles " and his fame reached the ears of Marcus Aurelius. The expedition to Rome was made in consequence of a summons from the Emperor, whose daughter Lucilla was afflicted by a devil (the symbolical gold-clad queen of the epitaph becomes the Empress). St Abercius successfully exorcised this evil spirit and commanded it to transport a great stone altar from the Roman hippodrome to his episcopal city, where it should provide materials for his tomb. Other episodes were added from the legends of other saints, and the writer appended to his tale a transcription of the original genuine epitaph of Abercius.

This epitaph was formerly regarded with nearly as much suspicion as the Life of which it formed a part, until in 1882 the English archæologist, W. M. Ramsay, discovered at Kelendres, near Smyrna, an inscribed stone bearing the equivalent of the date A.D. 216. It was a memorial inscription to one Alexander, the son of Antony, which was found to correspond almost word for word with the first and last verses of the epitaph of Abercius. In the following year Ramsay found, built into the wall of the baths at Hieropolis, further fragments which supplied much of the part of the epitaph of Abercius missing from the other stone. With these two inscriptions and the text given in the Life of the saint an authentic text of great value was restored. But the claim of Abercius to be a Christian saint was still not admitted by everyone to be established. On account of the symbolism with which it was expressed, interpreters of the inscription identified him as a priest of Cybele or of Attis or of some syncretistic cult, and it was only after long and lively controversies that it was generally admitted that the Abercius of the inscription was a Christian bishop whose traditional cult was justified. He has been venerated liturgically among the Greeks since the tenth century, and he is named to-day in the Roman Martyrology, but as bishop of Hierapolis (the see of St Papias) instead of Hieropolis, an error found in the bogus Life.

A considerable literature has been created by the inscriptions which Sir W. M. Ramsay found at Hieropolis, and which now, by the gracious act of the discoverer, adorns the Christian Museum at the Lateran. All the discussion which has since arisen has added very little to the interpretation which the Anglican Bishop Lightfoot, with sure scholarly instinct, published in vol. i of his *Ignatius and Polycarp* (1885). Such sceptical critics as G. Ficker and A. Dieterich have not produced a fragment of evidence which would raise a doubt regarding the Christian character of the inscription. The work of F. J. Dölger, *Ichthys* (see especially vol. ii, 1922, pp. 454–507), may be recommended as replying effectively, along with many other vindications written both by Catholics and non-Catholics, to the objections which have been urged. Dom Leclercq's article in the *Diction. d'Archéol.*, etc. (vol. i, cc. 66–87), provides good illustrations as well as a full bibliography. With regard to the Life of Abercius, the two more ancient texts of this Greek pious fiction have now been critically edited by T. Nissen, *S. Abercii Vita*, 1912. Though historically worthless, it contains geographical data of value, and its quotations from Bardesanes are of curious interest. The present writer would now be inclined to modify considerably certain views expressed by him in the second of two articles on St Abercius which appeared in *The Month* for May and July, 1890.

ST MELANIUS, OR MELLON, Bp. OF ROUEN, CONF.

c. A.D. 311

This saint was born in Britain towards the middle of the third century, probably near Cardiff, where a church dedicated in his honour (Llaneirwg) has given his name to a district. He is said to have been brought up a pagan and to have been sent when young as one of a mission to Rome in connection with the imperial taxes. He came into contact with Pope St Stephen I, was converted, baptised, and ordained priest. While still in Rome Melanius had a vision directing him to preach the gospel to the Gauls, and St Stephen having had a similar vision, he was consecrated bishop and began to evangelise Neustria. He established himself at Rouen and so is venerated as the first bishop of that city, and is the first British bishop recorded to have governed a foreign see. St Melanius worked with success for many years, his preaching and virtues being enforced by miracles. After his death he was buried where is now the church of St Gervais ; in 880 his relics were transferred to Pontoise, where they were destroyed at the Revolution.

There are three short Latin Lives of St Mellonus, which are printed in the *Acta Sanctorum*, October, vol. ix, or in Sauvage (*Actes de S. Mellon*, 1884), but, as Vacandard maintains (*Vie de Saint Ouen*, p. 92), these biographies date only from the twelfth century and can deserve no confidence. See also Duchesne, *Fastes Épiscopaux*, vol. ii, pp. 200–203 ; and Baring-Gould and Fisher, *Lives of the British Saints*, vol. iii, p. 466.

SS. NUNILO AND ALODIA, VIRGS. AND MARTS.

A.D. 851

The great era of the martyrs in Spain began in the year 850, under the Moorish caliph Abderrahman II, and these two maidens were among the numberless martyrs who in those days sealed their fidelity to the law of God with their blood. They were sisters, living at Huesca, their father being a Mohammedan and their mother a Christian. After the death of her first husband, she was so foolish as to take a second who was also a Mohammedan. Her two daughters, who had been brought up in the Christian faith, had much to suffer in the exercise of their religion from the brutality of their step-father, who was a person of importance. They were also pestered by many suitors to marry, but having decided to serve God in the state of virginity they obtained leave to go to the house of a Christian aunt, where they enjoyed an entire liberty as to their religion, and their devotions were only interrupted by necessary duties or other good works. When the laws of Abderrahman were published against the Christians, they were too well known by their family and the repute of their zeal and piety not to be soon arrested. They appeared before the cadi not only undaunted but with a holy joy. He employed flattery and promises to try to work them into compliance, and at length proceeded to threats. When these failed him, he put them into the hands of wicked women, hoping these would be able by their craft to insinuate themselves into the hearts of the Christian women. But Christ enlightened and protected them and after many trials the temptresses were obliged to declare to the judge that nothing could conquer their resolution. He therefore condemned them to be beheaded in their prison, which was accordingly done, and their passion is mentioned in the Roman Martyrology on this day.

A just and humble fear, the practice of penance, the most fervent use of the sacraments, prayer, and meditation on eternal truths, a contempt of the world and of the goods and evils of this life, and a constant attention to that which is to come, were the weapons with which the martyrs stood always prepared for the combat, and the source of the courage and strength which they obtained of God and by which they triumphed. But the spiritual persecutions of the world are often more dangerous than those of the sword, and they corrupt far more souls. The allurements of pleasure and riches, the vanity of publicity, and the snares of pride and ambition, murder more souls than the Neros and Diocletians and Abderrahmans murdered bodies. We run into the arms of certain death if we expose ourselves to our enemies without our weapons. Constant watchfulness, penance, prayer, and the other means mentioned above are the armour with which we must be always shielded that we may be invincible against the Devil.

Our information is all, practically speaking, derived from the *Memoriale Sanctorum* of Eulogius. The relevant passages are quoted and commented upon in the *Acta Sanctorum*, October, vol. ix.

ST DONATUS, Bp. of Fiesole, Conf.
A.D. 876

The tradition of Fiesole is that Donatus was a man of noble Irish birth who in the early part of the ninth century made a pilgrimage to Rome. On the return journey he arrived at Fiesole at a time when the clergy and people were gathered together to elect a new bishop, praying earnestly that the Holy Ghost would send them one who would be a true pastor in the manifold troubles with which they were beset. No one would have taken any notice of the stranger Donatus as he entered the cathedral, for he was an insignificant little man, but at the moment he crossed the threshold the bells began to ring and all the lamps and candles were kindled without human agency. This was taken to be a sign from Heaven in favour of Donatus, and he was unanimously acclaimed bishop.

The Life of St Donatus is interspersed with verses and an epitaph, supposed to have been written by himself, according to which he was an enthusiastic teacher of grammar and prosody and a trusted servant of the Emperor Louis I and King Lothaire. One of the poems describes the beauty of Ireland. The preface to the Life of St Brigid by the eighth-century monk Coelan was written by St Donatus of Fiesole, and his feast is observed to-day throughout Ireland.

There is a biography—in fact more than one—printed in the *Acta Sanctorum*, October, vol. ix. See further the *Dict. Nat. Biog.*, vol. xv, p. 216 ; Gougaud, *Christianity in Celtic Lands* (1932), p. 180 ; and M. Esposito in the *Journal of Theological Studies*, vol. xxxiii (1923), p. 129.

OCTOBER 23

ST THEODORET, Mart.

A.D. 362

JULIAN, uncle to the Emperor Julian and likewise an apostate, was by his nephew made prefect of the East, of which district Antioch was the capital. Being informed that in the treasury of the chief church there was a quantity of gold and silver, he determined to seize it and published an order by which he banished the clergy from the city. Theodoret, a zealous priest who had been very active during the reign of Constantius and who was keeper of the sacred vessels, refused to abandon his flock and continued openly to hold sacred assemblies with prayer and sacrifice. Julian commanded him to be apprehended and brought before him, when he charged him with having thrown down the statues of the gods and built churches in the foregoing reign. Theodoret owned he had built churches upon the tombs of martyrs, and reproved the prefect because, after having known the true God, he had abandoned His worship. Julian ordered him to be beaten on the soles of his feet and afterwards tied to four stakes, and stretched with cords and pulleys by his legs and arms : which was done with great violence. But the martyr still exhorted him to acknowledge the true God and Jesus Christ His Son, whereupon Julian ordered that he should be tormented on the rack, and when the blood was streaming from his wounds, said to him, " I see you do not feel your torments enough." The martyr replied, " I do not feel them at all, because God is with me." Julian had his sides burned with torches, and Theodoret, whilst his flesh was scorching, lifted up his eyes to Heaven and prayed that God would glorify His name throughout all ages. At these words the executioners fell on their faces to the ground, saying they saw four angels clothed in white with Theodoret. Julian in a rage ordered them to be thrown into the water and drowned, whereat Theodoret said to them : " Go before, my brethren. I will follow by vanquishing the enemy." The prefect asked him who that enemy was. " The Devil," said the martyr, " for whom you fight. Jesus Christ, the Saviour of the world, is He who giveth victory." He then explained to his tormentor at some length the mysteries of the Incarnation and Redemption, and when Julian threatened him with instant death retorted by prophesying for him an early and painful end. He was then sentenced to be beheaded, which sentence was duly carried out.

On the day of the martyrdom of St Theodoret, Julian, according to an order he had received from the Emperor, went and seized the goods of the great church of Antioch, having with him two officers. One of them, as he was viewing the magnificent vessels which the Emperors Constantine and Constantius had given to the church, impiously remarked, " Behold on what rich plate the Son of Mary is served." Julian also profaned the sacred vessels in the most out-rageous manner. The next morning he presented to the Emperor an inventory of what he had seized, and informed him of what he had done to St Theodoret. But the Emperor told him plainly that he did not approve his putting any Christian to death merely on account of his religion, and complained that this would afford an occasion to the Galileans to write against him and to make a saint and a martyr of Theodoret. The prefect, who little expected such a reception, was much upset, and that same evening was taken violently ill. He was in great agony for over forty days, and then came to a miserable end. St Theodoret is called Theodore in the Roman Martyrology.

Although the *passio* of this martyr is included by Ruinart amongst his *Acta Sincera* it is difficult to put confidence in the miraculous details recorded. The text, with variations and a full commentary, may be read in the *Acta Sanctorum*, October, vol. x. St Theodoret, as we may learn from the writings of St John Chrysostom, Sozomen and others, was held in much veneration at Antioch, and his name (in the form Theodore) is duly entered in the *Hieronymianum* under March 29. An earlier form of the *passio* has been discovered by P. Franchi de' Cavalieri. See his " Note Agiografiche " in *Studi e Testi*, vol. 33, (1920), pp. 86–88 and 91.

ST SEVERINUS, OR SEURIN, Bp. OF BORDEAUX, CONF.

c. A.D. 420

The account of this St Severinus given by St Gregory of Tours in the late sixth century makes him to have come from the East to Bordeaux, whose see St Amandus resigned for a time in his favour about the year 410. The Roman Martyrology, while putting his death at Bordeaux, calls Severinus " Bishop of Cologne." This has reference to an identification, now abandoned, of Seurin with a St Severinus of Cologne, also commemorated to-day. He distin-guished himself by his zeal against Arianism, and died at the begin-ning of the fifth century. According to the legend Severinus while a priest was walking in the fields when he heard a voice say, " Severinus, you will be bishop of Cologne." "When will that happen ? " he asked. "When your staff buds and flowers," was the reply. And his stick, stuck in the ground, took root and blossomed, and he was called to Cologne. At Tongres, says Gregory of Tours, he knew by revelation the death and glory of St Martin at the time of his departure from this life. In the midst of his labours against heresy he was again warned by a voice, this time that he was wanted in Bordeaux ; he went thither and was met by the bishop St Amandus who, also instructed by Heaven, yielded up his office to him. It is possible that St Severinus of Cologne was driven from his diocese by the Arian barbarians and took refuge in Aquitaine. The relics of St Severinus venerated in his church at Cologne are said to have been brought to Bordeaux, where the church of Saint-Seurin claims to have the rest of them : but there would seem to be no doubt that there were two holy bishops named Severinus, contemporaries, and not one as represented in the legends.

Modern research has clearly established that the only Life of St Severinus of any authority, and in fact the source from which the others have borrowed, is that written by Venantius Fortunatus. Identified and printed for the first time by Dom H. Quentin (*La plus ancienne Vie de S. Seurin*, 1902), it has been re-edited by W. Levison in the *M. G. H. Scrip. rer. Meroving.*, vol. vii, pp. 205–224. Severinus before coming to Bordeaux had apparently been bishop of Treves ; but there is nothing to connect him with Cologne. By a curious confusion, on which see the *Analecta Bollandiana*, vol. xxxviii (1920), pp. 427–428, Seurin seems to have been the original from which an imaginary bishop of Bordeaux " St Fort " was afterwards evolved.

ST ROMANUS, Bp. of Rouen, Conf.

A.D. 639

Not much that is certainly authentic is known of this bishop. His father, alleged to be a convert of St Remigius, was born of an illustrious French family, and Romanus was placed young in the court of Clotaire II. He was chancellor to that prince when, upon the death of Hidulphus, he was chosen archbishop of Rouen. The remains of idolatry exercised his zeal ; he converted the unbelievers and is said to have destroyed a temple of Venus at Rouen and three others in the diocese, dedicated to Mercury, Jupiter, and Apollo. Amongst many miracles it is related that, the Seine having overflowed a considerable part of the city, the saint, who happened to be at the court of Dagobert, upon hearing this news made haste to succour his flock. Kneeling down to pray on the side of the water, with a crucifix in his hand, the floods retired gently within the banks of the river. The name of St Romanus is famous in France on account of a privilege which the metropolitical chapter of Rouen exercised until the Revolution, of releasing in his honour a prisoner under sentence of death every year on the feast of the Ascension of our Lord. The chapter sent notice to the parliament of Rouen two months before to stop the execution of criminals till that time ; and on that day chose the prisoner who, being first condemned to death, was then set at liberty, to assist in carrying the shrine of St Romanus in the great procession. He heard two exhortations and then was told that in honour of St Romanus he was pardoned. The legend is that this privilege took its rise from St Romanus killing a great serpent, called Gargouille, with the assistance of a murderer whom he took out of his dungeon. No traces of this story are found in any Life of this saint or in any writings before the end of the four-teenth century ; the deliverance of the condemned criminal was probably intended for a symbol of the redemption of mankind through Christ. The custom was called *Privilège de la Fierté* or *Chasse de St Romain*. St Romanus was bishop for some ten years and died on this day about the year 640.

The servant of God finds in Him comfort in all events, reposing in Him a confidence which nothing can shake, and ever rejoicing in His holy will, to which with love and assurance he commits himself in life and in death. God's omnipotence all things obey, and His infinite goodness and mercy are always open and ready to meet us : His servant can never call to mind either these or any other attributes of God without an inexpressible interior joy and love. In filial fear and sincere sorrow for his sins he ceases not with confidence to call upon God, his redeemer, friend and protector, begging that He exert His might (which is nowhere so wonderfully manifested as in the pardon of sinners) and display His eternal and boundless mercy in bringing him to true repentance and salvation, and that He order all things with regard to him according to His will and to the greater glory of His name.

There are several short Lives of St Romanus, but not of a date which would lend them any historical value. The texts for the most part are printed or summarised in the *Acta Sanctorum*, October, vol. x, but a useful note upon the Lives and their authors is available in Vacandard, *Vie de St Ouen* (1902), pp. 356–358. Other references to St Romain occur *passim* in the text. See also Duchesne, *Fastes Épiscopaux*, vol. ii, p. 207 ; and L. Pillon in the *Gazette des Beaux-Arts*, vol. xxx (1903), pp. 441–454.

ST IGNATIUS, PATRIARCH OF CONSTANTINOPLE, CONF.

A.D. 877

The birth of this saint, one of the best bishops who ever ruled the church of Constantinople, was most illustrious : his mother Procopia was daughter to the Emperor Nicephorus I, and his father Michael, surnamed Rhangabé, was, on the death of his father-in-law, himself raised to the imperial throne. His reign was brief. In the year 813 the army deposed him in favour of Leo the Armenian, and his two sons were mutilated and shut up in a monastery. The younger of them became a monk and changed his former name, Nicetas, into that of Ignatius. He was at that time fourteen years of age. During his first years he underwent severe trial, being placed in a monastery which was governed by an unorthodox abbot from whom he had much to suffer ; but this became to him a spur to watchfulness and a continual exercise of patience, by which he learned to die more perfectly to himself. Upon the death of his persecutor he was chosen abbot, having already been ordained priest by the Bishop of Paros. In 842, the Empress Theodora became regent for her son Michael III, a minor, restored the holy images, expelled John VII, the iconoclast Patriarch of Constantinople, and raised St Methodius to that dignity. After his death, in 846, St Ignatius was taken from his monastery of Satyrus and made patriarch by canonical election, being recognised as such by the Pope, St Leo IV. His virtues shone brightly in this office, but the liberty which he used in opposing vice and reprimanding public offenders drew on him severe persecution. Bardas Cæsar, brother to the Empress, had a great share in the government, for which his abilities would have qualified him if the corruption of his heart had not rendered him unfit to be a member of decent society, much more to be entrusted with the care of the young Emperor. He was scandalously debauched in his morals, so that he put away his wife and incestuously took his own daughter-in-law into his house. The Patriarch could not bear such scandals, and exhorted this hardened sinner to have pity on his own soul. But Bardas was so far from giving ear to his charitable admonitions as impudently to present himself to receive holy Communion in the Great Church on the feast of the Epiphany in 857. Ignatius refused to admit him to the holy table. Bardas, stung with resentment, threatened to stab him, but the prelate remained firm. The young emperor, known ominously in history as Michael the Drunkard, was of no less depraved a heart, so that it had not been hard for his uncle, by flattering his passions, to gain an ascendency over him.　Bardas set himself to remove Theodora, who was still regent, and stood in his way and often checked his ambitions and designs.　He therefore persuaded Michael that it was time for him now to reign by himself and that he ought to send away his mother and sisters.　The youth relished this advice, that he might be more at liberty to follow his vicious inclinations, sent for the Patriarch (whom he had already insulted by openly caricaturing pontifical rites), and ordered him to cut off the hair of his mother and three sisters as a mark of their engaging in a monastic life.　St Ignatius refused, and Michael, when he had found a pretext for banishing Theodora to the monastery of Gastria, set himself with Bardas to remove the Patriarch.　With the help of an aggrieved bishop, Gregory of Syracuse, they trumped up charges and ordered Ignatius to be deposed and exiled as a traitor.　He was taken to the island of Terebinthos, where all means were used to extort from him a resignation of his dignity ; but he refused by such an act to deliver up his flock to wolves, and put his patriarchal cathedral (Sancta Sophia) under an interdict until he should return.　At last Bardas decided that his place should be taken by the chief secretary of state, the layman Photius.　This extraordinary man was of high birth, a prodigy of genius and learning, well skilled in all the profane arts and in ecclesiastical matters ; he ought to have been a great and respected figure in Christian history, but he took up an unjust cause, pursued it unscrupulously, and is remembered in the West primarily as an arch-schismatic.　It is possible that at first he accepted the responsibility genuinely against his will ; but at Christmas 857 he took the fatal step, and was made monk, lector, subdeacon, deacon, priest, and patriarch, in as many days, by the excommunicated Gregory of Syracuse.

The election of Photius having been made notoriously against the canons, efforts were still made to get St Ignatius to resign. When they failed he was treated with such brutality by his gaolers that Photius himself wrote in protest to Bardas.　Those bishops who were faithful to him assembled in the church of Irene at Constantinople and excommunicated Photius.　He held a counter-synod in the church of the Holy Apostles and, declaring that Ignatius's own election had been uncanonical, pronounced a sentence of deposition and excommunication against him.　St Ignatius was then, with many of his adherents, put on board a vessel in chains and sent to Mitylene in the isle of Lesbos. Photius now sent a letter to St Nicholas I in which he begged the Pope to send two legates, ostensibly to improve ecclesiastical discipline and again to condemn the iconoclasts.　The Pope received no messenger from St Ignatius, for his enemies did not suffer him to send any. He therefore answered very cautiously, and sent two legates to Constantinople, Rodoald, Bishop of Porto, and Zachary, Bishop of Anagni, with orders only to take information and to report to him. But he complains that Ignatius had been deposed without consulting the Holy See. Unhappily these legates were weak and unworthy, if not downright venal men. They were threatened and flattered by the Emperor, did not insist on hearing the case for Ignatius, and were completely won over from the start. A synod, therefore, was held in 861 in which, the legates exceeding their power and commission, St Ignatius was unjustly deposed, with much harsh and tyrannical usage, and in spite of his formal appeal to the Holy See. He was allowed to retire to his mother's house at Posis, whence he sent a letter to the Pope by the hand of the archimandrite Theognostus. But the Emperor decided to make Ignatius read his condemnation in the pulpit of the church of the Apostles, and then to have his eyes put out and his hand cut off. Pentecost was the occasion chosen for this outrageous project, and Ignatius made his escape only by putting on the clothes of a slave. In this disguise he went out in the night-time, being taken by the guards for a porter, and made his way to the islands of the Bosphorus, where he lived among the monks (who mostly upheld him), sometimes in one island, sometimes in another. The Emperor caused strict search to be everywhere made, and the admiral of the fleet was sent with six vessels in quest of him. But an earthquake which shook Constantinople terrified the citizens, who cried out that it was a punishment for the persecution of Ignatius. It is said that the Emperor and Bardas were both alarmed (Photius knew too much about the natural causes of earthquakes to be intimidated by it), and swore publicly that no harm should be done to Ignatius, and that he might with safety return to his own monastery ; which he did, under surveillance.

The Pope, after the return of his legates and after he had received the information of Theognostus, disowned what they had done, declaring he gave them no commission for the deposition of Ignatius or for the promotion of Photius (Rodoald and Zachary were subsequently degraded and excommunicated). He then wrote to Michael and Photius plainly stating that Ignatius must be restored, and in a letter to the Patriarchs of Alexandria, Antioch, and Jerusalem he says : "We enjoin and order you, by the apostolical authority, to hold with us in regard to Ignatius and Photius ; and to publish this letter in your dioceses that it may be known to all men." The decision of St Nicholas was confirmed by a council at Rome in 863, and

Photius was threatened with excommunication if he did not submit. In the meanwhile he reposed on the authority of his imperial master, Michael the Drunkard, who observing these controversies remarked : " There are three patriarchs. Mine is Theophilus Gryllus, the clown, Bardas Cæsar's is Photius, and the people's is Ignatius."

By the year 867 Photius was so fixed in rebellion as to pretend to excommunicate and depose Pope St Nicholas I ! But almost at once the Emperor Michael, who in the previous year had connived at the murder of Bardas, was himself murdered by his creature Basil, who became emperor. Not from respect for the Holy See or any love of justice but from motives of political expediency he banished his victim's patriarch Photius (who, unhappily for the Church, was to return eleven years later), and recalled St Ignatius. The persecuted prelate had been dispossessed for nine years, and his first act after his restoration was to ask Pope Hadrian II, who had succeeded St Nicholas, to hold a general council. This, a small assembly, was convened in 869 at Constantinople, the eighth œcumenical council and the fourth of that city. It solemnly condemned the exploits of Photius and his followers, including ten bishops, but treated them with very great leniency. For the remaining years of his rule St Ignatius applied himself to the duties of his office with vigilance and energy, but unfortunately not with perfect prudence, so that he became himself involved in a dispute with the Holy See concerning its patriarchal jurisdiction over the Bulgarians. He even went so far as to encourage their prince, Boris, to expel his Latin bishops in favour of Greeks. Pope John VIII was naturally indignant and was about to excommunicate Ignatius, but at this juncture he died, on October 23, 877. The personal holiness of his life, his fearlessness in rebuking the wickedness of emperors and nobles, and his patience under persecution for righteousness' sake caused his name to be added to the Roman Martyrology, and his feast is kept by the Latin Catholics of Constantinople as well as by the Byzantines.

A Greek biography by Nicetas, the Paphlagonian, recounts the main incidents in the history of the patriarch. The Greek text may be found in Migne, *P.G.*, vol. 105 ; a Latin translation with a very full commentary is in the *Acta Sanctorum*, October, vol. x. But the diplomatic correspondence and documents of the period are also of the first importance and must be sought in Mansi, or in Hefele-Leclercq, *Conciles*, vol. iv. The account given above, which reproduces the substance of Alban Butler's still more lengthy disquisition, reflects the tone of the Catholic apologetic of the eighteenth century. It should be noted that of recent years fuller research has tended to mitigate considerably the harshness of the judgement previously passed upon Photius. The matter cannot be discussed here, but the reader may be referred to such works as A. Lapôtre, *Le Pape Jean VIII* ; Fr. Dvorník,

" Le second schisme de Photios " in *Byzantion*, vol. viii (1933), pp. 425–474 ; Dvorník, *Les Légendes de Constantin et de Méthode* (1933) ; and P. Grumel, *Revue des Sciences philosophiques et théologiques*, vol. xxii (1933), pp. 432–457. There is a full article on the Patriarch St Ignatius in the *Dictionnaire de Théologie*, vol. vii (1922), cc. 713–722, but this, like Hergenröther's *Photius*, follows more conservative lines.

ST ALLUCIO, Conf.

A.D. 1134

Allucio, lesser patron of the diocese of Pescia in Tuscany, was a shepherd and herdman, who on account of the great interest he took in the almshouse of Val di Nievole was appointed master of it by his fellow-townsmen. He became in effect its second founder, and further devoted himself to the establishment of shelters at fords, mountain-passes, and so on, and to similar public works, such as the building of a bridge over the Arno ; he staffed the hospices with young men, who were afterwards known as the Brothers of St Allucio. A number of remarkable miracles were recorded of the saint and he was credited with bringing about a reconciliation between the warring cities of Ravenna and Faenza. In 1182, forty-eight years after his death, the relics of St Allucio were enshrined (they are now in the cathedral at Pescia), the almshouse was given his name, and in 1344 the Bishop of Lucca approved the *cultus :* it was confirmed by Pope Pius IX by the granting of a proper Mass for the saint.

The cult of St Allucio seems to be adequately attested by documents, one of which takes the form of a public instrument summarising the principal episodes of his life. They are given in the *Acta Sanctorum*, October, vol. x. See also the *Dictionnaire d'Hist. et de Géog.*, vol. ii, col. 627.

BD. JOHN BONUS, Conf.

A.D. 1249

There are two holy men who, though only given the title of " Blessed," are distinguished by inclusion in the Roman Martyrology this month ; one is John Leonardi (9th), the other is John Bonus, or " the Good." In spite of his name, which he inherited from his family, the Buonuomini, his earlier life was not conspicuous for religion. When his father died he left his home at Mantua and made his living as an entertainer at the courts, palaces, and wealthy establishments of Italy, leading a licentious and debauched life, though ever pursued by the prayers of his devoted mother. In 1208, when he was about forty years old, he had a serious illness which brought him near death, and when he had recovered he took the warning to heart and was soon a changed man. He had made a resolve during his sickness to mend his ways and, a less common thing than such resolutions, he kept it. He opened his heart to the Bishop of Mantua, who imposed a penance on him and allowed him to try a hermit's life, which he began near Cesena. John set himself to conquer his insurgent flesh in solitude and acquire habits of devotion and virtue with such success that he soon had the reputation of a saint, and disciples began to gather round him. For a time they lived according to regulations which Blessed John made on the spot as need arose, but when a church had been built and the community taken definite shape papal approval was sought and Innocent IV imposed the Rule of St Augustine as their basis.

Blessed John received many supernatural enlightenments in prayer, performed a number of most remarkable miracles, and did not allow advancing age to lessen his austerities ; he kept three lents every year, wore only one light garment in the coldest weather, and had three beds in his cell, one uncomfortable, another more uncomfortable, and the third most uncomfortable. He continued to suffer very violent temptations from the Devil, and was moreover slandered by malicious persons, calumnies which he opposed merely by a simple denial. The number of his penitents so increased and so many people came to see him out of curiosity that Blessed John made up his mind to go away secretly to a more quiet place ; but after having walked all night he found himself at dawn once more before the door of his own cell, so he concluded that it was God's will that he should stay where he was. John died at Mantua in the year 1249 and was buried in the church of St Agnes, where his tomb was illustrious for miracles. His congregation of penitents did not survive long as an independent organisation. Under the name of *Boniti* they had eleven establishments within a few years of their founder's death, but in 1256 they were united with the other congregations of which Pope Alexander IV formed the order of Hermit-friars of St Augustine ; one of the Boniti, Lanfranc of Milan, was its first prior general. The feast of Blessed John Bonus is accordingly kept by the Augustinian friars and the Augustinians of the Assumption.

The Bollandists, in the *Acta Sanctorum*, October, vol. ix, fill nearly two hundred folio pages with the documents which bear on the history of Blessed John Bonus. These comprise a relatively lengthy biography written at the beginning of the sixteenth century by the Augustinian, Ambrose Calepinus, and also the depositions of witnesses who in 1251, 1252, and 1254 gave evidence with a view to John's canonisation. They describe *inter alia* his immunity from the effects of great heat, for he stood for several minutes shuffling his bare feet about without injury in a heap of red-hot ashes. See *The Month* for February, 1932, pp. 146–147.

BD. BARTHOLOMEW BREGANZA, Bp. of Vicenza, Conf.

A.D. 1271

Blessed Bartholomew studied in his youth at Padua and about the year 1220 received the Dominican habit from the hands of the founder of the order himself, in his native town of Vicenza. He prudently directed a number of houses as prior, and while preaching with Father John of Vicenza at Bologna in 1233 established a military order, called *Fratres Gaudentes*, for the preservation of peace and of public order ; it spread to other towns of Italy and existed till the eighteenth century. At this time the near East was in particular need of holy bishops in view of the abuses of the Crusades, and Blessed Bartholomew was appointed to a see in the isle of Cyprus. From here he visited St Louis of France at Jaffa, Sidon, and Acre, and formed a deep friendship with the King, who urged him to visit him in France. This he was able to do a few years later when he was sent as papal legate to the King of England. Henry III was then in Aquitaine, where Blessed Bartholomew presented himself and accompanied the King to Paris. Here he was welcomed warmly by St Louis and given a relic of the true cross and of the crown of thorns. In 1256 Pope Alexander IV translated Blessed Bartholomew to the see of Vicenza, wherein he was soon involved in troubles with the violent and evil Ghibelline leader, Ezzelino da Romano. For a time he was in exile from his diocese, but on his return devoted himself with increased energy to purifying the faith and morals of his flock, rebuilding the churches ruined by Ezzelino, and striving for the peace of the distracted cities of Veneto.

Four years before his death Blessed Bartholomew assisted at the second translation of the relics of St Dominic, and preached the panegyric on that occasion. It is often said that he was Master of the Sacred Palace to Gregory IX, legate of Innocent IV to St Louis in the East, and named Latin Patriarch of Jerusalem ; but there is no mention of these offices in his testament, wherein he states what posts of importance he had filled. He died on July 1, 1271, and was buried in the church of the Holy Crown, which he had built at

Vicenza to house the relics presented by St Louis. He was greatly venerated by the people and commonly called Blessed Bartholomew, a *cultus* that was confirmed by Pope Pius VI in 1793.

A sufficient account will be found in the *Acta Sanctorum*, July, vol. i. See also G. T. Faccioli, *Vita e Virtu del b. Bartolommeo*, 1794 ; B. Altaner, *Dominikanermissionen des 13 Jahrhundert* (1924), pp. 40 *seq.* ; M. de Waresquiel, *Le B. Barthélemy de Breganze* (1905) ; and Procter, *Lives of Dominican Saints*, pp. 297–301.

OCTOBER 24

ST RAPHAEL THE ARCHANGEL

OF the seven archangels, who in both Jewish and Christian tradition are venerated as pre-eminently standing before the throne of God, three only are mentioned by name in the Bible, Michael, Gabriel, and Raphael. These have been venerated in the Church from early times, especially in the East, but it was not till the pontificate of Pope Benedict XV that the liturgical feasts of the two last were made obligatory throughout the Latin Church.

It is recorded in the sacred book of the history of Tobias that St Raphael was sent by God to minister to the old Tobias, who was blind and greatly afflicted, and to Sara, daughter of Raguel, whose seven bridegrooms had each perished on the night of their wedding. And when the young Tobias was sent into Media to collect money owing to his father, it was Raphael who, in the form of a man and under the name of Azarias, accompanied him on the journey, helped him in his difficulties, and taught him how safely to enter into wedlock with Sara. " He conducted me," says Tobias, " and brought me safe again. He received the money of Gabalus. He caused me to have my wife, and he chased from her the evil spirit. He gave joy to her parents. Myself he delivered from being devoured by the fish ; thee also he hath made to see the light of Heaven ; and we are filled with all good things through him." The offices of healing performed by the angel in this story and the fact that his name signifies " God has healed " has caused Raphael to be identified with the angel who moved the waters of the healing sheep-pool (John v 1–4) ; this identity is recognised in the liturgy by the reading of that passage of the gospel in the Mass of St Raphael's feast. In Tobias xii 12 and 15, the archangel directly speaks of himself as " one of the seven who stand before the Lord," and says that he continually offered the prayers of young Tobias up to God.

Apart from the veneration of St Michael (on which see May 8 and September 29), the earliest liturgical recognition of the other great archangels seems to be found in the primitive Greek form of the Litany of the Saints. Mr. Edmund Bishop is of opinion (*Liturgica Historica*, pp. 142–151) that this may be traced back to the time of Pope Sergius (687–701). In it St Michael, St Gabriel, and St Raphael are invoked in succession just as they are to-day, the only difference being that they there take precedence, not only of St John the Baptist, but also of the Blessed Virgin herself. On the early mention of St Raphael in Christian documents and on the present commemoration, consult further Cardinal Schuster, *Liber Sacramentorum* (Eng. trans.), vol. v, pp. 189–191. On the archangels in art it will be sufficient to give a reference to Künstle, *Ikonographie*, vol. i ; though the subject has also been fully treated by A. Didron, van Drival, and others. In the *Ethiopic Synaxarium* (Ed. Budge, 1928), vol. iv, pp. 1274–1278, is a curious account of the dedication of a church to St Raphael in an island off Alexandria early in the fifth century.

ST FELIX, Bp. of Thibiuca, Mart.

A.D. 303

In the beginning of Diocletian's persecution, numbers among the Christians delivered up the sacred books into the hands of the persecutors that they might be burnt. Many even sought for pretences to extenuate or excuse this crime, as if it ever could be lawful to concur in a sacrilegious or impious action. Felix, a bishop in proconsular Africa, was so far from being carried away by the torrent that the falls of others were to him a spur to greater watchfulness and fortitude. Magnilian, magistrate of Thibiuca, ordered him to be apprehended, and commanded him to give up all books and writings belonging to his church, that they might be burnt. The martyr replied that the law of God must be preferred to the law of man, so Magnilian sent him to the proconsul at Carthage. This officer, offended at his bold confession, commanded him to be loaded with irons and, after he had kept him nine days in a foul dungeon, to be put on board a vessel to be taken to stand his trial before the prefect of the *prætorium* in Italy. The Bishop lay under hatches in the ship, between the horses' feet, four days without eating or drinking. The vessel arrived at Agrigentum in Sicily, and the saint was treated with great honour by the Christians of that island and in all the cities through which he passed. When the prefect had brought him as far as Venosa in Apulia he ordered his irons to be knocked off, and again put to him the questions whether he had the Scriptures and why he refused to deliver them up. Felix answered that he could not deny that he had the books, but that he would never give them up. The prefect without more ado condemned him to be beheaded. At the place of execution St Felix thanked God for all His mercies, and bowing down his head offered himself a sacrifice to Him who lives for ever and ever. He was fifty-six years old, and one of the first victims under Diocletian.

Nevertheless, the account of his being carried into Italy is an inter-
polation in his *acta* : he probably suffered at Carthage. Other
martyrs named with him by the Roman Martyrology are connected
with the " Twelve Brothers " (September 1) and the martyred Bishop
of Thibiuca has probably been confused with another Felix, put
to death at Venosa.

Many great, learned, and once holy men have, with the *traditores*,
fallen before the end of their course. At the sight of such examples,
who does not tremble for himself ? If we know ourselves, we shall
be certain that no one is weaker than we are. Can any creature be
more unworthy of the divine mercy than those who have repaid the
greatest graces with sloth and infidelities ? When, therefore, we
read of the fall or sins of others, we ought to turn our eyes upon
ourselves : to thank the divine mercy which has still borne with us
and is yet ready with stretched forth arms to embrace us ; to shake
off our sloth in the practice of virtue, enter upon a fervent penitential
life, and call upon God in fear and humility. He is our strength
and support, almighty and most desirous to save us, if our wilful
pride stand not in the way. He alone can effectually remove those
obstacles ; prayer and penitence will not fail to obtain this constant
grace. But to neglect these means is to perish.

In the *Analecta Bollandiana*, vol. xxxix (1921), pp. 241–276, Père
Delehaye has published a remarkable study of the text of this *passio*. The
materials previously edited in the *Acta Sanctorum*, October, vol. x, were
insufficient, and Delehaye, after printing representative forms of the two
great families into which the texts may be divided, supplies an admirable
restoration of the primitive document which lies at the base of all. As
stated above, the deportation of the martyr to Italy is a fiction of the later
hagiographers who unscrupulously embroidered the original text. Felix,
as Delehaye very positively asserts (in agreement with M. Monceaux,
Revue archéologique, 1905, vol. i, pp. 335–340), was put to death by the
Proconsul at Carthage, and his relics were subsequently laid to rest in the
well-known " basilica Fausti." The proper day of the martyrdom of
St Felix would seem to be the 15th or possibly the 16th of July. For
the confusions which led to its transference, first to July 30, and finally to
October 24, see Delehaye, and more fully Dom Quentin, *Les Martyrologes
historiques*, pp. 522–532 and 697–698.

ST PROCLUS, Bp. of Constantinople, Conf.

A.D. 447

St Proclus was a native of Constantinople, and was very young
were he was made a lector. The service of the church did not hinder

him from closely following his studies, and he was a disciple of
St John Chrysostom ; nevertheless he became secretary to St John's
opponent, Atticus, Bishop of Constantinople, who ordained him
deacon and priest. After his death many pitched upon Proclus as
the fittest person to be placed in that important see ; but Sisinnius
was chosen and he appointed Proclus bishop of Cyzicus, metropolis
of the Hellespont. The inhabitants of that city, being unwilling to
acknowledge the jurisdiction of Constantinople, refused to receive
him and chose Dalmatius, a monk. Proclus therefore continued at
Constantinople, where he got a great reputation by his preaching.
Upon the death of Sisinnius in 427 many again cast their eyes upon
him as the most worthy of that dignity ; but Nestorius was chosen,
who soon began to propagate his errors. St Proclus courageously
maintained the truth against him, and in 429 preached a sermon to
show that the Blessed Virgin ought to be styled the Mother of God ;
in the course of it he made use of the memorable phrase, " We do
not proclaim a deified man, but we confess an incarnate God."
Nestorius, who was present, publicly contradicted him in the church.
When that heresiarch was deposed in 431 Maximian was chosen to
succeed him, those that were for St Proclus being overruled by
those who maintained that his appointment would contravene the
canon which forbade the translation of bishops from one see to
another. But after Maximian's death in 434, as Proclus had never
been able in fact to take possession of the see of Cyzicus, he was
elected to that of Constantinople, a proceeding of which Pope St
Celestine I had approved some time before. The mildness with
which he treated even the most obstinate among the Nestorians,
Arians, and other heretics, was a distinguishing part of his character,
but he strenuously supported the Catholic faith and kept up correspondence and lived in close union and friendship with the Holy
See and St Cyril of Alexandria. The Armenian bishops consulted
him about the doctrine and writings of Theodore of Mopsuestia,
who was then dead, and whose name was in reputation in those
parts. St Proclus answered them in 436 by his *Tome to the Armenians*,
which is the most famous of his writings. In it he condemned the
doctrine mentioned as savouring of Nestorianism, and expounded
the faith of the Incarnation ; without, however, naming Theodore,
whose memory was revered by the Cilicians and who had died in
the communion of the Church. He exhorted them to adhere to the
doctrine of St Basil and St Gregory Nazianzen, whose names and
works were in particular veneration among them. Others carried
on this contest with greater warmth. Thus St Proclus saved the
Armenian church from the danger of Nestorianism ; but there was

no Proclus a hundred years later to save them from the opposed heresy of the Monophysites. In concert with the Empress Pulcheria, he translated the body of his old master St John Chrysostom from Comana Pontica to the Church of the Apostles at Constantinople. The whole city went out to meet the procession, and the remaining intransigent followers of St John submitted themselves to his gentle and orthodox successor.

A number of the letters and sermons of St Proclus are extant. " The style of this father," says Alban Butler, " is concise, sententious, and full of lively witty turns, more proper to please and delight than to move the heart. This sort of composition requires much pains and study ; and though this father was mighty successful in this way, it is not to be compared to the easy natural gravity of St Basil or the sweet style of St Chrysostom."

During the episcopate of St Proclus Constantinople was visited by a disastrous earthquake, and amid the ruins of many buildings men ran to and fro distracted with fear and horror, not being able to find any place of refuge or security. The inhabitants wandered in the fields, and St Proclus with his clergy followed his scattered flock, and ceased not to comfort them amidst their afflictions and to implore the divine mercy. The Greek Menology of Basil, on the authority of a chronicler who wrote three hundred and fifty years after the alleged event, refers to a legend that, as they thus prayed, crying out *Kyrie eleison*, a child was caught up out of sight into the air. When he came back to earth, the boy said he had heard the angelic choirs singing the words, " Holy God, holy Strong One, holy Deathless One " ; and straightway he died. The people repeated the words, adding, " Have mercy upon us," and the earthquake ceased. In consequence St Proclus introduced this invocation, the *Trisagion*, into the Liturgy. It is not known that he did this, but the first certain mention of the Trisagion is at the Council of Chalcedon, only a few years later, and it is quite likely that St Proclus and his people prayed in these famous words at the time of the earthquake.

Proclus is referred to by St Cyril of Alexandria as " a man full of religion, perfectly instructed in the discipline of the Church, and a careful observer of the canons." " In moral excellence," says the Greek historian Socrates, who knew him personally, " he had few equals. He was always gentle to everyone, for he was convinced that kindness advances the cause of truth better than severity. He therefore determined not to irritate and harass heretics, and so restored to the Church in his own person that mild and benignant dignity of character which had so often been unhappily violated. . . .

He was a pattern to all true prelates." St Proclus died on July 24 in the year 447.

A sufficiently full account of St Proclus. compiled from the church historians and other sources, is provided in the *Acta Sanctorum*, October, vol. x. But see also F. X. Bauer, *Proklos von Constantinopel* (1918), and Bardenhewer, *Geschichte der alt-kirchlichen Literatur*, vol. iv, pp. 202–208. Ever since the publication of the Syriac text of the *Book of Heraclides*, the question of Nestorius's real teaching has been revived, and a large literature has resulted ; for details see the article " Nestorius " in the *Dictionnaire de Théologie*.

ST EVERGISLUS, or EBREGISILUS, Bp. of Cologne, Mart.

c. A.D. 450 (590)

When St Severinus of Cologne was making a visitation at the church of Tongres in Limburg a young child was presented to him to be consecrated to the service of God. He saw in this boy, Evergislus, a chosen soul, took a personal interest in his education, and when he was grown up made him his archdeacon. Evergislus was present when St Severinus, as related by Gregory of Tours, had his vision of the entry of St Martin into Heaven, but the archdeacon himself saw and heard nothing, and sent a messenger to Tours to verify that Martin was dead. He succeeded his master as bishop of Cologne. One day when visiting the church of the " Golden Saints " he greeted the martyrs with the verse, " Exultabunt sancti in gloria," and at once the voice of an invisible choir responded, " Lætabuntur in cubilibus suis ! " While at Tongres in the discharge of his pastoral duties St Evergislus went at night to the church of the monastery of our Lady to pray ; here he was set upon by robbers, and met his death by an arrow.

This is the legend of the church of Cologne, recognised in the Roman Martyrology to-day, but it is doubtful if the Evergislus to whom it refers ever existed. St Evergislus actually lived a hundred years later and was active at the court of Austrasia. He was twice sent as a royal ambassador, by Queen Brunhild into Spain to the Visigothic King Reccared and by Childebert II to Guntramnus of Burgundy ; on the second occasion he accompanied St Gregory of Tours. St Evergislus was not a martyr. His relics are claimed by Cologne, but actually they seem to be those of St Ebregisilus of Maestricht, bishop there at the beginning of the seventh century ; he was buried at Saint-Trond and translated to the church of St Cæcilia in Cologne by St Bruno in the year 959. He is commemorated on this same day.

The data seem involved in hopeless confusion. What purports to be a Life of Evergislus is printed in the *Analecta Bollandiana*, vol. vi (1887), pp. 193–198, and also elsewhere ; but it was written only in the eleventh century and is historically worthless. See, however, the discussion of the problem by W. Levison in the *Festschrift für A. Brackman* (1931), pp. 40–63 ; and *cf.* Duchesne, *Fastes Episcopaux*, vol. iii, p. 176.

ST ARETAS AND THE MARTS. OF NAGRAN, AND ST ELESBAAN, KING AND CONF.

A.D. 523

About the middle of the fifth century the Aksumite Ethiopians extended their power over the Arabs and Jews of Himyar, across the Red Sea, and in the beginning of the sixth century imposed a new dynasty upon this tributary people. Taking advantage of the death of the local ruler or viceroy, a member of the displaced Himyarite family, called Dunaan (Dhu-Nowas), rose in revolt. He was a convert to Judaism, and with the support of his co-religionists he seized Safar (Taphar), massacred the garrison and Christian clergy, and turned the church into a synagogue. Elesbaan, the Aksumite king, prepared to put down the rebellion and in the meantime Dunaan laid siege to Nagran (Nedjran), a stronghold of Christianity. It put up a strong defence and Dunaan, in despair of taking it, offered an amnesty if it would surrender. The offer was accepted, but the terms were repudiated : the town was given over to Dunaan's soldiers to sack, and death was decreed for every Christian who would not apostatise. The leader in the defence had been Abdullah ibn Kaab, chief of the Beni Harith (whence he is called St *Aretas* in the Roman Martyrology), with 340 of his tribe ; these were all beheaded. All priests, deacons, ministers, and consecrated virgins were burnt without trial, being thrown into pits that were filled with burning fuel. Daumeh, wife of Aretas and the most beautiful woman in the city, excited the desire of Dunaan. She repulsed him, and he had her daughters executed before her eyes and their warm blood poured into her mouth, before her own head was struck off. The Roman Martyrology mentions a boy of five years who jumped into the fire in which his mother was dying in agony. Four thousand other men, women, and children were slain, and even the bones of the bishop Paul, dead for two years, were dug up and scattered.

An episcopal envoy of the Emperor Justin I was at the camp of an Arab tribe on the Persian frontier when the tale of his achievement was brought from Dunaan, and the bishop at once sent an account of it to the imperial court at Constantinople. At the same time refugees from Nagran spread the news over Egypt and Syria. It made a profound and awful impression, which lasted for many generations.* The Patriarch of Alexandria wrote to the bishops of the East recommending a liturgical commemoration of the martyrs and prayers for the survivors, and urging that the Jewish elders of their school at Tiberias should be held responsible for what had happened : a suggestion more forcible than just. Both the Emperor and the Patriarch wrote urging immediate action upon the Aksumite king, Elesbaan (whom the Syrians call David and the Abyssinians Caleb). He required no encouragement, and set off across the straits with a punitive force to avenge the slaughtered saints and to recover his power in Himyar. In the ensuing campaign Elesbaan was victorious, Dunaan being killed in battle and his chief town occupied, and a Christian viceroy appointed. Alban Butler says that Elesbaan, " having by the divine blessing defeated the tyrant, made use of his victory with great clemency and moderation." This can hardly be maintained. He restored Nagran and built several new churches, but both in the field and in dealing with the Jews who had encouraged the massacre he conducted himself with that cruelty and rapacity which are only to be looked for in the barbarous prince of a semi-pagan nation. However, towards the end of his life he resigned his throne to his son, made a present of his royal crown to the church of the Holy Sepulchre in Jerusalem, and himself became an exemplary monk. Thus St Elesbaan earned the eulogy which is accorded him in the Roman Martyrology on the 27th of this month ; he died about the year 555.

The names of the Nagran martyrs and of St Elesbaan were introduced into the Roman Martyrology by Baronius in spite of the fact that all of them were probably, at least materially, Monophysites.

The Greek text of the *passio* has been printed in the *Acta Sanctorum*, October, vol. x, and we have also the Syriac account written by Symeon of Beth Arram. See further, Guidi in the *Atti della Accad. dei Lincei*, vol. vii (1881), pp. 471 *seq.* ; Deramey in the *Revue de l'Histoire des religions*, vol. xxviii, pp. 14–42 ; the *Revue des études juives*, vols. xviii, xx, and xxi, which contain papers by Halévy and Duchesne's reply ; and Nöldeke in *Göttingen Gel. Anzeiger*, 1899, pp. 825 *seq.* A more recent work by A Moberg, *The Book of the Himyarites, Fragments of an unknown Syriac work* (1924), does not add much to our knowledge. It belongs to the usual type of hagiographical romance.

---

* Mohammed mentions the massacre in the Koran and condemns its perpetrators to Hell (*sura* lxxxv).

ST SENOCH, Abbot and Conf.

A.D. 579

This saint was a contemporary of St Gregory, Bishop of Tours, who knew him personally and wrote his Life. Senoch (Senou) was born of pagan parents at the village of Tiffauges in Poitou, and having been converted to Christ left his home with the intention of becoming a hermit. He wandered into Touraine, and found there a suitable place, where is now the village of Saint-Senou. He installed himself in some ruins, said to have been the remains of a monastery, with the stones of which he built a dwelling for himself and a small chapel, which was consecrated by the Bishop of Tours, St Euphronius. Senoch was joined by three disciples, but he preferred to be quite alone and spent most of his time shut up in his own cell; he fasted on barley-bread and water, always went barefooted, and loaded his body with fetters. The austerities of the new hermit earned him a great reputation for sanctity, and many visitors came to the place who insisted on making offerings, which St Senoch devoted to the relief of slaves and other needy people. When St Euphronius died in 573 Senoch went to Tours to pay his respects to his successor, St Gregory, with whom he exchanged the kiss of brotherhood and then returned quietly to his cell. But soon after he made another journey, to visit his friends and relatives at Tiffauges, and met with such signs of respect and veneration while he was away that he came back rather proud of himself. St Gregory noticed this and rebuked him sharply, reminding him of the words of St Paul, that he would glory in nothing but his infirmities in order that the power of Christ might dwell in him, for in himself he was nothing. Senoch humbly accepted the reprimand and as a penance and to avoid appearance of singularity he agreed no longer to withdraw himself from the company of his brethren except during Advent and Lent. St Gregory narrates a number of miracles of healing vouchsafed by God at the prayer of St Senoch, who died in his arms after an illness of three days' duration; Gregory had been told of it and hurried to the hermit's bedside, where he arrived an hour before the end. The Bishop officiated at his funeral, for which an immense crowd gathered, and when he celebrated the Mass of the month's mind a paralytic was cured at St Senoch's grave. His feast is kept in the dioceses of Tours and Luçon.

Most of what we know concerning St Senoch comes from Gregory of Tours. All the relevant material will be found in the *Acta Sanctorum*, October, vol. x.

ST MARK, Conf.

c. A.D. 580

The Roman Martyrology to-day mentions this Mark, a solitary in Campania, and refers to his famous deeds chronicled by St Gregory. In his *Dialogues* St Gregory says that many of his friends knew Mark personally and had been present at his miracles, and that he had heard much of him from his predecessor, Pope Pelagius II. Mark lived alone in a small cave on Mount Marsica (Mondragone), and after miraculously overcoming the lack of water had for three years the daily company of the Devil, in the form of a serpent ("his old friend"). When he first took up his quarters in the cave the hermit fastened one end of a chain to his ankle and the other to the rock, so that he could not wander wantonly from his habitation. Word of this came to St Benedict at Monte Cassino (where Mark is said to have been a monk), and he sent a message in which the authentic voice of Benedict can be heard speaking : "If you are God's servant, let yourself be held by the chain of Christ, not by any chain of iron." St Mark accordingly loosed himself and later gave the chain to his followers when they complained that the bucket rope of the well kept on breaking. There was a great rock overhanging Mark's cave and his neighbours were much afraid that it would fall and crush him. Therefore one Mascator came with a number of people and offered to remove it. Mark refused to budge from the cave while it was done, telling them nevertheless to do whatever they thought necessary, and they set to work in fear and trembling with him inside. But when the rock was loosed it bounced harmlessly over the cave and rolled safely down the mountain-side.

On October 22 the Roman Martyrology speaks of "the holy MARK THE BISHOP, a most noble and learned man, who was the first Gentile to undertake the government of the Church of Jerusalem. Not long after he gained the martyr's palm under the Emperor Antoninus," about the year 156. His martyrdom is not mentioned by Eusebius and it is questionable.

The Dialogues of St Gregory the Great are our only source of information.

ST MAGLORIUS, Bp. and Conf.

c. A.D. 586

St Umbrafel, who later became a monk under his nephew St Samson on Ynys Pyr (Caldey) and then an abbot in Ireland, was married to Afrella, daughter of Meurig, the prince of Morgannwg ; they had a son, born in Glamorgan, whom they named Maelor, who is called in French Magloire and in Latin Maglorius. According to his late Life, which contains much fabulous matter, he was entrusted while young to the care of St Illtyd at Llanilltyd Fawr, where also was his cousin St Samson. On reaching manhood Maglorius returned to his home, where Samson visited him and spoke so fervently of the things of God that he also left the world to become a monk and companion to Samson, who ordained him deacon and took him into Brittany. Here Maglorius was given charge of a monastery at Kerfunt, shared the missionary labours of St Samson, and when he died succeeded him as abbot and bishop at Dol. He discharged his new duties with vigour for three years, but he was getting an old man, and about 565 he resigned his responsibilities into the hands of his disciple St Budoc, son of the Breton prince Judual. Maglorius then retired to a remote spot on the coast, but even here his life was soon made a misery by the crowds of people who came to be cured of their ills or to see a miracle. Among them was the chieftain of Sark, Loescon, whom Maglorius healed of a skin disease, and in gratitude he gave the saint and his monks a part of his island, whither they went to live. But the resources of the place, principally sea fowl and fish, were insufficient to support the increased population, and there was friction between Maglorius and Loescon, which ended in Loescon leaving the island altogether. St Maglorius built a monastery where is now the *Seigneurie* of Sark, and organised the people to resist the barbarian raiders from Germany, whom they successfully kept at bay. The saint also visited Jersey, for the purpose of delivering that island from a " dragon," in return for which service he was granted land there as well. Throughout these activities he lived a life of great austerity, fasting every day and not eating at all on Wednesdays and Fridays ; for the last months of his life he interpreted literally the words of the Psalmist, " This will I seek after, that I may dwell in the house of the Lord all the days of my life," and never stirred out of the church except for necessity. During the plague and famine of the year 585 he worked heroically for the people, and God is said to have come to their help with miracles at the intercession of the saint. He died shortly after and in the ninth century his relics were translated to Lehon on the mainland and thence to Paris, where some still remain, confused with others at the time of the Revolution, in the church of St James *du Haut Pas.*

The feast of St Maglorius is observed in the Rennes diocese, and as the other chief centre of his *cultus* is the Channel Islands

he has a commemoration to-day throughout the diocese of
Portsmouth.

We have several short medieval biographies, on which see the *Bibliotheca
Hagiographica Latina*, nn. 5139–5147. There is a full notice by Miss
Bateson in the *Dict. of Nat. Biog.*, vol. xxxv, pp. 323–324 ; and another in
Baring-Gould and Fisher, *Lives of the British Saints*, vol. iii, pp. 407 *seq.* ;
but the most valuable contributions to the subject come from such continental
scholars as A. de la Borderie and F. Duine. Consult the former's *Histoire de
Bretagne*, vol. i (1896) and the latter's *Inventaire*, as well as his *Memento des
sources hagiographiques de Bretagne*.

ST MARTIN OF VERTOU, ABBOT AND CONF.
END OF THE SIXTH CENTURY

Very little beyond speculation is known of this saint, for his
two extant Lives were written some centuries after his death and
consist chiefly of miracles, and there has been confusion between
him and St Martin of Braga, who was abbot of Dumium in Portugal
while this Martin was a hermit in the forest of Dumen in Brittany.
He was born at Nantes, but of a Frankish family, and was ordained
deacon by St Felix, who sent him to preach in Poitou. The legend
says that after much effort he had succeeded in converting only the
master and mistress of the house wherein he dwelt, so, warning
them to flee from the wrath to come, he left the town where he had
laboured wallowing in its iniquities, and it was straightway visited
by an earthquake which swallowed it up and waters flowed over its
site. This place is now known as Lac de Grand Lieu, and the village
of Herbauges at its edge is the successor of the destroyed town.
Moreover, near by is to be seen a *menhir*, which is the pillar of stone
into which the fleeing woman was transformed because she looked
back at the doomed town. Of which story may be said what Camden
temperately remarks about a similar tale concerning Llyn Safaddan
in Breconshire : " All which I suspect as fabulous, and not to be
otherwise regarded."

After his failure as a missioner St Martin retired to a lonely
forest on the left bank of the Sèvre, and about the year 575 established the hermitage which grew into the Benedictine abbey of
Vertou. He evangelised this district, and other monastic foundations are attributed to him, including a nunnery at Durieu, where
he died. The monks of Vertou are said to have stolen his body
while it was awaiting burial in the church at Durieu and the nuns were
singing the Office for the Dead at night. Among the stories told of

St Martin (by confusion, in this case, with Martin of Braga) is that an unnamed British prince had a daughter who was fearfully tormented by evil spirits. One of them said through her mouth that they would be overcome by the prayers of a holy man called Martin, and the prince thereupon sent messengers in all directions to find such an one. At length they came to Vertou, told their errand, and the saint agreed to accompany them. He had hardly landed in Britain when the demons knew of his arrival and, unwilling to wait for him, tormented their victim for the last time and fled. She of course received the nun's veil from her deliverer.

On October 8 is commemorated St Martin Cid, first abbot of the Cistercian monastery of Belfuente, between Zamora and Salamanca. He died in 1153.

The Bollandists in the *Acta Sanctorum*, October, vol. x, seem to have printed all the texts which bear upon the life and miracles of this rather nebulous saint.

BD. JOHN ANGELO PORRO, Conf.

A.D. 1506

The city of Milan has the honour of being the birthplace of this ornament of the order of the Servants of Mary, who soon after his profession and ordination was sent first to Cavacurta and then to the cradle of his order on Monte Senario as being more suited to a life of prayer and silence than to the works of the active ministry. Here he practised penitential austerities, having always in his mind the passion of our Lord and the sorrows of His Mother. Having remained there in great holiness for some years he was drawn from his solitude to be master of novices at Florence, an office he fulfilled so well that he is venerated in his order as a patron of novice-masters. After nine years of this work he was made prior of Monte Senario, and when his period of office was over he returned to Milan, hoping to escape the crowds of visitors whom his reputation for miracles attracted. Wherever he was stationed he spent much time in giving instruction in Christian doctrine, especially to the poor and unlearned; in Milan he went about the streets gathering in children for this purpose, a work which was to be organized in the same place by St Charles Borromeo in the next generation. While at Monte Senario Blessed John Angelo learned in a vision of the death of his sister and that he too must go back home as his death was near. Accordingly he returned to his native Milan, worn out with work and hardships, and died there in the

Servite priory of our Lady in 1506. The *cultus* of Blessed John Angelo Porro was approved by Pope Clement XII in 1737.

A Life by Philip Albericius has been reproduced in the *Acta Sanctorum*, October, vol. x, with the usual introduction and commentary ; but Father Soulier, O.S.M., in the *Monumenta Ordinis Servorum B.M.V.*, vol. viii, pp. 121–211, and vol. ix, pp. 5–222, has been able to glean a few additional data. It must be confessed, however, that the career and personality of the *beato* still remain veiled in great obscurity. A popular Life in Italian by L. Raffaelli (1906), aims primarily at edification and can make no pretence to critical scholarship.

BD. ANTONY MARY CLARET, BP. AND CONF.

A.D. 1870

A notice of this holy archbishop, who was beatified by Pope Pius XI in 1934, will be found printed as an appendix to this volume, p. 382.

SS. CHRYSANTHUS AND DARIA, MARTS.

A.D. 283 (?)

THAT these two martyrs were actual persons who gave their lives for Christ is attested by the evidence of their early veneration at Rome, but their *passio* is a fanciful compilation of the fifth century.   It says that Chrysanthus was the son of a patrician named Polemius, who came with his father from Alexandria to Rome in the reign of Numerian.   He was instructed in the faith and baptised by a priest called Carpophorus.   On discovering this, Polemius was indignant and subjected his son to the blandishments of five young women, hoping that he would lose his chastity and with it his new religion.   When this device failed, Polemius proposed a marriage between Chrysanthus and a certain Daria, a virgin of Vesta.   How this was to be brought about is not explained, but Daria proved acceptable to Chrysanthus, converted her, and they entered into a virginal union.   Between them they made a number of converts in Roman society, and were denounced to the prefect Celerinus, who committed them to the charge of the tribune Claudius.   He handed Chrysanthus over to a company of seventy soldiers, with instructions to make him sacrifice to Hercules by any means which they chose.   They subjected him to a number of torments, under which he remained so constant that the tribune himself was constrained to confess Christ, and with him his wife Hilaria and their sons Jason and Maurus.   The seventy soldiers likewise followed their example, and by order of the Emperor all were slain together except Hilaria, who was put to death later while praying at their tomb.   St Claudius and his companions are commemorated in the Roman Martyrology on December 3.   Daria in the meanwhile had been consigned to a brothel, where she was defended from harm by a lion, which escaped for the purpose from the amphitheatre.   To get rid of the beast the house had to be set on fire, and then the girl with her husband was taken before Numerian himself.   After being tortured they were condemned to death, and were stoned and buried in an old sand-pit on the Via Salaria Nova. On the first anniversary of their passion some of the faithful met together in this pit, and while they were praying in the crypt where the martyrs were buried emissaries of the Emperor closed up the entrance with rocks and earth, so that they were all entombed. These are the SS. Diodorus the priest, Marianus the deacon, and their fellows, commemorated on December 1.

The statement that SS. Chrysanthus and Daria were stoned and buried in a sand-pit is probably true. Later their tomb, with the bones of the other martyrs, was said to be discovered, and St Gregory of Tours has left a description of the shrine that was made of it. In the ninth century apparently its site was still known, for in the year 844 the relics of SS. Chrysanthus and Daria were translated to Prüm in Rhenish Prussia and four years later to Münstereifel, where they still are. The tomb was probably in the neighbourhood of the *Cœmeterium Jordanorum* on the New Salarian Way, where are a number of ancient sand-pits.

There is both a Latin and a Greek text of this fanciful legend. Both are printed in the *Acta Sanctorum*, October, vol. xi. An exceptionally full discussion of the historical data will be found in Delehaye's commentary on the *Hieronymianum* under August 12, on which day these martyrs are there specially commemorated, but their names also recur on December 20, and in this connection Delehaye points out that the assignment of their feast in the Roman Martyrology to October 25 seems to be due to a statement made in an account of a translation of their relics that October 25 was not only the date of the translation but the actual day of their martyrdom. The marble calendar of Naples (*c.* 850) seems to confirm this. Pope St Damasus is recorded to have written an inscription for their tomb, but that which was at one time attributed to him must certainly be of later date. See further, J. P. Kirsch, *Festkalender* (1924), pp. 90–93 ; and Leclercq in *Diction. d'Archéol.*, etc., vol. iii, cc. 1560–1568.

SS. CRISPIN AND CRISPINIAN, MARTS.

c. A.D. 285

The names of these two martyrs were famous throughout northern Europe in the Middle Ages, but are to-day known in England chiefly from the great speech which Shakespeare puts into the mouth of King Henry V on the eve of Agincourt (*Henry V*, Act iv, Scene 3). Their *passio* unfortunately cannot be relied on, though the era and place of martyrdom is probably correctly stated. It says that they came from Rome to preach the faith in Gaul toward the middle of the third century, together with St Quintinus and others. Fixing their residence at Soissons, they instructed many in the faith of Christ, which they preached publicly during the day at reasonable times ; and, in imitation of St Paul, worked with their hands at night making shoes, though they are said to have been nobly born (and brothers). The infidels listened to their instructions and were astonished at the example of their lives, and the effect was the conversion of many to the Christian faith. They had continued this employment several years when, the Emperor Maximian coming into Gaul, a complaint was lodged against them. He, perhaps as much to gratify their accusers as to indulge his own superstition and cruelty, gave orders that they should be taken before Rictius Varus, an implacable enemy of the Christians. He subjected them to various torments and in vain tried to kill them by drowning and boiling ; this so infuriated him that he took his own life by jumping into the fire prepared for them ! Thereupon Maximian commanded that they be beheaded, and this was done. Later a great church was built over their tomb, and St Eligius the Smith embellished their shrine. SS. Crispin and Crispinian are supposed to have plied their trade without taking payment unless it was offered, and thereby disposed men to listen to the gospel. They are the traditional patrons of shoemakers, cobblers, and other workers in leather.

The local tradition which associates these martyrs with the little port of Faversham in Kent is not mentioned by Alban Butler, though it must have been well known in his day, for it is still a living tradition among the people. They are said to have fled thither to escape the persecution, and followed their trade of shoemaking at a house on the site of the Swan Inn, at the lower end of Preston Street. A Mr. Southouse, writing about the year 1670, says that in his time this house had " considerable visits paid to it by the foreigners of that gentle calling," so it looks as if the tradition was also known abroad. There was an altar dedicated in honour of SS. Crispin and Crispinian in the parish church of our Lady St Mary.

From the example of the saints it appears how foolish is the pretences of many Christians who imagine that the care of a family, the business of a farm or a shop, the attention which they are obliged to give to their worldly profession, are impediments which excuse them from aiming at perfection. Such, indeed, they make them ; but this is altogether owing to their own sloth and weakness. Many saints have made these very occupations the means of their perfection. St Paul made tents ; SS. Crispin and Crispinian were shoemakers ; the Blessed Virgin was taken up with the care of her cottage ; Christ Himself worked with His reputed father ; and those saints who renounced all commerce with the world to devote themselves totally to the contemplation of heavenly things made mats, tilled the earth, or copied and bound books. The secret of their sanctification was that, fulfilling the words of Christ, they studied to subdue their passions and die to themselves ; they with earnestness and application obtained of God and improved daily in their souls a spirit of devotion and prayer ; their temporal business they regarded as a duty which they owed to Him, and sanctified it by a pure and perfect intention, as Christ on earth directed everything He did to the glory of His Father. In these very activities they improved themselves in virtue, by the occasions which called it forth at every moment and in every action. Opportunities for every kind of good work never fail in any circumstances ; and the means of sanctification may be practised in every state of life.

The Bollandists in the *Acta Sanctorum*, October, vol. xi, print the *passio* and supply a very full commentary. The historical fact of the martyrdom seems sufficiently guaranteed by the entry on this day in the *Hieronymianum* " in Galiis civitate Sessionis Crispini et Crispiniani." On the popularity of these saints as patrons, see J. Neubner, *Die heiligen Handwerker* (1929) ; G. Amadio, *Le Mie Pagine Sparse* (1933), pp. 378–383 ; Bächtold-Stäubli, *Handwörterbuch des deutschen Aberglaubens*, vol. ii ; and Künstle, *Ikonographie*, vol. ii.

SS. FRONTO AND GEORGE, Bps. AND CONFS.
FOURTH CENTURY (?)

Though without doubt these two saints really existed and were early apostles of Périgueux, their legends, which can be traced only to the ninth century, seem to have been fabricated or altered with the object of giving an apostolic origin to the see of Périgueux. Fronto, it is said, was of the tribe of Juda and was born in Lycaonia. He was converted by the testimony of our Lord's miracles, was baptised by St Peter, and became one of the Seventy-two. After the death and assumption of our Lady he accompanied St Peter to Antioch and Rome, and was sent thence with the priest George to preach to the Gauls. On the way George died, but, like St Maternus of Trier and St Martial of Limoges, he was brought to life again by the touch of St Peter's staff. St Fronto preached with conspicuous success in Aquitaine and Lorraine, and several fantastic miracles and inconsistent particulars are given of his mission. His centre was at Périgueux, whereof he is venerated as the first bishop. Later legends import into his life an incident recorded of quite another St Fronto, who was in fact a hermit in the Nitrian desert. St George evangelised the Velay and is accounted the first bishop of Le Puy.

He is referred to only as a priest by the Roman Martyrology, which says that St Fronto was consecrated bishop by St Peter.

The pages devoted to this legend in the *Acta Sanctorum*, October. vol. xi, may be said to have been superseded by the very careful examination of the documents in the *Analecta Bollandiana*, vol. xlviii (1930), pp. 324–360 —" La Vie ancienne de St Front," by M. Coens, S.J. He there edits the text of an earlier legend of St Fronto, already recognised as more primitive by Mgr Duchesne (see *Fastes Épiscopaux*, vol. ii, pp. 130–134). In this, Fronto is not described as born in Lycaonia, but at Leuquais in the Dordogne, not very far from the Perigueux, he was destined to evangelise. The extravagances and anachronisms are much the same as those in the legend summarised above, but there are signs that the earlier compiler did use some historical material, and a seventh-century Life of St Géry undoubtedly speaks of a tomb of St Fronto venerated in Perigueux at that date.

ST GAUDENTIUS, Bp. of Brescia, Conf.

c. A.D. 410

He seems to have been educated under St Philastrius, Bishop of Brescia, whom he styles his father. His reputation was very high and he travelled to Jerusalem, partly on pilgrimage and partly hoping by his absence to be forgotten at home. In this, however, he was mistaken. In a monastery at Cæsarea in Cappadocia he met with the sisters and the nieces of St Basil, who bestowed on him relics of the Forty Martyrs and other saints, knowing that he would honour those sacred pledges as they had honoured them. During his absence St Philastrius died, and the clergy and people of Brescia chose Gaudentius for their bishop. Fearing obstacles from his humility, they bound themselves by an oath to receive no other for their pastor. The bishops of the province met and with St Ambrose, their metropolitan, confirmed the election. St Gaudentius only yielded to the threat of refusal of communion by the Eastern bishops if he refused to obey. He was ordained by St Ambrose with other bishops of the province about the year 387 ; the sermon which he preached on that occasion expresses the profound humility with which his youth and inexperience inspired him.

The church of Brescia soon found how great a treasure it possessed in so holy a pastor. He never ceased to break the Bread of life, and to feed souls with the truths of salvation. A certain nobleman named Benevolus, who had been disgraced by the Empress Justina because he refused to draw up an edict in favour of the Arians, had retired to Brescia, and being hindered by sickness from attending some of the sermons of St Gaudentius, requested that he would commit them to writing for his use. By this means were preserved ten out of the twenty-one sermons of the saint which are extant. In the second, which he made for the neophytes at their coming from the font on Holy Saturday, he explained to them the mysteries which he could not expound in presence of the catechumens, especially the Blessed Eucharist, of which he says : " The Creator and Lord of Nature, who brings the bread out of the ground, makes also of bread His own body ; because He has promised, and is able to perform it. And He who made wine of water, converts wine into His own blood." Gaudentius built a new church at Brescia, which he named the " Assembly of the Saints," and to the dedication of which he invited many bishops and in their presence made the seventeenth sermon of those which are extant. In it he says that he had deposited in this church the relics of the Forty Martyrs, of St John Baptist, St Andrew, St Thomas, St Luke, and others, affirming that a portion of a martyr's relics is in virtue and efficacy the same as the whole. " Therefore," he says, " that we may be succoured by the patronage of so many saints, let us come and supplicate with an entire confidence and earnest desire, that by their interceding we may deserve to obtain all things we ask, magnifying Christ our Lord, the giver of so great grace." In 405, St Gaudentius was deputed with some others by Pope St Innocent I and by the Emperor Honorius to go into the East to defend the cause of St John Chrysostom before Arcadius, for which Chrysostom sent him a letter of thanks. St Gaudentius and the deputies were ill received, and imprisoned for some time in Thrace ; their papers were forcibly taken from them, and bribes were offered if they would declare themselves in communion with the bishop who had supplanted St John Chrysostom. St Paul is said to have appeared in a vision to one of their deacons to encourage them. They eventually arrived back safely in Italy after four months away, though it is supposed their enemies intended them to be cast away at sea, for they were put on a most unseaworthy vessel. St Gaudentius seems to have died about the year 410, and Rufinus styled him " the glory of the doctors of the age wherein he lives." He is honoured on this day in the Roman Martyrology, which mentions on October 14 another St Gaudentius. He was an Ephesian, who came to Italy and was elected bishop of Rimini. With other Catholic prelates he was persecuted by the Arian synod of Sirmium, and was slain by those heretics in the year 359. His feast is kept by the Canons Regular of the Lateran.

There seems to be no formal biography of St Gaudentius, but from contemporary allusions and letters a tolerably full account is furnished in the *Acta Sanctorum,* October, vol. xi. The activities of the saint have occasionally been made the subject of contributions to the local ecclesiastical journal, *Brixia sacra, e.g.* vol. vi and vol. vii (1915–16). See also Lanzoni, *Diocesi d'Italia* (1927), vol. ii, pp. 963–965 ; and the *Journal of Theological Studies,* vol. xii (1914), pp. 593–596.

BD. THADDEUS MACHAR (MACARTHY), CONF.
BISHOP OF CORK AND CLOYNE
A.D. 1497

Of the early life of this bishop, the only Irishman beatified between the canonisation of Lorcan o'Toole in 1228 and the beatification of Oliver Plunket in 1920, very little is known. He belonged to the royal MacCarthys in the part of Munster later known as the Desmond country, his father being lord of Muskerry and his mother a daughter of FitzMaurice, lord of Kerry ; Thaddeus (Tadhg) was a baptismal name in this house for seven hundred years. He is said to have begun his studies with the Friars Minor of Kilcrea and to have then gone abroad, and he seems to have been in Rome when, in 1482 at the age of twenty-seven, he was appointed bishop of Ross by Pope Sixtus IV. Three years later when Henry Tudor became ruler of the three kingdoms, the Yorkist Geraldines made a determined effort to have their own representative in the see of Ross. Ever since the appointment of Thaddeus MacCarthy there had been a rival claimant in the person of Odo o'Driscoll, his predecessor's auxiliary, and it was now alleged that Thaddeus had intruded himself under false pretences, with other charges added. The Earl of Desmond seized the temporalities of the see, and its bishop took refuge at the Cistercian abbey of Fonte Vivo, which was given him *in commendam* by the Bishop of Clogher. By the machinations of the Geraldines Thaddeus was in 1488 declared suspended by the Holy See, and he set off to Rome to plead his cause in person. After two years of investigation and delay Pope Innocent VIII confirmed the bishopric of Ross to Odo, but nominated Thaddeus to the united dioceses of Cork and Cloyne, then vacant by the resignation of the Norman William des Roches, a personal friend of Thaddeus.

Cork and Cloyne was one of the most important bishoprics of Ireland, and was held by a succession of Norman and English prelates. When Blessed Thaddeus arrived to take possession of it he found his cathedral closed against him and the see's endowments in the hands of the Geraldines, Barrys, and others. In vain he endeavoured to assert his canonical rights and to obtain peaceful control of his charge : there was nothing for it but to go again to Rome and appeal to the Holy See. The Pope condemned the lay tyrants and provided Blessed Thaddeus with letters to the Earl of Kildare, then Lord Deputy of Ireland, to the heads of the Bishop's own clan, and to others, exhorting them to protect and aid his just cause. With these Blessed Thaddeus set out for home as a pilgrim on foot, and in the evening of October 24, 1497, reached Ivrea, at the foot of the Alps, where he stayed at the hospice of the canons regular of St Bernard of Menthon. The next morning he was found dead in his bed.

When an examination of his luggage showed who the dead pilgrim was, the matter was reported to the Bishop of Ivrea, who ordered that he should be buried with the utmost solemnity. The story of the episcopal pilgrim travelling *incognito* and on foot soon got around, and the cathedral was crowded with people from the neighbourhood who came to the funeral. They continued to visit the tomb, and the popular *cultus* of Blessed Thaddeus, encouraged by many miracles, was thus begun. In 1742 the relics were examined and translated to below the high altar, and the Bishops of Ivrea and Cork having co-operated in the forwarding of his cause, the *cultus* of Blessed Thaddeus was confirmed by Pope Leo XIII in 1895. His feast is now kept in the dioceses of Ivrea, Ross, Cork, and Cloyne.

Not very much seems to be known concerning this *beato*. In the *Irish Ecclesiastical Record* no mention is made of the decree of confirmation of *cultus* (1895), but in the following year the lessons sanctioned for the Office of his festival are printed, pp. 859–861. The decree confirming *cultus* may be read in the *Analecta Ecclesiastica*, vol. iii (1895), p. 456. It gives very little biographical detail, but dwells principally on the miracles worked at the shrine at Ivrea.

OCTOBER 26

ST EVARISTUS, POPE AND MART.

c. A.D. 107

ST EVARISTUS succeeded St Clement in the see of Rome in the reign of Trajan and governed the Church about eight years, being the fourth successor of St Peter. The *Liber Pontificalis* says that he was the son of a Hellenic Jew of Bethlehem, and, certainly incorrectly, that he divided Rome into several " titles " or parishes, assigning a priest to each, and appointed seven deacons for the city. He is usually accorded the title of martyr, but his martyrdom is not proved ; it is practically certain that St Evaristus was buried near St Peter's tomb on the Vatican.

The immediate disciples of the Apostles were so swallowed up in the life to come that they seemed no longer inhabitants of this world but of Heaven, where their thoughts and affections were placed and whither they directed all their actions, even their necessary attention to temporal concerns. The generality of Christians now set their hearts so much on earthly goods and so easily lose sight of eternity that they are no longer animated by the spirit of the primitive saints, and are become children of this world, slaves to its vanities and to their own passions. If we do not correct this disorder of our hearts and conform our interior life to the spirit of Christ we cannot be entitled to His promises.

There is a notice in the *Acta Sanctorum*, October, vol. xi, but the text and notes of Duchesne's edition of the *Liber Pontificalis* tell us nearly all there is to be known. See, however, an interesting comment by Father von Nostiz-Rieneck on the " Brevierlektionen der Päpste Evaristos und Alexander I " in the *Zeitschrift für Katholische Theologie*, vol. xxix (1905), pp. 159–165.

SS. LUCIAN AND MARCIAN, MARTS.

A.D. 250

Lucian and Marcian while living in the darkness of idolatry applied themselves to the study of black magic, but were converted to the Faith by finding their charms lose their power against a

Christian maiden and evil spirits defeated by the sign of the cross. Their eyes being thus opened, they publicly burned their magical books in the city of Nicomedia ; and when they had effaced their crimes by Baptism they distributed their possessions among the poor and retired together into solitude, that by mortification and prayer they might subdue their passions, and strengthen in their souls that grace which they had just received. After a time they made frequent excursions abroad to preach Christ to the Gentiles and gain souls to the kingdom of His love. The edicts of Decius against the Christians being published in Bithynia in 250, they were apprehended and brought before the proconsul Sabinus, who asked Lucian by what authority he presumed to preach Jesus Christ. " Every man," said the martyr, " does well to endeavour to draw his brother out of a dangerous error," and Marcian likewise gloried in the power of Christ. The judge commanded them to be cruelly tortured, whereupon they reproached him that, whilst they worshipped idols, they had committed many crimes and made open profession of practising magic, without incurring any chastisement ; but when they were become Christians and good citizens they were barbarously punished. Sabinus threatened them with more torments. " We are ready to suffer," said Marcian, " but we will not renounce the true God, lest we be cast into a fire which will never be quenched." At this Sabinus condemned them to be burned alive, and they went joyfully to the place of execution, singing hymns of praise and thanksgiving to God. This story is a romance woven round a group of martyrs at Nicomedia, whose leader was a St Lucian ; they are given as Lucian, Florius, and their companions in the Roman Martyrology. For some unknown reason the Spaniards claim them for Catalonia and an alleged finding of their relics took place at Vic d'Osona in the year 1050.

The *passio* of these martyrs is preserved to us both in Latin and in Syriac ; the Greek text, which is probably the original, seems to have perished. The Latin *passio* is printed in the *Acta Sanctorum*, October, vol. xi ; the Syriac was edited by S. E. Assemani (in his *Acta SS. Mart. Orientalium*, vol. ii, pp. 49 *seq.*) from a manuscript written in the sixth, or possibly even the fifth century. The Syriac *breviarium* of the early fifth century also commemorates these martyrs on October 26, but assigns them to Antioch, and gives the name Silvanus in place of Lucianus. They are, however, correctly named, and attributed to Nicomedia, in the *Hieronymianum*, and the whole question is fully discussed by Delehaye in his commentary, p. 572.

ST RUSTICUS, Bp. of Narbonne, Conf.

A.D. 461

He was a native of southern Gaul and the son of a bishop named Bonosus. A letter written by St Jerome about the year 411 is supposed to be addressed to him; the recipient is recommended to leave his home and to submit himself to the direction of Proculus, Bishop of Marseilles. Rusticus went to Rome, where he was a successful orator, but returned to Gaul to become a monk at Lérins. He was ordained priest by Proculus and attached to his cathedral, and then was elevated to the bishopric of Narbonne. His diocese was in a very unsatisfactory state : the invading Goths were spreading Arianism and the orthodox were quarrelling among themselves, and eventually St Rusticus wrote to Pope St Leo I, setting forth his difficulties and asking to be allowed to resign. The Pope dissuaded him from this and sent him an important letter about the government of the diocese. St Rusticus built a cathedral at Narbonne and the inscription he put up recording its foundation is still in existence. He was held in high regard by his brother-bishops, but of his activities little is known, except that he attended the synod at Arles which approved St Leo's " tome " condemning Monophysism and another which adjudicated between Theodore, Bishop of Fréjus, and the abbey of Lérins.

There is no formal Life of St Rusticus, but from scattered references the Bollandists have compiled a sufficient notice in the *Acta Sanctorum*, October, vol. xi. The letter addressed to Pope Leo seems to have been occasioned by the difficulties arising out of a synod convoked by Rusticus in 458. A particular interest attaches to this Gaulish bishop because his name appears in four different inscriptions discovered at Narbonne or in the immediate neighbourhood. The first and most complete tells us, incidentally, that not only was he the son of Bishop Bonosus, but that an uncle, his mother's brother, was also a bishop called Arator. Another inscription, only discovered in quite recent years, contains the words *Orate pro me Rustico vestro* (pray for me your Rusticus). See on these inscriptions Leclercq, *Dict. d'Archéol., etc.*, vol. xii (1935), cc. 828 and 847–854. *Cf.* also Duchesne, *Fastes Épiscopaux*, vol. i, p. 303.

ST EATA, Bp. of Hexham, Conf.

A.D. 685

When St Aidan came from Iona to his mission in Northumbria he selected twelve English boys to be trained under himself to work in the service of Christ, and of these twelve Eata was one. He became abbot of Melrose, and received St Cuthbert there as a novice, and when St Colman and some of his monks left Northumbria after their defeat at the Synod of Whitby, Eata was put in charge of those who remained at Lindisfarne. St Bede reports on hearsay that St Colman himself asked King Oswy to make this appointment because Eata was a personal disciple of St Aidan. When in 678 St Wilfrid was driven from his see and Northumbria divided into two dioceses, St Eata was appointed bishop of the Bernicians in the north. He was consecrated at York by St Theodore of Canterbury and as he had the choice of Hexham or Lindisfarne for his see he chose Lindisfarne. Three years later Tumbert was consecrated for Hexham, and when he was deposed St Cuthbert was named in his place. He, however, preferred to be at Lindisfarne, whither he had gone as a monk with St Eata, and so an exchange was made, Eata going to Hexham. Here he remained for the short space of life that remained to him, and after his death was revered as a saint by the grateful people among whom he had laboured. Bede says of him that he was a most venerable man, meek and simple. He was buried in his cathedral church, from whence the Archbishop of York in 1113 proposed to translate his relics to York Minster. But he desisted from his intention when St Eata appeared to him in a dream at Hexham, asking that his body might be left to rest in the church which he had governed.

There is a Life of St Eata which has been printed by Raine in his *Priory of Hexham* and a summary by Capgrave in the *Acta Sanctorum*, October, vol. xi; but there is little to add to what may be gathered from the text and notes of Plummer's edition of Bede. See also Stanton's *Menology*, pp. 514–515.

BD. BONAVENTURE OF POTENZA, Conf.

A.D. 1711

He was born at Potenza in the kingdom of Naples in the year 1651 and at the age of fifteen became a Conventual friar minor at Nocera. As an illustration of the implicit obedience that he gave to his superiors it is related that, the key of the sacristy being lost, it was reported to be at the bottom of the cistern, and Brother Bonaventure was told to get hook and line and fish it out. This he did, and after angling for a time hauled up the key. This is recorded of him as a miracle, but whether the miracle lay in the key being transported into the cistern, or in the amazing dexterity of Brother

Bonaventure, does not appear. He was stationed at a number of friaries, but the eight years which he spent at Amalfi was the most fruitful period of his life and he worked there with great profit to the people and his own soul. Several times it was proposed to make him guardian, but at his own earnest wish he was never given any office of authority but that of master of novices. Blessed Bonaventure's devotion to our Lady was particularly directed towards her as conceived without original sin (he lived nearly two hundred years before that dogma was defined), and he would often express the wish that he was another Duns Scotus that he might as effectively defend the truth of the Immaculate Conception.

Blessed Bonaventure died at Ravello on October 26, 1711, and he is one of the saints of the Naples district whose blood is recorded to have flowed freely after he was dead. "It was the will of God that His servant should give an example of obedience even after death. Long after he had expired, the bishop's vicar general asked the surgeon to bleed him in the arm, and he said, ' Father Bonaventure, give us your arm.' The body remained motionless, so turning to the superior the vicar general said, ' Father Guardian, command him in the name of holy obedience to give us his arm.' No sooner had the guardian given the order than the blessed man raised his right arm and presented it to the surgeon. It may be imagined with what fear and admiration the bystanders beheld this action " (*Auréole Séraphique*). From the fuller evidence which was at their disposal the Bollandists have raised a disturbing doubt as to whether Blessed Bonaventure was actually dead when these things happened. Thirty years later his body was found to be incorrupt and the limbs flexible. He was beatified in 1775.

In the *Acta Sanctorum*, October, vol. xii, Father V. de Buck has compiled a Life of the *beato* from the materials supplied in earlier biographies of this devoted Franciscan Conventual, notably from the accounts published by G. M. Rugilo (1754) and G. L. Rossi (1775). See also Léon, *Auréole Séraphique* (Eng. trans.), vol. iii, pp. 423–429. In connection with the blood prodigy referred to above, it is noteworthy that Blessed Bonaventure died at Ravello, a Neapolitan town, in which the annual liquefaction of the blood of St Pantaleon rouses intense popular enthusiasm. See the July volume of this series, pp. 373–375.

OCTOBER 27

ST FRUMENTIUS, Bp. and Conf.

Apostle of Ethiopia

c. A.D. 380

SOMEWHERE about the year 330 a certain philosopher of Tyre, named Meropius, out of curiosity and a wish to see the world and improve his knowledge, undertook a voyage to Ethiopia, which we now call Abyssinia. He took with him two young men, Frumentius and Ædesius, with whose education he was entrusted. In the course of their voyage homeward the vessel touched at a certain port, probably Adulis, to take in provisions and fresh water. The natives fell out with some of the sailors, attacked them, and put the whole crew and all the passengers to the sword, except the two boys, who were studying their lessons under a tree at some distance. When they were found they were carried to the king, who resided at Aksum in the Tigre country. He was attracted by the bearing and knowledge of the young Christians, and not long after made Ædesius his cupbearer and Frumentius, who was the elder, his secretary of state, entrusting him with the public writings and accounts. They lived in great honour with this prince, who on his death-bed thanked them for their services and, in recompense, gave them their liberty. The queen, who was left regent for her eldest son, entreated them to remain and assist her in the government of the state, wherein she found their fidelity, abilities, and integrity her greatest support. Frumentius had the principal management of affairs and, desiring to promote the faith of Christ, induced several Christian merchants who traded there to settle in the country. He procured them privileges and all conveniences for religious worship, and by his own fervour and example strongly recommended the true religion to the infidels. When the young king, whose name was Abreha, came of age and, jointly with his brother Asbeha, took the reins of government into his own hands, the Tyrians resigned their posts, though he invited them to stay. Ædesius went back to Tyre, where he was ordained priest and told his adventures to Rufinus at Antioch, who incorporated them in his continuation of the *Church History* of Eusebius. But Frumentius, having nothing so much at heart as the conversion of the whole

343

nation, took the route to Alexandria, and entreated the bishop, St Athanasius, to send some pastor to that country, ripe for conversion to the faith. St Athanasius called a synod of bishops, and by their unanimous advice ordained Frumentius himself bishop of the Ethiopians, judging no one more proper to finish the work which he had begun. Thus began the dependence of the Christians of Abyssinia on the church of Alexandria which has continued to this day.

The consecration of St Frumentius took place probably just before the year 340 or just after 346. Joined eventually by Ædesius, he went back to Aksum and gained great numbers to the faith by his preaching and miracles ; seldom did any people embrace Christianity with greater ardour or defend it with greater courage. The two kings themselves received baptism, and by their fervour were a spur to their subjects in the practice of every religious duty ; they are venerated as saints in the Abyssinian kalendar. But the Arian emperor Constantius conceived an implacable suspicion against St Frumentius, because he was linked in faith and affection with St Athanasius ; and when he found that he was not even to be tempted, much less seduced by him, he wrote a letter to the two converted kings, in which he commanded them to deliver up Frumentius into the hands of George, the intruded bishop of Alexandria, who would be responsible for his " welfare." The Emperor also warned them against Athanasius as guilty " of many crimes." The only result was that this letter was communicated by the kings to St Athanasius, who has inserted it in his *apologia* against the Arians. The conversion even of the Aksumite kingdom was not completed during the lifetime of St Frumentius. After his death he was called *Abuna*, " Our father," and *Aba salama*, " Father of peace," and *abuna* is still the title of the primate of the dissident Church of Abyssinia.

In every age, from Christ down to this very time, new nations and peoples have been added to His fold, and the apostasy of those that have forsaken the path of truth, such as the Ethiopians, has been repaired by fresh acquisitions. This is the work of the Most High, the wonderful effect of all-powerful grace. It is owing to the divine blessing that the heavenly seed fructifies in the hearts of men, and it is God who raises up and animates with His Spirit zealous successors of the apostles, whom He vouchsafes to make His instruments in this great work. We are indebted to His gratuitous mercy for the inestimable benefit of this light of faith. If we do not correspond faithfully, with fear and love, to so great a grace, our punishment will be so much the more dreadful.

The story told by Rufinus may be read with other matter in the *Acta Sanctorum*, October, vol. xii. This other matter includes a copy of a long Greek inscription found at Aksum, commemorating the exploits of Aïzanas, King of the Homeritae, and his brother Saïzanas. Now it was precisely to Aïzanas and Saïzanas that Constantius addressed his letter, of which St Athanasius has preserved the text, demanding the surrender of Frumentius. There can consequently be no doubt that the last-named really was at Aksum preaching the Christian faith. Although the earlier adventures of Frumentius, as Rufinus recounts them, may have been misunderstood or disfigured with legendary additions, his presence in Aksum, as a bishop, consecrated for this mission by St Athanasius, is a certain fact. See Prof. Guidi in the *Dictionnaire d'Histoire ecclés., etc.*, vol. i, cc. 210–212 ; Leclercq in *Dict. d'Archéol., etc.*, vol. v, cc. 586–594 ; Duchesne, *Histoire ancienne de l'Église*, vol. iii, pp. 576–578 ; and *cf.* the account given of St Frumentius in the *Ethiopic Synaxarium* (Ed. Budge, 1928), vol. iv, pp. 1164–1165.

ST OTTERAN, OR ODHRAN, ABBOT AND CONF.

A.D. 563

Otteran, " noble and without sin," was an abbot from Meath and one of the twelve who sailed with St Columba out of Loch Foyle to Iona ; Adamnan says he was a Briton. Soon after their arrival St Otteran felt death to be upon him, and he said, " I would be the first to die under the covenant of the kingdom of God in this place." " I will give you that kingdom," replied Columba, " and moreover this also, that whoever makes a request at my burial-place shall not get it until he prays to you as well." And Columba, unwilling to see his friend die, blessed him and went out of the house, and as he was walking in the yard he stopped, looking amazedly up to the heavens. Aidan o'Libir asked him at what he gazed, and St Columba answered that he saw strife in the upper air between good and evil spirits, and angels carrying off the soul of Otteran in triumph to Heaven. So he was the first by his death and burial there to seal Iona to the Irish monks, and the place of his burying, the only cemetery on the island, is still called *Reilig Orain*. Although this is all that is known of St Otteran his feast (as a bishop) is kept to-day throughout Ireland.

How little is known concerning St Odhran appears clearly from the glosses to the *Félire* of Œngus, which suggest more than one alternative as to Odhran's identity. A notice in very vague terms is printed in the *Acta Sanctorum*, October, vol. xii. See also Forbes, *Kalendars of Scottish Saints*, p. 426. In the Life of Ciarán of Saigher, Odhran is said to have made a famous monastic foundation at Leitrioch (Latteragh, Tipperary), and in the Annals of Ulster we are told that he died in the year 548.

OCTOBER 28

SS. SIMON AND JUDE, OR THADDEUS, APOSTLES
FIRST CENTURY

ST SIMON is surnamed the Cananæan or Zelotes in the holy Scriptures, words which respectively in Aramaic and Greek mean "the Zealous." Some have mistakenly thought that the first of these surnames was meant to imply that St Simon was born at Cana, in Galilee, and the Greeks say that it was at his marriage that our Lord turned the water into wine. The name refers to his zeal for the Jewish law before his call, and does not necessarily mean that he was one of that particular party among the Jews called Zealots, from the great care they professed for the honour of God and the purity of religion. No mention of him appears in the gospels beyond that he was adopted by Christ into the college of the apostles. With the rest he received the miraculous gifts of the Holy Ghost, but of his life after Pentecost we have no information whatsoever; it is not possible to reconcile the various traditions. The later Greek writers say he preached the gospel on the Black Sea, in Egypt and north Africa, and in the island of Britain; the Georgians claim his apostolate and martyrdom for Iberia and Colchis; the Abyssinians, mixing him up with St Simeon, one of the Seventy-two, make him the second bishop of Jerusalem. The Menology of Basil says that St Simon died in peace at Edessa, but the Western tradition, recognised in the Roman liturgy, is that after preaching in Egypt, he joined St Jude from Mesopotamia and that they went as missionaries for some years to Persia, suffering martyrdom at Suanir. They are accordingly commemorated together in the West on this day (in some martyrologies on July 1), but in the East separately and on various dates.

The apostle Jude, also called Thaddeus (or Lebbeus), is usually regarded as the brother of St James the Less, and therefore related to our Lord (Matt. xiii, 55). It is not known when and by what means he became a disciple of Christ, nothing having been said of him in the gospels before we find him enumerated in the catalogue of the apostles. After the Last Supper, when Christ promised to manifest Himself to His hearers, St Jude asked Him why He did not manifest Himself to the rest of the world; and Christ answered that He would visit all those who love Him and would admit them to intimate communications of grace. The history of St Jude after our Lord's ascension and the descent of the Holy Ghost is as uncertain as that of St Simon. There are traditions that he preached in Judea, Samaria, Idumæa, and Mesopotamia; St Paulinus says he planted the faith in Libya. St Jude's name is borne by one of the canonical epistles, which has much in common with the second epistle of St Peter. It is not addressed to any particular church or person, and in it he urges the faithful to " contend earnestly for the faith once delivered to the saints. For certain men are secretly entered in . . . ungodly men, turning the grace of our Lord God into riotousness, and denying the only sovereign ruler and our Lord Jesus Christ."

St Jude Thaddeus has often been confounded with the St Thaddeus of the Abgar legend (see Addai and Mari, August 5), and made to die in peace at Beirut or Edessa. As has been said above, according to Western tradition he was martyred with St Simon in Persia. Eusebius quotes from St Hegesippus (second century) a story that two grandsons of St Jude, Zoker and James, were brought before the Emperor Domitian, who had been alarmed by the report that they were of the royal house of David. But when he saw they were poor, hard-working peasants, and heard that the kingdom for which they looked was not of this world, he dismissed them with contempt.

We owe to God homage of praise and thanks for the infinite mercy by which He has established a Church on earth so richly endowed with every means of sanctity and grace : a Church in which His name is always glorified and countless souls are associated to the company of the blessed angels. It ought to be our first and constant petition to God, as we learn from our Lord's prayer, that for the glory of His holy name He will protect and preserve His Church : enlarge its borders, sanctify its members, and fill its pastors with the spirit with which He enriched His apostles, whom He was pleased to choose for the foundation of this sacred church. If we desire a share of those graces which God pours forth upon those souls which He disposes to receive them, we must remember that He imparts them only to those who sincerely try to die to themselves and to cast all inordinate attachments out of their hearts ; so long as any of these reign in a soul, she is one of that world to which God cannot manifest Himself. This is the mystery which Christ unfolded to St Jude. The world has not known Him. Few even among those who know God by faith attain to the experimental knowledge of

Him and the taste of His love, because few, very few, disentangle their affections from created things. So long as their hearts remain wedded to the world, they fall in some degree under its curse and are unable to extinguish its spirit.

There is what purports to be a *passio* of these two apostles, but in its Latin form it cannot be earlier than the latter part of the sixth century. It is attributed to a certain Abdias who is said to have been a disciple of Simon and Jude and to have been consecrated by them first bishop of Babylon. This no doubt explains the curious entry on this day in the *Félire* of Œngus : " Ample is their assembly : Babylon their burial ground : Thaddeus and Simon, huge is their host." On pseudo-Abdias see further R. A. Lipsius, *Die apocryphen Apostelgeschichten, etc.*, vol. i, pp. 117 *seq.* ; and Batiffol in *Dict. de Théologie*, vol. i, c. 23. The mention of SS. Simon and Jude together is found in the *Hieronymianum* for this day, and the scene of their martyrdom is said to be " Suanis, civitate Persarum," on which consult Delehaye's commentary, and Gutschmid, *Kleine Schriften*, vol. ii, pp. 368–369.

ST ANASTASIA, Virg., and ST CYRIL, Marts.

c. A.D. 260 (?)

Cardinal Baronius added the following entry to the Roman Martyrology under this date : " At Rome, the passion of the holy martyrs Anastasia the Elder, a virgin, and Cyril. This same virgin during the persecution of Valerian was bound with fetters by the prefect Probus, smitten with blows and tortured with fire and scourges ; and as she continued unmoved in the confession of Christ her breasts were cut off, her nails torn out, her teeth broken, her hands and feet hacked away. Then she was beheaded and, beautified with the jewels of so many sufferings, she passed to her Bridegroom. Cyril brought her water when she asked therefor, and received martyrdom for his reward." The traditions of the church of Rome know nothing of these martyrs, who were first venerated in the East. Their Greek *passio* appears to be a fictitious composition of the tenth century. It says that St Anastasia was a maiden of patrician birth, twenty years old, who lived in a community of consecrated virgins under a superior named Sophia. The soldiers of the prefect broke into the house, carried her off, and brought her before Probus, who ordered that she be stripped naked. On her protesting that this would shame him more than it would her, she was maltreated as the Martyrology sets out. After her execution Sophia secured and buried the body, which was afterwards translated to Constantinople.

The *passio* says that there were two Anastasias martyred at Rome, this virgin and a widow.

The *passio* exists both in Greek and in Latin. Both texts are printed in the *Acta Sanctorum*, October, vol. xii. J. P. Kirsch seems inclined to think that the only historical martyr was the widow who suffered at Sirmium, but that, as her feast was kept on a different date in the East, some Greek hagiographer thought it well to invent a new story of a virgin bearing the same name, which he embellished with the fantastic details recounted above. See *Lexikon für Theologie und Kirche*, vol. i (1930), c. 389.

ST FIDELIS, Mart.

A.D. 303 (?)

During the persecution of Maximian the imprisoned Christians of Milan were visited and ministered to by an army officer named Fidelis, a convert of St Maternus. He procured the freedom of five of them and, with two soldiers, Carpophorus and Exanthus, they tried to make their escape into the Alps. They were overtaken near Como, and the two last-named with their companions were executed on the spot, in a wood. Fidelis got away and reached Samolito, at the other side of the lake, but here he was captured by the soldiers, who had followed him in a boat. There they scourged and beheaded him. There is another version which says that SS. Fidelis, Carpophorus, and Exanthus were three Christian soldiers who when persecution began deserted the army and fled to Como, where they were apprehended and put to death. Carpophorus, Exanthus, and the five others are commemorated separately in the Roman Martyrology on August 7. St Peter Damian wrote a hymn and a panegyric in honour of St Fidelis, part of whose relics were translated from the abbey of Arona to a church in Milan in 1572.

A relatively sober text is printed in the *Acta Sanctorum*, vol. xii, from a fourteenth-century manuscript. It seems certain that a tomb of St Fidelis at Como was known to Ennodies in the sixth century. See Delehaye, *Origines du Culte des Martyrs*, pp. 380–381.

ST SALVIUS, or SAIRE, Conf.

SIXTH CENTURY (?)

This saint has been confused with St Salvius of Albi and St Salvius of Amiens (and they with one another), but he seems to have been a distinct person and a hermit in the forest of Bray in Normandy.

Nothing is known about him, but in a footnote to his account of St Salvius of Albi (September 10) Alban Butler gives an extract from a manuscript preserved in the castle of Saint-Saire (Eure et Loir) of the Counts of Boulainvilliers. It runs as follows :

" The titles of the metropolitan of Rouen prove that about the year 800, and near a century after, there was a place in the forest of Bray consecrated to the memory and honour of St Salvius, who had been a solitary there. Whether this saint was bishop of Albi or Amiens, or even whether he was any more than a hermit whose penitential life God glorified by divers miracles, is what must remain undecided : the memory of these facts is entirely lost. There remain, however, formal proofs of St Salvius being a solitary in an ancient MS. from five to six hundred years old, which contains the office of his feast. He is also represented in a pane of glass in an ancient subterraneous chapel in the dress of a hermit, on his knees, praying with his hands extended. The devotion of the people who visited the church or chapel which was built where his hermitage stood was supported by miracles and extraordinary cures which the divine power wrought there, insomuch that the reputation of it went very far. Some houses were built in the neighbourhood for the convenience of pilgrims ; but the nature of the country rendered it inaccessible, and the horror of the marshes, augmented by the woods which covered them, hindered the progress of the establishment, which the piety of particulars might have otherwise founded. The canons of Rouen were at the expense of clearing some of the more accessible lands for the subsistence of the priests, who there performed the divine office ; and this is the first origin of the parish of Saint-Saire, and the foundation of the lordship which the chapter of Rouen possesses there."

A brief notice of St Salvius may be found in the *Acta Sanctorum*, October, vol. xii. There is no biography of any sort.

ST FARO, Bp. of Meaux, Conf.
Seventh Century

The city of Meaux, situated on the Marne, thirty miles from Paris, is said to have received the first seeds of faith by the preaching of St Dionysius of Paris about the year 250. The eminent sanctity of St Faro, one of the first known bishops of Meaux, has rendered his name the most illustrious of all the prelates of this see who are mentioned in the kalendars of the Church. He was the brother of

St Chainoaldus of Laon and of St Burgundofara, first abbess of Faremoutier, and spent his youth in the court of King Theodobert II of Austrasia. Later he married, and in 613 passed to the court of Clotaire II, who reunited the whole French monarchy. When that prince, provoked at the insolent speeches of certain Saxon ambassadors, had cast them into prison and sworn he would put them to death, St Faro prevailed on him to defer the execution twenty-four hours, and afterwards to pardon them. Under Dagobert I he became chancellor, and used his influence with his prince to protect the innocent, the orphan, and the widow, and to relieve all that were in distress. The life which he led there was most edifying and holy, and when he was about thirty-five years old he determined, if his wife would agree, to enter the ecclesiastical state. Blidechild was of the same disposition, and she retired to a solitary place upon one of her own estates, which seems to have been at Aupigny, where some years after she died, after having persuaded her husband to persevere in his new vocation, which for a time he wished to abandon and return to her. St Faro received the tonsure among the clergy of Meaux, which episcopal see becoming vacant, he was chosen to fill it, about the year 626.

The holy prelate laboured for the salvation of the souls committed to his charge with unwearied zeal and attention, and promoted their advancement in Christian perfection and the conversion of those who had not yet forsaken idolatry. The author of his Life tells us that he restored sight to a blind man by conferring on him the sacrament of Confirmation, and wrought several other miracles. Excited by his example, many others of distinction entered into the same way of life. Soon after Faro's episcopal consecration St Fiacre arrived at Meaux from Ireland. The Bishop had a great regard for the Irish, having been brought up under the influence of St Columbanus, and he gave to Fiacre some land of his own patrimony at Breuil for a hermitage. Before his death he founded in the suburbs of the city of Meaux, where he possessed a large estate, the monastery of the Holy Cross, which later bore his name. St Faro placed in it monks of St Columbanus from Luxeuil, but the Rule of St Benedict was afterwards received here, and the abbey of Prüm, refounded by King Pepin in 762, was a filiation from this house.

The Life of St Faro, which was written 200 years after his death by another bishop of Meaux, Hildegar, is of no great historical value. It has been critically edited after Mabillon by Bruno Krusch in the *M. G. H. Scrip. rer. Meroving.*, vol. v, pp. 171–206. This text is undoubtedly the original of the shorter narrative printed in the *Acta Sanctorum*. There is reference in Hildegar's compilation to a ballad which, we are told, was sung by all the people in commemoration of Clotaire's victory over the Saxons, and which is known as the " Cantilène de St. Faron." As a supposed specimen of the early Romance language it has given rise to a very considerable literature, of which a full account, with bibliography, may be found in the *Dict. d'Archéolog., etc.*, vol. v, cc. 1114–1124. With regard to St Faro, see Beaumier-Besse, *Abbayes et Prieurés de France*, vol. i, pp. 304 *seq.* ; Duchesne, *Fastes Épiscopaux*, vol. ii, p. 477 ; and H. M. Delsart, *Sainte Fare, sa Vie et son Culte*, Paris, 1911.

ST NARCISSUS, Bp. of Jerusalem, Conf.

c. A.D. 220

ST NARCISSUS was already old when he was placed at the head of the church of Jerusalem. In 198 he and Theophilus, Bishop of Cæsarea, presided at a council of the bishops of Palestine held at Cæsarea concerning the time of celebrating Easter; it was decreed that this feast is to be kept always on a Sunday, and not with the Jewish passover as was then done by the Christians of Asia Minor. Eusebius says that the Christians of Jerusalem preserved in his time the remembrance of several miracles which God had wrought by this bishop, as when on one Easter-eve the deacons were unprovided with oil for the lamps in the church, Narcissus sent for water, pronounced a prayer over it, and then bade them pour it into the lamps. They did so, and it was immediately converted into oil. What was alleged to be some of this miraculous oil was kept there as a memorial at the time when Eusebius wrote. The veneration of good men for this holy bishop could not shelter him from the malice of the wicked, and some, disliking his severity in the observance of ecclesiastical discipline, laid to his charge a certain crime, which Eusebius does not specify. They confirmed their calumny by oath, but their accusation did not find credit. However, St Narcissus, notwithstanding the slander had made no impression on the people, made it an excuse for leaving Jerusalem, and spending some time alone, as had long been his wish. He spent several years undiscovered in his solitude and, that his church might not remain destitute of a pastor, the neighbouring bishops placed in it Dios, and after him Germanion, who was succeeded by Gordios. Whilst this last held the see, Narcissus appeared again like one from the dead. The faithful, delighted at the recovery of their pastor, induced him to resume the administration of the diocese. He acquiesced, but, under the weight of extreme old age, made St Alexander his coadjutor. This Alexander was a Cappadocian bishop who had been in prison for the faith and on his release visited Jerusalem. He succeeded St Narcissus, with the permission of the other bishops, and provides the first recorded instance both of an episcopal coadjutor and of a translation from one see to another. Narcissus continued to serve his flock by his prayers, being, as is said, at that time about one hundred and sixteen years old. The Roman Martyrology honours his memory on October 29.

The pastors of the primitive Church, animated with the spirit of the Apostles, were faithful imitators of their virtues, having the same zeal, the same contempt of the world, the same love of Christ. If we truly respect the Church as the spotless bride of our Lord, we shall incessantly pray for its exaltation and increase, and beseech the Almighty to give it pastors according to His own heart, like those who appeared in the infancy of Christianity. And that no obstacle on our part may prevent the happy effects of their zeal, we should learn to regulate our conduct by the instructions which they give us ; we should regard them as the ministers of Christ ; we should listen to them with docility and attention ; we should make their faith the rule of ours.

The Bollandists in the *Acta Sanctorum*, October, vol. xii, have brought together from Eusebius and other sources all that is known, or likely to be known, about St Narcissus, Bishop of Jerusalem.

ST THEUDERIUS, OR CHEF, ABBOT AND CONF.

c. A.D. 575

He was born at Arcisia (Saint-Chef-d'Arcisse) of one of the noble families of the country of Vienne and by the interior call of the Holy Ghost forsook the world. Having long exercised himself in the practices of a monastic life at Lérins and been ordained priest by St Cæsarius at Arles, he returned to his own country and, being joined by several disciples, built for them first cells and afterwards a monastery near the city of Vienne in Dauphiné. It was anciently a custom in monasteries that the priest who sang the community Mass spent the week in which he discharged that office in close retirement in his cell in contemplation and penance, that he might be the better prepared to offer daily the tremendous sacrifice and more faithfully acquit himself of his mediatorship between God and His people. It was an extension of this custom at Vienne in the sixth century that some monk of whose sanctity the people entertained a high opinion was chosen voluntarily to lead the life of a recluse ; he was walled up in a cell and spent his whole time in fasting and praying to implore the divine mercy in favour of himself and his country. This practice would have been an abuse and superstition if any persons, relying on the prayers of others, were themselves remiss in prayer or penance. St Theuderius was asked to undertake this penitential state, which obligation he willingly took upon himself, and discharged with much fervour at the church of St Laurence during the last twelve years of his life. An extraordinary gift of miracles made his name famous. He died about the year 575, and was buried in the monastery of St Laurence, whence his relics were translated to the church of his birthplace.

A Life, first printed by Mabillon and the Bollandists, has been again edited by Bruno Krusch in the *M. G. H. Scrip. rer. Meroving.*, vol. iii, 526–530. As it was written by Ado in the ninth century, it merits no great confidence. It is not, however, true, as was formerly believed, that Ado inserted the name of Theuderius in his martyrology. See Dom Quentin, *Martyrologes historiques*, p. 477.

ST COLMAN OF KILMACDUAGH, Bp. and Conf.

a.d. 632

The feast of this Colman is kept throughout Ireland on this day according to the custom of the diocese of Kilmacduagh, it having been transferred from the 27th to the 29th under Benedict XIV, though the old Martyrology of Donegal assigns it also to February 3. He was born at Corker in Kiltartan about the middle of the sixth century and lived first on Arranmore and then, for greater solitude, at Burren among the mountains of County Clare. He is said to have hidden himself there because he had been made a bishop against his will ; he had one disciple, and they subsisted for many years on wild vegetables and water. He then founded a monastery at the place called after him Kilmacduagh (the cell of the son of Duach), and is venerated as the first bishop there and over all the territory of Hy Fiachrach Aidhne. The land was given him by his near relation King Guaire of Connacht, who had discovered Colman's retreat, according to the legend, through his Easter dinner being whisked away and carried by angels to the cell of the hermits at Burren. Among other fanciful stories about St Colman is that he was waited on by a cock, a mouse, and a fly : the cock woke him for the night office, the mouse prevented him from going to sleep again, and the fly acted as an indicator and book-marker ! The saint died and was buried at Kilmacduagh about the year 632.

In the Bollandists, October, vol. xii, there is a copious notice of Colman, borrowed for the most part from Colgan's *Acta Sanctorum Hiberniæ*. See also O'Keeffe in *Ériu*, vol. i, pp. 43–48 ; and Whitley Stokes in the *Revue*

Celtique, vol. xxvi, pp. 372–377. This Colman's name does not occur in the text of the *Félire* of Œngus, but "Colman mac Duach" is entered first on February 3 in the Martyrology of Tallaght, which equally dates from about the year 800. Colman was a very common Irish name. There are no less than twelve Colmans mentioned in the Tallaght Martyrology during the single month of October.

ST ETHELNOTH, Abp. of Canterbury, Conf.

A.D. 1038

The reign of the Danish king Canute in England during the earlier part of the eleventh century was a period of peace and prosperity for the Church, and among the men who directed it at that time this St Ethelnoth was conspicuous. While dean of the cathedral church of Christ at Canterbury his learning and holiness caused him to be known as "Ethelnoth the Good," and on the death of the metropolitan Living in 1020 he was appointed in his place. Two years later Ethelnoth was in Rome, where Pope Benedict VIII received him "with great worship and very honourably hallowed him archbishop," by which may be understood that he invested him with the *pallium*. In the following year Ethelnoth translated the relics of his predecessor St Elphege, martyred by the Danes near Greenwich in 1012, from London to Canterbury. The cost of a worthy shrine was defrayed by King Canute, at the instance of his wife and the archbishop, his father's men having been guilty of the murder. St Ethelnoth enjoyed the favour of Canute, and he encouraged the King's liberality to promote several other religious undertakings, among them the rebuilding of Chartres cathedral and the due payment of "Peter's pence" to the Holy See. Ethelnoth governed his see in peace for eighteen years.

Ethelnoth is one of those Anglo-Saxon ecclesiastics whose claim to saintship is very contestable. His name does not seem to occur in any medieval calendar, and there is no other evidence of *cultus*. The Bollandists, however, following the example of Mabillon (*Acta Sanctorum O.S.B.*, vol. vi, part 1, pp. 394–397), have devoted a notice to him (under the spelling "Ædelnodus") on October 30 (vol. xiii). In the absence of any early biography they have pieced together an account from contemporary and later chroniclers. See further the *Dict. Nat. Biog.*, vol. xvii, p. 25 ; and Stanton's *Menology*, pp. 517–518.

THE MARTYRS OF DOUAY
Sixteenth and Seventeenth Centuries

In the year 1568 the English College at Douai was founded by William Allen (afterwards cardinal ; the anniversary of his death in 1594 is kept on the 16th of this month). Its original object was to train young men for the priesthood with an eye to the needs of England when the Faith should be re-established there, but within a short time these priests were being sent back to their country as missionaries—the " seminary priests " at whom legislation was aimed. These began to arrive in 1574 and on November 29, 1577, their first martyr, Blessed Cuthbert Mayne, suffered at Launceston. During the next hundred years more than one hundred and sixty priests from the college (which from 1578 till 1594 was transferred to Reims) were put to death in England and Wales, and of these over eighty have been beatified ; they are referred to under their respective dates in these volumes. For these martyrs from Douay a special collective feast is kept in the dioceses of Westminster and of Hexham and Newcastle. When the Revolution made it impossible to carry on the college in France, it was re-established in 1794 at St Edmund's, Old Hall Green, for the south of England, and at Crook Hall, Durham (in 1808, St Cuthbert's, Ushaw), for the north, which colleges are respectively in the above dioceses. " Kindle in us, O Lord, the spirit to which the blessed martyrs of Douay ministered, that we too being filled therewith may strive to love what they loved and do as they taught " (collect for the feast).

The Douay Diaries, with the exception of the sixth volume which is lost, have now all been published. The first two appeared as *Records of the English Catholics under the Penal Laws*, vol. i (1878), and were edited by Father T. F. Knox. They extend from 1568 to 1593. The third, fourth, fifth, and seventh diaries have been printed by the Catholic Record Society as vols. x, xi, and xxviii of their publications.

OCTOBER 30

ST SERAPION, Bp. of Antioch, Conf.

c. A.D. 212

THE fourth-century Syriac document called the *Doctrine of Addai* refers to Serapion as having been consecrated by Zephyrinus, Bishop of the City of Rome, but he had in fact been bishop of Antioch for some years before the pontificate of St Zephyrinus began. The Roman Martyrology says he was famous for his learning, and it is chiefly for his theological writings that he is remembered. Eusebius gives an extract from a private letter written to Caricus and Ponticus, in which he condemns Montanism, which was being propagated by the pseudo-prophecies of two hysterical women, and encloses the treatise of Apollonius of Ephesus against the sect. He also wrote expostulating with a certain Domninus, who had apostatised under persecution and turned Jew.

During the episcopate of Serapion trouble arose in the church of Rhossos in Cilicia about the public reading of the so-called *Gospel of Peter*, an apocryphal work of Gnostic provenance. At first Serapion, not knowing its contents and trusting to the orthodoxy of his flock, permitted it to be read. Then he borrowed a copy from the sect who used it, "whom we call Docetæ" (that is, illusionists, because they affirmed that our Lord's humanity was not real but an illusion), and having read it wrote to the church at Rhossos to forbid its use ; for he found in it, he says, "some additions to the true teaching of the Saviour." According to the tradition of the *Doctrine of Addai*, after the death of St Addai and his successor Aggai, there was no bishop in East Syria, so their disciple Palut came to Antioch and was there consecrated third bishop of Edessa by St Serapion. But the truth of this is as uncertain as the origins of the East Syrian church : if Addai, who (they say) made Palut priest, was a personal disciple of our Lord, as the legend claims, obviously he could not have been consecrated bishop at the end of the second century. An even more surprising thing about St Serapion is that his feast is kept by the Carmelites on the ground that he belonged to their order. He has no *cultus* in the East.

All, practically speaking, that is known concerning St Serapion of
Antioch is recounted and commented upon by the Bollandists in vol. xiii
for October. The references to this name, however, contained in the
Doctrine of Addai, had apparently not attracted their attention, but these, as
pointed out above, are quite unreliable. It is interesting to note that in
the early Syriac *breviarium*, we have mention on May 14 of " Serapion,
Bishop of Antioch."

ST MARCELLUS, Mart.

A.D. 298

Particulars of the passion of St Marcellus, one of the isolated
martyrs before the outbreak of the great persecution of Diocletian
in the year 303, are preserved for us in his extant authentic acts.
This brief document runs as follows (translation of the Reverend
E. C. E. Owen) :

In the city of Tingis [Tangier], during the administration of
Fortunatus as governor, the time came for the birthday of the
Emperor. When all in that place were feasting at banquets and
sacrificing, a certain Marcellus, one of the centurions of the Trajan
legion, deeming those banquets to be heathen, cast away his soldier's
belt in front of the standards of the legion which were then in camp,
and testified in a loud voice, saying : " I serve Jesus Christ the
Eternal King." He also threw away his vine-switch [the distinctive
badge of a centurion] and arms, and added : " Henceforward I cease
to serve your Emperors, and I scorn to worship your gods of wood
and stone, which are deaf and dumb idols. If such be the terms
of service, that men are forced to offer sacrifice to gods and emperors,
behold I cast away my vine-switch and belt, I renounce the standards,
and refuse to serve."

The soldiers were dumbfounded at hearing such things ; they
laid hold on him, and reported the matter to Anastasius Fortunatus,
the commander of the legion, who ordered him to be thrown into
prison. When the feasting was over, he gave orders, sitting in
council, that the centurion Marcellus should be brought in. When
Marcellus, one of the centurions of Asta [a city of southern Spain],
was brought in, Anastasius Fortunatus the governor said : " What
did you mean by ungirding yourself in violation of military discipline, and casting away your belt and vine-switch ? "

MARCELLUS : On July 21, in presence of the standards of your
legion, when you celebrated the festival of the Emperor, I made
answer openly and in a loud voice that I was a Christian and that I

could not serve under this allegiance, but only under the allegiance of Jesus Christ the Son of God the Father Almighty.

FORTUNATUS : I cannot pass over your rash conduct, and therefore I will report this matter to the Emperors and Cæsar. You yourself shall be referred unhurt to my lord, Aurelius Agricolan, deputy for the prefects of the Guard.

On October 30 at Tingis, Marcellus, one of the centurions of Asta, having been brought into court, it was officially reported : " Fortunatus the governor has referred Marcellus, a centurion, to your authority. There is in court a letter dealing with this case, which at your command I will read." Agricolan said : " Let it be read." The official report was as follows : " From Fortunatus to you, my lord, and so forth. This soldier, having cast away his soldier's belt, and having testified that he was a Christian, spoke in the presence of all the people many blasphemous things against the gods and against Cæsar. We have therefore sent him on to you, that you may order such action to be taken as your eminence may ordain in regard to the same." After the letter had been read, Agricolan said : " Did you say these things as appear in the official report of the governor ? "

MARCELLUS : I did.

AGRICOLAN : Did you hold the rank of a centurion of the first class ?

MARCELLUS : I did.

AGRICOLAN : What madness possessed you to cast away the signs of your allegiance, and to speak as you did ?

MARCELLUS : There is no madness in those who fear the Lord.

AGRICOLAN : Did you make each of these speeches contained in the official report of the governor ?

MARCELLUS : I did.

AGRICOLAN : Did you cast away your arms ?

MARCELLUS : I did. For it was not right for a Christian, who serves the Lord Christ, to serve the cares of the world.

Agricolan said : " The acts of Marcellus are such as must be visited with disciplinary punishment." And he pronounced sentence as follows : " Marcellus, who held the rank of centurion of the first class, having admitted that he has degraded himself by openly throwing off his allegiance, and having besides put on record, as appears in the official report of the governor, other insane expressions, it is our pleasure that he be put to death by the sword."

When he was being led to execution, he said to Agricolan : " May God bless thee ! For so ought a martyr to depart out of this world." And when he had said these words he was beheaded, dying for the name of our Lord Jesus Christ, who is glorious for ever and ever. Amen.

There end the *acta* of St Marcellus. There is a note added to the proceedings before Fortunatus that " the shorthand-writer who took down the official proceedings was Cæcilius." We know that before Agricolan it was Cassian, for he also is venerated as a martyr, having refused to carry out his duties when he saw the constancy of St Marcellus, as is narrated on December 3.

We justly honour the martyrs, whom God Himself honours. Martyrdom is the most heroic act of divine love, and the most perfect and entire sacrifice man can make of himself to God, for of all the goods of this life man has nothing more precious and dear than his life and honour. And what stronger proof can he give of his fidelity to the law of God than to accept an ignominious and cruel death rather than consent to sin ? Nor does anything require a more heroic degree of courage and firmness than to suffer torments at the very thought of which we shudder. God proportions His rewards and crowns to the measure of our sufferings and love for Him. How great, then, is the glory, how abundant the recompense which attends the martyrs. They rejoiced when their sufferings were increased, because they had before their eyes the incomparably greater increase of grace, divine love, and eternal glory. If we shrink under the smallest sufferings (as we do) it is plain that our faith and our idea of everlasting bliss must be very weak and our love cool.

Although it is generally admitted that the Acts of Marcellus are representative of the most trustworthy class of such documents (*cf.* for example Harnack, *Chronologie*, vol. ii, pp. 473–474), still the text printed by Knopf from which Mr. Owen has translated is not free from faults. See Père Delehaye's revision in the *Analecta Bollandiana*, vol. xli (1923), pp. 357–387, a setting which has been duly taken into account in G. Krüger's 3ᵈ edition of Knopf's *Ausgewählte Martyrerakten* (1929). See also P. Franchi de' Cavalieri in *Nuovo Bulletino de Arch. Crist.*, 1906, pp. 237–267.

ST ASTERIUS, Bp. of Amasea, Conf.

c. A.D. 400

All that is known about the life of this saint, apart from his episcopate, is from his own statement that he was educated by a very able Scythian or Goth, who had himself been educated at Antioch, and that he was a barrister before receiving holy orders. St Asterius was a preacher of considerable power, and twenty-one of his homilies are extant. In that on SS. Peter and Paul he teaches and often repeats the prerogative of jurisdiction which St Peter received over all Christians from the East to the West ; and says that Christ made him His vicar and left him the father, pastor, and master of all those who should embrace the Faith. In his panegyric of St Phocas, he established the invocation of saints, the honouring of their relics, pilgrimages to pray before them, and miracles wrought by them. In the following sermon, on the holy martyrs, he says : " We keep their bodies decently enshrined as precious pledges : vessels of benediction, the organs of their blessed souls, the tabernacles of their holy minds. We put ourselves under their protection. The martyrs defend the Church as soldiers guard a citadel. The people flock from all quarters and keep great festivals to honour their tombs. All who labour under the heavy load of afflictions fly to them for refuge. We employ them as intercessors in our prayers, whereby the hardships of poverty are eased, diseases cured, the threats of princes appeased. A parent, taking a sick child in his arms, puts off the doctors and runs to some one of the martyrs, offering his prayer to the Lord and addressing him whom he chooses for his mediator in such words as these : ' You who have suffered for Christ, intercede for one who suffers by sickness. By that great power you have, offer a prayer on behalf of fellow-servants. Though you are now removed from us, you know what men on earth feel in their sufferings and diseases.' If another is going to be married, he begins his new life by asking the prayers of the martyrs. Who, putting to sea, weighs anchor before he has invoked the Lord of the sea through the martyrs ? " St Asterius describes with what magnificence and crowds of people the feasts of martyrs were celebrated over the whole world. He says the Gentiles and the Eunomian heretics condemned the honours paid to them and their relics, and he answers, " We by no means worship the martyrs, but we honour them as the true worshippers of God. We lay their bodies in rich sepulchres and erect stately shrines of their repose that we may be stirred up to an emulation of their honours." These Eunomians, he says, do not honour the martyrs because they blaspheme the King of martyrs, making Christ unequal to His Father. He tells them that they ought at least to respect the voice of the evil spirits who are forced to confess the power of the martyrs. " Those," said he, " whom we have seen bark like dogs, seized with frenzy, and are now come to their senses, prove by their cure how effectual the intercession of the martyrs is."

This St Asterius is not named in the Roman Martyrology, but

there is another therein on October 21 who is said to have taken the body of St Callistus from the well into which it was thrown. He himself was cast into the Tiber and so gave his life.

There is no formal Life of St Asterius, but various references to him have been brought together in the *Acta Sanctorum*, October, vol. xiii. Some of his discourses have been made the subject of separate discussion. See, for example, A. Bretz, *Studien und Texte zu Asterius von Amasea*, and more generally Bardenhewer, *Geschichte der altkirchlichen Literatur*, vol. iii (1912), pp. 228–230.

ST GERMANUS, Bp. of Capua, Conf.

c. A.D. 540

This holy prelate was sent by Pope St Hormisdas as legate to the Emperor Justin in 519 to persuade the Orientals to put an end to the schism which had continued thirty-five years, having been fomented by the Emperors Zeno and Anastasius, both favourers of heretics, and by Acacius and other patriarchs of Constantinople. The embassy was attended with the desired success ; the heretics were condemned and the schism ended by the signature of the Pope's famous " Formula." St Germanus and his fellow-legates suffered much from the heretics, but escaped out of their hands. St Gregory the Great relates on the authority of " his elders " that Germanus saw St Paschasius, the deacon of Rome, long after his death, in Purgatory for having adhered to the schism of Laurence against Pope St Symmachus, and that he was purging his fault as an attendant at the hot springs of Angelum, whither Germanus had been sent to bathe for the good of his health. Within a few days Paschasius was released by the Bishop's prayers. St Germanus was a personal friend of St Benedict who, again according to the account of St Gregory, when he was at Mount Cassino saw in a vision the soul of Germanus, at the hour of his departure, carried by the ministry of angels to eternal bliss. His death happened about the year 540.

A manuscript of the eleventh century at Monte Cassino preserves a short Life of St Germanus which has been printed in the *Acta Sanctorum*, October, vol. xiii. It is not entirely certain, though it is no doubt probable, that this Germanus is identical with the envoy sent to Constantinople by Pope Hormisdas. See, further, Lanzoni, *Diocesi d'Italia*, vol. i, p. 203.

BD. BENVENUTA BOJANI, Virg.

A.D. 1292

It has been said that the life of Benvenuta Bojani was "a poem of praise to our Blessed Lady, a hymn of light, purity, and joy, which was lived rather than sung in her honour." This life began in the year 1254, on May 4 (it was centuries before this month had become specially associated with the Queen of Heaven), at Cividale in Friuli, and there were already six young Bojani, all girls. Her father Conrad naturally hoped for a boy this time, and when he learned he had yet another daughter he is said to have exclaimed, "Very well! Since it is so, let her too be welcome." And so she was called Benvenuta. Her devotion to our Lady was noticeable from very early years, and she would repeat the Hail Mary, in the short form, ending at "Jesus," as then used, many times in the day, accompanying each repetition with a profound inclination such as she saw the Dominican friars make so often in their church. Like Blessed Magdalen Panattieri, commemorated this month (13th), Benvenuta was happy in belonging to a family whose members were as truly religious as herself, rejoicing in her goodness and devotion, and who, when she wished to bind herself to perfect chastity and become a tertiary of the Dominicans, put no obstacles in her way. But unlike Blessed Magdalen she took no part in the public life of her town, emphasising the contemplative rather than the active side of the Dominican vocation. Her spirit of penitence, in particular, made her inflict most severe austerities on herself. She would sometimes discipline herself three times in a night, and when she was only twelve she tied a rope (the "cord of St Thomas"?) so tightly round her loins that the flesh grew around it. The suffering it caused became intolerable, and she feared that the only way to remove it was by a surgical operation, till one day when she was asking God to help her about it she found the rope lying unbroken at her feet. Benvenuta confided this miracle to her confessor, Friar Conrad, who mitigated her penances and forbade her to undertake any without his approval. For five years she suffered from serious bad health and could scarcely leave her room, during which time she was furiously tempted to despair, and in other ways; but the worst trial was being unable to assist at Mass, except when occasionally carried, and at Compline with its daily singing of *Salve Regina* by the Dominican friars. Eventually she was suddenly and publicly cured in church on the feast of the Annunciation, having vowed to make a pilgrimage to the shrine of St Dominic at Bologna if she recovered. This she carried out with her sister Mary and her youngest brother.

Blessed Benvenuta's patience and perseverance in sickness and temptation were rewarded by numerous graces, visions, and raptures in prayer. A delightful story is told (though belonging to her youth) that she went into a church one day just after her mother had died, and saw there a child, to whom she said, " Have you got a mother ? " He said he had. " I haven't now," said she, " But since you have, perhaps you can already say the Hail Mary ? " " Oh yes," replied the child, " can you ? "—" Yes, I can."—" Very well then, say it to me." Benvenuta began the Hail Mary in Latin, and as she ended on the name Jesus, " It is I," interrupted the child, and disappeared from sight. Cheerfulness and confidence were the marks of the life of Blessed Benvenuta, but she had to go through one more assault of the Devil, tempting her to despair and infidelity as she lay dying. She overcame triumphantly, and died peacefully with the name of Mary on her lips, on October 30, 1292. Her *cultus* was approved in 1763, but her burial-place at Cividale is lost.

As we may learn from the full account in the *Acta Sanctorum*, October, vol. xiii, a Life of this *beata*, written in Latin shortly after her death, was translated into Italian and published in 1589. This biography figured largely in the Process which ended in the formal *confirmatio cultus*, and the original Latin is printed in full by the Bollandists. See also M. C. de Ganay, *Les Bienheureuses Dominicaines* (1913), pp. 91–108 ; and Procter, *Lives of Dominicon Saints*, pp. 302–306.

ST DOROTHEA OF MONTAU, WIDOW

A.D. 1394

She takes her name from Montau (Marienburg) in Prussia, where she was born of peasant parents in 1347. At the age of seventeen Dorothea married one Albert, a swordsmith of Danzig, by whom she had nine children, of whom only the youngest survived, and became a Benedictine nun. Albert was an ill-tempered and overbearing man, and during their twenty-five years of married life his wife suffered much on this account ; but her own kindliness and courage modified his disposition considerably, and in 1382 she induced him to take her on a pilgrimage to Aachen. Thenceforward they often went on pilgrimage together, to Einsiedeln, Cologne, and elsewhere, and they were planning to go to Rome when Albert fell ill. Dorothea therefore went alone, and at her return her husband had just died. Thus left a widow at the age of forty-three, she went to live at Marienwerder, and in 1393 became a recluse in a cell by the church of the Teutonic Knights. She was there only a year before her death, on May 25, 1394, but long enough to gain a great repute for sanctity and supernatural enlightenment. Numerous visitors sought her cell, to ask advice or in hope of obtaining a miraculous cure of their ills. Her Life, in Latin and German, with an account of her visions and revelations, was written by her director, from whom we learn that Dorothea had a very intense devotion to the Blessed Sacrament, and was often supernaturally enabled to look upon It, which she greatly desired to do. In the Middle Ages very great importance was attached to seeing the Body of the Lord, especially at the elevation at Mass, and the Life of St Dorothea shows that in her time It was exposed all day for this purpose in some churches of Prussia and Pomerania. Among her revelations from Heaven is said to have been the rule of life which she adopted at Marienwerder. She was greatly revered by the people and soon after her death the cause of canonisation was begun, but as soon dropped. Nevertheless the *cultus* spread to Poland, Lithuania, Bohemia, and elsewhere, and St Dorothea is still popularly regarded as the patroness of Prussia.

Regarding this very interesting mystic a good deal of information is available. In the *Acta Sanctorum*, October, vol. xiii, more than a hundred folio pages are devoted to her, and this was supplemented by the publication in the *Analecta Bollandiana* of the work called the *Septililium*, compiled from the revelations and utterances of Blessed Dorothea by her confessor John Marienwerder. This was printed by instalments in vols. ii, iii, and iv of the *Analecta* (1883–1885). More than one biographical sketch seems to have survived, for the most part written shortly after her death, and compiled with a view to the process of her canonization. See also F. Hipler, *Johannes Marienwerder und die Klauserin Dorothea*, 1865 ; and Ringholtz, *Geschichte von Einsiedeln* (1906), pp. 268 *seq.*, and 689 *seq.*

BD. JOHN SLADE, Mart.

A.D. 1583

Blessed John Slade was born in Dorsetshire, educated at New College, Oxford, and became a schoolmaster. His zeal in upholding the Faith led to his arrest on a charge of denying the royal supremacy in spirituals, and he was brought up for trial at Winchester, together with Blessed John Bodey (November 2), in April 1583. They were both condemned, but there was a re-trial on the same indictment at Andover four months later, which Cardinal Allen imputed to a consciousness in their prosecutors of the first sentence having been unjust and illegal. But the result was the same, the sentence was repeated, and Blessed John Slade was hanged, drawn, and quartered at Winchester on this day in the year 1583.

See Challoner, *Memoirs of Missionary Priests* (Ed. Pollen), pp. 83–85 ; and Burton-Pollen, *Lives of the English Martyrs*, second series, vol. i, pp. 1–7.

ST ALPHONSUS RODRIGUEZ, CONF.

A.D. 1617

There are two well-known canonised lay brothers commemorated this month, but in other external circumstances there were considerable differences between St Gerard Majella and St Alphonsus Rodriguez. For instance, at the age when Gerard was dead, Alphonsus was still a married man, living with his family ; while the one died before he was thirty, the other lived to be nearly ninety ; during his three years of profession Gerard served in several houses of his congregation and was employed in a variety of ways, but Alphonsus was porter at the same college for forty-five years. Diego Rodriguez was a well-to-do cloth and wool merchant in Segovia, and Alphonsus was his third child in a big family, a family moreover well known in the town for the religious care with which the parents conducted it. When in 1541 Blessed Peter Faber and another Jesuit came to preach a mission at Segovia they stayed with Diego, and at the end accepted his offer of a few days' holiday at his country house. Young Alphonsus, then about ten, went with them and was prepared for his first Communion by Blessed Peter. When he was fourteen he was sent with his elder brother, Diego, to study under the Jesuits at Alcala, but before the first year was out their father died, and it was decided that Alphonsus must go into the business, which his mother was going to carry on. She retired and left him in sole charge when he was twenty-three, and three years later he married a girl called Mary Suarez. The business had been doing badly and his wife's dowry did not do much to improve it ; Alphonsus was not an incapable business man, but " times were bad." Then he lost his little daughter, and, after a long illness following the birth of a boy, his wife too. Two years later his mother died, and this succession of misfortunes and losses made Alphonsus give very serious thought to what God was calling him to do in the world. He had always been a man of devout and righteous life, but he began to realise that he was meant to be something different from the numerous men of business who led exemplary but unheroic lives in Segovia. He discovered that if he sold his business he would have enough for himself and his little son to live on, so he did this and went to live in a part of his father's old house, where his two maiden sisters had long resided. These two, Antonia and Juliana, were a very pious couple and taught their brother the rudiments of mental prayer, so that he was soon meditating two hours every morning and evening on the mysteries of the rosary. Alphonsus began to see his past life as very imperfect when regarded in the light of Christ and, following a vision of the glories of Heaven, he made a general confession and set himself to practise considerable austerities as well as going to confession and communion every week. After some years his son died, and the edge of Alphonsus's sorrow was turned by the consideration that the boy had been saved from the danger and misery of ever offending God.

He now contemplated, not for the first time, the possibility of becoming a religious and applied to the Jesuits at Segovia. They unhesitatingly refused him : he was nearly forty, his health was not good, and he had not finished an education good enough to make him fit for sacerdotal studies. Undaunted, he went off to see his old friend Father Louis Santander, S.J., at Valencia. Father Santander recommended him to get ordained as soon as possible, and as a first step to learn Latin. So, like St Ignatius Loyola before him, and with like mortifications, he put himself to school with the little boys. As he had given nearly all his money to his sisters and to the poor before leaving Segovia, he had to take a post as a servant and supplement his earnings by begging alms in order to support himself. He met at the school a man of his own age and inclinations, who induced him to consider giving up all idea of becoming a Jesuit and to be instead a hermit. During a vacation Alphonsus went to visit this man at his hermitage in the mountains, but suddenly seeing the suggestion as a temptation to desert his real vocation, he returned to Valencia and confessed his weakness to Father Santander, saying, " I will never again follow my own will for the rest of my life. Do with me as you think best." In 1571 the Jesuit provincial, Father Cordeses, recognising a saint and over-ruling his official consultors, accepted Alphonsus Rodriguez as a lay-brother, or temporal coadjutor, as such is called in the Society. On the evening before his formal reception he had a visit from his hermit friend, who was in so furious a rage and upbraided him in such a tone that Alphonsus was henceforward convinced that the man was really a manifestation of the Devil. Six months later he was sent from Spain to the College of

Montesion in the island of Majorca, and soon after his arrival was made hall-porter.

St Alphonsus carried out the duties of this post till he became too old and infirm, and the reputation he had in it was summed up once for all by Father Michael Julian in his exclamation, " That brother is not a man—he is an angel ! " Every minute left free by his work and what it entailed was given to prayer, but though he achieved a marvellous habitual recollection and union with God his spiritual path was far from an easy one. Especially in his later years he suffered from long periods of desolation and aridity, and with terrifying regularity he was seized with pain and sickness whenever he set himself formally to meditate. Added to this, he was beset with violent temptations, just as though for years he had not curbed his body by fierce austerities, which now had to be made even more vigorous. But he never despaired, carrying out every duty with exact regularity, knowing that in God's own time he would be seized again in an ecstasy of love and spiritual delight. Priests who had known him for forty years used to say that they had never noticed a word or action of Brother Alphonsus which could justly receive adverse criticism. In 1585, when he was fifty-four years old, he made his final vows, which he used to renew every day at Mass. A hall-porter is not to be envied at the best of times, and when a boys' school is part of the establishment he needs to have a firm hand and an extra fund of patience ; but the job has its compensations : the porter meets a variety of people and is a link between the public world without and the private world within. At Montesion, in addition to the students, there was a constant coming and going of clergy of all sorts, of nobles and professional men and members of their families having business with the Jesuit fathers, of the poor wanting help and merchants and tradesmen from Palma wanting orders. All these people got to know, to respect, and to love Brother Alphonsus, whose opinions and advice were sought and valued as well by the learned and holy as by the simple, and his reputation was known far beyond the boundaries of the college. The most famous of his " pupils " was St Peter Claver, who was studying at the college in 1605. For three years he put himself under the direction of St Alphonsus who, enlightened by Heaven, fired his enthusiasm for and urged him on to that work in America which was eventually to gain for St Peter the title of " Apostle of the Negroes."

St Alphonsus had always a very deep devotion towards the Mother of God, and particularly as conceived free from original sin, a doctrine that had been defended in Majorca three hundred years before by Blessed Raymund Lull. For a time it was believed by many that the Little Office of the Immaculate Conception had itself been composed by Alphonsus, but his disciple and biographer Father Colin says it was known in Spain before his time ; Alphonsus had a great regard for this office and popularised its use among others, from which fact arose the mistake that he was its author. Nor did he write the famous treatise on the *Practice of Perfection and Christian Virtues :* this was the work of another Jesuit of the same name, who has not been canonised. But St Alphonsus left some fugitive writings, set down at the command of his superiors, full of the simple, solid doctrine and exhortation that one would look for from such a man. In our relations with others he tells us to " think well of all but poorly of yourself. Remember the good qualities of others, pass over the bad ones ; if you must notice them, excuse them. But dismiss any good that you may see in yourself, for you do not know if it be pleasing to God. Be pleasant and cheerful to all." He preached as he practised. When he was over seventy and very infirm, his rector, Father Alvarez, told him one day, just to see what he would do, to go on duty to the Indies. St Alphonsus went straight down to the gate and asked for it to be opened for him. " I am ordered to the Indies," he said, and was going there and then to look for a ship at the port of Palma, but was told to go back to the rector. That during the later part of his life he suffered from spiritual dereliction and violent assaults of the Devil has been mentioned above, and to these were added the trials of ill-health and physical suffering, and at last he was practically confined to his bed. But his invincible perseverance and patience brought consolations " to such a degree that he could not raise his eyes in spirit to Jesus and Mary without their being at once before him." In May of 1617 the rector of Montesion, Father Julian, was down with rheumatic fever, and asked for the prayers of St Alphonsus. He spent the night interceding for him, and in the morning Father Julian was able to say Mass. In October he knew that his end was at hand, and after receiving Holy Communion on the 29th all pain of mind and body ceased. He lay as it were in an unbroken ecstasy until, at midnight of the 31st, a terrible agony began. At the end of half an hour composure returned, he looked around lovingly at his brethren, kissed the crucifix, uttered the Holy Name in a loud voice, and died. His funeral was attended by the Spanish viceroy and nobility of Majorca, by the bishop, and by crowds of the poor, sick, and afflicted, whose love and faith were rewarded by miracles. In the following year the viceroy drew the attention of Pope Paul V to the heroic virtues of Alphonsus Rodriguez, but the suppression of the Jesuits in Spain and elsewhere helped to delay his beatification till 1825. He was canonised by Pope Leo XIII in 1888.

The documents printed for the Congregation of Sacred Rites in view of the beatification and canonisation of St Alphonsus are very copious owing to the objections raised by the Promotor Fidei in connection with the saint's early occupations and his writings. These documents, with the autobiographical notes, which he wrote down by order of obedience between the years 1601 and 1616, supply the most valuable materials for his Life. The notes in question are printed at the beginning of his *Obras Espirituales*, which were edited in three volumes by Father J. Nonell at Barcelona in 1885–1887. The same Father Nonell wrote in Spanish what is still perhaps the best biography of the saint, *Vida de San Alonso Rodriguez*, 1888 ; and this was largely used by Father Goldie in the English Life which he published in 1889. In the *Acta Sanctorum*, October, vol. xiii, the Bollandists have reprinted the earliest published Life of Alphonsus, that by Father Janin, which appeared in 1644 and was written in Latin. On the saint's connection with the Little Office of the Immaculate Conception, often erroneously printed under his name, see Uriarte, *Obras Anonimas y seudonimas, S.J.*, vol. i, pp. 512–515 ; and on his ascetical teaching see Viller, *Dictionnaire de Spiritualité*, vol. i (1933), cc. 395–402. The latest published Life seems to be that by I. Casanovas, *San Alonso Rodriguez*, 1917.

BD. ANGELO OF ACRI, Conf.

A.D. 1739

The fame of St Leonard of Port Maurice as a mission-preacher in Tuscany and northern Italy during the first half of the eighteenth century has gone far beyond the boundaries of his own order and country, but his contemporary preacher in Calabria, Angelo of Acri, also a Franciscan, is not so well known, though he was as famous in the south as St Leonard in the north. He was born at Acri in the diocese of Bisignano in 1669, and when he was eighteen was accepted as a postulant by the Capuchins, but the austerity of their life was too much for him and he left. But he was not satisfied, and after a time was permitted again to try his vocation in the same order. And again he failed to persevere. Thereupon his uncle, a priest, pointed out to him that he was obviously intended by God for a secular life and had better marry. Angelo was still unconvinced : he had a strong attraction to the religious life and a corresponding aversion from trying to settle down " in the world," and in 1690 he made a third attempt with the Capuchins. This time he overcame his difficulties by the aid of urgent prayer, and after a rather stormy novitiate was professed and began his studies for the priesthood. His superiors saw thaf he still stood in need of strict discipline and treated him with considerable severity, and at the same time he was greatly tried by temptations against chastity; he overcame both trials and so profited by them that it is said that during the celebration of his first Mass he was rapt in ecstasy. It was not till 1702 that he was first entrusted with public preaching, when he was sent to preach the Lent at San Giorgio. He prepared his course with great care, but in the pulpit his confidence and memory deserted him and he failed so lamentably that he gave up and returned to his friary before it was over. Meditating on his failure and asking God's help in his trouble, he one day seemed to hear a voice saying, " Be not afraid. The gift of preaching shall be yours." " Who art thou ? " asked Father Angelo, and the reply came, " I am who I am. For the future preach simply and colloquially, so that all may understand you." Father Angelo did as he was told ; he laid aside all his books of oratory and with them the flowers of speech and flights of learning, and prepared his discourses only with the help of his Bible and crucifix. His new manner was immediately successful with the common people, but these were the days before St Alphonsus Liguori and his Redemptorists had simplified the style of preaching prevalent in Italy, and more refined people were contemptuous of the straightforwardness and familiar phrasing of Father Angelo. The attention of these was won in a rather dramatic way when, in 1711, Cardinal Pignatelli invited him to preach the Lent at the church of St Eligius in Naples. His first sermon there provoked the usual superior amusement among the gentry, and the two following days the church was almost empty. The parish priest asked him to discontinue the course, but Cardinal Pignatelli said he was to continue, and this " incident " stimulated curiosity, so that the church was crowded next day. At the end of his sermon Father Angelo asked the congregation to say a Hail Mary for the soul of somebody in the church who was about to die. As they left the building, speculating about the prophecy, a well-known lawyer, who had made himself conspicuous by his raillery at the preacher, fell dead from a stroke. This happening, which was followed by others equally remarkable, made Father Angelo's reputation in Naples ; for the future there were more listeners than the church could hold, and many who came merely from curiosity received the grace of God and were brought to their knees.

For the next twenty-eight years Blessed Angelo preached as a missioner in the kingdom of Naples and particularly up and down his own province of Calabria. His discourses on the Passion and the Four Last Things brought thousands to penance and amendment of life, and wherever he preached he had a calvary set up in the open air as a reminder, after he had gone, of the truths he had preached there. His mission was emphasised by many miracles, especially of healing the sick, and examples of seeming supernatural agility or of bilocation are recorded of him. He had insight into the souls of men, reminding them of forgotten or concealed sins, and several times, as at Naples, predicted future events with exactness. He continued his labours to within six months of his death, when he became blind, but was able to say Mass daily till the end, which came peacefully at the friary of Acri on October 30, 1739. A flow of blood in the veins and movement of an arm at the word of the father guardian, similar to the phenomena reported of Blessed Bonaventure of Potenza (October 26), are stated to have taken place three days after death. Blessed Angelo of Acri was beatified by Pope Leo XII in 1825.

The Bollandists have supplied a full account of this *beato* in the *Acta Sanctorum*, October, vol. xiii. They have drawn almost entirely upon the evidence presented in the beatification process. See, however, also the Lives written by Ernest de Beaulieu, Paris, 1899, and Giacinto da Belmonte, Rome, 1894. A summary in English may be read in Léon, *Auréole Séraphique* (Eng. trans.), vol. iv, pp. 1–7.

OCTOBER 31

ST QUINTINUS, OR QUENTIN, MART.

A.D. 287

ST QUINTINUS was a Roman who, full of zeal for the kingdom of Jesus Christ and burning to make His name and His love and mercy known among the infidels, left his country and, attended by St Lucian of Beauvais, made his way to Gaul. They preached the faith together in that country till they reached Amiens in Picardy, where they parted. St Quintinus stayed at Amiens, endeavouring by his prayers and labours to make that country a portion of our Lord's vineyard, and the reward of his charitable labours was the crown of martyrdom, which he received in the beginning of the reign of Maximian. The prefect Rictius Varus heard what great progress the Christian faith had made at Amiens, and he ordered St Quintinus to be seized, thrown into prison, and loaded with chains. The next day the holy preacher was brought before the prefect, who tried to win him over with promises and threats ; finding him proof against both, he ordered him to be whipped and confined to a dungeon without the liberty of receiving comfort or assistance from the faithful. The *passio* of St Quintinus is a worthless recital of tortures and marvels. It says that his limbs were stretched with pulleys on the rack till his joints were dislocated, his body torn with iron wire, boiled pitch and oil were poured on his back and lighted torches applied to his sides. By the ministry of an angel he escaped from prison but was taken again while preaching in the market-place. When Rictius Varus left Amiens he commanded Quintinus to be conducted to Augusta Veromanduorum (now Saint-Quentin), where he made fresh attacks upon the confessor of Christ. Ashamed to see himself vanquished by his courage, Rictius Varus ordered his body to be pierced with two iron wires from the neck to the thighs, nails to be stuck under his finger-nails and in his flesh, and lastly his head to be cut off, whereupon a dove issued from his gaping neck and flew away into the heavens. The martyr's body was watched by soldiers till night, and then thrown into the river Somme : but it was recovered by the Christians and buried near the town. Fifty-five years after it was discovered by Eusebia, a

devout lady who built a chapel to enshrine the relics. The knowledge of the place was again lost till, in the beginning of the year
641, St Eligius, Bishop of Noyon and the Vermandois, caused the
relics to be sought, and when they were discovered they were translated to his cathedral.

Happy are they whom God allows to seal their fidelity to Him
by their blood. Great is the honour and happiness for a mortal
man and a poor sinner to lay down his life for Him, who, out of
infinite love for us, gave His most precious life. Martyrs are holo-
causts offered to the divine love and glory. They are witnesses, as
the word imports in Greek, bearing testimony to the infinite power
and goodness of God, in which they place an entire confidence,
and to the truth of His holy revealed faith, which they confirm with
their blood. No testimony can be more glorious to God, more
edifying to the faithful, or more striking to infidels. It is by the
constancy of martyrs that our religion is established in men's hearts.

Since St Gregory of Tours already speaks of a church dedicated in honour
of St Quintinus, there can be little reason for questioning the fact that he
was an authentic martyr. But the story has been embellished with all
sorts of legendary excrescences and is preserved to us in a great variety of
forms, of which a list is given in the *Bibliotheca Hagiographica Latina*,
nn. 6999–7021. Several of these texts, including accounts of the translations
of relics, are reproduced in the long article devoted to St Quintinus in the
Acta Sanctorum, October, vol. xiii. Others have since been discovered,
notably a number of Carolingian metrical effusions which have been printed
in the *Analecta Bollandiana*, vol. xx (1901), pp. 1–44. It is interesting to
note that the legend of St Quintinus had apparently found its way into
England before the end of the ninth century and forms a paragraph in the
Anglo-Saxon martyrology edited for the Early English Text Society by
G. Herzfeld.

ST FOILLAN, Bp. and Mart.

c. A.D. 655

St Foillan was the brother of St Fursey, of whom an account is
given herein under date January 16. They came to England together
about the year 636 and established a monastery at Burghcastle, near
Yarmouth, from which they did missionary work among the East
Angles. After a time Fursey retired to a hermitage, where another
brother of his, St Ultan, was already living, leaving the monastery
and missions in charge of Foillan and two other priests. A year
later Fursey crossed over to Gaul, where he died about the year 648.
Meanwhile East Anglia was overrun by the Mercians under Penda,
and when the monastery at Burghcastle had been pillaged by the

invaders, Foillan and Ultan determined to follow the example of their brother. With what was left of their community they came into Neustria where, like Fursey before them, they were well received by Clovis II and his mayor of the palace, Ercinwald. From Péronne St Foillan went to Nivelles, where he was given some land at Fosses by Blessed Ita, widow of Blessed Pepin of Landen, who had founded the monastery at Nivelles of which their daughter St Gertrude was abbess. Here he established a monastery for the monks he had brought with him, and at the same time became visitor or director to the abbey of Nivelles, where he exercised a very great influence. St Foillan also engaged himself in missionary work among the Brabanters, and left a strong impression upon the religious life of the place and time ; he is one of the best remembered of the lesser Irish missionary monks on the continent.

A number of texts have been printed in the *Acta Sanctorum* bearing on the history of St Foillan, but one still more valuable is a short document which appears in some MSS. as an appendix to the earliest Life of St Fursey. Bruno Krusch who has edited it in the *M. G. H. Scrip. rer. Meroving.*, vol. iv, pp. 449–451, believes it to have been written by an eye-witness, probably an Irish monk in the service of the nuns at Nivelles. It describes the death and burial of St Foillan. See also Kenney, *Sources for the Early History of Ireland*, vol. i, pp. 503–504, and Crépin, " Le Monastère des Scots de Fosses " in *La Terre Wallonne*, vols. viii (1923), pp. 357–385, and ix (1923), pp. 16–26 ; with Gougaud, *Christianity in Celtic Lands*, pp. 147–148.

ST BEGA, OR BEE, VIRG.
SEVENTH CENTURY

In the fourth book of his *Ecclesiastical History* St Bede the Venerable refers to St Heiu, who, he says, was regarded as the first woman in Northumbria to become a nun and who founded a monastery at Hartlepool. This was taken over by St Hilda and Heiu went to live at Tadcaster. A little further on he makes mention of St Begu who, after being a religious for over thirty years, had in the nunnery at Hackness a vision of the departing of the soul of its foundress Hilda. St Bega (Begh, Bee) has been identified with either or both of these holy women, as was done by Leland and the Bollandists ; the identification has not been confirmed but rather seems to have been disproved. She is the heroine of a legend which makes her the daughter of an Irish king, sought in marriage by a son of the King of Norway. She had, however, vowed herself a virgin to Christ, and had been given by an angel a bracelet marked with a cross as a token of her heavenly betrothal. The day before she was to be given to the prince, while her suitor and her father were revelling in the hall, she escaped with the help of this bracelet and, seated on a clod of earth, was navigated across the sea and landed safely on the coast of Cumberland. For a time she lived as an ankress, and the sea-gulls, guillemots, and gannets brought food for her sustenance, but human marauders were less kind, and she was advised by the King of Northumbria, St Oswald, to become a nun. She therefore received the veil from St Aidan (Bede says it was he who consecrated Heiu) and established a monastery at St Bees (Copeland) which afterwards became a cell of the Benedictine abbey of St Mary at York.

Whatever background of truth there may be in the legend of St Bega, there is no doubt that she existed and was greatly venerated in Northumbria. The promontory on which she lived is named after her St Bee's Head, and she was the powerful patroness of the people of the neighbourhood, ground down between the exactions of their lords and the raids of the border Scots. They claimed even to possess her miraculous bracelet, and treasured equally the stories of how St Bega in her earthly life had been devoted to the poor and oppressed and had cooked, washed and mended for the workmen who built her monastery. St Bega was venerated in Scotland and Norway, and she may be the same as the " Becga, daughter of Gabhran, virgin," who is named in the Martyrology of Donegal on February 10.

About the year 655, on the eve of the feast of St Quintinus, St Foillan sang Mass at Nivelles and then set out with three companions to visit St Ultan at Fosses. While passing through the forest of Seneffe they were set upon by outlaws, robbed, murdered, and their bodies left lying. These were not found till the following January 16, when St Gertrude ordered them to be taken up and buried at the abbey which St Foillan had founded. A solemn procession in his honour takes place every seven years at Fosses, near Charleroi. As he was slain while journeying on the business of the Church, St Foillan is commemorated as a martyr in several places of Belgium ; he is believed also to have been a bishop, though the time and place of his consecration are not known.

It is very difficult to establish the truth where we have no sort of guarantee of the reliability of our sources. The legend of St Bega in its fuller form rests entirely upon one MS. (Cotton, Faust., B. iv), which Hardy in his *Descriptive Catalogue*, i, p. 223, dates twelfth century. The story is supported by the lessons in the Aberdeen Breviary. See Forbes, *Kalendars of Scottish Saints*, p. 278, and the *Acta Sanctorum*, September, vol. ii. C. Plummer, a very careful scholar, familiar with Irish as well as Anglo-Saxon sources, says quite positively that the Bega of Bede (Bk. iv, ch. 23) " is not to be confounded, as is often done, with Hein, or with the very mythical Irish saint Bega whose name is preserved in St Bees." See also *Dict. Nat. Biog.*, vol. iv, pp. 128–129, and Stanton, *Menology*, p. 519. In the *Lives of the English Saints*, Father Faber, then an Anglican, has recounted in graceful terms the legend of St Bega, and he has cited in an appendix Wordsworth's "Stanza" on the headland of St Bees. The Latin text of the Cotton MS. was first printed and translated by G. C. Tomlinson in the *Carlisle Historical Tracts*.

ST WOLFGANG, Bp. of Ratisbon, Conf.

A.D. 994

St Wolfgang came of a Suabian family and was born about the year 834. His education at seven years of age was put into the hands of a neighbouring ecclesiastic, but some time after he was removed to the abbey of Reichenau, on an island in Lake Constance, which was at that time a flourishing school of learning and furnished many churches with eminent pastors. In this house Wolfgang became friendly with a young nobleman called Henry, brother to Poppo, Bishop of Würzburg, who had set up a great school in that city, and engaged an Italian professor, Stephen of Novara, to lecture there. This Henry persuaded Wolfgang to bear him company to this new school at Würzburg, where the ability of the young Suabian soon provoked jealousy as well as admiration. In 956 Henry was elected archbishop of Trier, and took Wolfgang with him, making him a teacher in the cathedral school. At Trier he came under the influence of the reforming monk Ramwold, and entered wholeheartedly into Henry's efforts for the improvement of religion, discipline, and morality in his diocese. Upon the death of the archbishop in 964 Wolfgang became a Benedictine in the monastery of Einsiedeln, governed at that time by George, an Englishman. The abbot soon found the reputation of Wolfgang to be less than his merit, and appointed him director of the school of the monastery, which under his care became the most flourishing in the country. St Ulric, Bishop of Augsburg, now ordained St Wolfgang priest, and with his ordination he received an apostolic missionary spirit. Having obtained his abbot's leave, he went with a select number of monks to preach the faith to the Magyars in Pannonia. The results of this undertaking did not correspond to his zeal, and the Bishop of Passau recommended him to the Emperor Otto II as a person qualified to fill the see of Ratisbon (Regensburg) which was then vacant. He was conducted to the Emperor at Frankfort, who gave him the investiture of the temporalities, though the saint entreated him to allow him to return to his monastery. Being sent back to

Ratisbon at Christmas 972 he was consecrated and enthroned. He never quitted the monastic habit, and practised all the austerities of a religious life when in the episcopal dignity. The first thing he did after regulation of his own household was to settle a thorough reformation among all his clergy, and in all the monasteries of his diocese, especially two disorderly nunneries. One of the sources of revenue of the see was the abbey of St Emmeramus at Ratisbon, which the bishops held *in commendam*, with the usual bad results. St Wolfgang restored its autonomy and called Ramwold from Trier to be its abbot. He was indefatigable in preaching and, being a man of prayer, possessed the art of touching the hearts of his hearers. Every duty of his office he discharged with vigilance and fidelity during twenty-two years' administration. Several miracles are recorded of him and his generosity to the poor was proverbial. Once when the vintage had failed, some ignorant priests took to using water in the chalice at Mass. The bishop was naturally horrified, and distributed wine from his household stocks throughout the diocese. He helped St Aurelia, who is said by some to have been a princess of the house of Capet, to take up a solitary life at Strasburg ; she is commemorated on the 15th of this month.

At one time St Wolfgang deserted his see and retired to a solitary place, where he was found by some huntsmen and brought back. But his desire for a monastic quiet did not prevent him from a careful discharge of his secular duties, and he attended several imperial diets as well as accompanying the Emperor on a campaign into France. The territory of Bohemia being part of his diocese, he found it too extensive and gave up a great part of it for a bishopric in that country ; and procured St Adelbert to be placed in it as first bishop of Prague. Henry, Duke of Bavaria, held St Wolfgang in the highest veneration, and entrusted to him the education of his four children, namely, St Henry, afterwards emperor, Bruno, who died bishop of Augsburg, Gisela, Queen of Hungary, and Bridget, who died abbess at Ratisbon. He was taken ill while travelling down the Danube into Lower Austria and died at a little place called Pupping, not far from Linz ; at his own request he was carried for his last moments into the church of St Othmar. St Wolfgang was canonised by Pope St Leo IX in 1052 ; his feast is kept in many dioceses of central Europe, and also by the Canons Regular of the Lateran because he restored the canonical life for his clergy according to the regulations of St Chrodegang of Metz.

We are well informed regarding St Wolfgang. The book of Arnold the monk concerning St Emmerammus and the biography of Wolfgang by Othlo, with some other supplementary materials, are reliable sources, and they have been edited very carefully of late years in the *Acta Sanctorum*, November, vol. ii, part 1. See also a popular, but not uncritical volume by Otto Häfner, *Der hl. Wolfgang, ein Stern des X Jahrhunderts*, 1930 ; and also the archæological study of J. A. Endres, *Beiträge zur Kunst-und Kultur-geschichte des mittelalterlichen Regensburgs* as well as I. Zibermayr, *Die St. Wolfganslegende in ihrem Entstehen und Einflusse auf die österreichische Kunst*, 1924.

BB. CHRISTOPHER OF ROMANDIOLA AND THOMAS OF FLORENCE, Confs.

A.D. 1272 AND 1447

The feast of these two *beati*, though they have nothing to do with one another, is kept together on this day by the Friars Minor and the Capuchins. Blessed Christopher (often called " of Cahors ") was a personal disciple of St Francis of Assisi. He was a parish priest in the diocese of Cesena, and when about forty years of age he resigned his benefice and joined the newly formed order of Friars Minor, among whom he was distinguished for his bodily austerities and his devotion to the lepers. He was eventually sent into Gascony where he preached against the Albigensians and established his order at Cahors. He died here in 1272, at a great age, and his *cultus* was approved by Pope Pius X in 1905.

Blessed Thomas Bellacci, a native of Florence, was a Franciscan lay-brother, who as a young man had led a wild and disorderly life. Realisation of the futility of it all and the wise words of a friend wrought a change in him and he was accepted—with some trepidation, for his excesses were notorious—by the friars of the Observance at Fiesole. But his penitence equalled his former sinfulness, and in time, for all he was only a lay-brother, he was made master of novices, whom he trained in the strictest ways of the Observance. St Bernardino of Siena sent subjects to be formed by him, and when in 1414 the commissary, Friar John of Stroncone, went to spread the reform in the kingdom of Naples he took Blessed Thomas with him. He laboured there for some six years, strengthened with the gift of miracles, and then, authorised by Pope Martin V, he undertook, in company with Blessed Antony of Stroncone, to oppose the heretical *Fraticelli* in Tuscany. While engaged in this campaign he made a number of new foundations, over which St Bernardino gave him authority, his own headquarters being at the friary of Scarlino. Here he established a custom of going in procession after the night office to a neighbouring wood, where each friar had a little shelter of boughs and shrubs wherein they remained for a time in meditation. In 1427 Blessed Thomas went for a year to Corsica, where he established the Observant friars with the help of his friend Blessed Antony ; then he came back to Scarlino and continued to direct his Tuscan houses until 1439.

In that year, as a result of the " reunion council " at Florence, Friar Albert of Sarzana was sent as papal legate to the Jacobites and other Monophysite heretics of the East, and he took Blessed Thomas with him, although he was in his seventieth year. From Persia Albert commissioned him to go with three other friars into Ethiopia. Three times on their way they were seized by the Turks, who imprisoned them and treated them with great cruelty. But Blessed Thomas insisted on preaching to the Mohammedans, and eventually they had to be ransomed by Pope Eugenius IV, just before their captors were going to put them to death. Grieved that they were not deemed worthy of the crown of martyrdom they returned to Rome, where they were honourably received by the Pope, and Blessed Thomas retired to a friary at Monte Piano in the Abruzzi. He could not get over that God had refused the proffered sacrifice of his life for the Faith, and in 1447, aged as he was, he set out for Rome to ask permission to go again to the East. But at Rieti he was taken ill, and died there on October 31. Many agitated that he should be canonised with St Bernardino of Siena, whose cause was then in process. To prevent the delay that would have resulted St John of Capistrano, it is said, went to Thomas's tomb at Rieti and commanded him in the name of holy obedience to cease his miracles until the canonisation of Bernardino should be achieved. They stopped for three years, but Blessed Thomas has never been canonised. His *cultus* was approved by Pope Clement XIV in 1771.

The Bollandists on October 31 relegate this holy friar among the *prætermissos* on the ground that no sufficient evidence had then been produced for his continued *cultus*. The decree of confirmation, which includes some biographical details, may be read in the *Analecta Ecclesiastica* for 1905, p. 206. There is a Life by Bernard of Bessa in the *Analecta Franciscana*, vol. iii, pp. 161–173. See also the biography of L. de Chérancé, Paris, 1907.

APPENDIX

OCTOBER 24

BD. ANTONY MARY CLARET, Bp. and Conf.

A.D. 1870

DESPITE the imposing form in which his name is sometimes presented—Antonio Maria Claret y Clará—this holy archbishop was of relatively humble origin. Born in 1807 at Sallent in the north of Spain, he practised for a time his father's trade of cloth-weaving, and with such success that he came to occupy an important post at Barcelona. He had always been a singularly devout youth, but a narrow escape from drowning, which he attributed to our Lady's intercession, led him in 1829 to enter the ecclesiastical seminary at Vich, where he was ordained priest in 1835. After a few years in the diocese he began to entertain the idea of a Carthusian vocation, but as that seemed to be beyond his physical strength, he proceeded to Rome and eventually entered the Jesuit noviciate with the idea of consecrating his life to the foreign missions. Here, however, his health broke down and he was advised by Father Roothan, the Jesuit Father-General, to return to Spain and busy himself with the evangelisation of his countrymen. This course he adopted and for ten years he was engaged in giving missions and retreats throughout Catalonia. His zeal inspired other priests to join in the same work, and in 1849 he was mainly instrumental in founding the Congregation of " Missionary Sons of the Immaculate Heart of Mary." The institute, commonly known by his name as " the Claretians," has spread and flourished, not only in Spain, but in California, Texas, Arizona, Illinois, and other regions, with a superior-general living in Rome. It now numbers 210 houses and residences, with some 1150 priests. Almost immediately after this great work had been inaugurated, Father Claret was appointed Archbishop of Santiago de Cuba. The task was one of exceptional difficulty, in which his efforts to bring about a much-needed reform were resisted by a powerful organisation of disorderly and anti-Christian fanatics. Several attempts were made upon his life, and in one instance a serious wound was inflicted by an assassin infuriated by the loss of his mistress who had been won back to her religious duties. It was the intercession of the Archbishop himself which obtained from the authorities the remission of the death sentence. In 1856, at the request of Pope Pius IX, Blessed Antony returned to Spain to become confessor to Queen Isabella II, then reigning. He resigned his Cuban archbishopric, but avoided residence at the Court for any longer than his official duties required, devoting himself to missionary work and the diffusion of good literature, especially in his native Catalan. To him Spain owes the foundation of the " Libreria Religiosa " in Barcelona, which has exerted immense influence in reviving a true Catholic spirit. In the course of his life Bd. Antony is said to have preached 10,000 sermons and to have published 200 books or pamphlets for the instruction and edification of both clergy and people. His continual union with God was rewarded by many supernatural favours not only in the way of ecstasies and the gift of prophecy, but also by the miraculous cure of bodily diseases. In the revolution of 1868 he was banished from Spain together with the Queen. He then visited Paris, and afterwards Rome, where he made his influence felt in promoting the definition of papal infallibility. An attempt was made to bring him back to Spain, but he never lived to reach it, for a fatal illness came upon him in France and he went to his reward in the Cistercian monastery of Fontfroide, near Narbonne, on October 24, 1870. He was declared Blessed by Pope Pius XI on February 25, 1934.

A number of Lives in Spanish and Catalan have appeared since the death of Blessed Antonio Maria. Those by M. Aguilar (1894), G. Blanch (1908), and J. Puigdesens (1928) seem specially worthy of mention. In the *Acta Apostolicæ Sedis*, vol. xxvi (1934), pp. 173–179 and 198–201, will be found two official decrees both containing a biographical summary. There is also an account in the Appendix to the *Catholic Encyclopedia*, vol. xvi, p. 26 ; and an illustrated brochure was produced by the Claretian Fathers of Los Angeles, California, as " A Souvenir of the Triduum to commemorate the Beatification," 1934.

INDEX TO VOLUME X

[The figures in brackets give, as nearly as may be, the date of the Saint's death.]

A

Abercius, Bp. of Hieropolis, conf. (end of second century), 299.

Acca, Bp. of Hexham, conf. (742), 276.

Agilbert, Bp. of Paris, conf. (*c.* 685), 152.

Alacoque, *see* Margaret-Mary.

Alexander Sauli, Bp. of Pavia, conf. (1593), 159.

Allucio, conf. (1134), 312.

Alodia, virg. and mart. (851), 301.

Alphonsus Rodriguez, conf. (1617), 367.

Ammon the Great, conf. (*c.* 350), 53.

Anastasia, virg., and Cyril, MM. (*c.* 260 ?), 348.

Anastasius of Cluny, conf. (1085), 229.

Andrew of Crete, mart. (766), 277.

Andronicus, mart. (304), 144.

Andronicus, conf. and Athanasia, matron (fifth century), 112.

Angadrisma, virg. and abbess (*c.* 695), 193.

Angelo of Acri, conf. (1739), 371.

Angels, The Holy Guardian, 14.

Anstrudis, virg. and abbess (688), 242.

Antony Mary Claret, bp. and conf. (1870), 382.

Appolinaris, Bp. of Valence, conf. (520), 59.

Aquilinus, Bp. of Evreux, conf. (*c.* 695), 264.

Archangel, *see* Raphael the Archangel.

Areopagite, *see* Dionysius the Areopagite.

Aretas and the Marts. of Nagran, and Elesbaan, king and conf. (523), 322.

Artaldus, or Arthaud, Bp. of Belley, conf. (1206), 88.

Artemius, mart. (363), 275.

Arthaud, *see* Artaldus.

Asterius, Bp. of Amasea, conf. (*c.* 400), 361.

Athanasia, matron (fifth century), 112.

Attilanus, Bp. of Zamora, conf. (1009), 32.

B

Bacchus, mart. (303), 84.

Balthasar of Chiavari, conf. (1492), 244.

Bartholomew Breganza, Bp. of Vicenza, conf. (1271), 314.

Bavo, conf. (*c.* 653), 7.

Bee, *see* Bega.

Bega, or Bee, virg. (seventh century), 376.

Benvenuta Bojani, virg. (1292), 364.

Bercharius, mart. (696), 226.

Bertrand, Bp. of Comminges, conf. (1123), 229.

Bertrand, *see* Louis Bertrand.

Bojani, *see* Benvenuta.

Bonaventure of Potenza, conf. (1711), 341.

Bonus, *see* John Bonus.

Borgia, *see* Francis Borgia.

Breganza, *see* Bartholomew Breganza.

Bridget of Sweden, widow (1373), 90.

Bruno, conf. (1101), 68.

Bruno the Great, Abp. of Cologne, conf. (965), 155.

Burchard, Bp. of Würzburg, conf. (*c.* 754), 194.

The Mayflower Press, Plymouth. William Brendon & Son, Ltd.